JUL 0 2 1998	DATE		

ANNE BRONTË

by

WINIFRED GÉRIN

ALLEN LANE

This new edition first published in 1976

Allen Lane
Penguin Books Ltd
17 Grosvenor Gardens, London s w 1
ISBN 0 7139 0977 3 (cased)
ISBN 0 7139 0978 1 (paper)

Printed in Great Britain by
Lowe & Brydone (Printers) Ltd, Thetford, Norfolk

PREFACE

DURING the short time that Acton Bell came before the public as a writer—from 1846-9—she received considerable notice. In the case of her controversial novel, *The Tenant of Wildfell Hall*, she even achieved a *succès de scandale* (a second edition had to be rushed through within a month from publication), while *Agnes Grey* disturbed critics and readers alike with its unfaltering truth.

Since then, as the pseudonym was discarded and Anne Brontë emerged, she has been passed over—both as a writer and as an individual—by successive Brontë biographers as less than nothing, or dismissed with a gesture of condescension as affording only a pale replica of her sisters' genius.

The epithet "gentle", once applied to Anne Brontë by the family's intimates, would seem to have repelled sympathy rather than aroused it and has been allowed to stick to her like a burr which nothing can dislodge and no other word replace. There have been those even—and May Sinclair was of them—who chose to interpret gentle as meaning weak, and who have denied to the bravest of the Brontës those very qualities of forthrightness and independence which made her novels and poems so startling to the readers of her day and age.

Not only on the social plane was Anne Brontë greatly daring as a writer, portraying vice with a frankness from which even a Thackeray shrank, and claiming for women equal legal rights totally denied them at the time, but she penetrated into the very mysteries of religious dogma and proclaimed beliefs which even ten years later were to shock Victorian society when treated by Dean Farrar. And all this without any intention of shocking, but merely from the promptings of a heart that scorned injustice and that was as honest as it was kind.

The quality of heart and mind of the chosen confidante of Emily Brontë should not need defending here or anywhere, yet the fact remains that, with few exceptions, less than justice has been paid to Anne Brontë by the critics. Because of this and because she is worth knowing—both as a writer and as an individual—I offer no apology to the public for adding yet another volume to the store of

Brontëana (except in so far as it falls short of my intention) since as yet no biography of Anne Brontë exists.

The material upon which this book has been based falls into four categories : the ascertainable facts of Anne's life ; the original documents, the letters, diaries and reminiscences of Anne herself and her immediate circle ; her published works ; and the places and people among whom she passed her days.

All facts connected with her life have been checked to their source, such as the date of her birth recorded by Miss Firth in her diary for 17th January 1820 ; her christening on 25th March 1820, entered in the registers of St James's church, Thornton ; her death at Scarborough for which we have her death-certificate and also the entry in Ellen Nussey's unpublished diary for 28th May 1849 ; her obituary in the *Leeds Mercury* for 9th June 1849, etc.

The decision taken by Charlotte Brontë to destroy the greater number of her dead sisters' papers (an act dealt with in its proper place in the text and notes of this book) has left us with few MSS belonging to Anne herself. Of her letters, which must have been numerous during her two years of schooling away from home and the subsequent five years spent away as governess, only four have come down to us, and these are addressed to outsiders, three to Ellen Nussey and one to Mr Williams, the reader for Charlotte's firm of publishers, Smith, Elder & Co.[1] Happily six other documents have been preserved constituting some of the "diary papers" written conjointly with Emily at four-yearly intervals on family occasions to report on home events ; four in the handwriting of Emily, two in Anne's. Wherever the originals of such documents exist in this country (in particular the four above-mentioned letters of Anne's and two of the diary papers which are in the Brontë Parsonage Museum and the British Museum) I have consulted them. For other originals now in the U.S.A. I have asked to see exact transcripts.

Anne's literary remains are of essential biographical interest. Their autobiographical character is not only implicit in their very style of composition—that of reminiscence written in the first person—but it is explicitly acknowledged by Anne herself in her two novels. As to the intensely personal inspiration of the poems she herself has given us a clue when she confesses in *Agnes Grey* :

[1] These are preserved at the Brontë Parsonage Museum, Haworth, and in the Ashley Library at the British Museum.

"When we are harassed by sorrows or anxieties, or long oppressed by any powerful feelings which we must keep to ourselves, for which we can obtain and seek no sympathy from any living creature . . . we often naturally seek relief in poetry. . . ." Anne has very exactly described here the conditions in which so much of her adult life was spent and in which the only relief she could find for her pent-up feelings was in writing poetry. Though more often transposed upon a purely imaginative plane than any of the incidents in the novels, the poems reveal her inner life, and when their dates can be compared with the outward current of events, furnish an eloquent comment upon them. This is the easier, that to sign and date even a fragment of composition was a Brontë trait developed in childhood and continued through adult life.

The sum of Anne's literary remains amounts to two novels and fifty-nine poems, but a close study of fiction and poetry alike can, indeed, tell us a very great deal about their author. Anne Brontë herself vouched for the veracity of many a passage, as in *Agnes Grey* when she wrote: "Shielded by my own obscurity, and by the lapse of years, and a few fictitious names I do not fear to venture, and will candidly lay before the public what I would not disclose to the most intimate friend." Readers of Mrs Gaskell will remember how completely Charlotte endorsed her sister Anne's scrupulous adherence to truth, even when the truth seemed too hard to accept.

While much of Anne's poetry is dramatic in form and "Gondal" in theme (twenty-one poems out of a total of fifty-nine), the majority of her poems is not only largely but intensely personal in inspiration. This is particularly evident in the poems of religious experience and the five poems commemorating her love for Willy Weightman.

Anne's poetry is very little known to the general reader. Only a limited number of the poems have from time to time been published in selected anthologies (the complete texts of the Wise and Symington editions and that of C. K. Shorter are long ago out of print) ; that is why I have quoted largely from them wherever applicable in the narrative, so that the silence of this singularly reticent girl should at last be broken for us, and that we should come to understand her better.

As a Brontë biographer I am particularly privileged to live in Haworth. In addition to the authentic MSS belonging to my subject I have been able to draw upon the personal relics—the furniture, pictures, drawings, books, embroidery, the very china

out of which the family drank and the utensils of their admirable
Yorkshire kitchen, all still preserved in the Brontës' old home.
There, too, stand the books that formed Anne's small library—
books of devotion and study to remind us that she was a scholar as
well as a poet and a Christian ; the portfolios of her drawings
(notable these), the ponderous albums of her music, all minutely
annotated in her hand ; the sampler finished, as all good samplers
should be, by the tenth year of the little seamstress and reminding
us, if we were likely to forget, that the aunt who brought her up
was a Methodist. "My child," the words exhorted her as she daily
stitched, "despise not the chastening of the Lord ; neither be weary
of his correction. . . ."

There exists a body of local tradition in every village of considerable antiquity ; Haworth is peculiarly rich in this. I have the
advantage of knowing and counting as my friends the second
generation of Haworth families that were once connected with the
Brontës. By such close contacts has something of the spirit of that
family and of this place been able, I like to think, to enter into the
composition of this book.

Lastly, but far from least, among the sources that have gone to
its creation, I must mention the places, the schools, the homes, the
churches in any way connected with Anne Brontë, from her birth-
place at Thornton to the churchyard above the sea at Scarborough
where she lies. I have followed her everywhere to see what she
saw, to trace her passage and to pursue every available trail that
might give a feature and a shape to those persons who, at the
turnings in her life, accompanied her upon part of her way and
peopled her world—that world which every writer from Mrs
Gaskell down to the present time has represented as a kind of a void,
a social vacuum in which the Brontës moved alone without human
contact or sympathy of any kind. Thus the shadowy forms of the
Thornton godmother whose beautiful home, Kipping House, I was
privileged to visit ; the enlightened schoolmistress, Margaret
Wooler, whose traces I was not content to follow to Roe Head
and Heald's House only, but from whose neglected grave in Birstall
churchyard I could not rest till I had removed the tangle of ivy and
bramble ; the friend, Ellen Nussey, in her elegant homes at the
Rydings and Brookroyd, the pupils, the clergymen who taught and
influenced Anne, sprang to life for me. All these I have sought out
wherever the traces of them can be found, even to the humblest

relic. For sometimes it is from silent witnesses that much may be learned, as all, I think, will agree who have seen Aunt Branwell's lustre teapot with its text : "To me to live is Christ, to die is gain."

But when all has been visited it is from Haworth itself that the most can be learnt about the Brontës. From Haworth and the moors spreading about it for miles came the source of all exuberance and joy in a life spent all too much in the enforced pursuit of uncongenial tasks and in the society of alien minds. Without the moors Anne would never have been a poet ; without them and the sea she would never have attained to the religious vision by which, in the words of her sister Charlotte, "she was enabled to bear what was to be borne, patiently, serenely, victoriously." For in the last resort Anne Brontë must be judged by the high character which she displayed not only at the end but at every turning in her life. It is for what she was, quite as much as for what she created, that one wants to know more of her.

A tribute to Anne Brontë has long been overdue. In the phrase of George Moore, the champion who rose so belatedly and so singly in her defence, she has been left in the kitchen "as a sort of literary Cinderella, while criticism has raised up thrones for Charlotte and Emily" all too long. It is time the ashes were shaken off Anne's rags, that she was raised from her humble position on the hearth and seated—if not on a throne, then at least on a stout oaken stool —whether beside, behind or before her sisters matters little—but assuredly where the Immortals sit.

W.G.

Haworth, 1959

ACKNOWLEDGMENTS

I am happy to record my indebtedness to the following and to thank them for their help in the preparation of this book : the Council of the Brontë Society for granting me access to the documents in the Brontë Parsonage Museum, Haworth, and for affording me facilities for study and research there ; and to the Museum's custodian, Mr H. G. Mitchell, for his practical help during many months of research ; the Keeper of the Department of Manuscripts at the British Museum for allowing me to see the manuscripts in the Ashley Library relating to Anne Brontë ; the Curator of the Berg Collection in the New York Public Library and Miss Fannie E. Ratchford, Curator of the Rare Books Collection, University of Texas Library, Austin, Texas, for answering queries and for sending me transcripts of manuscripts of Anne Brontë's works in their keeping ; the Curator of the Castle Museum, York, the Curator of Scarborough Museum, the Chief Librarian of Scarborough Public Library, and the Honorary Secretary of the York Georgian Society, for supplying me with much valuable information relative to the antiquities of both towns ; the Rev. F. Northorp, formerly Vicar of Great with Little Ouseburn, York, for his active research on my behalf into the history of three generations of the Robinson family of Thorp Green Hall, Little Ouseburn, from the Parish Registers in his keeping and on other local matters ; The Rev. Canon F. E. Ford, formerly Vicar of St Mary's, Scarborough, for information respecting the churches in Scarborough in Anne Brontë's time, and for permission to copy the entry of her burial ; Canon W. R. M. Chaplin, Vicar of St Lawrence's, Appleby, for making investigations relating to Willy Weightman and his family ; Dr and Mrs Stewart of Kipping House, Thornton, and Mr and Mrs Lister of Heald's House, Dewsbury Moor, for kindly showing me over their homes ; Miss Susan Brooke, M.A., F.S.A., for much valuable information relating to the Ingham family of Blake Hall, Mirfield ; Miss W. M. Stancliffe of the Old Rectory, Mirfield, for particulars regarding the Ingham family and, particularly, regarding Blake Hall before its demolition ; Miss Frances Branwell of Penzance for most kindly supplying facts about the Branwell family.

I am also glad to thank the following for permission to quote extracts from the books listed : Professor Jacques Blondel, *Emily Brontë* ; Mrs Doris Long and Messrs. Hodder & Stoughton, Ltd., *The Brontës, Life and Letters* and *The Brontës and their Circle* by C. K. Shorter ; Miss Fannie E. Ratchford, *The Brontës' Web of Childhood* and *Gondal's Queen* ; Mr Ernest Raymond, *In the Steps of the Brontës* ; Miss Patricia Thomson, *The Victorian Heroine* ; Messrs. W. H. Allen & Co., Ltd., *Emily Brontë* by Mary Duclaux ; Mr C. D. Medley, *Conversations in Ebury Street* by George Moore ; Sir Isaac Pitman & Sons Ltd,. *In the Footsteps of the Brontës* by Ellis Chadwick ; The Shakespeare Head Press, *The Brontës, their Lives, Friendships and Correspondence* edited by T. J. Wise and J. A. Symington.

While every effort has been made to trace the owners of copyright in Brontë texts it has not always been possible to do so. If there are any others whose permission I should have sought before publishing this book, I beg to tender them my sincere apologies for the omission.

Finally, I should like to thank my husband, John Lock, whose vast knowledge of Brontë matters and of the religious background of their times has been invaluable to me.

W.G.

AUTHOR'S NOTE

Since this book was first published in 1959 the text of a hitherto unknown letter of Anne Brontë's was brought to my notice, and is now appended here. Written barely ten days after the death of Emily Brontë, in December 1848, the letter was addressed to Dr David Thom, a Liverpool divine, author of several works on "Universalism", who had evidently written to Acton Bell after the publication of *The Tenant of Wildfell Hall*. There followed more than one exchange of letters, since in the Preface to the Sermons of Dr Thom, published in 1863, the editor commented: ". . . In 1848 appeared *Jane Eyre* and we find this devourer of books yielding to the fascinating charms of Currer Bell. He had soon detected the sex of the author, and was tolerably well satisfied of her North of England residence. An interesting correspondence with the talented sister of Charlotte Brontë (Acton Bell) subsequently took place· on the subject of Universalism."

Anne Brontë's letter, preserved by the descendants of Dr Thom, was published in the *Times Literary Supplement* of 21st June 1923 by its owner, the late Walter Haydon, whose wife was a Miss Thom; it has not subsequently appeared.

A drawing of Anne Brontë's, dated 13th November 1839, is also reproduced here for the first time by kind permission of the Brontë Society.

The text for this new edition of the book has been revised and amended and supplied with additional notes to bring it into line with my more recent research in the field of Brontë studies.

Winifred Gérin

1974

CONTENTS

LIST OF PLATES

I DEDICATE THIS BOOK
TO JOHN
WHOSE LOVE OF ANNE BRONTË
FIRST INSPIRED MINE

Chapter One

THE GODMOTHERS

THE day Anne Brontë was born the other children stayed with Miss Firth at Kipping House. It was the 17th of January 1820— winter at its darkest, the days at their shortest, and Thornton, the suburb of Bradford where the Firths and Brontës resided, a prey to the bitter winds that swept down from the north.

Yet inside Kipping House, with its low raftered ceilings, oak-panelled walls, heavily recessed windows and gigantic hearths, nothing could be more snug or more welcome to the little group of children invited there for the day.

There were Maria, Elizabeth, Charlotte, Branwell and Emily— ranging in age from six years old to eighteen months—undersized, peaky children with perfect manners. Even at that time their idea of playing was sketching, story-telling and reading, and to children with such tastes, what could be more delightful than a long winter's day spent by the fire, indulging in all their favourite pursuits? Indulged, moreover, by their charming and kind young hostess and free to play as they liked all over that wonderful house, for Kipping, as their Papa and Mamma would have told them, was a truly historical place.

Kipping House, dating from the Restoration, is still an enchant-ing house today. It stands just off the main Halifax-Bradford road at the bend of a hollow lane, encircled by fields where, in summer, the air is heady with the scent of meadow-sweet. It is a house full of character, presenting its rear wall to the lane ; its dipping roofs, dormer-windows, irregular chimney-stacks of preternatural height, and postern gate, in no way preparing the visitor for the porticoed entrance door with Corinthian columns by which admission is gained at the front of the house. Here the gardens and grounds slope sharply down towards the river, meandering through what looks like a guard of honour of ancient beech, ash and elm. It is a place where time has, indeed, stood still, where not even the smoke from encroaching industrial centres has stained the air.

The great drawing-room at Kipping where Miss Firth enter-tained her little friends on that January day looks out over the gardens through three immensely high windows, towards the valley and the wooded slopes beyond.   One likes to think that the children pressed eager faces to those very panes, till dusk or falling snow blotted out the scene.   Then the warm damask curtains would be drawn and tea served, and they would crowd round their hostess with those attentive, unchildish faces to hear yet another tale.

For Maria, Elizabeth and Charlotte the ordeal of taking tea at Miss Firth's, though deeply impressive, was not entirely novel. Since the previous year the visits of "M. E. & C. Brontë" were already being entered in Miss Firth's diary when the children had obviously come, as on this occasion, unsupported by either parent. Maria, the eldest, not quite aged five when she first entered the Kipping drawing-room, had, as all who knew her relate, the persuasion and authority of a mother in handling her young sisters and brother.   Charlotte's fastidious manners and perfect taste, we cannot help reflecting, were formed at an early date and at a good school.   We see her, a diminutive child, like her own "Polly", silently absorbing the gracious atmosphere of Miss Firth's drawing-room and even then resenting, as she so violently did later, being taken up on that kind lady's lap and treated like a child.

Miss Firth, then aged twenty-three, made a habit of keeping a diary.   Since the age of fifteen she had noted down the small events that made up her daily life ; the comings and goings of her papa's visitors, her rare and rather unwilling readings of the fashionable authors—Scott, Goldsmith, Moore and Young—and the texts of the sermons of the two services she never failed to attend every Sunday at Thornton Chapel.

The "little Brontës' " papa was Curate-in-charge of Thornton's "Old Bell Chapel", as St James's Church was familiarly called, and by his functions, if not for any more personal considerations, had every claim on Miss Firth's neighbourly solicitude.   For the Firths were a pious family.   Miss Firth's papa was connected by marriage with a long line of pious and well-to-do persons.   A forbear of Mr Firth's had instituted prayer-meetings for the Independents in the great barn adjoining Kipping House, which still bears the date 1669 on its front.   By Mr Brontë's time the Firths, though supporting now the Established Church rather than the Independent Party within its ranks—the quality of their zeal in no way diminished —still continued unchallenged to lead religious society in Thornton.

To befriend the minister of Thornton Chapel, be he single, or married and much encumbered with family as young Mr Brontë was, remained a duty that Mr Firth and his daughter not only performed, but performed with alacrity.

For Miss Firth the Church, and all that pertained to the Church, was the overruling interest of her life, so that Mr Brontë was no sooner appointed to the "Old Bell Chapel" in May 1815 than he and all his family found themselves under her aegis.

Miss Firth's papa was a widower and she was keeping house for him at the time Mr Brontë arrived at Thornton. She was just eighteen and her mamma had been tragically killed the year before by being thrown from her gig at the very door of Kipping House. As the only daughter of well-to-do parents, Elizabeth Firth had had the advantage of a year's "finishing" at the Academy for Young Ladies run by Miss Mangnall at Crofton Hall near Wakefield— Miss Richmal Mangnall whose eminence as an educationalist was to be irrefutably established by the publication of her *Questions*, so soon to become the classic of the Victorian schoolroom. Elizabeth's connection with Crofton Hall was not to be without its influence on the fortunes of the two eldest Brontë girls as, later, her association with Cowan Bridge and Roe Head was to have its repercussion first on Charlotte and then on Anne Brontë. So early may be seen in the lives of the little Brontë girls the traces of their godmother's influence.

In Elizabeth's diary Mr Brontë's predecessor at Thornton Chapel, the Rev. Thomas Atkinson, figured largely. Her final meeting with him and his departure from Thornton are recorded in strains that remind us that the world into which the Brontë children were born, far removed though biographers would make it appear, was nevertheless the very world of Jane Austen, in which Elizabeth Firth's contemporaries, Catherine Morland, Fanny Price and Charlotte Lucas were, like herself, finding curates of palpitating importance in their rural societies.

Elizabeth Firth had a cousin four years older than herself, Fanny Walker, whose home was at Lascelles Hall, an early Georgian mansion at Kirkheaton outside Huddersfield, which, in due course, Charlotte and Anne Brontë were to visit. The two cousins were much together, Elizabeth staying at Lascelles Hall and Frances visiting Elizabeth at Kipping. Here on various occasions she must have met the Rev. Thomas Atkinson. For, while Elizabeth was entering verbatim in her journal the texts and headings of the gentleman's sermons and counting the number of times she met him in the week, the Rev. Mr Atkinson was counting the number of times he met Elizabeth's cousin. Esteeming them all too few, he suddenly asked his colleague Mr Brontë, then minister of Hartshead, if he would consent to an exchange of livings to enable Mr Atkinson to be within closer range of Miss Walker at Huddersfield.

Mr Brontë was perfectly prepared to oblige, the more so since this exchange would place Mrs Brontë considerably nearer the relatives then resident in Bradford to whom she was closely bound by every tie of affection. They were her Uncle and Aunt Fennell (her uncle had only recently been appointed to the Parish Church in Bradford) and their daughter, her cousin Jane who, on the same day and at the same altar rails as herself and Patrick Brontë, had married his best friend William Morgan. William Morgan had also recently been appointed vicar of Christ Church, Bradford, so here, within three miles of Thornton, was a whole circle of friends and relatives whose society would render life at Thornton infinitely more agreeable for young Mr and Mrs Brontë. Mr Atkinson's proposal was acceded to, his last sermon at Thornton preached (Elizabeth recording the event in her journal commented that the "Congregation appeared much affected at the singing of the Valedictory hymn, 'With all Thy power O Lord defend Him whom we now to Thee commend'") and Elizabeth herself, in very low spirits to judge by the tone of her entries, went to stay at Lascelles Hall with her successful cousin.

Her absence from home lasted for nearly six weeks, during which the new minister took up his functions. Mr Brontë, as all Thornton knew, had come, via various curacies, from Ireland. He was thirty-eight years of age and brought with him his wife, his wife's sister, Miss Branwell, and his two little girls—Maria aged about eighteen months and a four-month-old baby not christened as yet. On the very next day after her return home Elizabeth Firth recorded in her diary : "7th June. I called at Mr Brontë's."

"Mr Brontë's", as Elizabeth was always subsequently to call the parsonage as well as the family, was about eight minutes' walk from Kipping House. It was in Market Street—one of the twenty-three houses which made up the total number of habitations in Thornton's main street. So unspoilt, in fact, was Thornton in those days, that the chapel where Mr Brontë had come to officiate stood in the middle of fields with no access to it other than by field paths.

Many years later when looking back to that time Mr Brontë said that to think of Thornton was to "think of Kipping and of his dear friends there". Certainly the friendship seems to have been as immediate as it was to prove enduring. Within the first week of acquaintance Miss Firth is meeting the Brontës on four distinct occasions : she calls at the parsonage, she meets them out at dinner ; inevitably she meets them at church and, naturally, before the week is out, Mrs Brontë and her sister Miss Branwell return Miss Firth's visit by paying their first call at Kipping House.

As they stood on the cobbles before its doors on that June afternoon, they must have thought it very pleasant indeed. It was Monday, 12th June 1815 and, though politics and military matters were a passion with Patrick Brontë in those days, and the ladies of his family would be better informed on current affairs than many females of that time, neither of them could foretell that before the week was out a decisive victory would be won for England, and the rule of Napoleon in Europe overthrown for ever. To them, that Monday afternoon at Thornton, the name of Waterloo as yet meant nothing. If the truth were known, the ladies were more concerned with the particular ordeal before them than with any that might confront the continent of Europe. The young lady on whom they were calling was, despite youth, the acknowledged leader of Thornton society. As with her contemporary, Emma Woodhouse, upon her good graces much of the happiness of the clergyman's wife and her family would depend. However independent-minded the mother of the Brontës might be—and one has only to read her letters to her affianced lover to recognise in her the spiritual mother of Jane Eyre and Agnes Grey—she was a woman of her time ; she knew her social conventions and was well aware that the Lady Catherine de Bourghs of this world can poison the lives of those they deem their social inferiors, among whom curates and their wives were emphatically classed.

But, as the door of Kipping House opened and the two shy little ladies were ushered through the panelled lobby to the gracious drawing-room at its farther end, no Lady Catherine awaited them; not even Emma Woodhouse. The young and eager hostess who rose to greet them may have caused the mother of the future governesses—and authoresses—a moment's qualm, but it was soon dispelled.

One thing is certain : from that day not a week passed throughout the five years of the Brontës' residence at Thornton without frequent social engagements uniting the families from the parsonage and Kipping House. From this initial contact a circle of friends was formed which provided a background of benevolence, as it were, to the little Brontës' earliest days. The links thus formed, though inevitably loosened by time, were never to be quite lost. The godparents, as so many of this circle became, had their small parts to play even after the passage of years.

Within four months of the Brontës' coming to Thornton Mr Firth was married to a lady who seems to have been an exemplary stepmother to Elizabeth, who loved her devotedly from the first. With this pleasant addition to their society, no wonder the diary abounds in tea-drinkings, dinners, church-attendance, lecture-going and country walks, in *all* of which Mr Brontë bore his part and in *some* of which—dependent on her state of health— Mrs Brontë and her sister shared.

The intimacy, indeed, was so fast established that within three months of their first meeting Elizabeth Firth and her papa were standing godparents to the Brontës' second child, called in compliment to her two godmothers—her Aunt Elizabeth Branwell and Miss Firth—Elizabeth likewise.

The presence of "Aunt Branwell" as she later became known, at this early stage in the Brontë story, dispels the legend set going by Mrs Gaskell to the effect that she came north only on the occasion of the death of Mrs Brontë.

Elizabeth Branwell, of whom we shall hear much in the following pages, was seven years older than her sister Maria, and when the latter married Patrick Brontë on 29th December 1812 and another sister, Charlotte, married a cousin on the selfsame day in Penzance, she found herself the only unmarried member of a large family of four sisters and one brother. By her father's will she had been left a competence of £50 a year, a small independence that made her more marriageable than many another young lady in those days. Elizabeth Branwell seems to have had attractions and, according to Ellen Nussey who met her for the first time only in 1833, seems to have been extremely aware of those attractions. She undoubtedly counted on finding a husband as her sisters had done. With no one and nothing to keep her in her native Penzance she visited Maria in Yorkshire, ostensibly to help her through her confinements, but possibly also with an eye to matrimony.

Miss Branwell was with the Brontës when they came to Thornton, and stayed there for over fourteen months. Whether or no she left under a particular disappointment is not recorded, but we do know that she was very much affected in taking leave of her family and friends, as Miss Firth was to note in her diary. Judging by the character she later displayed, it may not perhaps have been so surprising that she left Thornton as she came, a maiden lady.

Since the days of Mrs Gaskell it has always been assumed that Mrs Brontë's married life must have been unhappy. The supposition, however, does not rest on evidence. Apart from the calamity of her early death, with its attendant nine months of stark suffering, Mrs Brontë's life was very much that of the young woman of her time and station. She had not expected to be rich and no doubt came to terms with her clerical poverty as well as, or even better than, many other young women married to clergymen on a stipend of £200 a year. That she was very much in love with her "Saucy Pat" her witty letters on the eve of their marriage attest. She had six children in seven years. Admittedly, by modern standards, this is dreadful, but it was nothing exceptional in the first decades of the nineteenth century. What differentiates Mrs Brontë from other young wives of the period is that she successfully survived her six confinements.

Nor was she, like her modern counterparts, destitute of domestic help. Ill-paid as Mr Brontë was, he did not leave his wife without a servant nor, after the birth of a third little girl, Charlotte, in 1816, without a children's nurse as well. Nancy Garrs, the predecesso. of the more famous "Tabby" and Martha Brown, took the little Brontës as nurslings when she herself was a girl in her teens. Her devotion to them was instantaneous and life-long.

There seems no reason to doubt that a true harmony reigned in the parsonage in Market Street. To Mrs Brontë, unwitting of the fate awaiting her at Haworth, Thornton brought beloved children and good friends. There was a whole host of them : Firths, Outhwaites, Ibbotsons, Jowetts and Elizabeth Firth's cousin Frances Walker and her affianced lover Mr Atkinson, Mr Brontë's successor at Hartshead. They were not yet married when, in June 1816, together with Elizabeth Firth, they stood sponsors to Charlotte,

born on 21st April of that year. Together with the Firths—
Mr Firth and his second wife, who stood sponsors to Branwell—
the Fennells and the Morgans (Jane Morgan and her mother, Jane
Fennell, were Emily's godparents, hence the "Emily Jane") they
were faithfully to befriend poor Mrs Brontë's children long after
she was gone.

By the time it was Anne's turn to be christened the happy
Thornton days were almost over. Within a month of her birth
her father was licensed as perpetual curate to Haworth—a moorland
village six miles to the north-west of Thornton—and the family's
removal there had become an inevitability instead of a disagreeable
contingency that, for the past year, had been facing Mr and
Mrs Brontë.

Mr Brontë was licensed to Haworth on 25th February 1820
but, as it turned out, the family did not move there until 20th April.

Anne's christening took place on 25th March, the Saturday
before Easter, the ceremony being performed by the Rev. William
Morgan, by now not only Mr Brontë's closest friend but the almost
official "celebrant" of every one of the family's sacraments. For
the third time Miss Firth stood godmother to one of the Brontë
babies. Together with her close friend of Crofton Hall days, Miss
Fanny Outhwaite—one of the intimates of the Brontës' Thornton
circle and daughter of a well-known Bradford doctor—Miss Firth
and her Papa stood sponsors for Anne. She was named after
Mrs Brontë's mother—then deceased—and an elder sister who had
died young.

Although as already said Anne's christening did not take place
till 25th March, in Miss Firth's cash accounts for January 1820 she
entered £1 as being given at "Anne Brontë's christening". In the
register of Anne's baptism at the Old Bell Chapel her father's
"profession" is entered for the first time as "Minister of Haworth".
The appointment was thus officially sealed and Thornton could no
longer be called the Brontës' home. In less than a month's time
the baby girl being held over the old stone font to receive the sign
of the cross from William Morgan's podgy finger, would be gone
to live in her father's new parish on the other side of Oxenhope
Moor. Of Thornton Anne Brontë would take nothing with her
but the loving solicitude of her two godmothers.

While the parsonage at Haworth was being made ready to
receive Mrs Brontë and the six little children (the eldest only six

and a half years old) they stayed for the last time at Kipping House. Tradition in the Firth family has it that it was from there that the final removal took place.

Mr Brontë may have retailed all the advantages to be derived from the very much more commodious house and garden awaiting them at Haworth, the bracing air and open situation of the village ; the grand and inspiriting scenery all around, at which he had as yet been able to cast only hurried glances on his rounds ; to Mrs Brontë a district without friends had no attractions, and nothing could make her consider the removal in any other light than that of a banishment. For her, indeed, it was to be an end. For the children also—although all, necessarily, looked on it as a beginning —it meant an end to the sheltered, halcyon days of early childhood, the familiar Thornton round, the benevolent smiling faces that, down the vista of the long five years, seemed always to have surrounded their daily goings out and comings in. None of them could have guessed that, for them, Haworth was to be a fulfilment.

On a fine spring morning, just three months after Anne Brontë was born, the hour of parting came. Waving tearful farewells to the dejected group standing about the door of Kipping, the little cavalcade set out for the unknown.

Chapter Two

A CHOICE OF STEPMOTHERS

ACCORDING to family tradition and the editor of Miss Firth's diary, Mr Brontë's correspondence with that lady subsequent to the family's removal to Haworth was destroyed "only . . . just before the Miss Brontës became famous". With the letters must have gone the entries of her diary for the years 1821–4 because, to our lasting loss, these are not forthcoming. Thus the precious evidence of a close friend on the events of the first momentous years at Haworth is lacking, and all the light we possess by which to illumine the scene derives from servants' gossip and hearsay which, amplified and distorted in later years before it reached the ears of Mrs Gaskell, has left such an ugly reflection on the character of Mr Brontë ; a reflection which, when the ascertainable facts at length emerge, appears to have been wholly unmerited.

The last glimpse the Thornton friends had of Mrs Brontë and her children as they drove away that April morning across the moors had been dimmed by tears. It is very doubtful if they ever saw her again. The Firths, who most probably intended later, when their friends should be finally settled in, to drive over and call on them in their new home, were themselves shortly to be preoccupied with the illness and then the death of Mr Firth on 27th December 1820, a date which almost coincided with the beginning of the calamities overtaking the Brontë family. On both sides the valedictions were thus final that 20th April when the Brontës drove away to Haworth. Happily neither party knew what was awaiting them.

The family moved in eight covered wagons, seven taking the furniture, and Mrs Brontë and the children travelling in the eighth. At the height of his physical powers as Mr Brontë then was, there is nothing remarkable in the description of him given to Mrs Chadwick by eye-witnesses, walking all the way by the side of the covered cart and occasionally lifting out one of the children to take a little exercise, for the rate of progress along the rough moorland road could only be slow.

10

Nowadays it takes half an hour to cover the eight miles by car. In 1820 it took the Brontë family all day.

Whether they struck Haworth over "the Brow" or approached it from the Halifax Road via Cross Roads, the formidable ascent of Main Street—Kirkgate, as it was called in those days—had to be undertaken. We are told that the inhabitants of Haworth stood on their door-steps to see the new incumbent's family arrive. Their presence could but emphasise the narrowness of a street already constricted by the height and unbroken frontage of the houses whose stone façades present a rampart to the view of those laboriously making the ascent.

In the Brontës' time there were no pavements at all ; the houses opened flush upon the street whose flagstones, then as now, were placed "end-ways" in order, as Mrs Gaskell said, "to give a better hold to the horses' feet". The sense of overwhelming power and permanence which Haworth Main Street still awakens in the newcomer could have struck Mrs Brontë and her children even then, seeing it for the first time on that spring evening. What they saw is almost identically what we see today, a village of considerable antiquity even in 1820, with the majority of its dwellings dating back to Stuart times.

No letters to any of the relatives and friends at Bradford, Thornton or Hartshead (the Rev. Thomas Atkinson had married Frances Walker in December 1817 and now lived permanently in Mr Brontë's old parish), or even to Elizabeth Branwell in far-off Cornwall, survive to tell us what were the reactions of Mr and Mrs Brontë on reaching their new home.

Human contacts would be lacking both to begin with and for the next few years, but there cannot have been two opinions on the great superiority of the Haworth parsonage over that at Thornton, and on the grandeur and magnificence of the surrounding country. The proximity of the moors which begin within five minutes' walk of the parsonage, and the parsonage garden itself— a luxury totally wanting at Thornton—must immediately have appeared to both parents as of incalculable benefit to the children.

In that garden, divided on two sides from the surrounding churchyard by high stone walls, meagrely planted with a few lilac and currant bushes, a laburnum and a cherry-tree and a patch of lawn in the centre, Anne's first staggering steps were made. The elders—the four big sisters and the only brother—were, from the very beginning, tenderly attached to the little sister, born so delicate that Charlotte recalled in after years that "from her childhood Anne seemed preparing for an early death."

Anne's particular trouble was asthma. It is worth noting that of all that family of ill-fated children she was the only one to be recognised as delicate and to be acknowledged as suffering from a congenital weakness. Whether it was that her mother already carried the seeds of her fell disease when she bore Anne, or whether she never fully recovered after Anne's birth (her sixth child in seven years) Mrs Brontë was taken mortally ill less than a fortnight after Anne's first birthday.

It was the 29th of January 1821, and she was not expected to survive the day. Unhappily for her she rallied and lived for yet another eight months of intolerable suffering. It was an internal cancer as the doctor, hurriedly fetched, told the distracted husband. Mr Brontë sent for more than one specialist during his wife's illness, refusing to accept the hopeless verdict, but of course nothing could be done to save her or even to alleviate her suffering. The little Brontës were suddenly plunged into the most tragic situation that children can know. For eight long months their mother lay dying in the new house which had not yet had time to become their home. The gracious presence which should have pervaded all its rooms and ordered its daily life never had time to be imprinted on its air.

Of the surviving children Charlotte, alone, in later life, was to remember her mother playing in the twilight with her only son. Neither that son himself, nor Emily nor Anne would preserve any memory of their mother.

Mrs Brontë died on 15th September 1821, a year and five months after the family had settled in Haworth.

In May Miss Branwell had arrived from Cornwall and had taken charge of the household, her brother-in-law and the six little children. Her coming was regarded as an unqualified blessing by both Mr and Mrs Brontë. A great affection had always bound the sisters, and Miss Branwell's presence could at least alleviate Mrs Brontë's worst anxiety on the score of her children. The two young servants, Nancy and Sarah Garrs, beloved of the children as they were, had neither the authority nor the experience to control them effectively.

Never one to scant her duty, Miss Branwell filled the immense void left by the invalid to the very best of her capacity. But not for a moment did she consider her sojourn in Haworth as other than temporary. She took an instant and irreducible dislike to the place, deploring its lack of amenities and strongly disapproving the independent and sturdy character of its inhabitants. As yet, during the hot summer months while her sister lay dying, no inkling of the rigours of the climate presented itself to her unsuspecting mind.

Then, as later, she found her chief solace in the pretty manners and endearing ways of her only nephew and her youngest niece. Miss Branwell loved Anne at sight.

There may have been more than one reason for this. More than any other of the Brontë children Anne resembled her mother (a comparison of Anne's portrait with that of her mother at fifteen corroborates this fact). Anne was unmistakably a Branwell. She was, moreover, from her earliest infancy "a darling child", "a quaint little child", "the darling of the home", as the servants said, promising early to be the prettiest of the little Brontë girls. She was a good little child with an exceptionally loving nature. From the first Miss Branwell hoped to shape her heart and mind after her own image.

Of Anne's babyhood one story remains. Nancy Garrs, the children's nursemaid, who lived to a great old age, used to recall how "when Anne was a baby, Charlotte rushed into her Papa's study to say that there was an angel standing by Anne's cradle, but when they returned it was gone, though Charlotte was sure she had seen it"—a tribute both to Charlotte's imagination and Anne's early character !

Branwell, as the only boy of the family, was qualified to gain his aunt's approbation which his elder, cleverer and already more stubborn sisters could not fail to forfeit even at this early hour ; Miss Branwell was nothing if not partial in her opinions.

With her advent at the parsonage, the number of persons living there rose to twelve. As always when considering the sleeping accommodation of the Brontës, one shudders to think of the seeds of disease sown through inadequate accommodation.

Haworth Parsonage is, emphatically, *not* the grim prison-house described by all too many of the writers who have cursorily visited it. It is a dignified, finely proportioned Georgian house, built in the seventeen-seventies, but it contained only five bedrooms, of which one was a narrow slip without a fireplace over the entrance-hall, and another little more than a box-room over the back. Into these five rooms Mr and Mrs Brontë, their six children, Miss Branwell, the two servants and Mrs Brontë's nurse had to be packed. In the worst room of all from the point of view of hygiene the four eldest girls slept in little camp-beds that were collapsed by day, when it was converted into the children's nursery. Here, until long after they were into their teens, the survivors slept, played, wrote and enjoyed unchallenged liberty. The dimensions of the room are 9 ft by 5 ft 7½ in.

Mrs Brontë's death left her widower financially crippled and the frightful problem unresolved of how best to act for his six children, the youngest of whom was only twenty months old.

The good friends he had made since he first came to Yorkshire, the Morgans, the Fennells, the Firths, the Outhwaites and the Atkinsons, came to his help now and sent him sufficient sums of money to pay off the immediate debts incurred by the long and—in those days—expensive illness of his wife.

The other problem could not so easily be resolved. Miss Branwell was prepared to bide his time and to allow a decent interval to elapse before expecting him to do what all his contemporaries did in a like situation—to take another wife—but she was not prepared to remain permanently in Yorkshire and to forgo the pleasant independence of her life in Penzance. To Miss Branwell, who had shared in the agreeable Thornton round, the question cannot have been so much whom he would marry, as when the marriage would take place.

Mr Brontë probably let a year elapse, but some time in 1822 the inevitable proposal was made : he asked Miss Elizabeth Firth to marry him. Though Mr Brontë and Miss Branwell had not our privilege of looking over the pages of her diary, they cannot fail to have entertained sanguine hopes of the result. Miss Firth's conduct since their first meeting in 1815 must have convinced the gentleman of her partiality—a partiality kept, naturally, well within bounds, but nonetheless perceptible to the discerning eye.

Miss Firth was the obvious, the ideal stepmother for the little Brontës ; from their birth, almost, she had cherished them with a peculiar tenderness. Miss Firth was, moreover, a very charming and gifted lady, by no means lacking in the essential feminine graces (it must not be forgotten that Mr Brontë was only forty-four, a vigorous man as yet in the prime of life) ; and, finally, Miss Firth had inherited a fortune in her own right. Could he have done better either for himself or for his poor little children ?

The incredible thing, to us as to him no doubt, is that Miss Firth refused him. Poor Mr Brontë must so confidently have written those letters whose destruction we deplore. Whether Miss Firth refused him outright or played for time, we shall never know. Until midsummer 1823 he does not seem entirely to have given up hope. But refuse him finally she did, and it is impossible not to reflect what would have been the history of the Brontë sisters if her answer had been different.

Would the conventional mind of Miss Firth have cramped the budding minds of genius ? Would her kindness have been compensation enough for the loss of that freedom which they achieved under the motherless régime of Haworth Parsonage ? Would her money, enabling them to dispense with the slavery of life as governesses, have been fatal to the poets within their breasts ? Who can tell ?

Certainly the rejection was not made in a wounding manner (unlike the second rejection to which the poor man was shortly to expose himself). Miss Firth, within two years to marry the Rev. James Clarke Franks, Vicar of Huddersfield (another old friend and member of the Thornton circle), was to remain the most amiable of correspondents and kindest of friends to Mr Brontë and his children until her death. Her influence, extending right through the adolescence of the Brontë girls, brought advice, choice presents and occasional holidays without which they would have been yet poorer than they were. Mr Brontë's impeccably courteous letters over the years allow no trace of pique to appear ; he was obviously only too thankful that his daughters had in Mrs Franks so true a friend.

It is not without interest to remember in this connection Mrs Gaskell's assertion regarding the complete social isolation in which the Brontë girls grew up. Knowing nothing about the wide circle of friends that Mr Brontë had made in his early days and preserved through life, she wrote : ". . . they grew up out of childhood into girlhood bereft, in a singular manner, of all such society as would have been natural to their age, sex and station."

It is believed that Mr Brontë made three attempts at finding a wife and was equally unsuccessful in all.

His mortifying rejection by Miss Mary Burder—a former sweet-
heart of his Wethersfield days—is sufficiently well known to need
no repetition here. This time the lady "added so many keen
sarcasms" to her refusal that she stunned Mr Brontë into silence
for over five months. Even then, still recalling how "affectionate,
kind, forgiving, agreeable in person and still more agreeable in
mind" Miss Burder had been fourteen years before when he had
lodged at her aunt's, Mr Brontë had the folly to return to the
charge. If she ever replied her letter is no longer extant.

All that is known of Mr Brontë's third attempt at matrimony
is an indirect allusion contained in a letter by a young lady of
Keighley, a Miss Isabella Dury, to a friend, in which she wrote:
"I heard . . . that I had quarrelled with my brother about Mr
Brontë. I beg if ever you hear such a report, you will contradict
it as I can assure you it is perfectly unfounded. I think I should
never be so very silly as to have the most distant idea of marrying
anybody who has not some fortune and six children into the
bargain. It is too ridiculous to imagine any truth in it." That
was in January 1824.

By the early spring of 1824 it had thus been sufficiently brought
home to Mr Brontë that he must make some *other* arrangement for
the care and upbringing of what he persisted in rather euphemisti-
cally calling his "small but sweet little family".

Whether on his representations or on the prompting of her own
pronounced sense of duty, Miss Branwell took up her permanent
abode at Haworth.

The decision was a momentous one. For the lady herself the
sacrifice proved greater than she could successfully make ; she
allowed it to embitter not only her own life but that of the young
creatures committed to her care. The imprint of Miss Branwell,
not only on the current of their days but upon the very colour of
their minds, was to be well-nigh indelible, particularly in the case
of Anne, and its removal achieved only after a life-long struggle.

Sad as their motherless childhood must have been, it need never
have been "oppressed by sin and woe" but for the gloomy regimen
of their maiden aunt.

Chapter Three

FUNERAL BELL

THUS the little Brontës' fate was decided. They were to have no stepmother, but a maiden aunt to rule over their home. For better or for worse the die was cast : the future, alone, would show with what results to themselves.

One of the first deliberate decisions taken by Miss Branwell was to insist that the two elder girls be sent away to school. Neither now nor later would Miss Branwell be made responsible for the education of her nieces. Fine sewing of every description she was willing and competent to instruct them in ; in the rudiments of their letters and grammar as well she was prepared to ground them. But to assume the onerous task of their education, as their mother, had she lived, would most certainly have done, Miss Branwell from the outset firmly declined to do. It was a period in which in nearly every home the mother assumed the education of her daughters, until their teens, when they were sent away for a year or two of schooling to acquire that "polish" which could never quite be achieved at home.

Thus, by the middle of the year 1823 the education of his elder daughters became the most pressing problem for Mr Brontë to resolve.

In view of the burden of blame usually cast on him for the Cowan Bridge tragedy it is only fair to recall that his first choice of a school for his daughters was unexceptionable. Certainly on the advice of Miss Firth—and probably at her expense—Maria and Elizabeth were sent to Richmal Mangnall's famous school, Crofton Hall near Wakefield, where Miss Firth and her friend Miss Outhwaite had themselves been educated.

Unfortunately they stayed only a short time at Crofton Hall. To the everlasting regret of their family—and of all Brontë lovers —they did not return there after the Christmas holidays. Possibly through one of his various clerical friends, Mr Brontë had received circulars of a new school whose curriculum was especially designed for the daughters of clergymen and whose fees were equally adjusted to their peculiar needs.

For the sum of £14 per annum "The Clergy Daughters' School" at Cowan Bridge, near Kirkby Lonsdale, in Westmorland, offered not only to educate but to clothe, feed, find in books and supply with medical attendance the daughters of any gentleman in holy orders. With five daughters needing shortly to be educated, is it surprising that Mr Brontë should have read the prospectus as something in the nature of an answer to prayer? Since Miss Branwell had no inclination towards pedagogy (her limitations in this field would be all too apparent hereafter) the little Brontë girls must go to school, and where could their father find better value than at Cowan Bridge? He could not, or would not perhaps, always be beholden to friends to send them to expensive schools like Crofton Hall. No, Cowan Bridge was the answer.

Mr Brontë was not the only desperate clergyman encumbered with daughters who jumped at that offer in January 1824. Forty-six children were enrolled in that first year and Mr Brontë hurried to enrol Maria and Elizabeth. They were not, however, able to join the school until the second term, on 1st July 1824, because of an epidemic of whooping-cough and measles which swept through Haworth and the parsonage that winter, and confined all the poor little Brontës to their beds for several weeks. None of them escaped the dual infection and they were all very ill.

Nancy Garrs maintained later that Maria and Elizabeth were given no chance to recuperate like the other children, who were allowed to run wild on the moors during that spring and early summer, and made an excellent recovery thanks to the good air. According to Nancy, whose testimony might excusably be biased (her considered opinion of Miss Branwell was that she was "a bit of a tyke"), their aunt kept the two little girls indoors all day in her stuffy bedroom sewing their new underclothes in preparation for going to school, so that they took with them to "Lowood" bodies already undermined by disease. It is the height of irony that the sewing, to which, according to Nancy, the poor little girls owed their decline, was found by the school authorities at Cowan Bridge to be so remarkably bad!

The registers of the Clergy Daughters' School at Cowan Bridge (later to be removed to Casterton) contain the entries made on the occasion of the arrival and departure of the four little Brontë girls. Against Maria and Elizabeth's names it is recorded that the one "works [sews] badly" and the other "works *very* badly".

Altogether, the Cowan Bridge registers do not redound to the credit of Miss Branwell's instruction. It must be remembered that, by the time the children entered school, their aunt had lived with them for over three years and the rudiments of their education had been in her hands. Maria (aged ten) was found to read "tolerably", Elizabeth (aged nine) to read "little". Only Emily (aged six) read "very prettily". Maria wrote "pretty well", so did Elizabeth, but Charlotte (aged eight) wrote "indifferently". Maria knew "very little Geography or History", Elizabeth knew "nothing of Grammar, Geography, History or accomplishments". Charlotte's ignorance of these subjects was complete, but it was noticed, even at Cowan Bridge, that she was "altogether clever of her age, but knows nothing systematically".

That would seem to be the general inference ; the children had been taught nothing systematically. Not only then, but for many years to come, Aunt was to hold them in her stuffy room, stitching at the fine calicoes and cambrics of their underwear, making accomplished needlewomen of them and hearing them repeat their lessons in spelling, grammar and arithmetic which, alone of their father's teaching, she was competent to supervise.

All the wealth of information that Maria, in particular, at this time and the others later acquired, came to them through contact with their father. Mr Brontë told Mrs Gaskell that he could converse with Maria on any subject of topical interest—political, military or literary—just as with an intellectual equal.

The precocity of *all* the children at this very time, from ten-year-old Maria to four-year-old Anne, could not be better exemplified than by the story of the "Masks" which Mr Brontë later reported to Mrs Gaskell. As an illustration of the children's maturity of mind, it is an eloquent commentary on the findings of the Cowan Bridge School authorities.

The story gives us a first clear image of Anne at four years old.

"When my children were very young," wrote Mr Brontë, "when, as far as I can remember, the oldest was about ten years of age, and the youngest about four, thinking that they knew more than I had yet discovered, in order to make them speak with less timidity, I deemed that if they were put under a sort of cover I might gain my end ; and happening to have a mask in the house, I told them all to stand and speak boldly from under cover of the mask.

"I began with the youngest (Anne, afterwards Acton Bell) and asked what a child like her most wanted ; she answered, 'Age and experience'. I asked the next (Emily, afterwards Ellis Bell) what I had best do with her brother Branwell, who was sometimes a naughty boy ; she answered, 'Reason with him, and when he won't listen to reason, whip him'. I asked Branwell what was the best way of knowing the difference between the intellects of men and women ; he answered, 'By considering the difference between them as to their bodies'. I then asked Charlotte what was the best book in the world ; she answered, 'The Bible'. And what was the next best ; she answered, 'The Book of Nature'. I then asked the next, what was the best mode of education for a woman ; she answered, 'That which would make her rule her house well'. Lastly, I asked the oldest what was the best mode of spending time ; she answered, 'By laying it out in preparation for a happy eternity'."

As though to forestall possible incredulity in his readers, Mr Brontë added : "I may not have given precisely their words, but I have nearly done so, as they made a deep and lasting impression on my memory. The substance, however, was exactly what I have stated."

It is the last picture we have of the six children together. On 1st July 1824 Maria and Elizabeth were taken to Cowan Bridge by their father. He put up at the school for the night, shared the children's meals next day and returned to Haworth perfectly satisfied with all he had seen and heard. Since his experience of girls' schools was nil, he could have no standard of comparison. He paid an entrance fee of £7 for each child and £4 for books and clothing.

His good impressions were obviously not contradicted by any ill reports from the little girls themselves, for on 10th August he returned to Cowan Bridge, taking Charlotte with him. Emily, doubtless not yet sufficiently recovered, did not follow her sisters till 25th November. She had turned six on 30th July. This reprieve allowed her to witness a natural phenomenon on the moors of Haworth which probably left a lasting impression on her mind.

Less than a month after Charlotte's going from home, on a Thursday afternoon (the date was 2nd September 1824) Branwell, aged seven, Emily, aged six, and Anne, aged four years and eight

months, were taken by Nancy and Sarah Garrs for a walk on the
moors. What happened there is much better told in Mr Brontë's
own words :

"As the day was exceedingly fine, I had sent my little children,
who were indisposed [author's italics] accompanied by the servants,
to take an airing on the common." [The "common" of Mr Brontë's
account and of Emily's poem,

A little and a lone green lane
That opens on a common wide

is not the open grazing ground usually designated by the word.
The common at Haworth is swelling, heathy ground rising
immediately behind the parsonage and merging within a distance
of three hundred yards with the open moor. It is reached by a
flagged way across the fields.]

Nancy and Sarah, like typical nursery-maids, did not confine
their walk to the common, as their reverend employer supposed,
but walked their little charges, "indisposed" or not indisposed, a
matter of four miles over the moors, as the sequel shows. No
wonder that, to resume Mr Brontë's story, "they stayed rather
longer than I expected. I went to an upper chamber," he continues, "to look out for their return. The heavens over the moors
were blackening fast. I heard muttering of distant thunder, and
saw the frequent flashing of the lightning. Though, ten minutes
before, there was scarcely a breath of air stirring, the gale freshened
rapidly, and carried along with it clouds of dust and stubble : and
by this time, some large drops of rain clearly announced an
approaching heavy shower. My little family had escaped to a
place of shelter, but I did not know it. I consequently watched
every movement of the coming tempest with a painful degree of
interest. The house was perfectly still. Under these circumstances
I heard a deep distant explosion, something resembling, yet something differing from thunder, and I perceived a gentle tremor in the
chamber in which I was standing and in the glass of the window
just before me, which, at the time, made an extraordinary impression
on my mind ; and which, I have no manner of doubt now, was the
effect of an Earthquake at the place of eruption."

In this sermon, expressly written to point the moral of this
"solemn visitation of Providence" and delivered in Haworth Church
on Sunday, 12th September 1824, Mr Brontë was describing the

bog-burst which has since been known locally as the Crow Hill Bog Eruption.

The physical scars of this tremendous upheaval can still be seen today. Deep pits, like shell-holes, seam the peaty ground for miles about the centre of the occurrence which, being on high ground, sent hurtling down into the valleys below gigantic boulders of the blue-grey millstone grit of which this rocky soil is formed. The detonations must have echoed and re-echoed within the circle of these hills where the thunder gets trapped, like a wild beast in a cage, and goes roaring around for hours. The mere volume of noise must have been overwhelming to childish ears. At the same time, according to eye-witness accounts, a great gush of mud, released by the burst above, began slowly to advance, "its solid, oncoming front black and sticky : a man had time to count his sins thrice over whilst the monster crept stealthily toward him. There are those about the moorside who remember seeing the spectacle : and they say that it seemed as if the whole moor top were turning over on its side and rolling downward."

If, on his own avowal, "an extraordinary impression" was made on Mr Brontë's mind (at a distance of four miles) what must have been the effect upon young children ? Not one of terror, as the whole sequel of their lives was to demonstrate. An acceptance of nature in *all* her moods was to be a characteristic of Emily and Anne in particular ; an acceptance and a reverence bordering upon worship. They were never to be fair-weather admirers of hers, but instruments so finely attuned to her moods that she could play on them as she pleased. As a prelude to a lifetime spent in closest communion with her, can one doubt that the experience to which the children were exposed that day gave them an early insight into the forces at work behind the universe ?

The short interval between Charlotte's going to school and Emily's following her was the first time that Emily and Anne had been closely thrown together. A momentous circumstance when their eventual devotion is considered ; a devotion which, according to Ellen Nussey, could be compared only to that uniting twins.

Emily at this time, as the Superintendent of the Clergy Daughters' School was to observe and to remember years later, was "a darling child", all curls and impetuosity. The instinct to protect the weak and oppressed was born with her. For the first time she stood alone in the position of elder sister to Anne, whose delicacy even at that early time called out everything that was chivalrous in Emily. For an all-too-short interval of three months they were thrown together as never before and then, on 25th November, Emily was driven away to Cowan Bridge. Not for seven months could Anne hope to see her again.

Another painful change was about to take place in Anne's world, a change particularly affecting to a child of her age. Mr Brontë decided, for financial reasons, to get rid of Nancy and Sarah Garrs. Anne had never known home without either of these kind creatures whose love for her was as lasting as it was entire.

The decision had probably to be reached because Nancy was leaving in any case, to get married, and because, as Mr Brontë himself said, he wanted an "elderly woman" in place of "two young ones" (the latter decision smacks more of Miss Branwell than of Mr Brontë). However the change originated, it coincided with Emily's going to school.

The "elderly woman" who took the place of the Garrs sisters has played a very big part in the Brontë story. Her name was Tabitha Aykroyd and, if only Anne could have known it then, her coming was to bring untold happiness to the parsonage children. She was a widow, aged fifty-three, a Haworth woman with several relatives in the village. With her advent, in November 1824, the pattern of life at the parsonage took on a new form, with which Tabitha Aykroyd—or, as she soon became known, "Tabby"—was to be indissolubly linked until her own death at the age of eighty-four.

It is probable that, but for the events which were soon to break over the family's heads, Anne would in due course have followed her sisters to the Clergy Daughters' School at Cowan Bridge.

How that establishment appeared to a child we know from the pages of *Jane Eyre*.

In letters written on various occasions during her adult life, Charlotte spoke of Cowan Bridge ; her judgments therein expressed may be taken to represent her matured opinion written neither under the sting of suffering nor heightened for purposes of fiction. Her final judgment on "Lowood" can best be found in a letter to Miss Wooler dated 28th August 1848 : "My personal knowledge [of the Clergy Daughters' School] is very much out of date, being derived from the experience of twenty years ago ; the establishment was at that time in its infancy, and a sad, rickety infancy it was. Typhus fever decimated the school periodically, and consumption and scrofula in every variety of form, which bad air and water, and bad, insufficient diet can generate, preyed on the ill-fated pupils. I understand it is very much altered for the better since those days."

In a letter to her publisher written in later years, Charlotte said : "I was never at Cowan Bridge but for one little year as a very little girl. I am certain I have long been forgotten : though for myself I remember all and everything clearly. Early impressions are ineffaceable. . . . My career was a very quiet one. I was plodding and industrious, perhaps I was very grave, for I suffered to see my sisters perishing. . . ."

The question to which there seems no satisfactory reply returns hauntingly every time one considers the case : Why did the children never write home to complain ? That Mr Brontë and Miss Branwell would have overlooked complaints of so serious a nature is unthinkable. Selfish father as Mr Brontë's detractors would make him out to be, he was, by all the tangible evidence to hand, a uniformly fond and proud parent. The inescapable conclusion is that none of the little girls ever wrote to complain. Whether they were prevented from doing so, one can only surmise.

Once during the course of that calamitous year the children received a visit at Cowan Bridge. Miss Firth, married to the Rev. James Franks on 21st September 1824, noted in her diary that, in the course of their honeymoon, she and her husband called at the school to see the three little girls (Emily had not joined them as yet) and left them each a tip of half a crown. Unhappily the visit occurred far too early in the children's sojourn for any startling symptoms of disease to have made themselves manifest as yet. Mr and Mrs Franks probably only added unwittingly to the fool's paradise in which Mr Brontë lived by writing encouraging reports of the little girls.

On 14th February 1825 Maria left Cowan Bridge "in ill-health" as the school registers report, but did not die until 6th May. Four other girls left the school "in ill-health" on the days immediately before or following Maria, and in two cases their deaths preceded hers. (Altogether twenty-eight girls out of a total of seventy-seven left Cowan Bridge in the course of that year.)

On 31st May Elizabeth left Cowan Bridge "in ill-health". Some facts relative to her journey home have been preserved in the accounts of the Clergy Daughters' School. She was sent home in the company of the school housekeeper, Mrs Hardacre. The items entered read as follows :

Elizabeth's fare home, guard & coach man	13	0
Mrs Hardacre's fare	18	0
Horse, gig, pikes and men	2	6
Mrs Hardacre's bed at Keighley	1	0
2 letters	1	$4\frac{1}{2}$

The alarm caused by Elizabeth's collapse, so shortly following upon Maria's death, seems to have galvanised the school authorities. On the same day that Elizabeth was sent home Charlotte and Emily were dispatched to a holiday home owned by the school—or rather, by its Principal, the Rev. Carus Wilson, at Silverdale, near Morecambe Bay. The house, which was called "The Cove", was within sight of the sea, but the little Brontë girls, arriving late at night and hurriedly put to bed in a room at the back of the house, were destined not to see the sea on that occasion. Early in the morning Mr Brontë arrived to fetch his children home. Elizabeth's dying look must now have convinced the wretched father of the school's utter unsuitability for his delicate children.

Under such heart-breaking circumstances were Anne's sisters restored to her. A fortnight after the return of Charlotte and Emily, on 15th June, Elizabeth died and in her turn was carried into the old church to be buried at the side of her mother and elder sister.

What the effect of the deaths of Maria and Elizabeth must have been upon their sisters and brother, only those can guess who have lost a beloved elder brother or sister in childhood. The very foundations of life are undermined. That someone young, almost as young as oneself, should die seems impossible. Aunts die, uncles die, characters in fiction die, but not the admired model on whom the pattern of one's own life has been formed ; the elder who, while dispensing justice and advice like a parent, is yet so much nearer than a parent at that age.

The Brontë children, already bereft of a mother's love, had set their affections upon Maria who had so gallantly tried to fill that mother's place. That she was "grave, thoughtful and quiet to a degree beyond her years", the servants attested ; that her father could converse with her on any of the leading topics of the day with as much freedom and pleasure as with any grown-up person, Mr Brontë himself told Mrs Gaskell. To her younger sisters and brother Maria had been the source of all happiness and love. With her death tenderness went out of their lives.

Nor, in their terrible sorrow, were the children spared any of the physical aspects of the calamity. In lines written many years later Branwell recalled vividly all the paraphernalia of mourning which nineteenth-century custom was pleased to impose upon the bereaved, and from which the elders had neither the psychology nor the sensibility to exempt the young children.

To see Maria in her coffin, Branwell and, undoubtedly, Anne were inexorably led. By the time Elizabeth died, Charlotte and Emily were also at home to share in the ghoulish rites.

Every detail of that fearful experience was branded upon Branwell's memory, to be recalled later, in 1841, in his poem "Caroline". Probably only then, when he was twenty-four, did Branwell dare to face and exorcise that nightmare of his childhood. It might explain much of his subsequent instability. The verses are his valediction to Maria.

Caroline

I stooped to pluck a rose that grew
Beside this window, waving then ;
But back my little hand withdrew,
From some reproof of inward pain ;
For she who loved it was not there
To check me with her dove-like eye,
And something bid my heart forbear
Her favourite rose-bud to destroy.
Was it that bell—that funeral bell,
Sullenly sounding on the wind ?
Was it that melancholy knell
Which first to sorrow woke my mind ?
I looked upon my mourning dress,
Till my heart beat with childish fear,
And frightened at my loneliness,
I watched, some well-known sound to hear.
But all without lay silent in
The sunny hush of afternoon,
And only muffled steps within
Passed slowly and sedately on.

There lay she then, as now she lies—
For not a limb has moved since then—
In dreamless slumber closed, those eyes
That never more might wake again.
She lay, as I had seen her lie
On many a happy night before,
When I was humbly kneeling by—
Whom she was teaching to adore :
Oh, just as when by her I prayed,
And she to heaven sent up my prayer,
She lay with flowers about her head—
Though formal grave-clothes hid her hair !
Still did her lips the smile retain
Which parted them when hope was high,
Still seemed her brow as smoothed from pain
As when all thought she could not die
And, though her bed looked cramped and strange,
Her too bright cheek all faded now,
My young eye scarcely saw a change
From hours when moonlight paled her brow.
And yet I felt—and scarce could speak—
A chilly face, a faltering breath,
When my hand touched the marble cheek
Which lay so passively beneath.

My father's stern eye dropt a tear
Upon the coffin resting there.
My mother [read "Aunt"] lifted me to see
What might within that coffin be ;
And to this moment I can feel
The voiceless gasp—the sickening chill—
With which I hid my whitened face
In the dear folds of her embrace. . . .

There lay she then.

Branwell has told us everything we need to know about the
anguish those children underwent.   In less than four years after the
death of their mother they were bereft by a double blow of the
beings whom after their father they had grown to love best.
   With no comparable genius at mothering the little ones Charlotte
assumed the uneasy succession of Maria, rather as an intellectual
leader than as a moral one, and the depleted ranks of children clung
together.   Inevitably Branwell gravitated towards Charlotte, and
Anne to Emily as the natural and unquestioned protectors to whom,
in the terrifying insecurity of life, they henceforward had to look.

Chapter Four

INTIMATIONS OF MORTALITY

ANNE was five and a half years old when the disaster occurred, an age at which, by modern standards, she would have been exempt from all possible contact with the tragedy. But as we have seen, this was not so in 1825, especially not in a home ruled over by a Methodist aunt and an Evangelical father. To understand the full importance of such an event in precisely such a household we have to know something more about the aunt to whose care Anne's childhood was almost entirely committed.

Miss Branwell was forty-five when her sister died leaving her the virtual mistress of Haworth Parsonage. Seven years older than that sister, her roots were all the more deeply imbedded in the way of life known to her in her native Penzance, a way of life that would appear to have been a strange mixture of worldliness and piety. Religion and the pleasant social round—in which Miss Branwell allowed it to be understood that she had shone—were the over-ruling interests of her life to which she clung with a tenacity that made any attempt at transplantation a dismal failure. To the out-moded fashions of her prime, as to the fervour of a religious revival that had swept all Cornwall in her formative years, Miss Branwell remained unrelentingly committed to the last day of her life.

Young Ellen Nussey meeting her for the first time in 1833 saw only the quaint exterior : the disproportionate size of her caps, her "auburn" front of curls, her propensity to snuff, her "clicking" about the house in pattens, her reminiscences of the past, all the innocent foibles of someone she regarded as a very "antiquated little lady". But behind that exterior there lurked a gloomy mind, so unrelievedly gloomy that in all the numerous allusions to "aunt" in the girls' letters she is never once reported as smiling—far less laughing—but very often indeed as "cross".

Her melancholia was probably constitutional, although many have attributed it to the doctrines of the denomination in which she had been brought up, forgetting in saying so that the outward forms of early Methodism, at least, were cheerful. To Methodism in all its manifestations "Aunt Branwell" had early been initiated. Her native Cornwall, though in the beginnings of Methodism "notorious for the most flagrant opposition to the Gospel", had, in the fifty years of John Wesley's ministry, become the very stronghold of the movement. Between his first visit there in 1742 when he found "the strongest opposition to Methodism in the country", and his last in 1789 when he could say : "Methodism had conquered Cornwall more completely than any other county", the whole status of religion—and of the religious-minded—had been revolutionised. On Wesley's first visits he and his followers had been stoned and not a crust of bread offered them. "This is the best country I ever saw," he then said good-humouredly, "for getting a stomach, but the worst I ever saw for getting food. Do the people think that we can live by preaching ?" What Wesley and his horse had actually lived on in those early days were the brambles bordering the lanes. By 1779 and the late eighties when he returned for his last spectacular meetings, the whole prospect had changed. If on his last visit of all in 1789—two years before his death—he spoke to crowds of about 60,000 persons, it was in a great measure due to supporters like the Branwells, professional people and upper tradesmen, that his triumph had been achieved. Wesley's patriarchal appearance, the rapt silence of his auditors, the beauty of the setting in which he spoke—a natural amphitheatre hollowed out of the cliff-side and overlooking the sea—were images which would impress themselves for ever on young minds like that of Elizabeth Branwell, then aged thirteen, whose girlhood had been passed in the very thick of manifestations such as these and whose family were becoming increasingly implicated in the prospering fortunes of the "Society of People Calling themselves Methodists".

Already in the generation preceding hers there were several members of her family who were "active" workers in the Society. Highly respected among their townspeople, with records going back to the mid-seventeenth century, the Branwells were noticeable for public spirit, holding posts in the liberal professions, the services and in civil administration. Elizabeth Branwell's father, Thomas, had been a member of the Town Council, without actually attaining the status of alderman. According to Mrs Gaskell, on the evidence of his descendants living in her day, Thomas Branwell "possessed more than ordinary talents", which he bequeathed in particular to his daughter Maria, later Mrs Brontë. His wife Anne Carne was the daughter of a prosperous silversmith. They had for long years before their deaths in 1808 and 1809 respectively been members of the Society of Methodists in Penzance. One sister of Thomas Branwell—Elizabeth—had married a shopkeeper, by name John Keam, whose obituary in the *Methodist Magazine* for 1826 reported of him that he had been a "fervent Methodist for thirty-six years", which places his admission to the Society in 1790. In that same year another sister of Thomas's, Jane, married that shining Wesleyan light, the schoolmaster and Wesleyan "Class-leader", John Fennell, at whose school, Woodhouse Grove, Anne Brontë's parents eventually met, fell in love and married. Of the generation of Mrs Brontë and Aunt Branwell themselves, their own sister Jane married one of the Methodist preachers of Penzance, John Kingston, whose missionary experiences in the West Indies had won him particular mention at the Annual Methodist Conference and special reports in the *Methodist Magazine* for 1799.

With all their relatives so closely caught up in the Methodist movement, it goes without saying that Mrs Brontë and her sisters were brought up according to its precepts. The views of John Fennell—"Uncle Fennell" as he was to Maria and Elizabeth Branwell —on how a young Methodist woman should comport herself are of particular interest when one remembers the life-long family connection he was to have with the Brontës.

Reporting in the *Methodist Magazine* for December 1801 on the death at nineteen of Susanna Taylor of Penzance, who died "last Saturday in the full triumph of faith", John Fennell improves the occasion by portraying the "defunct" as a model for other young women. "Her deportment was grave and serious—no lightness or trifling—no foolish or vain conversation, so frequently seen and lamented among young professors. She saw that God must be feared and loved at all times. When among her young companions she generally employed the time in telling them what God had done for her soul. As she met sometimes in my class . . . I had an opportunity for observing her. . . ."

A lifetime of precept and example was to demonstrate how fully Miss Branwell shared her uncle's views. In the matter of dress, however, she did depart somewhat from the model laid down and retain certain mundane propensities that, though they made her nieces laugh at her, must surely have brought her nearer to them than her many virtues can have done. Ellen Nussey noted that

Aunt Branwell not only always wore silk dresses, shawls and laces (some of which can yet be seen at the Parsonage Museum) but indulged in the disturbing habit of taking snuff, "out of a very pretty gold snuff box". John Wesley's views on such worldliness were clear, condemnatory and final. In prescribing a very plain garb for his followers (though "singularity like that of the Quakers was to be eschewed") he laid down that they should wear "no gold or pearls or other precious jewels, use no curling of hair or costly apparel, how grave soever . . . no velvet, no silks, no fine linen, no superfluities, no mere ornaments, though ever so much in the fashion . . ." and, what was more, he particularly censured the use of snuff. The evidence of Miss Branwell's will would, in due course, show that in addition to the silk dresses and the snuff, she both possessed and prized jewels made of "gold and precious stones", whose threat to her nieces' eternal weal she so little regarded, apparently, as to bequeath these treasures to them at her death.

In considering the strong Methodist atmosphere in which the girlhood of Mrs Brontë and her sisters was passed, it must not be overlooked that at that time the Methodists had not broken away from the Established Church. To be a Methodist in those years did not in any way argue that one was not a good churchman or churchwoman. On the contrary : the most fervent Anglicans and clergy of the Established Church up and down the country were enthusiastic helpers of the Methodist Movement and the latter lent their pulpits to the itinerant preachers—as Grimshaw did at Haworth, and Crosse at Bradford, to quote only two famous examples—seeing in Methodism nothing but a much-needed and admirable return to primitive piety.

Thomas Branwell and his family were typical of this period of compromise. While attending church regularly on Sundays—he had his pew in Madron Church—he and the women of his family attended the week-day meetings of the Methodists, held first in private houses and later in the New Road Meeting House. After Thomas's death a larger chapel was built in 1814 in what became known as Chapel Street, at No. 25 of which Aunt Branwell had her home. But while the Miss Branwells were members of the Methodist "Class" directed by John Fennell, and very certainly taught, sewed and otherwise "witnessed" to their zeal in the cause, the family births, marriages and burials continued to be celebrated in the old church of Penzance and there existed no thought in their minds of having forfeited membership of the Church of England. Right up to his death in 1791 John Wesley himself never admitted to such a parting of the ways, though necessity and the impatience of his followers were fast pushing him to it, as when in 1784 he took on himself to ordain ministers for work in America. The severance of his "Society" from the Church was a contingency he had strenuously sought to avoid throughout his ministry ; it was altogether abhorrent to his brother Charles. It was not till after their deaths, in the years 1811–12, that his successors decided to hold their own services in church hours, thus imposing on their followers the choice which had not previously existed of going either to chapel or to church. Unlike her sister Maria who married a clergyman of the Established Church and had inevitably, when the severance came, to opt for church rather than chapel, as Uncle Fennell had likewise to do, Elizabeth Branwell, if nothing had taken her from her native Cornwall, might well have opted for the Methodists as the rest of her family did. As it was, the influence of half a lifetime of devotion was too profound ever to be modified by any change of surroundings. As she came to Haworth so she died : though she attended her brother-in-law's church and asked to be buried in it to be near her sister, at heart she remained a Methodist to the end.

In one of her temperament this was a circumstance that was to have a lasting and, on the whole, an unhappy repercussion on her nieces.

The religion of Aunt Branwell had none of the persuasive tenderness of little Maria whose precocious piety, with its sweet singing of hymns and bed-time prayers and tales, remained for ever a cherished memory for Charlotte and Branwell. With all the dogmatism of an arid temperament, Miss Branwell expounded the tenets of a religion of love as though it were first and foremost a religion of fear.

She belonged, herself, to the Wesleyan or Arminian branch of Methodism whose doctrine of "Redemption for All" was diametrically opposed to that of the Calvinist Methodists, those followers of George Whitefield and the Countess of Huntingdon who believed in redemption only for the "Elect". Their divergences had been the rock on which the Evangelical Revival had split. This was the burning question debated year in, year out among Methodists from every field-cart, by every extempore preacher in the land, and in every issue of the Society's official organ, the *Methodist Magazine*. This was the question that was to haunt Anne Brontë all her life, and to be the main source of all her suffering. The prospects of salvation, even the relatively hopeful prospects of salvation expounded by her aunt, appeared bleak indeed to Anne as a little child. So much was required of the sinner, so little she could do, so stupendous the forces leagued against her !

Anne herself has described what her state of mind was like as a young child, reared on this regimen :

> I see, far back, a helpless child,
> Feeble, and full of causeless fears,
> Simple and easily beguiled
> To credit all it hears . . .

The crushing sense of sin from which it took her all her life to extricate herself, dated undoubtedly from this time. She lived, at the most impressionable period of childhood, under a sense of the daily imminence of death and, something that her aunt made more dreadful still than death, the imminence of Judgment, with all the concomitant emotions that such a prospect aroused. Only the sinless could escape damnation, and who could say they were devoid of sin ?

The question was deeply branded upon the child's shrinking mind ; she was marked by it for life.

> Oppressed with sin and woe,
> A burdened heart I bear. . . .

These opening lines of one of her best-known poems expressed but too truly the persecution which this recurrent idea exercised over her' mind ; it was the source of much of her sorrow in adult life. Though she was ultimately to attain to a religion widely removed from her aunt's, the old leaven still, from time to time, worked to undermine her hardly won peace and all too often to poison for her the source of light and joy.

She early revolted against the doctrine of damnation as applied to others, but of her own salvation she remained sadly long in doubt.

If it is queried why the main charge against the oppressive religious upbringing of the little Brontës—and of Anne in particular —should be laid at Miss Branwell's door and not, rather, at their father's, the answer is that there is evidence on this very head which exonerates him.

Anne was to remain a prey all her life to the dread doctrines of "Election" and "Reprobation", around which the battle between Wesleyan and Whitefield Methodists waged throughout the eighteenth century, echoes of which would reach her directly from her aunt. Mr Brontë's views on these subjects are known : he vigorously opposed both. When applying for a curate to his old friend, the former Miss Firth's husband, the Rev. J. C. Franks, he wrote in a letter of 10th January 1839, ". . . I could not feel comfortable with a coadjutor who would deem it his duty to preach the appalling doctrines of personal election and reprobation . . . I should consider these decidedly derogatory to the attributes of God. . . ." One of Mr Brontë's chief reasons for liking the curate with whom he was finally supplied—the famous Willy Weightman, of whom much will be heard in these pages—was precisely because Willy Weightman's religion was a joyous one. "He did not see," Mr Brontë said of him, "why true believers, having the promise of the life that . . . is to come, should create unto themselves artificial sorrows, and dis-figure the garment of gospel peace with the garb of sighing and sadness. . . ."

In spite of the silk dresses, such would appear to have been the habitual "garb" of Miss Branwell. Her theories of education and principles of religion, applied to such exceptionally imaginative children as the little Brontës, went very far, in the case of Anne particularly, to breaking the fragile vessel she so earnestly sought to fill with Grace Abounding.

The place of "home-education" in the Wesleyan scheme cannot be over-estimated. The formation of character, as distinct from the acquisition of knowledge (which Wesley himself, and Miss Branwell after him, almost despised) was the be-all and end-all of moral instruction. Wesley's views on the bringing-up of children were uncomplicated and held in few words. "Break their wills betimes, begin this work before they can run alone, before they can speak plain, perhaps before they can speak at all. Whatever pains it costs, break the will, if you would not damn the child. Let a child from a year old be taught to fear the rod and to cry softly ; from that age make him do as he is bid, if you whip him ten times running to effect it. . . ."

Miss Branwell's most potent weapon was not the rod. Apart

from locking up a rebellious child in a dark room where recently a death had occurred, she is not ever reported to have used violence on her nieces. She was not actively unkind or harsh. She did not need to be. She ruled by a tyranny of the spirit, exercising her dominion by a strong appeal to the emotions over which, in the case of children with such heightened imaginations, she had an easy victory.

Her influence, naturally enough, was paramount over Anne's infancy and childhood. A delicate little child, orphaned of her mother at the age of twenty months, Anne inevitably became Miss Branwell's first care. She conceived a great affection for the poor little girl and, in a person of her nature, such a feeling was bound to be coupled with a resolution to do her best spiritually even more than materially by her charge—by Anne, in particular, more than by the other children, because Anne since "early childhood", as Charlotte later remembered, "seemed preparing for an early death".

If the *earthly* prospects of her favourite niece appeared increasingly poor, the salvation of her soul became, proportionately, the chief purpose of the pious lady's life.

While her sisters were at Cowan Bridge and Branwell at Haworth Grammar School (from which he was later removed), Anne was entirely committed to the society of her aunt. It has already been seen how Miss Branwell dealt with children recovering from whooping-cough and measles. For Anne, suffering from chronic asthma, the régime would have been the same. Her days would be spent in her aunt's airless room and, worse still, her nights as well. Even when fully grown up, Anne could not avoid sleeping with her aunt, except during the prolonged absence of either of her sisters. Even after the return of Charlotte and Emily from Cowan Bridge, Anne would never share in her family's cosy bed-times. While Charlotte and Emily joyfully elaborated their "Secret Plays" in the little room over the hall, and Branwell luxuriously read by candle-light in his room at the back of the house, poor Anne lay in the great gaunt chamber where her mother had died, with no other prospect than Aunt's coming to bed to cheer the darkness for her.

Mortality was a subject on which the Methodists were peculiarly eloquent. In their war against the flesh every aspect of corruption served to heighten the end they had in view : to disgust their followers with this life and speed them into the next. The recounting of death-bed scenes was a regular feature of their weekly meetings, and the more harrowing the details the more edifying they were held to be. The lessons to be derived from the early deaths of young children were regarded as salutory above all others. With such a mentor as Aunt Branwell, what profit would not have been derived from that first lesson in mortality that was provided for the little Brontës by the deaths of their sisters Maria and Elizabeth !

To Aunt Branwell the Everlasting Fire was a furnace of very real substance and combustible power ; the likelihood of an infant falling into it was just as great as of her falling into the nursery fire. And whereas worldly people set up fire-guards to protect the unwary child, Miss Branwell surrounded Anne by every protective device that preaching and prayer could erect. Without her vigilance Anne might so very easily be lost.

A lady who could drink tea daily out of a lustre teapot on whose chubby sides were enamelled the words of Grimshaw's favourite text, "To me to live is Christ, to die is gain", is not likely to have interpreted any of the articles of her religion in a figurative light. Hell was very real and damnation certain for the vast majority of mankind. To seek to turn away from everlasting perdition the persons committed to one's care—and especially the young, ignorant and idle—was the whole duty of a Christian gentlewoman. And Miss Branwell did not flinch from fulfilling that duty, as the very text of the sampler chosen for her little niece's first clumsy attempt at stitching reminds us feelingly. Anne Brontë had early branded on her mind the exhortation from Proverbs 3:9-18 : "My child despise not the chastening of the Lord ; neither be weary of his correction. For whom the Lord loveth he correcteth, even as a father the son in whom he delighteth."

Even at five years old a child who has seen her elder sister in her coffin can be made acutely sensible of the insecurity of her own mortal tenure. The frequency and alarming nature of Anne's attacks of asthma were made the reminders that death is ever on the pounce for the unprepared and that the Good Child must daily hold herself in readiness for a confrontation with the king of terrors.

To gauge the power exercised over impressionable minds by doctrines such as these one has only to turn the pages of the early numbers of the *Methodist Magazine* to read in what dramatic terms all the approaches of death could be presented. We know from Charlotte and Mrs Gaskell that Miss Branwell's reading had been chiefly derived from this journal, the *Ladies' Magazine*, the *Ladies' Diary* and a few other periodicals of the same calibre. The "light literature" of Caroline Helstone's aunt, in *Shirley*, was very exactly that of Aunt Branwell, composed of ". . . some venerable *Lady's Magazines*, that had once performed a sea-voyage with its owner, and undergone a storm, and whose pages were stained with salt water ; some mad *Methodist Magazines*, full of miracles and apparitions of preternatural warnings, ominous dreams, and frenzied fanaticism, the equally mad letters of Mrs. Elizabeth Rowe from the Dead to the Living ; a few old English classics—from these faded flowers Caroline had in her childhood extracted the honey—they were tasteless to her now. . . ." In a letter to Hartley Coleridge of December 1840 Charlotte has some further illuminating comments to make on her aunt's taste in literature. "I am sorry", she writes, "I did not exist forty or fifty years ago when the *Ladies' Magazine* was flourishing like a green bay tree. In that case, I make no doubt, my aspirations after literary fame would have met with due encouragement . . . I recollect, when I was a child, getting hold of some antiquated volumes and reading them by stealth with the most exquisite pleasure. You give a correct description of the patient Grisels of those days. My aunt was one of them; and to this day she thinks the tales of the *Ladies' Magazine* infinitely superior to any trash of modern literature."

The *Methodist Magazine*, founded by John Wesley in 1778 as the *Arminian Magazine* and published monthly with a fine engraved frontispiece portrait of a "preacher of the Gospel", was the official organ of the movement and had a tremendous circulation. To it such collaterals of the Branwell family as John Kingston and John Fennell repeatedly contributed, and its place on the shelves of the Miss Branwells was an obligation. The set-up of the *Methodist Magazine* followed a regular pattern which included in every month's issue—running serially over several months sometimes—the relation of death-bed scenes vouched for by eye-witnesses, accounts of "conversions" (names and addresses fully given), descriptions of missionary activities, letters from readers dealing with specific aspects of faith ; the texts of outstanding sermons (often Wesley's own), reviews of new theological books and "special features" such as "An Extraordinary Instance of divine Providence exerted in the Preservation of two Infants", or of "Thirty-five mariners at sea", or of the "Preservation from fire of a Whole Family", with many occurrences of a miraculous and supernatural character, the whole totalling forty-eight pages monthly.

"Among the variety of subjects which have found a place in your excellent and useful publication," wrote one contributor to the September issue of 1801, "I find the absolute Eternity of the Torments of Hell is one. You have inserted a sermon on that subject in Vol XVI . . . wherein the author has proved the certainty of that awful truth in the clearest and most convincing manner. . . . These, with some other pieces which have appeared in the *Methodist Magazine,* give your readers much useful information on the subject. But there is still room, if I mistake not, to add one Argument more . . ." and the contributor eagerly supplies further irrefutable proof of the eternity of damnation.

From such a source were Anne Brontë's first lessons in reading taken.

.

Of especial interest in recalling Anne's life-long devotion to the poet Cowper is the fact that much of his poetry of Calvinistic despair found its way into the *Methodist Magazine.* In her lines "To Cowper" written at one of the turning-points of her life she recalls :

> Sweet are thy strains, Celestial Bard ;
> And oft in childhood's years
> I've read them o'er and o'er again
> With floods of silent tears.
>
> The language of my inmost heart
> I traced in every line ;
> *My* sins, *my* sorrows, hopes and fears,
> Were there—and only mine.

and concludes :

> Yet, should thy darkest fears be true,
> If Heaven be so severe,
> That such a soul as thine is lost—
> Oh ! how shall I appear ?

With Anne Brontë Miss Branwell's task was not difficult. She was an unusually good little child, with a sweet and clinging disposition which, to begin with at least, found perfect happiness in obedience.

She has written in *Agnes Grey* of that early time which, to her sensitive nature, appeared as a régime of love, compared with what life yet held in store. "In my childhood," she says, comparing herself to her hardened little pupils, "I could not imagine a more effective punishment than for my mother [for mother read aunt] to refuse to kiss me at night ; the very idea was terrible. More than the idea I never felt, for, happily, I never committed a fault that was deemed worthy of such a penalty. . . ."

Anne never complained of her aunt's treatment of her as a child, but Mrs Gaskell has something to say on the subject that gives us food for thought. "Next to her nephew," wrote Mrs Gaskell, "the docile, pensive Anne was her favourite. Miss Branwell had taken charge of her from her infancy ; she was always patient and tractable, and would submit quietly to occasional oppression, *even when she felt it keenly*" [author's italics]. If she were responsible for nothing else, Miss Branwell must be answerable for Anne's acute sensibility to suffering.

To sum up the effects of Aunt's early training on the little Brontës, their ultimate attitude to one aspect at least of Methodism is eloquent and needs no further comment. Their condemnation of anything approaching mass emotion was implicit in the reticence which all three were to observe on the question of their personal religion. To the obligation laid on the earliest Methodists to "testify" in public to their state of mind and the weekly progress of religion in their hearts, the Brontë sisters were to oppose an absolute silence. Emily Brontë's comment to Mary Taylor when at school is well known. Asked by someone of what religion she was, Mary had answered that that was between God and herself ; to which Emily, lying on the hearth-rug, had simply nodded and said, "That's right." After Anne's death Charlotte, writing of the event to their faithful servant at the parsonage, had felt obliged to give some reassurance of Anne's piety, so little had she ever allowed it to obtrude. "It was not her custom," wrote Charlotte, "to talk much about religion, but she was very good. . . ." To us who can now read Anne's intensely personal verse, no such assurance is required : one thing is certain, religion was the mainspring of her life—though after much self-torment it was not to be the religion of Aunt Branwell.

Chapter Five

EMILY'S WORLD

THE influence of Aunt Branwell on Anne cannot be overrated. It was paramount for the first five years of her life, and because of that early impress would never be totally effaced. But with Emily's return from school and permanent residence at home, its undisputed ascendency was over and a new influence opposed to it which was in every particular its diametrical opposite. This came not only from Emily herself—strong as she was—but from that wide and radiant world outside, which was Emily's domain and into which she soon initiated her younger and favourite sister. When the world of nature was first revealed to Anne, Aunt's influence waned. From then on there would exist dual forces warring within Anne's breast which, like the personified abstractions of the old Morality plays, would seem to stand visibly on either side of her, tugging two ways : Aunt representing all that was conventional in religion, all that was lowering, debilitating in a rule of life ; Emily everything that was kindling, joyous and free. Between two such conceptions it would take a lifetime of suffering for Anne to find a compromise in the end.

Never at any time in the Brontë story is there a single reference to Miss Branwell walking on the moors. With Mr Brontë, a great walker himself, exercise was an essential of health, and we have seen how, even when very young, the little Brontës were sent out in care of the nurse-maids. Later Tabby accompanied them on the moors, carrying Anne over the stony places and becks in those early days when she was still too small to catch up with the others running ahead. With the growth of longer legs and the return of her sisters from school a new life began for Anne, of which the daily walk over the moors became an integral part. Accompanied by Tabby or, in Tabby's default, by Branwell, the girls spent the long summer afternoons in roaming at will in the wide and wonderful world that lay at their door. The habit of a lifetime was formed in those early years. When they grew up neither the deepest snow nor hardest frost was ever to keep Emily and Anne off the moors.

It was the *proximity* of the moors which made it possible for the Brontë children to run out of doors (as other children run into their garden) and fling themselves without let or hindrance—and above all, without witnesses—into the arms of nature.

Between Miss Branwell and Anne there was thus erected, imperceptibly and unintentionally, a barrier through which Miss Branwell was never to pass and beyond which Anne would out-distance her beyond recall.

For Anne already :

> Brightly the sun of summer shone
> Green fields and waving woods upon,
> And soft winds wandered by ;
> Above, a sky of purest blue,
> Around, bright flowers of loveliest hue,
> Allured the gazer's eye. . . .

Poetic feelings were born with all these children ; in Charlotte and Branwell they received the igniting spark from heroic, dramatic, essentially human examples ; in Emily and Anne nature above and beyond any other influence was paramount in kindling their imagination. From the day Anne could run freely with Emily on the moors, Aunt's unquestioned rule suffered its first imperceptible suspension.

At six years old deductions may not be clearly drawn, but Anne was to develop into a relentless little logician, and, formless and unspoken as the reflection may have been, the contrast between Aunt's cosmos and these radiant stretches cannot have escaped her childish observation.

Everything she saw out of doors appeared beautiful, friendly, consoling, precious, lovable—lovable before all else. A single primrose, a tiny bird, instantly her heart warmed to them. Their perfection and their fragility found in her a natural champion. What she felt as a child she expressed in after years. "A little girl loves her bird—Why ? Because it lives and feels ; because it is helpless and harmless ? A toad, likewise, lives and feels, and is equally helpless and harmless : but though she would not hurt a toad, she cannot love it like the bird, with its graceful form, soft feathers, and bright, speaking eyes. . . ."

To fall in love with the pretty creatures on the moors, to pity and wish to protect them was a first and inevitable effect of her new-found liberty. Though the operation would take years, out of this very sentiment would grow the first challenge against Aunt's theology : these pretty and helpless creatures were *not* born for "our convenience" but created by God, like ourselves, to lead a free life, over which man's only dominion should be to exercise a merciful care.

The bright and beautiful world stretching around her home she would love quite as instantly and *almost* as much as the animal world with which every day now brought her into closer intimacy. So the poet's eye was enchanted as the childish heart was warmed by the great daily encounter with the natural scene ; and what God had made became divine by simple implication. The God of Calvin would no longer appear to her on his arid Cross suffering in a vacuum ; gradually in her growing mind the image of a Redeemer took shape whose presence made itself seen and felt in a world vocal with birds and carpeted with flowers.

The moors are starred with flowers during long months of the year, the pastures with clover-heads. In early summer the shattering song of birds fills the air from first light to late dusk ; linnets and skylarks, lapwings and curlews predominate in the concert in which the distant crowing of cocks and bleating of lambs play an essential undertone.

In such a world every sight and sound was a potential playfellow ; the linnet swinging on the spray of heather ; the hummocks of bilberry just big enough to seat Emily and herself on a single tuft ; the plash and patter of water as it rilled between the rocks— cool water in which small hot hands delighted to dabble. All these were close at hand ; between them and the children a daily communion grew. Nothing but *joyful* recollections remained in after-life of those childish days.

> . . . Summer days were far too short
> For all the pleasures crowded there . . .

Inevitably, what she saw with the eyes of six years old were things within her grasp ; flowers in particular ; all her poetry was to be strewn with nostalgic recollections of these early loves— harebells, violets, primroses, ling—

> A fine and subtle spirit dwells
> In every little flower. . . .

There is a silent eloquence
In every wild blue-bell,
That fills my softened heart with bliss
That words could never tell. . . .

. . . Oh, that lone flower recalled to me
My happy childhood's hours
When blue-bells seemed like fairy-gifts,
A prize among the flowers. . . .

Primroses, as all readers of *Agnes Grey* will remember, preserved a singular power of enchantment over her.

As in the days of infancy,
An opening primrose seemed to me
A source of strange delight. . . .

"I could hear the sweet song of the happy lark," she wrote in *Agnes Grey*, "then my spirit of misanthropy began to melt away beneath the soft pure air and genial sunshine ; but sad thoughts of early childhood and yearnings for departed joys . . . arose instead. As my eyes wandered over the steep banks covered with young grass and green-leaved plants . . . I longed intensely for some familiar flower that might recall the woods, dales or green hillsides of home. . . . At length I descried, high up between the twisted roots of an oak, three lovely primroses peeping so sweetly from their hiding-place that the tears already started at the sight. . . ."

Her love of nature grew from an association of delight with the outdoor world. From the butterflies and pretty birds that first captivated her childish fancy, her growing sense looked beyond to the higher hills, the farther rocks, the wider stretches of moor. In later years, as Charlotte recollected, "the distant prospects were Anne's delight, and when I look round, she is in the blue tints, the pale mists, the waves and shadows of the horizon. . . ."

It was in this expansion of her spirit that she came under the leadership of Emily. First exercised out of doors in an intense and close partnership with all the life of the moors, it was shortly to be transferred to the life within, where, in the creation of that imaginary world in which the children first found their poetic wings, the influence of Emily over Anne was to become as paramount as ever, formerly, Aunt Branwell's had been.

Chapter Six

THE PALACE OF THE GENII—1826-31

FOR the six years following the deaths of Maria and Elizabeth the children lived by what appeared an immutable rule of monotonous days from which they found their own means of escape into an unconfined exotic clime where, in place of the shabby walls of home, they lived in a gorgeous palace in a city entirely made of glass on the equator's line. In between these two existences they came and went with all the facility of fabled genii.

Days at the parsonage began with "Prayers" read by Mr Brontë to the assembled family in his study. Then followed breakfast, the only meal—with the exception of an occasional tea—that Mr Brontë took with his children, in the "dining-room", as the main parlour was always called. The evidence of Emily's and Anne's subsequent "diary papers" would suggest that the girls all had some allotted household task to perform immediately after breakfast ; making the beds, sweeping the carpets, lending Tabby a hand in the kitchen, are all mentioned. But the bulk of the morning was, naturally, devoted to lessons with their father in his study. Mr Brontë taught his children all the major subjects—English, history, geography, arithmetic — and divinity — and Miss Branwell taught them grammar, spelling and, above all, how to sew.

From her Wesleyan upbringing Aunt Branwell retained that sense of "method" applied even to the smallest household task that caused the villagers of Haworth to say in later years that they could set their clocks by what was going on at the parsonage. When Emily and Anne were grown-up young women they would still in certain contingencies talk of drawing up a "regularity paper" by which to order their days. If, in some respects, Charlotte, Emily and Anne were more punctual, tidy and diligent than other young women of their age and time, this was due to Miss Branwell's training. Although *by nature* they were not easily any of these things, the impress of her early teaching was too deep ever to be effaced. Considering the necessity they were under of earning their own livings, such discipline could only have stood them in good stead.

Dinner was early according to the standards of that day, taken at two o'clock. Mr Brontë, for the sake of peace (Mrs Gaskell said, for his digestion's sake), invariably dined alone in his study. The accusation of eccentricity so often levelled at the Brontë family seems never to have been more merited than in the instance of family meals. Miss Branwell, not to be outdone by her brother-in-law, and probably just as thankful as he for an hour's quiet, frequently had her meals served to her in her bedroom. This left the children to the blissful obligation of dinner in the kitchen with Tabby. At the period of which we are now speaking this seems to have been the general rule, Miss Branwell aiming at keeping the dining-room "neat and tidy" for the possible visits of neighbouring clergy and their wives.

The old story, propagated by Mrs Brontë's nurse, of the children being deprived of meat has long ago been discredited. Nancy Garrs vehemently denied the accusation and Ellen Nussey, who visited the parsonage over a period of fifteen years, utterly refuted the foolish charge. Tabby fed her young charges plentifully ; they had meat and vegetables, suet puddings and the inevitable milk puddings. The only thing never served at the parsonage was pastry and the only economy exercised was on butter (a heavy item for a poor clergyman). Otherwise the diet was normal and sufficiently varied. The Brontës were very partial to tripe and onions and were regularly regaled on that dish by Tabby.

Immediately after dinner came the afternoon walk on the moors.

Back to tea in the spotless kitchen (how cosy, in all their writings, are the "interiors" described by the Brontës), and then the lugubrious hour with Aunt, sewing in her room.

Of open rebellion to her rule there is absolutely no evidence. The children submitted to her decrees in silence. Only in one particular was she foredoomed to failure with all three nieces alike, and that was in her worldly wisdom. Whereas they could, and did, respect her moral judgment, they very early mocked at her faded gentility. In all else—in their out-moded speech and clothing, the tight crimped hair and ugly formal clothes which have been laid to the charge of Mr Brontë—they allowed themselves to be guided by Miss Branwell. To the whole household the same unyielding maxims were applied : one did not make friends of servants, nor pets of animals : to do so was to transgress the ordinances of God who had fixed a station for all.

It was on this plane that, inevitably, the battle with Miss Branwell was early engaged by all the little girls, especially Emily and Anne, because of their passionate love of animals. It was they who fed the dogs from their own portions of porridge and milk at breakfast and who, in defiance of her strictures, brought home wounded fledglings from the moors. They knew that in such matters they had the support of their animal-loving father. Aunt's revenge in getting rid of Emily's pet hawk, Hero, while she was at school in Brussels, shows that long after the girls were grown up the battle over the animals was still being waged.

By 1829, at least, thanks to their father's taste, the children enjoyed the immense benefit of his—or Branwell's—reading aloud, very often while they sewed in Aunt's room, from the best literary periodicals of the day, as well as from the daily papers. "We take 2 or 3 newspapers a week," Charlotte could proudly boast in that same year. "We take the *Leeds Intelligencer*, Tory, and the *Leeds Mercury*, Whig, and see the *John Bull* : it is high Tory, very violent. Dr Driver lends us it, as likewise *Blackwood's Magazine*, the most able periodical there is. The editor is Mr Christopher North, an old man 74 years of age. The 1st April is his birthday, his company are Timothy Tickler, etc." Thus Charlotte at the age of twelve, revelling in the biographical data of her literary idols. The change from early readings in the *Methodist Magazine* was stimulating indeed.

If to modern children this sounds dreary, it is certain that none of the Brontës found it so, for a keen awareness of and interest in the contemporary political scene is apparent in all their games and in their earliest writings. Violently partisan they all were ("High Tories" to a man, in Papa's footsteps) ; their knowledge of the personalities of the day, in the political as well as in the literary world, far excels that of the average adult today. Is it surprising that, nurtured on such fare, the children not only knew the names of the public characters of their day, but thought of them as personal acquaintances ? Between this and making them the *dramatis personae* of their games was but a step to go.

There was a period in every day when, after the lessons were done—and it was considered too late or too cold for the children to run out again on the moors—they were allowed to do what they liked. For that period even Miss Branwell was thankful to be relieved of the onus of their welfare. Between the hours of five and seven they might go and play in the "nursery" (the tiny room in which so many of them had slept and which was still Charlotte's and Emily's bedroom), or in the kitchen if it were winter and a fire indispensable.

This was "the very witching hour" of day for them. In it they entered on a life completely different from, yet deeply influenced by, the routine life of the parsonage and their free life on the moors. It was like a third plane of existence upon which they moved, not as children subjected to the rule of their elders but as deities dispensing Night and Day to attendant multitudes.

They created for themselves a microcosm reflecting every aspect of public life, political, military, judicial and social. This escapist paradise completed that liberation of their spirits begun by an early and close contact with the natural scene about their home. Like all creations of the spirit it was a spontaneous growth arising, in the most natural manner in the world, out of their games.

The origin of these "Plays", which were not only to absorb the years of their adolescence but to colour so much of their adult writings, was a present of a box of wooden soldiers given to Branwell by his father in the midsummer of 1826. A year after the deaths of Maria and Elizabeth an entirely new direction was thus given to the children's lives.

Let Charlotte describe the incident. "Papa bought Branwell some wooden soldiers at Leeds," she writes. "When Papa came home it was night, and we were in bed, so next morning Branwell came to our door with a box of soldiers. Emily and I jumped out of bed, and I snatched up one and exclaimed : 'This is the Duke of Wellington ! This shall be the Duke !' When I had said this Emily likewise took one up and said it should be hers ; when Anne came down, she said one should be hers. Mine was the prettiest of the whole, and the tallest, and the most perfect in every part. Emily's was a grave-looking fellow, and we called him 'Gravey'. Anne's was a queer little thing, *much like herself*, and we called him 'Waiting-boy'. Branwell chose his, and called him Buonaparte."

The portrait of Mr Brontë that emerges from this scene is not that of the selfish recluse withdrawn from all his children's play and pleasures. On the contrary, we read that he brought back with him from that journey to Leeds, not only the wonderful soldiers for Branwell, but a "set of ninepins, a toy village and a dancing doll" which he gave Miss Branwell for the little girls. If Charlotte and Emily probably had some difference of opinion over the relative desirability of the ninepins and the toy village, neither will have disputed the appropriateness of the dancing doll for Anne.

However the presents were apportioned, Mr Brontë's purchase of the twelve soldiers from Leeds was a momentous circumstance in the young Brontës' lives.

As yet, the great rage of writing that was totally to possess the children within a year or two had not established its hold. True to the evolution of all literary forms, invention was at the "mime" stage and the spoken word had not yet been replaced by the written one. The children were still performing their stories and not yet sufficiently in control of their pens—and of their active bodies—to impose on themselves the discipline of sedentary composition.

Round the soldiers was soon reared a dramatic cycle, at first derived from the omnivorous reading of the young performers but increasingly impregnated with pure fantasy as their imaginations ran wild.

What these earlier stages of the young Brontës' creative urge were like, and how they affected even such sensible bodies as Tabby, has been related.

The passion and fire which the young actors put into their performance were, apparently, quite alarming. There came a day when, according to Francis Leyland—Branwell's subsequent friend, who had it from eye-witnesses—their dramatic frenzy passed all bounds and when, Papa and Aunt being respectively out and resting, Tabby, left all alone with her young charges, felt suddenly afraid. She ran all the way to her nephew's cottage and called for help. "William ! William ! Yah mun goa up to Mr Brontë's for aw'm sure yon childer's all goo'in mad, and aw darn't stop ith 'house ony longer wi' em ; and aw'll stay here woll yah come back." William, plodding up to the parsonage to pacify his aunt was greeted with "a great crack o' laughing" from the children, at Tabby's expense. Nothing could be more gratifying to the young performers than to receive such proof of the horrifying power of their playing. It is a pleasant picture to set against the Cowan Bridge tragedy.

There is an air of summer about it ; the house-door is open and the screaming, gesticulating children are tearing about the parsonage garden, so dear to Emily and Anne and featuring in so many of their thumb-nail sketches of home.   It was not much of a garden, "that little spot" as Anne wrote in after years :

> With grey walls compassed round
> Where knotted grass neglected lies,
> And weeds usurp the ground,

but it was a kingdom to them.   Ellen Nussey, describing it as she first saw it in 1833, said : "The garden was nearly all grass, and possessed only a few stunted thorns and shrubs, and a few currant bushes which Emily and Anne treasured as their own bit of fruit-garden. . . ."

Immediately outside Mr Brontë's window there was a cherry-tree.   Here, on one such occasion as that related above, Emily hid all day, playing at being Charles II after the Battle of Worcester. In scrambling back through Papa's window (Papa was naturally out) she snapped off a branch.   Nothing daunted, the young Brontës enlisted the help of the sexton (a stonemason by profession, whose yard was just across the lane from the parsonage) to paint over the raw wood.   But for all their ingenuity Papa saw through the artifice.   History does not relate whether he pronounced judgment on the offenders.

In such dramatic fashion were the children's first tales invented, with the "Young Men", or "The Twelves" as the twelve soldiers became known, for protagonists.   Between June 1826, when Mr Brontë's revolutionary present was made, and December of the following year the children elaborated three "Great Plays" ("The Young Men", "Our Fellows" and "The Islanders"), which, as Charlotte duly noted in her "History for the Year 1829", were the three Great Plays that were *not* kept secret : the others that she elaborated with Emily in bed by night, being strictly so.

Everything the children saw, heard or read became grist to their mill ; fresh incidents and new characters could be added endlessly to the saga and one play be made to last for months.

Thus "Our Fellows" was the direct outcome of a first reading of Aesop's *Fables.*   In this play each child had his own island inhabited by giants six miles high.   From *The Arabian Nights* they "lifted" the convention of the genii, whose rôles they themselves assumed, taking the titles of "Chief Genii Brannii, Tallii, Emmii and Annii", and investing themselves with fabulous powers such as resuscitating the dead after peculiarly sanguinary battles !

Branwell describes them thus, seated in solemn conclave very reminiscent of *Paradise Lost* (an early passion with the young Brontës) : "I am the Chief Genius Branii. With me are three others. She, Wellesley, who protects you, is named Tallii ; she who protects Parry is named Emmii ; she who protects Ross is called Annii. . . . We are the guardians of you all. . . ." At every turning-point in their heroes' evolution the Chief Genii would appear.

How one such play was invented we know from a vivid description by Charlotte in a passage where, already, the young author (aged twelve and a half) shows her gift for setting a dramatic scene.

"The Play of the Islanders was formed in December 1827 in the following manner," she wrote barely two years later.

One night, about the time when the cold sleet or stormy fogs of November are succeeded by the snow-storms, and high piercing night-winds of confirmed winter, we were all sitting round the warm blazing kitchen fire, having just concluded a quarrel with Tabby concerning the propriety of lighting a candle, from which she came off victorious, no candle having been produced. A long pause succeeded, which was at last broken by Branwell saying, in a lazy manner, "I don't know what to do." This was echoed by Emily and Anne.

Tabby : "Wha ya mun go t' bed."
Branwell : "I'd rather do anything than that."
Charlotte : "Why are you so glum tonight, Tabby ? Oh, suppose we had each an island of our own."
Branwell : "If we had I would choose the Island of Man."
Charlotte : "And I would choose the Isle of Wight."
Emily : "The Isle of Arran for me."
Anne : "And mine should be Guernsey."

We then chose who should be chief men in our islands. Branwell chose John Bull, Astley Cooper, and Leigh Hunt ; Emily, Walter Scott, Mr Lockhart, Johnny Lockhart ; Anne, Michael Sadler (sic), Lord Bentinck, Sir Henry Halford. I chose the Duke of Wellington and two sons, Christopher North and Mr Abernathy. Here our conversation was interrupted by the, to us, dismal sound of the clock striking seven, and we were summoned off to bed.

What strikes the reader most in this passage is the equal part which all four children sustain. The collaboration of the four eager minds here shows itself as complete. Between Charlotte aged eleven and Anne aged seven there is no perceptible gulf of ignorance fixed. If Islands are to be the subject of the game, Islands it shall be and from the eldest to the youngest of the party clear-cut decisions shall be made, not only in the matter of a choice of islands but in that of the islands' chief inhabitants. That Charlotte should choose members of the Wellesley family for her chief islanders was a foregone conclusion ; as was Branwell's choice of predominantly literary characters, and Emily's, reflecting the growing passion for all things Scottish in that household ; but one remains perplexed indeed at the choice of seven-year-old Anne. One asks oneself what had these three gentlemen in common to recommend themselves to a very small girl ? The answer is : they were all three benefactors of their fellow-men. With this particular small girl such qualities were always going to outweigh the merely glamorous in human reputation.

If Branwell's toy soldiers furnished the *dramatis personae* of the children's earliest stories (with the four genii Tallii, Brannii, Emmii and Annii directing their destinies) the Rev. J. Goldsmith's *Grammar of General Geography*, with its fascinating coloured maps, movement of tides, solar calendar and exquisite engravings, gave them the stage upon which to set up their scenes. The acquisition of this truly spell-binding book was to be every whit as momentous in the creation of the little Brontës' imaginary world as that of "The Twelves" or the first intoxicating perusal of *Aesop's Fables* and *The Arabian Nights*.

Like a heady wine, the first contact with the continents and oceans, the cities and seas of those coloured maps and charts went to their heads and set up a ferment that could overflow only in poetry. Invention was let loose like a gale in the Atlantic sweeping everything before it. The Rev. J. Goldsmith's atlas lied ! There were islands in the sea he had not charted, oceans he had not plumbed, cities towering above plains he had left blank in his maps . . . Years of industry could not exhaust the countless wonders of those coasts and climes. In the copy of this precious book preserved at the Brontë parsonage, Anne was to list the invented place-names of her and Emily's kingdoms of "Gondal" and "Gaaldine".

Africa was the continent of their choice ; had it not put itself in the forefront of the news, for young explorers like themselves, with the voyages and heroic death of Mungo Park navigating the Niger in 1806 ? The little Brontës fell upon it like the most mercenary young prospectors and carved out for themselves, their protégés and eventual colonists, whole provinces to exploit.

First, the "Young Men", the original twelve soldiers from

Leeds (for every one of whom names had now been found), were
wrecked at the mouth of the Niger river and driven inland. From
then on colonisation, with all its sequel of partition, administration
and construction, wholly absorbed the activity of the genii.

Here again, as in the original "play" of the islanders, all four
children assumed an equal rôle. In the four "Chief Men" of the
original twelve we recognise Charlotte's Wellington and an
unsavoury individual wished on Branwell, called "Sneaky" ; while
Emily's and Anne's choices are again distinguished by some
originality ; they choose the names of two contemporary explorers
for their heroes, William Edward Parry and John Ross. In the
partition of the African territory into kingdoms for these earliest
colonists, we find Charlotte's "Wellingtonsland", Branwell's
"Sneakysland", Emily's "Parrysland" and Anne's "Rossesland",
each with its appropriate capital : "Wellington's Glass Town",
"Sneaky's Glass Town", "Parry's Glass Town" and "Ross's Glass
Town". The game could—and did—go on *ad infinitum*—the
essential fact emerging from all this rage for creation being that the
children worked *in concert* at elaborating a complete society of their
own.

For this brave new world rulers had to be found, governments
elected, armies trained. A whole complex system of justice had to
be established, laws promulgated, decrees adopted. The life of
court, camp and city alike had to find its chroniclers and soon a
body of journalists, essayists and poets would be recording the chief
events of the year in the Great Glass Town Confederacy, as the
Union over which the four Genii watched was eventually named.

Of Emily's and Anne's written contributions to these earliest
chronicles there remains now not a trace. All the writing—and
illustrating—is in the hands of Charlotte and Branwell, whose tiny
booklets need a strong magnifying glass to be deciphered.

The reason for first adopting the infinitesimal italic script for all
their "secret" writing may have been the humiliating one of scarcity
of paper at the parsonage, but when they founded "Blackwood's
Young Men's Magazine" in August 1829 a desire to imitate print
as nearly as possible would be a strong motive with the young
authors. A secondary reason—which later became the overruling
one with Emily and Anne—was a wish for secrecy. In their case
the habit outlasted childhood and applied to the greater part of
their poetry to the end of their lives.

While the four Genii were supervising the erection of their Glass Towns in an atmosphere of exotic enchantment, the four little Brontës pursued a very even course within the walls of the parsonage. The dividing line between their real and imagined worlds was so fine that to the outsider it was invisible and to *them*—with unhappy consequences for some—it soon became non-existent. Nowhere is this more clearly noticeable than in the diary papers that they seem to have kept on special occasions, and with which Emily and Anne were to persist into adult life.

The earliest to be preserved is Charlotte's "History of the Year 1829" written on 12th March 1829.

"While I write this," says Charlotte, aged twelve and a half, "I am in the kitchen of the Parsonage, Haworth ; Tabby, the servant, is washing up the breakfast things, and Anne, my youngest sister . . . is kneeling on a chair, looking at some cakes which Tabby had been baking for us. Emily is in the parlour, brushing the carpet. Papa and Branwell are gone to Keighley. Aunt is upstairs in her room, and I am sitting by the table writing this in the kitchen. Keighley is a small town four miles from here. Papa and Branwell are gone for the newspaper, the *Leeds Intelligencer*, a most excellent Tory newspaper. . . .'

Whenever the curtain is lifted for a moment on the interior scene, the domestic group presented to our view is as cosy and natural as it well can be where there are children lacking the first requisite of a home—a mother.

By the fortunate preservation of certain relics, we can piece together a simple picture of daily life more eloquent of the truth than any theorising can be.

There exists a series of tiny drawings, executed by Charlotte and Branwell for Anne when she was a tot of seven or eight, that furnishes a charming comment on the children's mutual devotion. Here are the big brother and sister, aged ten and eleven, already proficient draughtsmen, so obviously sitting down to draw pretty pictures for the small sister, not yet advanced enough to do so for herself. They represent Gothic ruined towers in the high romantic vein, and thatched cottages, the obvious copperplate models for young beginners, but each touchingly inscribed "for Anne" and solemnly dated and signed by the budding artists.

Anne preserved these drawings all her life. The time came when these touching memorials to the precocity and affection of his little children would be peculiarly treasured by Mr Brontë. In his old age, when all but he were gone, he gave them to Martha Brown, knowing that they could not fall into better hands, with the following Deed of Gift. "Certain drawings by my children that were given to my daughter Anne, and left in her box, I have given to my servant Martha Brown, as fond mementos, reserving to myself any of these which I might claim for any particular purpose. If I should not claim them, they will be entirely at her disposal. P. Brontë, A.B. Incumbent of Haworth, Yorkshire."

The drawings can, happily, still be seen at the Brontë Parsonage Museum today.

When Anne was eight Charlotte wrote her first story, to which she gave no other title than : "There was once a little girl and her name was Ane." It was a domestic tale, fully illustrated in water-colour, destined, no doubt, like the ruined towers and the thatched cottages, for the amusement of her little sister. The heroine, it might be noted, had been born in the village of "Thorn" and "was a good girl not too much indulged".

Echoes of the now remote Thornton days reached the children from time to time during these very years when all their thoughts were turned upon so different a world. Miss Outhwaite made Anne the present of a Prayer Book, a handsome red morocco-bound book, in which she wrote : "Miss Outhwaite to her goddaughter Anne Brontë, July 13th, 1827."

Emily's godmother Jane, kind Uncle Morgan's wife, died young in September 1827. Seated in Miss Branwell's room the little girls, occupied at their sewing, would overhear Papa and Aunt discuss the sad event. The names "Firth", "Atkinson", "Outhwaite", "Morgan" would fall on the children's ears, evoking in their case not memories but imagined beings with faces and clothes very far removed from the actual faces and clothes of the ladies and gentlemen known to them chiefly by hearsay. Since the far-away Thornton days the little Brontës had met few of their godparents.

In the early summer of 1829 Emily's other godmother, Mrs Fennell, was to die and as an indirect consequence of this the children were for the first time to leave home on a visit to relatives. Miss Branwell, who was, it will be remembered, a niece of the bereaved widower's, for the first and only recorded time, took all the children with her to stay with Uncle Fennell at his parsonage at Crosstone in the September of that year. How they spent their time we know since Mr Brontë preserved a letter Charlotte wrote him on the occasion.

Dated from the Parsonage House, Crosstone, 23rd September 1829, "My dear Papa," it runs, "At Aunt's request I write these lines to inform you that 'if all be well' we shall be at home on Friday by dinner-time, when we hope to find you in good health. On account of the bad weather we have not been out much, but notwithstanding we have spent our time very pleasantly, between reading, working and learning our lessons, which Uncle Fennell has been so kind as to teach us every day. Branwell has taken two sketches from nature, and Emily, Anne, and myself have likewise each of us drawn a piece from some views of the lakes which Mr Fennell brought with him from Westmoreland [sic]. The whole of these he intends keeping. Mr Fennell is sorry he cannot accompany us to Haworth on Friday, for want of room, but hopes to have the pleasure of seeing you soon. All unite in sending their kind love with your affectionate daughter, Charlotte Brontë."

Emily and Anne's earliest extant drawings are copies of studies of birds, drawn in this same year 1829 when they turned, respectively, eleven and nine years old. The drawings were copied from a book which made a profound and lasting impact on their imaginations. It was Bewick's *History of British Birds*, published in 1804, a book which Mr Brontë evidently bought for his children, for a copy was eventually sold at the parsonage sale after his death. It abounded in beautiful and poetical engravings and so captured the imaginations of the little Brontë girls that it achieved the distinction of a mention in two of their ultimate novels—in *Jane Eyre* and *The Tenant of Wildfell Hall*.

It is Bewick that Jane Eyre is reading hidden behind the curtain, sitting cross-legged like a Turk, when her horrid cousin John Reed attacks her. And it is again Bewick that Helen Huntingdon's little boy is given to keep him quiet while his mamma and Gilbert Markham have their final explanation at the end of *Wildfell Hall*. "Look, Mr Markham," says young Arthur, proudly exhibiting his book, "a natural history with all kinds of birds and beasts in it, and the reading as nice as the pictures!"

The year 1830 would appear to have been one of prodigious output for Charlotte and Branwell. Between August and December Charlotte brought out six numbers of "Blackwood's Young Men's Magazine"—totalling 11,000 words—in addition to which she started a new series of "Character Sketches", completed in five days and running to 6,000 words. Branwell's output over the same period was equally prodigious and—to judge by a timely confession —quite prostrating. Reviewing a "Commentary on Ossian, 20 vols. folio", in the "Young Men's Magazine", he had to admit that "This is one of the most long-winded books that have ever been printed, we must now conclude for we are dreafully tired." "Dreafully tired" the thirteen-year-old Editor might well occasionally be !

That the collaboration between all four children was still as close as ever the following verses written by Branwell at this time attest :

> I see, I see appear
>   Awful Brannii, gloomy giant
> Shaking, o'er earth his blazing spear,
>   Brooding on blood with drear and vengeful soul
> He sits enthroned in clouds to hear his thunders roll.
> Dread Tallii next like a dire eagle flies
> And on our mortal miseries feasts her bloody eyes—
> Emmii and Annii with boding cry
> Famine and war foretell and mortal misery.

Alas ! for Charlotte the glorious period of untrammelled creation was drawing to its close. A decision reached in the course of the year 1830 and put into execution in the January of 1831 was going to shake the very foundations of the Genii's Palace. Thanks to a generous offer made by her godparents, Mr and Mrs Atkinson, Charlotte was to be sent to boarding-school. The news must have deprived the young Genii of their magic powers for several days after it was first received.

The end of an epoch had been reached. Never again would the four Chief Genii work in collaboration. They would never again completely share any experience. Henceforward they would divide ; the elder sister and brother pursuing, in renovated trappings, "the old ideas, the old faces, and the old scenes in the world below", while the younger sisters, turning their eyes upon a fresh horizon, were to discover a new world which they called Gondal but whose hills would be the hills of home. Unlike Charlotte's and Branwell's "Angria"—the exotic empire into which the Great Glass Confederacy merged—the permanence of Gondal lay in the fact that it was *not* a world at several removes from reality but only a slightly blurred print of the landscape of home.

Chapter Seven

GONDAL'S SHORE

> . . . long ago I loved to lie
> Upon the pathless moor,
> To hear the wild wind rushing by
> With never ceasing roar ;
>
> Its sound was music then to me,
> Its wild and lofty voice
> Made my heart beat exultingly
> And my whole soul rejoice. . . .

THOSE lines occur in the earliest verses of Anne Brontë's to be preserved ; she wrote them when she was sixteen years old. Their chief interest for us—whatever their literary merit—is in their strong biographical content. They show us Anne in her middle teens *looking back* nostalgically to a life that *had* been hers for years already. They show her revelling in the freedom which the natural surroundings of her home bestowed so bountifully upon the children of the parsonage. They show her "whole soul" rejoicing in the beauty of that scene, and, quite obviously, liberated from the spiritual dominion of Aunt.

"Oh, happy life !" she sings :

> To range the mountains wild
> The waving woods—or ocean's heaving breast,
> With limbs unfettered, conscience undefiled,
> And choosing where to wander, where to rest.

The choice, indeed, was wide.

> Beneath this lone and dreary hill
> There is a lonely vale,
> The purling of a crystal rill,
> The sighing of the gale.
>
> The sweet voice of the singing bird,
> The wind among the trees,
> Are ever in that valley heard ;
> While every passing breeze

> Is loaded with the pleasant scent
> Of wild and lovely flowers ;
> To yonder vales I often went
> To pass my evenings hours. . . .

Behind Haworth Parsonage, by the field-path that leads to the moors, the wanderer's eye is confronted by three valleys buried deep in declivities of the hills. There, where heath and bracken and ling cover the bare shoulders of the rocky heights, water rills down in runnels and cascades before it drops perpendicularly into the hollows to form those "becks" whose tinkle and flash fill the eye and ear delightfully for so many miles around.

Here Emily and Anne, from the first melting of snow in early spring to the last gales of autumn which strip every leaf from the crouching thorns on the flank of the pastureland, would daily come to "pass their evening hours".

With the departure of Charlotte to school a new régime was inaugurated at the parsonage. Whereas every hour of leisure had hitherto been organised by Charlotte to promote the glory and grandeur of the Great Glass Town Confederacy by intensive hours of scribbling within doors, Emily and Anne, casting off the yoke of Branwell (he was thirteen and going through a "sanguinary" phase wholly repugnant to his little sisters), asserted their complete independence and now turned their precious play time to quite other purposes. No matter how wild the weather, they were always happier out of doors than shut up inside. Winter, as well as summer, at all available hours of daylight in the intervals of lessons, they stretched their colt-like young limbs upon the moors. They tumbled in the high grasses and cast themselves down in the ling. To them all the voices of nature were friendly and spoke a recognisable language. Thus, to Anne, the north wind seemed to say :

> I have passed over thy own mountains dear,
> Thy northern mountains, and they still are free ;
> Still lonely, wild, majestic, bleak, and drear,
> And stern and lovely, as they used to be.
>
> When thou, a young enthusiast,
> As wild and free as they,
> O'er rocks, and glens, and snowy heights,
> Didst often love to stray. . . .

I've blown the pure, untrodden snows
In whirling eddies from their brows ;
And I have howled in caverns wild,
Where thou, a joyous mountain-child,
Didst dearly love to be. . . .

In "the young enthusiast", the "joyous mountain-child", it is difficult to recognise the little girl, Anne Brontë, so subdued to the dark teachings of Aunt Branwell that her frightened mind could barely contemplate any other prospect than that of early death and everlasting damnation. Inevitably, through the closer ties of youth and love, ardent imagination and generous sentiments, Emily had won in the second round of the contest for Anne's soul. Emily and Anne were too deeply alike, kindred in temperament, warmth, passion, enthusiasm, for any influence to be able to rival Emily's over the growing Anne. For the time being, at least, it *must* be paramount.

The nostalgic evocation contained in all Anne's teen-age verse of the time when she had run upon the hills of home—"as wild and free as they"—is not this poetry's only surprising characteristic. Each poem is signed with a fictitious name, in addition to her own in full, together with the date of composition. The authors of the poems from which the above extracts are taken would appear to be young ladies respectively named "Lady Geralda", "Alexandrina Zenobia" and "Marina Sabia"—shortly "Olivia Vernon" would be added to their number. In the names of these interesting heroines, the relation of whose loves and losses, wanderings and imprisonments would stretch over a period of full ten years, Anne would sign sixteen out of the total fifty-nine of her preserved poems. Many more, very certainly, were composed and either destroyed by Charlotte after Anne's death or have not yet come to light. By those that remain it is clearly demonstrable that a plot of great complexity had been elaborated into which these persons and situations fitted, but of which they were only a very small part. Anne's major figures, Alexandrina Zenobia and her lover Alexander Hybernia, were only two of the protagonists of a drama in which she and Emily not only created but performed in their own persons the salient incidents.

Quite obviously Charlotte's going from home did Emily and Anne great good. It threw them upon their own initiative and allowed them growing time in which to find, and to establish, their own individualities.

Before ever a literary cast was given to the new world Emily and Anne inhabited—the Kingdom of Gondal which they peopled with their heroes and heroines—they first of all ran wild in it in their own persons.

When Charlotte left home Emily was twelve and a half and Anne eleven, both already taller than Charlotte and fast growing such long legs that they would always be remarked on wherever they went as taller than most young ladies of that time.

The rule was that Branwell had to accompany them on their walks if Tabby could not do so, but it is quite obvious, from the contrivances of young Cathie in *Wuthering Heights* that the Brontë girls were adepts at giving their escorts the slip.

The moors above Haworth are perpetually clothed in splendour, no matter at what season of the year. In summer their texture is of a sombre richness that recalls the vast canvasses of Veronese. The heavy, velvet green of moss half covers the rocky structure of the earth ; the amber and topaz of the bilberry clumps stretches, hummock upon hummock, over every hill ; the heaving, breathing, swaying mass of heather (the colour of plum-bloom, umber and of wine) that ruffles like a fur in the low breeze, sweeps on all sides to the horizon's verge ; the emerald green of bracken and the silver green of the bent, lithe swathes of the grasses ; the smoke-blue of the harebells and the pink of clover-flowers and the butter yellow of Emily's "Yellow-star of the mountains" enamel the ground at one's feet, while the sky is resonant with the cries of the lapwing and the song of the late and early lark. From the grey, far-flung farmsteads blue smoke rises, cocks crow, young cattle low, sheep-dogs bark and, far away on the hillsides, the bleating of sheep answers the bleating of lambs. There is a nobility in this stretch of country that is an enemy to petty thoughts ; the whole scene is nothing less than elevating. Above all, skies of an illimitable vastness illumine and fleck, with their ever-passing procession of high clouds, the rolling stretches of moorland, vale and hill, evoking a wealth of colour from the ground that is as varied as it is beautiful.

With the life of the moors Emily and Anne became so deeply impregnated that it shaped their thoughts, coloured their imaginations and quickened their feelings as no other influence in their lives would ever do. To Emily, nature became an end in itself ; to Anne, a pathway to God ; to both of them it became a necessity.

Of such scenery is the poetry of Gondal composed. The

loneliness, the grandeur and the wild romantic charm could not long remain unpeopled for girls like Emily and Anne who *had* to transpose the limitations of their own Victorian society into one where boldness, freedom and daring were not reprehensible attributes in young women but essential safeguards.

On the moors of Haworth, in the course of their daily walks, the elaborate settings and incidents of their Gondal drama were found. Playing at outlaws, fugitive lovers and dethroned sovereigns themselves, the characters and crises of the plot sprang to life in the most natural way in the world.

> We know where deepest lies the snow,
> And where the frost winds keenest blow
> On every mountain brow. . . .

sang Anne.

> We long have known and learnt to bear
> The wandering outlaws toil and care. . . .

The outlaws' life—to which it is so easy to imagine one belongs, sitting upon a high ledge of rock jutting out over a deep and narrow chine where not a movement of sheep or the shadow of a curlew sailing overhead can pass unnoticed—becomes necessarily one of acute observation and caution.

The very spirit of that time haunts all Anne's Gondal verse :

> I was roaming light and gay
> Upon a breezy summer day,
> A bold and careless youth. . . .

It was a life of bliss, imagining one was a bold outlaw :

> . . . we had wandered far that day
> O'er that forbidden ground away :
> Ground, to our rebel feet how dear.
> Danger and freedom both were there !

What were all the tempting states of being compared with that of the free ranger over the wild hills ?

> It may be pleasant to recall the death
> Of those beneath whose sheltering roof you lie,
> But I would rather press the mountain-heath
> With nought to shield me from the starry sky.

Freedom and nature are more than victory or revenge to *this* outlaw
at least.

> I'd rather listen to the skylark's songs
> And think on Gondal's and my father's wrongs. . . .

There can be no doubt that it was the long hours spent lying in
the high encompassing heather, the vigils passed at the head of the
precipitous valleys, the lazy noons and long summer evenings spent
by the waterfalls that made of Emily and Anne—not poets, because
poetry was born with them—but such close participators in the
natural scene.   Here, in one of her earliest poems, Anne describes
those halcyon days :

> Zenobia, do you remember
> A little lonely spring
> Among Exina's woody hills
> Where blackbirds used to sing ?
>
> And when they ceased as daylight faded
> From the dusky sky,
> The pensive nightingale began
> Her matchless melody.
>
> Sweet bluebells used to flourish there
> And tall trees waved on high,
> And through their ever sounding leaves
> The soft wind used to sigh.
>
> At morning we have often played
> Beside that lonely well,
> At evening we have lingered there
> Till dewy twilight fell. . . .

The "little lonely spring" which "Alexander Hybernia" situated
among "Exina's woody hills" was the Sladen valley waterfall
where probably the happiest hours of the girls' lives were spent.
There Ellen Nussey, Charlotte's new-found school friend, was taken
on her first visit to Haworth in the summer of 1833, shortly after
Charlotte had come home for good.   Recalling that first memorable
visit to the place, Ellen wrote : "In fine and suitable weather
delightful rambles were made over the moors, and down into the
glens and ravines that here and there broke the monotony of the
moorland.   The rugged bank and rippling brook were treasures of
delight.   Emily, Anne, and Branwell used to ford the streams, and

sometimes placed stepping-stones for the other two [i.e. Charlotte and herself], there was always a lingering delight in these spots— every moss, every flower, every tint and form, were noted and enjoyed. Emily especially had a gleesome delight in these nooks of beauty—her reserve for the time vanished. One long ramble made in those early days was far away over the moors to a spot familiar to Emily and Anne, which they called 'The Meeting of the Waters'. It was a small oasis of emerald green turf, broken here and there by small clear springs ; a few large stones served as resting-places ; seated here, we were hidden from all the world, nothing appearing in view but miles and miles of heather, a glorious blue sky, and brightening sun. A fresh breeze wafted on us its exhilarating influence ; we laughed and made mirth of each other, and settled we would call ourselves the quartette. Emily, half-reclining on a slab of stone, played like a young child with the tadpoles in the water, making them swim about, and then fell to moralising on the strong and the weak, the brave and the cowardly, as she chased them with her hand. *No serious care or sorrow had so far cast its gloom on nature's youth and buoyancy, and nature's simplest offerings were fountains of pleasure and enjoyment*" [author's italics].

The world of Emily and Anne, as even Ellen Nussey saw, was *not* limited by the parsonage walls or the bounds of a modest garden. It was *not* tyrannised over by Aunt or embittered by the eccentricity of their father. It was *not* circumscribed by poverty or overshadowed by ill-health. It was a dazzling, unbounded, part make-believe world in which they themselves acted the chief heroic parts, against a scenic background which they might call "Gondal", but which, in all its mountainous and misty range, had not a thorn-bush, a reedy pool, a rocky dell or a heaving tract of heather that could not be identified upon their own moors of home. The overall impression left on Ellen Nussey by Charlotte's sisters was one of zestful cheerfulness and unchallenged independence.

By the time Charlotte returned from school, as this passage shows, Emily and Anne were the family's acknowledged guides for all excursions across the moors.

By then Gondal was an established fact. Why "Gondal", one asks ? Had the girls been studying the map of India and found the Gondal in the Kathiawar Peninsula ? We shall never know.

It was probably to greet Charlotte on her return from boarding-school in the summer of 1832 that Emily and Anne set down, in orderly fashion, those essential particulars about Gondal which were necessary for its comprehension by a neophyte. At this stage in the development of their new imaginary world there was no question of keeping Gondal secret or of excluding Charlotte from the game. On the contrary, Emily's diary paper of 1837 shows that the four young people continued to participate in each other's games so far as to be kept informed of salient events, even if neither pair took an active part in the policy-planning of the other any more.

For Charlotte's better comprehension of the Gondal scene, two lists—at least—were drawn up (only two have come down to us) ; the one of places, the other of personalities, both written by Anne. One she inserted in the "Vocabulary of Proper Names" at the end of that old friend to invention, Goldsmith's *Grammar of General Geography*, written in the tiny italic script all the children had cultivated for their "secret" writing. We learn that "Alexandia" is a Kingdom of Gaaldine—as are "Almedore", "Elseraden", "Ula", "Zelona" and "Zedora". "Gaaldine", we read, was "a large Island newly discovered in the South Pacific" ; "Gondal" (the mother island) was situated in the North Pacific, its capital being called "Regina".

These high-sounding Arabic names, chosen with an evident relish for the alliterative liquid consonants, are of special interest to us in that they recur constantly throughout Emily's and Anne's poetry. Emily's royal hero, Julius Brenzaida of Angora (in Gondal) became by conquest King of Almedore in Gaaldine—the tremendous Queen of Gondal, Augusta Geraldine, being born of the family of Almedore.

Anne's chief hero and heroine, Alexander Hybernia and Alexdrina Zenobia, both derive from Exina in Gondal, a place which in Emily's poetry is to become of capital importance to the Gondal plot in the person of its king, Gerald Exina, cousin and victim of Julius Brenzaida.

Anne's list of principal Gondal characters, pencilled on a scrap of paper measuring four inches by three, shows how the *dramatis personae* figuring in both the girls' poetry belonged to one or other of the reigning families of the island kingdoms of Gondal and Gaaldine. Chief among these are the families of Exina, Hybernia, Sophona, Vernon, Angora, Alzerno—all of which appear in Anne's poetry and some of them in Emily's. The great part played by them in the girls' poems would, alone, make it necessary to follow every available clue as to their identity. But their rôle will not be confined to literature alone ; they will intrude into the world of reality, as an examination of the diary papers left by Emily and Anne will show, and exist as unquestionably for them as the daily woman laundering in the back-kitchen.

In July 1833 Ellen Nussey paid her first visit to the parsonage. From her account we get the first glimpse of the Brontës by an outsider. The ages of the girls were : Charlotte seventeen, Emily just turned fifteen and Anne thirteen and a half ; Ellen herself was a year younger than Charlotte.

Her visit had been ardently awaited even by Emily, since Charlotte had not only elected her for her bosom friend at school but had been to stay at her home, "The Rydings", at Birstall in the previous year—the occasion on which Branwell, who had escorted his sister, is reported to have exclaimed : "I leave you in Paradise !"

The Nusseys' circle was, indeed, very different from that of the Brontës. Their home was luxurious and their fine collection of paintings sufficient of itself to arouse Branwell's fervour. Ellen was the youngest daughter of a large family (there were twelve children) which for three generations past had lived in the same fine house, "The Rydings". The great-grandfather had been a dyer ; and they were a family of prosperous cloth-manufacturers owning, between them, the three best properties in the district : "The Rydings", "White Lea" and "Brookroyd" (Ellen's eventual home). Two Nusseys struck out in a line of their own : an uncle going to London and becoming "Apothecary to H.R.H. the Prince Regent", and a brother of Ellen's becoming Court Physician, living in Cleveland Row, London.

Ellen's father had died in 1826 and, at the time of her visit to Haworth, she lived at "The Rydings" with her mother, her three sisters, Ann, Sarah and Mercy, and her brothers, Henry and George.

She was considered a pretty girl ; two unsigned drawings of her (believed to have been executed by Charlotte on the occasion of this visit) show a ringleted head, a slender neck, champagne shoulders and wide-apart eyes—too wide apart for intellectual beauty. An elegant frock of some filmy texture contributes to the general impression of a soft and sleepy nature. Ellen was sweet-tempered, loyal and lovable, and in the course of years all three Brontë girls gave her, in varying measure, a genuine affection.

(2,056)

Ellen drove over to Haworth in her mother's carriage accompanied by a man-servant, an ex-sailor whom Mr Brontë took pains to put at his ease.

Dutifully she introduces the elders and wonderful old Tabby before coming to the description we so impatiently await of her first impressions of Emily and Anne. She must have been just as impatient as we to meet Charlotte's sisters, of whom she had heard so much ; Branwell's acquaintance she had already made, but we are never told that she had even a passing interest in him as strong-minded Mary Taylor was, so surprisingly, to have later on. Ellen Nussey's taste—though catholic in numbers—was always to be restricted to "the Cloth".

Here was Ellen, standing in the stone-flagged entrance hall at the parsonage with its beautiful arch framing the staircase beyond, and Mr Brontë coming out of his study on the right, overwhelming in his white cravat and his old-world courtliness. How Mr Brontë comported himself to young ladies we know from *Shirley*. ("Perfectly easy and gallant, in his way, were his manners always to young ladies, and most popular was he amongst them ; yet, at heart, he neither respected nor liked the sex, and such of them as circumstances had brought into intimate relation with him had ever feared rather than loved him.")

What did Ellen think ? Ellen was very cautious. "Even at this time," she writes, "Mr Brontë struck me as looking very venerable with his snow-white hair and powdered coat-collar." (Mr Brontë was fifty-six at the time.) "His manner and mode of speech always had the tone of high-bred courtesy. He was considered somewhat of an invalid, and always lived in the most abstemious manner. His white cravat was not then so remarkable as it grew to be afterwards. . . . Mr Brontë's health caused him to retire early. He assembled his household for family worship at eight o'clock ; at nine he locked and barred the front door, always giving as he passed the sitting-room door a kindly admonition to the 'children' not to be late ; half-way up the stairs he stayed his steps to wind up the clock, the clock that in after days seemed to click like a dirge in the refrain of Longfellow's poem 'The Old Clock on the Stairs'.

Forever—never !
Never—forever !"

One definite judgment she passed then and there on her host ; it entirely concurs with Charlotte's portrait of him in *Shirley* : "He was not diabolical at all. The evil simply was—he had missed his vocation ; he should have been a soldier, and circumstances had made him a priest." "Mr Brontë's tastes," says Ellen, "led him to delight in the perusal of battle scenes, and in following the artifice of war ; had he entered on military service instead of ecclesiastical he would probably have had a very distinguished career. The self-denials and privations of camp-life would have agreed entirely with his nature, for he was remarkably independent of the luxuries and comforts of life."

Ellen Nussey's portrait of Miss Branwell we have already seen. The postscript to it, however, is of importance in that animal-loving home. "During Miss Branwell's reign at the Parsonage," writes Ellen, "the love of animals had to be kept in due subjection. There was then but one dog, which was admitted to the parlour at stated times. Emily and Anne always gave him a portion of their breakfast, which was, by their own choice, the old North Country diet of oatmeal porridge." (This would be "Grasper", whose portrait Emily executed in January 1834. Mr Brontë paid a dog-tax as from 1831. "Grasper" probably lived till the end of 1837 or early 1838, when his famous successor "Keeper" appeared on the scene.)

Since the visit lasted throughout the best part of July when Emily's birthday occurred, Ellen's portrait of her is as she was when just turned fifteen. "Emily," she writes, "had by this time acquired a lithesome, graceful figure. She was the tallest person in the house, except her father. Her hair, which was naturally as beautiful as Charlotte's, was in the same unbecoming tight curl and frizz, and there was the same want of complexion. She had very beautiful eyes—kind, kindling, liquid eyes ; but she did not often look at you : she was too reserved. Their colour might be said to be dark grey, at other times dark blue, they varied so. She talked very little. She and Anne were like twins—inseparable companions, and in the very closest sympathy, which never had any interruption." That last sentence has its importance in assessing the value of Anne. Not only did Emily find her the perfect companion in her early teens, but throughout life. Ellen Nussey was well placed to judge ; she knew them both to the very hour of their deaths.

"Anne," continues Ellen, "dear, gentle Anne, was quite different in appearance from the others. She was her aunt's favourite. Her hair was a very pretty, light brown, and fell on her neck in graceful curls. She had lovely violet-blue eyes, fine pencilled eyebrows, and clear, almost transparent complexion. She still pursued her studies, and especially her sewing, under the surveillance of her aunt. Emily had now begun to have the disposal of her own time. . . ."

Exactly a year later Charlotte was to essay her hand at a portrait of Anne in water-colours, which, if it renders the detail of Ellen Nussey's description—the pretty hair, the finely pencilled brows, the lovely eyes—falls far short of the charm conveyed in the verbal picture. Ellen Nussey was immensely taken with Emily and Anne, and was never to lose the almost poetic fervour with which she first regarded them. She had enough perception to sense that in these girls there was a quality derived in no degree from externals. Describing the lack of all curtains, carpets and ornaments in the parsonage, she concludes : "Scant and bare indeed, many will say, yet it was not a scantness that made itself felt. *Mind and thought, I had almost said elegance, but certainly refinement, diffused themselves over all, and made nothing really wanting*" [author's italics]. Where the Brontës were concerned, Ellen Nussey could sometimes be inspired.

Out of doors, she had noted how Emily's reserve had, for the time being, vanished, and how deep was both girls' delight in every growing thing and living creature, how at home—in the deepest sense of the words—they were upon the moors.

It was never their learning that impressed her—as Charlotte's did even at their first meeting at school. They were children of nature, Blake-like creatures, strangely unsophisticated on the one hand and percipient on the other to a quite unusual degree.

> I loved the free and open sky
> Better than books and tutors grim,

Anne recalls was her state of mind at that time.

The mixture of apparent childishness and profound natural wisdom which Ellen Nussey certainly perceived in Emily and Anne is very apparent in the first of their diary papers to be preserved and which is dated Monday, 24th November 1834.

I fed Rainbow, Diamond Snowflake Jasper phaesent (alias) this morning Branwell went down to Mr. Drivers and brought news that Sir Robert Peel was going to be invited to stand for Leeds Anne and I have been peeling Apples for Charlotte to make an apple pudding and for Aunts nuts and apples Charlotte

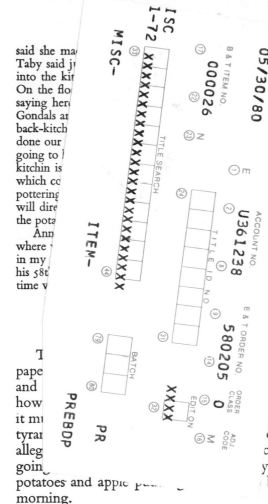

said she ma
Taby said j
into the ki
On the flo
saying her
Gondals ar
back-kitch
done our
going to l
kitchin is
which co
pottering
will dire
the pot;
Ann
where
in my
his 58t
time v

but limited intellect
ato) Aunt has come
nne Anne answered
ave Branwell a letter
t and Charlotte—The
osley is washing in the
e not tidied ourselves,
go out to play we are
nd apple-pudding The
done our music exercise
en in her face. Ya pitter
dear, O dear, O dear I
a pilling (finished pilling
cted
nd what we shall be and
—in which year I shall be
Branwell will be going in
we shall all be well at that

hily and Anne
ovember the 24 1834

T cefully written scrap of
pape en table over a hundred
and s uninhibited avowal of
how eir teens. For ever now
it m nourishment and parental
tyrar ole fabric of Mrs Gaskell's
alleg children meat. "We are
goin y, "Boiled Beef Turnips,
potatoes and appie p   bad menu for a Monday
morning.

The vignette it affords of Anne is also particularly worth noting. Aunt has asked "Where are your feet Anne?" And Anne has answered "On the floor Aunt." So Jane Eyre would have answered, or Maggy Tulliver, or any other naughty spirited girl in fiction or out of it, who has been admired since books were made and read, for ticking off tiresome aunts who ask obvious questions. A few years before it would have been unthinkable; at any time it may surprise those who underestimate Anne Brontë's forthright character. The whole picture is to be treasured for the contentment it displays. It is only in its conclusion that this first diary paper makes sad reading today, with its hopeful looking forward to the future.

Chapter Eight

ROE HEAD

FROM the midsummer of 1832 (when she returned home from school) to the midsummer of 1835 Charlotte taught her sisters at home. She handed on to them all the fresh acquirements she had gained at Miss Wooler's admirable establishment : history, English, grammar, geography, French, German, drawing. From her recommendations sent to Ellen Nussey at the time on what to read and what not to read in English literature we can judge a little how she directed her own sisters' studies. Charlotte's was a violently prejudiced list and her reasons for recommending some books and excluding others cannot fail to make some readers raise their eyebrows today.

"If you like poetry," wrote Charlotte, "let it be first-rate," and then goes on to include Campbell, Southey, Scott, Thomson and Goldsmith in the same list as Shakespeare, Milton, Pope and Byron, to prohibit *en bloc* the comedies of Shakespeare and the "Don Juan" of Byron, adding : "that must, indeed, be a depraved mind which can gather evil from *Henry VIII*, *Richard III*, from *Macbeth*, and *Hamlet* and *Julius Caesar.* . . ." Was the corollary that evil *would* be derived from a perusal of *Twelfth Night*, *As You Like It* and *The Merchant of Venice*? The dread lest Anne and Emily were effectually debarred from the joy of reading Shakespeare's comedies is set at rest by Anne herself who, in almost the opening words of *Agnes Grey* quotes from *Much Ado*. Shakespeare indeed she was to read and know so well as to be constantly quoting in her books ; which was not so general a practice with early Victorian young ladies as with those of today.

"For history, read Hume . . ." wrote Charlotte. "For fiction, read Scott alone ; all novels after his are worthless. For biography, read Johnson's *Lives of the Poets*, Boswell's *Life of Johnson*, Southey's *Life of Nelson*, Lockhart's *Life of Burns*, Moore's *Life of Sheridan*, Moore's *Life of Byron*. . . . For natural history, read Bewick and Audubon, and Goldsmith, and White's *History of Selborne*." A narrow list, but containing some nuggets of gold.

The interesting point about it is that the titles nearly all figure on the list of the library of the Keighley Mechanics' Institute which was the young Brontës' chief source of books. Founded in 1825 by the Earl of Burlington (Lord of the Manor of Keighley), the Rector, the Rev. Theodore Dury, and three or four more local benefactors, the library numbered some 362 members and was early subscribed to by Mr Brontë. From 1831 certainly the girls were regularly fetching books from its shelves, making the eight miles to and from Keighley an object for their walks.

Another fine library to which it is known they had access was that of their friends the Heaton family at Ponden Hall, the Jacobean mansion on the edge of the moors which stood model to both Emily and Anne for their "Thrushcross Grange" and "Wildfell Hall" respectively. There, in particular, the world of French literature was opened to them, which was to be of such initial service to Charlotte and Emily in preparing them for their schooldays in Brussels.

The collection of books at the parsonage itself remained a small one—Miss Branwell's contribution to it has already been examined. The essential classics—Homer, Virgil, Milton—could be found on Mr Brontë's shelves and the young people owned some Scott and Ossian and a few of the poets, in addition to the favourites of their childhood : *Aesop's Fables*, *The Arabian Nights* and Bewick's *British Birds*. But this is not surprising at a time when the price of new books was so exorbitant. The family's main reading was derived from the literary magazines of the day : *Blackwood's*, *Fraser's*, *Chambers* (and later the *Cornhill*), which Mr Brontë and Aunt took regularly and of which they were all, from the oldest to the youngest, assiduous students.

The girls, while young, were thus in continuous contact with what was best in contemporary writing.

To trace the origin of an author's style in his reading is a fascinating pursuit (who does not hear the voice of Fielding in Dickens ?) Yet with them, more than with most writers, it is impossible to trace the origins of their styles to any particular literary influence. So far as we can judge from the foregoing, Charlotte, Emily and Anne had equal opportunities of reading the acknowledged masters of English prose ; yet their three styles remained profoundly dissimilar.

Their mentality was allied, the field of their experience restricted and *restricted in the same manner* ; their moral judgments were akin, creating a psychological affinity which their first critics were swift to seize on ; but their writing remained distinct from first to last.

In neither Emily nor Anne would rhetorical passages, such as abound in Charlotte's books, ever be found.

The tersely satirical observations on her characters in which Anne excelled, would be replaced in Emily by a drier brevity which did not set out to amuse.   There is humour in the portrayal of Joseph and of Zillah—the wry humour of an unsmiling philosopher contemplating man in all his meannesses and follies—but there is no satire, whereas in *Agnes Grey* the style is buoyantly satirical in places, but never humorous.   The difference, of course, is as much one of character as of style.

Anne achieved a distinct style of her own—always fresh and lucid, very often sparkling, and sometimes illumined by a flash of self-betrayal which, in its naïveté, homely wisdom and felicity of phrase, recalls Goldsmith more than any other writer in the English language.   Anne Brontë did not hesitate to laugh at herself, to show how gullible she had been, how easily hoodwinked by the worldly-wise—and to make others laugh with her in a manner as disarming and lovable as Goldsmith's own.   This, above all, is the point of style which differentiates her from her sisters and is the true hall-mark of her writing.   Jane Eyre might confess to being plain just as Agnes Grey "could discover no beauty in those marked features, that pale hollow cheek, and ordinary dark brown hair", but it needed the touch of Irish temperament in Anne to make her heroine say "I always lacked common sense when taken by surprise" and promptly show her folly.

Without stretching the point too far, the likelihood of her having read the best of Goldsmith is great. His *Citizen of the World*, *Collected Poems* and *Natural History* all happen to figure in the catalogue of the Keighley Mechanics' Institute Library.

So, also, does the work of another Irish writer to whose novels, rich in satirical portraiture and homely wit, Anne's bear a marked affinity : Maria Edgeworth, all of whose books, including the latest, *Helen* (1832), had appeared before Anne went to school. Maria Edgeworth's preoccupation with pedagogy might have made her books of particular interest to the prospective governess Anne resolved to be. Something like a malicious echo of the earlier writer's optimistic strain seems to sound in this passage at the opening of *Agnes Grey* : ". . . And then, how charming to be entrusted with the care and education of children ! Whatever others said, I felt I was fully competent to the task . . . I had but to turn from my little pupils to myself at their age, and I should know, at once, how to win their confidence and affections. . . .

> —Delightful task !
> To teach the young idea how to shoot !"

As a prelude to her experiences as governess to the little Bloomfields the passage could not be more ironically apt.

Perhaps in Anne Brontë the Irish ancestry of the family found its outlet.

As a young girl Anne's favourite reading was undoubtedly poetry. Wordsworth's nature poetry found a ready echo in her heart, so early given to the beauty surrounding her home, and, indeed, so coloured her mind, that, consciously or unconsciously, she imitated it in such lines as these :

> While on my lonely couch I lie,
> I seldom feel myself alone,
> For fancy fills my dreaming eye
> With scenes and pictures of its own—

And again :

> As in the days of infancy,
> An opening primrose seemed to me
> A source of strange delight—

Cowper she so loved that, out of sympathy there grew up something more than understanding : a communion of thought and experience of which she herself became aware and which she expressed in the verses dedicated to him, thus :

> The language of my inmost heart
> I traced in every line ;
> My sins, my sorrows, hopes, and fears,
> Were there—and only mine—

Music she probably held in an equal love to poetry ; it was a passion with her all her life. Precisely how proficient she was is difficult to assess today when the standard of amateur playing is so much lower than that of Anne's day. Ellen Nussey, who heard both Emily and Anne play over a number of years, drew a sharp distinction between their performance. Of Emily she said that she "played with brilliancy" and that, after studying in Brussels with a first-class professor, her playing "was quite professional". Of Anne's achievement Ellen said : "She also played, but preferred soft melodies and vocal music. She sang a little ; her voice was weak, but very sweet in tone."

Music occupied a great part of Anne's life. It was not economy only, or the need to supply her pupils with fresh pieces, which made her copy so many airs into her manuscript books : it was love of the art itself, and the pleasure of adding to her own repertory, for it is obvious from *Agnes Grey* that Mr Brontë, at least, delighted in her singing.

Her albums of published music—a number of which are still preserved with the fingering most minutely pencilled in—would argue, by modern standards, a great proficiency.

When Ellen Nussey first visited Haworth in the summer of 1833 the girls had no piano. "A little later," wrote Ellen, "there was the addition of a piano" (the "elderly cabinet piano" so well described in *Wildfell Hall* and which can still be seen today at Haworth Parsonage), the famous piano round which crowded the passionate music-lovers that all the young Brontës were—Branwell, Emily and Anne in particular—in the enjoyment of many a light-hearted hour. The memory of one such has been preserved in a letter of Charlotte's. Writing to Ellen on 7th June 1838, describing a visit of Mary and Martha Taylor to the parsonage, she concludes : "They are making such a noise about me I cannot write any more. Mary is playing on the piano ; Martha is chattering as fast as her little tongue can run ; and Branwell is standing before her, laughing at her vivacity. . . ."

By the date of the diary paper of November 1834 Emily and Anne were obviously having music lessons. Some of their preserved music bears a much earlier date, as though they took lessons and, possibly, practised at their teacher's house. The girls possessed the scores of most of Handel's oratorios (Branwell's favourite music), often arranged as duets for organ and piano ; Beethoven's piano sonatas and a keyboard scoring of his overtures. It was a period when overtures were fashionable playing, and Emily and Anne possessed a fine collection of duet and solo settings of Weber's, Mozart's, Haydn's and Rossini's operatic works. The emphasis certainly seemed to be on light and brilliant music requiring undeniable technique in the performers. Anne was buying new music regularly up to the end of her teaching days in 1845. By the very high standard of amateur performance in her day she may not have distinguished herself, but her devotion to music was life-long and by present-day standards her ability would undoubtedly be considered high.

For the other chief "accomplishment" she would be required to teach—drawing—she also had more than a talent. It will be remembered that together with her three elders she had drawing lessons from the Leeds artist William Robinson whom Mr Brontë engaged at a fee of two guineas a visit to teach his children at home. A good number of her sketches still exist. Though conventional in subject—they are mostly copies of Classical Italian landscape—they show great skill in the medium and an obvious sensuous pleasure in form. Where she quite excels is in studies of children's heads. A few romantic studies of landscapes with figures, obviously original in composition, show that she could also have illustrated her own stories had she so wished. An attempt at character-drawing, where the facial expressions are remarkable, show that she was not content with aping the criteria of beauty. One such drawing of a girl with a singularly spiteful, savage and louring expression she has endorsed : "A very bad picture." A piece of self-criticism that reminds one that the author of *Agnes Grey* and *Wildfell Hall* was a searcher after the truth, however unvarnished it might be.

The experience of teaching her sisters gave Charlotte a certain assurance, and certainly further advanced her own studies as her mind matured, but what it did not do was to bring her in a penny. How completely destitute the Brontë girls were even of pocket-money is shown by Charlotte's apologies to Ellen Nussey in the pre-penny post days, for not being able to pay her own letter carriage. Writing to her on 4th July 1834 she says : "You will be tired of paying the postage of my letters, but necessity must plead my excuse for their frequent recurrence." More wounding still to her pride than having to accept the price of a stamp from a friend was having to accept the presents of clothing from time to time. "I *must* thank you for your very handsome present," she pursues in the same letter, "the bonnet is pretty, neat and simple, as like the giver as possible—I wish I could find some other way to thank you for your kindness than words. The load of obligation under which you lay me is positively overwhelming, and I make no return."

Mr Brontë housed and fed his daughters, possibly he paid for the *materials* of their clothes, but their confection was an absolute obligation from which they only escaped when they earned enough to buy their own bonnets and shawls and dresses. Over a period of many years, years when sensibility is at its acutest, they had to accept presents of clothes, possibly even of cast-off clothes from their godmothers, and write dutifully to acknowledge them, a gesture it went hard with any Brontë to make. Here is a letter of Charlotte's written while at school at Roe Head to Mrs Franks (the former Elizabeth Firth) :

"To Mrs. Franks, Huddersfield. Roe Head May 1831. Dear Madam—I beg to acknowledge receipt of the parcel which arrived the other day from Huddersfield, and to thank yourself for the frock and muslin and Miss Outhwaite for the shawl which she has so kindly sent me. My chilblains are quite well. I am sorry I was out when Mr. Atkinson called the other day. Pray give my love to Mrs. Firth, and present my thanks to her for her welcome note. The Miss Woolers desire their kindest respects to you. . . ."

Courage, pride and independence, characteristics of all three girls, may have sprung in undue proportion perhaps as a result of repeated obligations such as these. The lesson learned early in life was that independence was preferable to anything, no matter at what cost obtained.

Charlotte early resolved to earn her own living. In the midsummer of 1835 an opportunity offered. A teacher was wanted at her old school, Roe Head ; she applied for the post and was given it in exchange for free schooling for one of her sisters. She naturally offered this benefit to Emily, the elder of the two.

That Emily was psychologically unequal to such an effort Charlotte had yet to learn. The knowledge she aspired to for herself, the intellectual stimulus she craved from contact with other superior minds, were not the objectives of Emily. By force of circumstances they had to become those of Anne, but they were not *naturally* so. Emily and Anne could have been well content with very much *less* in life than Charlotte, provided they were given liberty—mental and physical—in a world of their own choosing. Their essentially poetic natures had to suffer violent coercion to fit them to live any sort of a practical life. In Emily's case, she never succeeded in doing so, even partially.

The decision to break up the family in the summer of 1835

coincided with Branwell's going to the Royal Academy Schools in London. It would be nearer the mark to say : with his projected departure for the Academy Schools, for he never actually entered them.

Branwell's godparents had been Mr Firth and his second wife who, from the far-away Thornton days, seem ever to have maintained a genuine friendship for Mr Brontë and his children. Mrs Firth made Mr Brontë the generous offer to pay for Branwell's training as a painter and for his expenses in London. Fully believing in his son's ability, Mr Brontë accepted.

Charlotte, writing to Ellen on 2nd July, thus announces the plan : "We are all about to divide, break up, separate. Emily is going to school, Branwell is going to London, and I am going to be a governess." Teasingly she withholds until the end of her letter the fact that her new post would bring her back to within four miles of Ellen, "at a place neither of us is unacquainted with, being no other than the identical Roe Head . . . where I was myself taught. . . . Miss Wooler made me the offer and I preferred it to one or two proposals of private governess-ship which I had before received."

Mr Brontë, reporting on the same matter to his old friend Elizabeth Franks (to whose good offices he recommends Charlotte and Emily), adds that, for the time being "my dear little Anne I intend to keep at home for another year under her Aunt's tuition and my own."

At fifteen and a half Anne was once again relegated to the sole companionship of the elders of the family ; her beloved Emily was to go away from her at the very age when most there is a need to confide one's bursting heart. For the girl she had now become, deeply sentimental, tender-hearted to excess, poetical in all the outpourings of a spirit daily more attuned to beauty, what a bleak prospect was this !

At the height of her poetic powers and mind's maturity Anne, looking back to this time of her early youth, saw the particular predicament of such an over-trusting, over-feeling nature as hers and wrote in the remarkable poem "Self-Communion" thus about herself :

> A tender heart too prone to weep,
> A love so earnest, strong, and deep
> It could not be exprest.

Poor helpless thing ! what can it do
Life's stormy cares and toils among ;
How tread this weary desert through,
That awes the brave and tires the strong ?
Where shall it centre so much trust ? . . .
That soul that clings to sympathy
As ivy clasps the forest tree,
How can it stand alone ?
That heart so prone to overflow
E'en at the thought of other's woe,
How will it bear its own ?
How, if a sparrow's death can wring
Such bitter tear-floods from the eye,
Will it behold the suffering
Of struggling, lost humanity . . . ?

True sympathy, such as she was endowed with, could but *add* to—not alleviate—the burden of the suffering in which she shared. It was one of her great and lasting causes of unhappiness that, except in the perfect sympathy of mind she met in Emily, there was so general a want of response to her intensest feelings :

And sometimes it was grief to know
My fondness was but half returned.
But this was nothing to the woe
With which another truth was learned :—
That I must check, or nurse apart
Full many an impulse of the heart
And many a darling thought :
What my soul worshipped, sought, and prized,
Were slighted, questioned, or despised ;
This pained me more than aught. . . .

From Emily's point of view, too, a more unhappy arrangement than the present one could not well be imagined. School was irksome enough to a girl of her mettle, but to be torn from Anne was misery indeed. In addition to both these sources of suffering there was her inner torment ; the growing demands of her compelling genius that exacted a certain condition of life for its expansion. That condition could be and was perfectly fulfilled at Haworth, and, as her all-too-short existence was to teach Emily, at Haworth and nowhere else.

Charlotte and Emily left home on 29th July 1835. It was the day before Emily's birthday. If any circumstance could add to the heart-break of departure, this would be it. One is tempted to see in this first severance of the girls on the eve of Emily's birthday the origin of that custom of the inseparables to write each other diary papers on that date, of which only two precious examples remain in each girl's handwriting.

Charlotte obviously believed that she could make the situation tolerable to Emily. The note of confidence in her powers to do so sounds in the confession : "the idea of being together consoles us somewhat".

Nothing could console Emily. Years later Charlotte tried to give a credible account of what Emily's sufferings had been at Roe Head. It had nothing to do with Roe Head. Only Charlotte knew, by intuition and fellow-feelings, that what nearly brought Emily to the grave was the severance from Haworth. And even then Charlotte dared not avow—what applied in her own case as well—that it wasn't *home* they missed so terribly, but the stimulus to creative writing which the moors of home afforded. The timeless days Emily, in particular, lived out upon the heath, the unbounded horizons that drew her ravished eyes, were the only setting possible for a soul like hers, suspended between two worlds.

"Liberty was the breath of Emily's nostrils," wrote Charlotte, "without it, she perished. The change from her own home to a school, and from her own very noiseless, very secluded but unrestrained and inartificial mode of life, to one of disciplined routine (though under the kindest auspices) was what she failed in enduring. Her nature proved here too strong for her fortitude. Every morning when she woke the vision of home and the moors rushed on her, and darkened and saddened the day that lay before her. Nobody knew what ailed her but me—I knew only too well. In this struggle her health was quickly broken : her white face, attenuated form, and failing strength threatened rapid decline. I felt in my heart she would die, if she did not go home, and with this conviction obtained her recall. She had only been three months at school. . . ." Mr Brontë was not going to risk a second Cowan Bridge ; he acted swiftly and decisively on this occasion ; Charlotte's report of her sister's condition was no sooner received than Emily was sent for.

It was mid-October. What Anne's feelings would be in welcoming Emily home can be easily guessed. But she was to have no time to nurse her favourite sister. Possibly even before Emily left Roe Head a quick decision had had to be reached : in default of Emily a free schooling in exchange for Charlotte's services was offered Anne.

It was instantly accepted. In view of all Anne's subsequent conduct, the likelihood is that the acceptance was strongly urged by herself; Mr Brontë and Miss Branwell had not wished her to leave home for another year. At no time and under no circumstances did Anne ever trade on her delicacy; like her own Agnes Grey she fought preferential treatment and firmly and persistently shouldered her own burdens.

The resolution which had grown up in her ever since the problem of their future had been raised that summer, swayed all her actions now. For the first time in her life she conceived an ambition. She resolved to fit herself, as well as *either* of her sisters, to earn her living as a teacher and to be a burden to nobody. To that resolution she adhered unflinchingly to the end.

Her very earliest poem to be preserved, the "Verses by Lady Geralda", though dated 1836, relates emotionally to this autumn of 1835 when, suddenly, the course of her life was changed. The depression subsequent on Emily's going away, the altered aspect of the familiar haunts provoked by her loneliness, are feelingly described; but then a new prospect dawns and the spark of ambition is fired and in that "cherished hope" she finds the courage to break away and face a new life. The verses are so autobiographical as to need quoting at some length :

> O why are things so changed to me ?
> What gave me joy before
> Now fills my heart with misery
> And nature smiles no more.
>
> And why are all the beauties gone
> From this my native hill ?—
> Alas ! my heart is changed alone,
> Nature is constant still.
>
> For when the heart is free from care,
> Whatever meets the eye
> Is bright, and every sound we hear
> Is full of melody. . . .
>
> But the world's before me now,
> Why should I despair ?
> I will not spend my days in vain,
> I will not linger here !

There is still a cherished hope
To cheer me on my way,
It is burning in my heart
With a feeble ray.

I will leave thee then my childhood's home,
For all thy joys are gone,
I leave thee through the world to roam
In search of fair renown.

From such a hopeless home to part
Is happiness to me,
For nought can charm my weary heart
Except activity.

Thus "to live to some purpose", as she eventually wrote in one of her last letters, had already now become the "cherished hope" of Anne Brontë.

We know by the evidence of a drawing of hers preserved by Miss Wooler that she reached Roe Head some time before 27th October 1835.

It was a journey of fourteen miles to the other side of Bradford, since Roe Head stood at the junction of the Bradford-Leeds roads into Huddersfield. In those days the surrounding countryside was very pleasant, as it still is in parts today, and the nature-loving Brontë girls might, indeed, have fallen upon stonier ground. The journey could be undertaken all the way by hired gig, or by gig to Bradford and on from there by the stage-coach to Huddersfield. As we know, from subsequent occasions, that Mr Brontë did not hesitate to send his daughters all the way by gig, we may suppose that on this first journey to school Anne travelled so.

The districts through which she passed, once Bradford was left behind, were mostly rural. The whole way from then onwards was punctuated by names familiar to her. The very sign-posts were like welcoming hands, waving her on to her father's former curacies at Dewsbury and Hartshead and, where not directly associated with him, were associated with the names of the few people who then filled Anne Brontë's restricted world. At Bradford itself lived her godmother, Miss Fanny Outhwaite, at Eldon Place, where Mr Brontë had so often called and where one wonders if Anne stopped now to break her journey. At Bradford also lived, of course, the children's "Uncle Morgan", who had married their

(2,056)

parents and christened all of them and, alas ! buried some of them too. He was well known even to the younger generation for he had made frequent visits to the parsonage at Haworth.

Now, as the wooded undulating scene unfolded at her feet, every church tower rising from its shroud of autumnal boughs spoke of her father's colleagues, the Buckworths, the Atkinsons, the Franks, who had either preceded or followed him in the surrounding parishes. Did the driver take her via Hightown on the long dip down towards Mirfield and Roe Head ? There, facing Clough Lane, stood, and still stands, the first home of her parents, where Maria and Elizabeth were born—a place of sacred memory for any of the Brontë girls and one to which Charlotte and Anne will have walked on Sunday evenings when free to attend service at Hartshead Church, the low-towered, broad-beamed little church where Maria was christened. Below Hartshead the road dipped sharply down towards Mirfield and the valley where the Calder flowed, lost now in autumnal mists and the great wall of smoke thrown out by Huddersfield. As the hill dropped more sharply still a long low wall lay to her right, over which she could see through the branches of beech and oak the rambling roof-tops and chimney-pots of the building the driver told her was Roe Head. In less than five minutes more she was turning through the wide stone-pillared gate and up the winding drive. It swept in a circle round towards the house, whose pleasant front faced south over sloping lawns, with trees flanking it and sheltering it from the rear.

The house to which Anne went on that late autumn day was a beautiful grey-stone house, two storeys high, with a double bow-windowed front, standing in its own extensive grounds. At that time of the year the giant oaks that screen it from the north would yet have retained their panoply of copper-coloured leaves. Beyond the fact that it was spacious and many-windowed, what more would a frightened girl see on her first arrival ?

The autumn day was drawing towards dusk when she arrived.

There was Charlotte, all solicitude, to welcome the traveller, and there, no doubt, imposing in their charming drawing-room, were the Miss Woolers, to whom Anne must be brought at once to pay her respects.

There had originally been five Miss Woolers, daughters of a prosperous local mill-owner. Two had married and at the time Anne arrived she would have had to confront only three Miss

Woolers in the beautiful bow-windowed drawing-room of Roe Head.

"Miss" Wooler—Margaret—the principal of the establishment, always deferentially addressed as "sister" by her juniors, was forty-three at that time. In person she was "like a lady-Abbess", according to Ellen Nussey. She always wore white well-fitting dresses, trimmed with some kind of embroidery. "Her long hair plaited, formed a coronet, and long large ringlets fell from her head to shoulders. She was not pretty or handsome, but her quiet dignity made her presence imposing." With her were probably "Miss Catherine", aged thirty-nine, to whom, in after years, Charlotte paid the doubtful compliment of comparing Madame Heger; and the youngest, Eliza, aged twenty-seven, the most "severe and proper" of the Miss Woolers, according to the testimony of their own nephew.

The married sisters were both of them wives of clergymen : Miss Susan who, some five years before Anne's arrival, had married the Rev. Edward Nicholl Carter, curate of Mirfield, who had prepared Charlotte for Confirmation when she first went to school, and with whom Anne was to have personal dealings ; and Miss Marianne, whose marriage to the Vicar of Dewsbury, the Rev. Thomas Allbutt, that same summer of 1835 had created the very vacancy Charlotte had been engaged to fill. Though married, neither of these ladies lived at any distance and still attended Roe Head in the capacity of "visiting teacher".

The Miss Woolers were reputed for their learning and piety, and yet it would be creating quite a false impression to imply that Roe Head had any affinity with "Minerva Lodge" or Mirfield with "Cranford". The Miss Woolers were practical women, living not in an effete past but in a progressive present. Though rural beauties surrounded the school on every side, their life-stream was drawn from the big manufacturing centres of Huddersfield, Heckmondwike, Birstall and Gomersal. Their pupils, though undoubtedly drawn from wealthy families, were a "mixed bag". Miss Amelia Walker of Lascelles Hall, a niece of Mrs Atkinson and a young lady of consequence not only in her own eyes but in those of all Huddersfield, whose father was a *nouveau riche* of two generations back, had to rub shoulders with the daughters of woollen manufacturers whose new wealth was even then in the making. The district was strongly Non-conformist, and although the Miss

Woolers themselves were ardently Church of England they were too practical not to admit pupils from conspicuous Dissenting families like the Taylors of Gomersal.

Miss Wooler did not believe in sequestering young women from the world ; on the contrary, enjoying robust health herself, she took every opportunity of walking them outside the walls of their "nunnery" and showing them the active noisy world smoking and clanking all about them in the valleys, where the lives of their fathers and brothers were spent and where the money that paid their fees was being earned.

Roe Head stands, as has already been mentioned, at the junction of the main Bradford and Leeds roads ; in no sense, therefore, were the girls cut off from sights and sounds of an active outer world. "Huddersfield Market day," writes Mrs Gaskell, "was still the great period for events at Roe Head. Then girls, running round the corner of the house and peeping between tree-stems, and up a shadowy lane, could catch a glimpse of a father or brother driving to market in his gig ; might perhaps exchange a wave of the hand. . . ." Might, and did, as the letters of Charlotte Brontë are there to prove. "I wish," she writes to Ellen in the course of the following year, "you could know the thrill of delight which I experienced when, as I stood at the dining-room window, I saw your brother George as he whirled past toss your little packet over the wall." Brother George passed that way very often and packets of letters between Charlotte and Ellen were continually being entrusted to him. There was also the weekly, Sabbath, thrill of meeting the Nusseys or Taylors at morning service in one or other of the numerous outlying churches which Charlotte and Anne attended during their school days.

The most important thing about Miss Wooler as a mentor of the young was the humanity and good sense she displayed towards her pupils. The following incident, also related by Ellen Nussey, shows that she was a good psychologist—as well as a capable teacher. Hearing the girls talk about the school ghost—a lady in rustling silks who was supposed to haunt the upper stories of the house—she adopted an effective measure for putting their credulity to the proof. "She would," said Ellen, "select one or other from among us to ascend the stairs after the dimness of evening hours had set in, to bring something down which could easily be found. No ghost made herself visible even to the frightened imagination of the

foolish and the timid ; the whitened face of apprehension soon
disappeared, nerves were braced, and a general laugh soon set us all
right again."

Miss Wooler was an excellent linguist and taught Italian as well
as French and German. As a teacher her methods sound almost
modern when compared with those of her contemporaries. "Miss
Wooler," wrote Mrs Gaskell, "had a remarkable knack of making
her pupils feel interested in whatever they had to learn. They set
to their studies, not as to tasks or duties to be got through, but with
a healthy desire and thirst for knowledge, of which she had
managed to make them perceive the relishing savour. They
did not leave off reading and learning as soon as the compulsory
pressure of school was taken away. They had been taught to think,
to analyse, to reject, to appreciate".

How Miss Wooler's recollections of the Luddite Riots and the
encroachment upon rural life of the Industrial Revolution affected
Charlotte is well known to all readers of *Shirley*. There can be no
doubt that Miss Wooler was an educative influence, opening her
young scholars' eyes, not only to the perfection of continental
literature but to the restless changing social fabric of life about
them. It was just such a teacher that Anne needed most to bring
her to grips with the material world in which she must, before
many years were out, make her own way.

Chapter Nine

A BURDENED HEART

ANNE went to Roe Head resolved to learn all she could, and, to judge by results, she must have done well at her studies. When it came to earning her own living she was able to offer the essential "accomplishments"—music, singing, drawing, as well as French, Latin, German, history, English, arithmetic, geography.

In acquiring Latin so well as to be able later to teach it, Anne was rather singular for her time. Neither Charlotte nor Emily did as much. Anne doubtless had the opportunity, which the others missed, of sharing Branwell's Latin lessons with their father and getting a good grounding before going to school.

Anne's copy of VALPY'S *Latin DELECTUS* that she used with her Thorp Green pupils still exists today. It contains pencilled notes and shows that she was competent to take her pupils well beyond those rudiments with which most young ladies of her day contented themselves.

It was a liberal, nay, generous régime at Roe Head. There were excellent food, regular exercise and even organised games on the pleasant lawns before the house. Miss Wooler's Young Ladies might indeed consider themselves favoured in all essential respects : as a boarding-school it could not well have been bettered.

As might be expected Anne's conduct was perfect and earned her a prize at the end of her first year. The inscription in Miss Wooler's hand reads : "A Prize for good conduct presented to Miss A. Bronte with Miss Wooler's kind love, Roe Head, Dec. 14th 1836." The choice of book for a girl of sixteen—Watt's *On the Improvement of the Mind*—would suggest that Miss Wooler saw in Anne a very serious-minded young person ; she seems never to have penetrated the extreme reserve behind which the shy girl hid.

Anne was profoundly unhappy at school, but with Emily's example before her would not admit defeat. The causes of her unhappiness were not the same as those affecting either of her sisters, but they went back as far, were quite as deep.

To begin with, the presence of Charlotte which should have

been some guarantee of happiness for Anne had quite the contrary effect : it proved a misfortune rather than a blessing.

Their relative ages and positions in the school served rather as a barrier than as a point of contact. Anne was fifteen years and ten months old when she arrived at Roe Head. Charlotte was four years older than Anne and one of the teachers now. This post of authority which a girl of less rectitude than Charlotte would have used to the benefit of her younger sister she used with the utmost impartiality. Not only did Charlotte not seek to obtain any favours for Anne, but she would rigorously have opposed any semblance of latitude where rules were concerned, or indulgence in the matter of half-holidays and outings, had the Miss Woolers even offered them.

The many notes to Ellen written in the deserted schoolroom, long after "all the house was retired", show that there was never any question of Anne sitting up with her. She went to bed with the other girls at whatever was the appointed hour for the boarders to go.

Anne's misfortune—for nothing short of a misfortune it proved —was that her schooldays coincided with a great emotional crisis in Charlotte's life. Charlotte not only loathed her work as teacher and regarded her pupils with impatience and virulence, but she suffered torments of frustration at being debarred from doing the work she loved. At a moment when she was becoming fully conscious of her powers, she found herself almost totally deprived of the leisure essential to writing.

From the very first Anne's situation was made uncomfortable by the consciousness of Charlotte's sacrifice on her behalf ; if we are to believe Mary Taylor, Charlotte was exploited in the affair. Discussing the point many years later with Mrs Gaskell, Mary Taylor said :

"I heard she had gone as a teacher to Miss Wooler's. I went to see her, and asked how she could give so much for so little money, when she could live without it. She owned that, after clothing herself and Anne, there was nothing left, though she had hoped to be able to save something. She confessed it was not brilliant, but what could she do ? I had nothing to answer. She seemed to have no interest or pleasure beyond the feeling of duty, and when she could get the opportunity used to sit alone and 'make out'."

How and what Charlotte "made out" the papers of her Roe Head

"Journal" reveal. Seldom has frustration found such anguished expression ; seldom has genius been so clear-eyed a witness of its own birth-throes ; seldom has the artist's suffering been dissected with a more pitiless knife ; seldom has the rebellion of a heart nearing bursting-point been expressed in more memorable language.

"I am just going to write because I cannot help it," she cries, casting about her a last contemptuous glance. "A. Cook on one side of me, E. Lister on the other and Miss W[ooler] in the background. Stupidity the atmosphere, school-books the employment, asses the society, what in all this is there to remind me of the divine, silent, unseen land of thought, dim now and indefinite as the dream of a dream, the shadow of a shade. There is a voice, there is an impulse that wakens up that dormant power which smites torpidity I sometimes think dead."

The voice of the wind raging outside the house reminded her of Angria. "O it has wakened a feeling that I cannot satisfy—a thousand wishes rose at its call which must die with me for they will never be fulfilled."

"The spirit of all Verdopolis," she cries (Verdopolis was the capital Glass City of the new state of Angria), ". . . came crowding into my mind. If I had had time to indulge it I felt that the vague sensation of that moment would have settled down into some narrative better at least than anything I ever produced before. But just then a dolt came up with a lesson. I thought I should have vomited." The intrusion of reality is like a searing iron applied to quivering flesh.

How much of her inner life, of its passionate needs and struggles, did she reveal to Anne ? Nothing at all if one can judge from her "Journal". The sense of Anne's presence penetrates only very rarely and as through a mist. Suddenly, at the end of a fragment in which she has introduced a new character into Verdopolitan society— Jane Moore—she herself makes the point. "The quick glance of her eye indicating a warm and excitable temperament, the mingled expression of good-natured pride, spirit and kind-heartedness predominating in every feature, all these are as clearly before me as Anne's quiet image, sitting at her lessons on the opposite side of the table."

In that passage we have as good a picture as we shall get of the relationship between Charlotte and Anne in their Roe Head days ;

Charlotte abandoned to her dream, Anne trying to concentrate on her lessons.

The great wind roaring down the chimneys and battering at the shutters of the schoolroom, that brings all Verdopolis before Charlotte's eyes, unites her for a moment with Anne as joint exile, from a cherished past. "That wind," she writes, "pouring in impetuous current through the air, sounding wildly unremittingly from hour to hour, deepening its tone as the night advances, coming not in gusts, but with a rapid gathering stormy swell, that wind I know is heard at this moment far away on the moors at Haworth. Branwell and Emily hear it and as it sweeps over our house down the churchyard and round the old Church, they think perhaps of me and Anne."

Emotionally starved as she found herself at this time, Charlotte allowed herself to be more and more dominated by the piety of her friend, Ellen Nussey, to whom she confided only so much of her troubles as were avowable. The mere fact that Ellen was her chosen confidante at this period and not Anne shows how little the sisters were in touch. Charlotte's letters to Ellen are as frequent as they are verbose. They all show a great perturbation of mind and dissatisfaction, both with her situation and with herself.

"Don't deceive yourself by imagining that I have a bit of real goodness about me. My darling, if I were like you, I should have to face Zionward. . . . If you knew my thoughts ; the dreams that absorb me ; and the fiery imagination that at times eats me up and makes me feel society, as it is, wretchedly insipid, you would pity me and I daresay despise me. . . ."

"If I could always live with you," she writes to Ellen on another occasion, ". . . I might one day become better, far better than my evil wandering thoughts, my corrupt heart, cold to the spirit and warm to the flesh will now permit me to be. . . ."

Where the "evil wandering thoughts" and the "corrupt heart" took refuge was in scenes like this, confided at fever-heat to the separate crumpled sheets that composed her journal.

"All this day I have been in a dream, half-miserable and half-ecstatic—miserable because I could not follow it out uninterruptedly, ecstatic because it showed almost in the vivid light of reality the ongoings of the infernal world." (Charlotte always referred thus to Angria.) "I had been toiling for nearly an hour with Miss Lister, Miss Marriott, and Ellen Cook, striving to teach them the dis-

tinction between an article and a substantive. The parsing lesson
was completed ; a dead silence had succeeded it in the school-room,
and I sat sinking from irritation and weariness into a kind of
lethargy. . . . A sweet August morning was smiling without.
The dew was not yet dried off the field. . . .

". . . After tea we took a long weary walk. I came back
exhausted to the last degree for Miss L[ister] and Miss M[arriott]
had been boring me with their vulgar familiar trash all the time
we were out. If those girls knew how I loathed their company
they would not seek mine as they do. The sun had set nearly a
quarter of an hour before we returned and it was getting dusk.

"They . . . went into the school-room to do their exercises
and I crept up to the bed-room to be alone for the first time that
day. Delicious was the sensation I experienced as I laid down [sic]
on the spare-bed and resigned myself to the luxury of twilight and
solitude. The stream of thought checked all day came flowing free
and calm along its channel. My ideas were too shattered to form
any definited picture *as they would have done in such circumstances at
home* [author's italics].

"The toil of the day," continues Charlotte, "succeeded by this
moment of divine leisure had acted on me like opium and was
coiling about me a disturbed but fascinating spell such as I never
felt before. What I imagined grew morbidly vivid. I remember
I quite seemed to see with my bodily eyes a lady standing in the
hall. . . ."

And she is off.

Added to the unappeasable cravings of the artist there rose up
out of a childhood dominated over by Aunt the voice of conscience
terrifying in its promptings. "I abhor myself," wrote Charlotte
to Ellen, "I despise myself; if the doctrine of Calvin be true,
I am already an outcast. . . ." This was the very language most
certain to affect Anne ; with her sister in this state of mind, no
wonder her own resistance became undermined, and eventually
crumbled.

At fifteen and a half Anne found herself suddenly deprived of
the sustaining presence, not only of the being she most loved in the
world, but of a way of life as free as it was inspiriting. With all
the resolution of a proud and honourable character she set herself
to overcome their loss and to bear the homesickness and panic
incident to such a change in her circumstances—and on the surface

succeeded in doing so. The need to learn had become an end in itself; the resolve to go out when the time was ripe and earn her own living enforced on her now the obligation to stand the test of absence. It was a challenge she was proud to meet.

But Charlotte's defection was something she could not have foreseen. Charlotte might—and did—hold her sister at arm's length where the unappeasable craving of her imagination was concerned, but as the religious crisis rose and overwhelmed Charlotte, inevitably the wave broke over Anne as well, and because, in this particular, Anne was more vulnerable than Charlotte, it had more fatal effects.

Charlotte, until almost too late, remained unaware of the troubles besetting Anne, equally because of her own mental preoccupation and because of the stoical front Anne succeeded in presenting. Yet, from the very beginning, Anne, like Charlotte, was confiding her griefs to paper.

The sharpest of these was, as might be expected at the outset, for her loss of liberty. With her removal to Roe Head the theme of imprisonment, later to be uppermost in so much of her poetry, takes a prominent place.

Like Charlotte hungering and thirsting for her imaginary world, Anne, caught up in the routine of a young ladies' seminary, was day and night yearning after Gondal. There can be no doubt that from this period date the poems : "A Voice from the Dungeon", "The Captive's Dream" and "The North Wind".

The authority and fire of all these pieces are astonishing in a schoolgirl of sixteen. Dramatised as the situations are to fit in with the general scheme of Gondal, the feeling is personal and very real. How inevitably must this message have come to her lying in her dormitory bed at Miss Wooler's, listening to the invocation of the north wind :

> I have passed over thy own mountains dear,
> Thy northern mountains, and they still are free :
> Still lonely, wild, majestic, bleak, and drear,
> And stern and lovely as they used to be. . . .
>
> No voice but mine can reach thy ear,
> And Heaven has kindly sent me here
> To mourn and sigh with thee,
> And tell thee of the cherished land
> Of thy nativity—

> Blow on, wild wind ; . . .
> Confined and hopeless as I am,
> Oh ! speak of liberty !
> Oh, tell me of my mountain home
> And I will welcome thee !

Throughout Anne's poetry recurs the theme of shared misfortunes, of vicarious suffering. It is impossible not to ascribe this to her almost twin-like participation in the life of her sister Emily. Over and over again she expresses the resolution to bear her own lot with fortitude, so long as those she loves are spared similar trials. In these earliest poems the sentiment occurs for the first time.

> Oh, Heaven ! I could bear
> My deadly fate with calmness if there were
> No kindred hearts to bleed and break for me.

How hopeless the prospect sometimes seemed, she has described in the poem "A Voice from the Dungeon", written in her second year at school, in October 1837.

> I'm buried now ; I've done with life ;
> I've done with hate, revenge and strife ;
> I've done with joy, and hope, and love,
> And all the bustling world above—
>
> Long have I dwelt forgotten here
> In pining woe and dull despair,
> This place of solitude and gloom
> Must be my dungeon and my tomb—

The pity was that, suffering from almost identical maladies, Charlotte and Anne could not bridge the state of spiritual isolation in which they lived. On the material plane they came no closer together either.

Surrounded as they were by former friends of their father's—as well as by Charlotte's friends, the Nusseys and Taylors at nearby Birstall and Gomersal—they need not have lacked for more adult society had they so wished. But they were so wretchedly shy that when invitations did arrive from their godparents at the nearby vicarages of Hartshead and Huddersfield, they regarded them more as formidable ordeals than as pleasures and accepted them only, one senses, with a degree of heavy-hearted resignation. The visits, one feels certain, afforded them very little refreshment of spirit.

Charlotte was invited to spend the week-end with her godparents the Atkinsons, at Mirfield. In this case the presence of Anne would have been a welcome support to the agonisingly shy girl Charlotte was. But here Anne was not invited. The Atkinsons lived in a far better house than Mr Brontë had inhabited when minister of Hartshead. It was known as "The Green House" and stood in a fine garden of its own at hardly a quarter of an hour's walk from Roe Head on the main Huddersfield road. Here Charlotte, in the recollection of the Atkinson's old housekeeper, Mrs Abraham Hirst, would pass much of the time of her visits in shrinking timidity from her hosts and their other guests.

The Sunday services were among the few regular occasions when the sisters met. Sometimes Miss Wooler permitted them to walk over to Birstall and Gomersal to meet their friends at the morning services there, but mostly they were required to attend Mirfield Church where the Miss Woolers' brother-in-law, the Rev. Edward Carter, officiated and the Roe Head girls had their pews. With Charlotte supervising them they would set off across the fields, wet or fine.

Mirfield Church stood on a rise of ground overlooking the parklands of Blake Hall and the Calder valley some mile and a half from Roe Head and was reached by a pleasant lane cutting across fields. When Anne Brontë went there as a schoolgirl among other schoolgirls, the family from Blake Hall, who were the patrons of the church, must also have been attending divine service. They were called Ingham and at that time were composed of young Mr and Mrs Ingham, of a little boy aged three and of a baby girl who, less than four years later, were to become Anne's pupils and be immortalised by her as Master Tom Bloomfield and Miss Mary Ann Bloomfield in *Agnes Grey*. Is it too far-fetched to suppose that young Mrs Ingham may many a time have glanced towards the Roe Head pew and encountered the critical eye of her children's future governess?

In those days the scholastic year was literally divided into two, the "halves" extending from the end of July to Christmas and from the end of January until the middle or end of June. The two annual holidays were of a month each. This arrangement—by which the poor children were at home in July and worked right through the hot month of August—was chiefly dictated, in rural districts at least, by the exigencies of the harvest, when young and old alike were needed to help bring in the crops.

At the end of Charlotte's and Anne's first year, in June 1836, when the immediate prospect of going home was reviving them like rain after drought, an invitation came from Anne's godmother, Mrs Franks, to spend some portion of the holidays at Huddersfield. "Dear Madam," wrote Charlotte in reply, in a letter in which one senses the near-panic in which any prospect of a visit—and especially a visit standing between them and home—immediately plunged the Brontë girls, "Dear Madam, I have been obliged to delay answering your kind invitation until I could fix a time for accepting it. Till this morning Miss Wooler had not decided when her school should break up ; she has now fixed upon Friday, the 17th of this month for the commencement of the vacation. On that day, if all be well, Anne and I hope to have the very great pleasure of seeing you at Huddersfield" [a distance of some three miles from Roe Head]. ". . . We propose," continued Charlotte, "coming by the four or five o'clock coach on Friday afternoon and returning by an early morning coach on Monday, as Papa, I fear, will scarcely be willing to dispense with us longer at home, even though we should be staying with so valued a friend as yourself. Excuse what is faulty in this hasty scrawl, My Dear Madam, and do not think me negligent in having so long delayed to answer your kind note, because I really could not help it. Accept my own and my sister's respectful and sincere love, and believe me to be, affectionately yours, C. Brontë."

Mr Brontë was not disposed to be made the excuse for curtailing a visit which he considered so flattering and so beneficial to his children. On 13th June, having heard of Charlotte's arrangements to reduce to a minimum what was obviously a dreaded visit, he took up his pen to write to Mrs Franks and, incidentally, let the cat out of the bag. He was quite aware that Charlotte and Anne grudged every moment of their holidays not spent at home. "My Dear Madam," he wrote, "My dear little Charlotte has informed me that you and Mr Franks have been so kind as to invite her and Anne to pay you a visit for a week, but that through impatience, as is very natural, they have curtailed that invitation to a few days. I have written to them to countermand this intention. I esteem it as a high privilege that they should be under your roof for a time, where, I am sure, they will see and hear nothing but what, under providence, must necessarily tend to their best interest in both the worlds. You I have long known ; Mr Franks' character I am well acquainted with through the medium of authentic report, and hence

I come to this conclusion. I have written to Charlotte and Anne to this effect, but as my letter may not reach them (owing to a bye post) in due time, I will thank you to communicate to them this intelligence. I will send the horse and gig for them to your house, and if necessary they may return from thence by Roe Head." [To pick up their luggage no doubt.]

One can picture the consternation of the two shy creatures when their Papa's decree was communicated to them by their hostess. There was to be no reprieve. A whole week of their precious holidays was to be spent from home. "In these sentiments," Mr Brontë concluded his letter, "Miss Branwell perfectly agrees with me."

The former Miss Firth, whose marriage to the Vicar of Huddersfield, it will be remembered, had occurred in 1824 and whose visit to Cowan Bridge while on her honeymoon Charlotte was not likely to have forgotten, was now the mother of three fine children (two boys, John and Harry, and a little girl, Elizabeth) and, could her young visitors but have guessed it, had little more than a year to live at that time. None of her kindness or affection for Mr Brontë's children had diminished, and one would like to know that something more than their crippling timidity made itself apparent on this occasion, or that she had the penetration to see behind and beyond their reserve.

Their visit coincided with the restoration of Huddersfield Church, a circumstance which, in those clerical circles, could not have failed to arouse their interest, if only to report fully on the matter to their Papa.

An experience of a more mundane sort awaited them on the very day of their arrival at Huddersfield. Mrs Franks, it will be remembered, was related to the Walker family of Lascelles Hall. (It was her cousin Frances Walker who had married Mr Atkinson and stood sponsor to Charlotte Brontë.) The present owner of Lascelles Hall, Mr Joseph Walker, was a brother of Mrs Atkinson and a cousin of Mrs Franks. Of his four children, the two girls, Jane and Amelia, had been pupils at Roe Head at the same time as Charlotte Brontë, Ellen Nussey and Mary Taylor. Moving in very different spheres the old schoolfellows had gone their several ways, but now four years later, in this summer of 1836, whom should the Brontë girls find on arriving at Huddersfield Vicarage but the entire Walker family come over from Lascelles Hall. Looking back on what must have been an ordeal to both herself and Anne, Charlotte wrote quite humorously of the event to Ellen Nussey. "When I was at Huddersfield, whom do you think I saw ? Amelia Walker and her sister, and mamma, papa and brother were all at the Vicarage when we arrived there on Friday. They were wondrously gracious. Amelia was almost enthusiastic in her professions of friendship ; she is taller, thinner, paler, and more delicate-looking than she used to be, very pretty still ; very ladylike and polished, but spoilt, utterly spoilt by the most hideous affectation. I wish she would copy her sister, who is indeed an example that affable, unaffected manners and a sweet disposition may fascinate powerfully without the aid of beauty. We spent the Tuesday at Lascelles Hall and had on the whole a very pleasant day."

Lascelles Hall, barely two miles outside Huddersfield, is a fine example of mid-eighteenth century architecture, standing on a wooded slope overlooking the valley of Kirkheaton. A wall in places ten feet high hides it from the approaching lane and the house itself with its Palladian front is screened from view by a winding drive of beech, until at a turn one suddenly comes on it. A rambling array of coach-houses and offices flanks it on the west, and in the rear lie show-gardens sheltered from the winds by high walls of ancient brick covered with espaliered pears and plums.

Stepping from high french windows on to spacious lawns that led to the famous rose-garden at the rear of the house, Anne would receive her first impression of what was meant by the term "the stately homes of England". Whether she realised it then, or not, much of her adult life would be spent in settings similar to these.

Of the Hall's inmates Charlotte was to write : "Miss Amelia changed her character every half-hour ; now she assumed the sweet sentimentalist, now the reckless rattler. Sometimes the question was 'Shall I look prettiest lofty ?' and again, 'Would not tender familiarity suit me better ?' At one moment she affected to enquire after her old school-acquaintances, the next she was detailing anecdotes of high life. At last I got so sick of this I turned for relief to her brother W[illiam]."

Charlotte's description of her old school-fellow is of more than passing interest to the Brontë student since, in the portrait of Amelia Walker, we see the unmistakable origin of the "worldly young woman" portrayed not only by Charlotte in Ginevra Fanshawe but by Anne in Rosalie Murray. This young person's characteristics are a blend of impudence and good-nature, caprice and petulance, self-indulgence and sacrifice to the world's exigencies.

George Moore, in his enthusiasm for *Agnes Grey*, levelled some serious charges against Charlotte Brontë which bear directly upon this subject. Not only was she, in his opinion, responsible for starting the critics "on their depreciation of Anne" (a just criticism, this), but his "case against Charlotte" which did not "end with an implicit defamation of her sister" included the equally serious charge of plagiarism. According to George Moore, Charlotte stole Rosalie Murray from *Agnes Grey* to fit in to her own *Villette* (in the character of Ginevra).

Had George Moore read Charlotte's letter concerning her old school-fellow he might have reconsidered the latter part of his charge. In point of fact, neither Amelia Walker nor Rosalie Murray were the exact prototypes for Ginevra Fanshawe, strongly related though they be. The "worldly young woman" of Anne and Charlotte's day, like their predecessors and successors in the field of fashion, ran true to type ; they followed a pattern of which both Anne and Charlotte, in their different experience of society, were bound to meet examples—Anne, admittedly, more specifically so than Charlotte, since, in her situation at Thorp Green, she was to frequent a far more worldly circle than ever Charlotte was to do in any of her posts as governess.

Whatever the rights and wrongs of George Moore's findings, on that particular visit to Huddersfield in June 1836 Anne was to have her first glimpse of that "great world" of whose feints and foolishness she was to become so shrewd—and just—a critic and whose rigours she was, in her own person, so shortly to brave.

Quite as much as Emily, Anne needed the direct contact with nature such as surrounded her daily life at home. It was necessary not only to her happiness but to her sense of security. Behind the smiling face of nature she had come to see a God of love, very different from the awful justiciary of her aunt's early teachings—the

> Eternal Power, of earth and air,
> Unseen, yet seen in all around,
> Remote, but dwelling everywhere,
> Though silent, heard in every sound. . . .

Removed from such cheerful influences and the powerful stimulus of Emily's mind she fell a prey once more, in her second year at school, to the old dark teachings of her childhood. She entered on a period of acute doubt and despondency—not doubt of God's goodness, as she says, but despondency at her own unworthiness and dread of damnation.

She has described the conflict waging in her heart during these months of "darkly toiling misery" :

> I see one kneeling on the sod,
> With infant hands upraised to Heaven—
> A young heart feeling after God
> Oft baffled, never backward driven.
> Mistaken oft, and oft astray,
> It strives to find the narrow way,
> But gropes and toils alone ;
> That inner life of strife and tears,
> Of kindling hopes and lowering fears
> To none but God is known—

Neither at Roe Head—nor later, seemingly—was Charlotte the confidante of her sister's "inner life of strife and tears" ; she may have guessed at it partially but had to confess, when the task of sorting Anne's posthumous manuscripts devolved on her, that she found "mournful evidence that religious feeling had been to her but too much like what it was to Cowper". . . . Undoubtedly the revelation came as a shock to Charlotte, not only by the mere fact of Anne's *suffering* but for the *silence* with which she bore it. "I own," wrote Charlotte to the publisher of her sister's posthumous works, "to me they seem sad, as if her whole innocent life had been passed under the martyrdom of an unconfessed physical pain. . . ." The operative word in this text is "unconfessed" ; it illumines yet further the sisters' relationship and bears out Charlotte's view of Anne as "of a remarkably taciturn, still, thoughtful nature, reserved even with her nearest of kin. . . ." Charlotte may have been aware that with Emily Anne was none of these things ; but not until after Anne's death did she fully discover how "reserved" Anne had been with her—a state of things which undoubtedly began at Roe Head.

Evidence is lacking of the exact date at which Anne fell gravely ill, whether in the autumn of 1836 or in the spring of 1837, but it was sometime before June 1837, when the school was removed to Dewsbury Moor, since it is specifically stated that it happened while Anne was yet at Roe Head.

The date is of less importance than the circumstances of the illness, for which we have the evidence of the minister attending her. He was the Rev. James La Trobe (the descendant of a French Huguenot family), a Moravian bishop and minister of the Moravian Church at Mirfield (scarce a mile distant from Roe Head), who, on the publication of Mrs Gaskell's *Life of Charlotte Bronte* in 1857, was so struck with her account of the ultimate destiny of the Brontë girls that he set down in writing for a friend the circumstances attending his acquaintance with Anne.

They were sufficiently remarkable when one considers that Anne was the daughter of an Anglican clergyman, surrounded by Anglican divines, the friends and colleagues of her father—among them, Mr Franks, the husband of her own godmother ; Charlotte's godfather, Mr Atkinson ; Miss Wooler's brother-in-law, Mr Carter—all well known to herself. Yet the evidence shows that it was not to any of these but to a total stranger that she sent, and that stranger a dissenting minister moreover. It is impossible not to ask oneself : what made her do it ?

The answer must obviously be that her need was beyond conventional remedy. It was the truth she wanted ; help, not a palliative. The future creator of Helen Huntingdon could not be put off with ready-made replies. She would inquire for herself. Something stronger than the precepts of a lifetime told her that somewhere there must be help ; that somewhere the pity she felt in her heart for others would find a response commensurable with her plight ; that if now the time had come for her to die, the creed in which she had been brought up should stand the proof—or fail her utterly. And, unflinchingly, she recognised the fact that it was failing her now.

There had been a Moravian settlement at Mirfield since 1751. Benjamin Ingham—of the Ingham family of Blake Hall—the friend and fellow-evangelist of Wesley, had brought the Moravians over from the founder-colony which had existed since 1722 in Saxony. Admitted to set up several centres in England, including London and Oxford, the Moravian Brotherhood was given recognition as a Church by Act of Parliament in 1751. Their founder in England, Peter Böhler (a life-long friend of Wesley), and the majority of the early brethren who settled here were Bohemians, driven into exile by the persecution of their own rulers, but gradually nationals of other countries joined them and by the early nineteenth century their English proselytes were numerous and scattered far and wide.

In the essential difference between the Moravian doctrines and the Methodists' we may find one of the reasons that prompted Anne's request to see the Moravian bishop. There was a mystical quality in their religion which advocated silence and a passive waiting for revelation—which made them suspicious to Wesley and was one of the reasons for which he ultimately broke away from them in 1740. Theirs was essentially a religion of pardon and peace. They preached "Salvation by faith", where Wesley had preached "salvation by works"; they admitted a dual nature in man which accepted the fact that even in the righteous man there still existed side by side with the "New man" in his heart an "Old man" capable yet of sin and fallings away, whose presence, even in the best, they likened to an old tooth : "You may break off one bit and another and another ; but you can never get it all away. The stump will stay as long as you live and sometimes will ache too."

Wesley had preached the doctrine of perfectability by which on a sudden instant the redeemed were made aware that they were saved—from which state he had encouraged his followers to believe there must be no back-sliding. Anne Brontë, agonisingly conscious of the back-sliding in her own nature, may have felt that the doctrine the Moravian brothers preached was nearer the truth of imperfect human kind as she knew it. Whether she knew something of their tenets beforehand or had merely heard of the Rev. La Trobe's piety in particular, she sent for him at a moment of great spiritual crisis. Many years later the account he gave of those meetings was published by his friend William Scruton, the Thornton biographer of the Brontës, who, in his turn, related them to Ellen Nussey in her old age. It is thus that we can gather how Anne ever came to hear of the Moravian bishop.

According to Mr Scruton, Miss Wooler "had always been wont to speak of the members [of the Moravian congregation] to her pupils in terms of the greatest respect. Miss Nussey, when a girl, had herself been a pupil of the lady's academy . . . and she had several dear friends who were Moravians. Miss Nussey," Mr Scruton goes on to say, "was deeply interested in a letter which I had recently received from the Rev. James La Trobe, a Bishop of the Moravian church. . . . He was minister of the Moravian church at Mirfield from 1836-41 and sometime during that period he had been urgently requested by Anne Brontë to visit her at Roe Head at a time when she was prostrated by a very serious illness."

Mr Scruton goes on to give the text of the bishop's letter which is as follows : "She was suffering from a severe attack of gastric fever," he wrote, "which brought her very low, and her voice was only a whisper ; her life hung on a slender thread. She soon got over the shyness natural on seeing a perfect stranger. The words of love, from Jesus, opened her ear to my words, and she was very grateful for my visits. I found her well acquainted with the main truths of the Bible respecting our salvation, *but seeing them more through the law than the Gospel, more as a requirement from God than His Gift in His Son,* but her heart opened to the sweet views of salvation, pardon and peace in the blood of Christ, and she accepted His welcome to the weary and heavy laden sinner, conscious more of her not loving the Lord her God than of acts of enmity to Him, and, had she died then, I should have counted her His redeemed and ransomed Child" [author's italics].

The encounter between the Moravian minister and Anne Brontë came in the nick of time. With rare penetration he saw that, whatever the physical causes of her illness, it was the harsh and hopeless religion in which she had been brought up which was slowly breaking her heart. The fear of death was so aggravated by the terror of judgment that his first recourse must be to substitute in its place a gospel of mercy and love. In so doing he found that he was only confirming the inclination of a heart singularly compassionate, honest and courageous.

Bishop La Trobe made no attempt to *convert* Anne Brontë ; all he had to do was to convince her that the promptings of her heart were right instead of wrong. He was probably the first person of authority to do so and to bring her the assurance after which she had been seeking all her life, that the God she worshipped was as merciful as He was great. In the particular crisis through which she was passing she needed, more than anything, to be given just such an assurance, for she had been bred to mistrust all natural impulses as promptings of the devil and to regard all independence of judgment as a "Sin of Pride".

She had found a friend in need ; there is no doubt that he saved her then and that he quickened in her the gospel of hope to which she clung as her pole star through all future adversity.

Unhappily he could not entirely eradicate the implanted teaching of years; Anne would, at recurrent periods of her life, fall a prey to the old doubts and terrors :

> Oppressed with sin and woe
> A burdened heart I bear—

but they would not in the end prevail. She would always find the courage to fight them.

> With this polluted heart
> I dare to come to Thee,
> Holy and mighty as Thou art,
> For Thou wilt pardon me—

Thanks to the friend of that early crisis the darkest moments would, eventually, find illumination and the gospel of love dispel the gospel of fear.

The course of her life, so singularly beset with sorrows, would confirm the serious bent of a mind which, under another dispensation, would have been capable of much liveliness. Circumstances would never allow her for long to relegate the great questions of religion to the lumber-room, as it were, of memory; she would continually be forced to face them, and if much of her verse, as Charlotte said, makes sad enough reading with its deeply implanted sense of personal sin, yet the final message was to be one of hope as in the memorable lines :

> Far as this earth may be
> From yonder starry skies,
> Remoter still am I from Thee ;
> Yet Thou wilt not despise.
>
> In my Redeemer's name
> I give myself to thee,
> And all unworthy as I am
> My God will cherish me.
>
> Oh, make me wholly Thine
> Thy love to me impart,
> And let Thy holy spirit shine
> For ever on my heart.

Chapter Ten

HEALD'S HOUSE

CHARLOTTE and Anne returned home on 14th December. A few days later Tabby fell on the ice of the steep main street of Haworth and broke her leg. It could not be set till the next morning and the complicated fracture left her "in a very doubtful and dangerous state", as Charlotte wrote to Ellen, regretfully postponing the projected visit of her friend.

After Papa, Tabby was certainly the person the young Brontës were fondest of in the world.

Her caustic tongue had enlivened their youth, as her kind heart had soothed their childhood. They had played tricks on Tabby since their nursery days, and thrown back at her her own racy language in argument. She was the most wholesome influence in their lives, sane, natural and hearty, completely dependable and unblushingly frank. There was nothing she had not done for them, and there was nothing they would not do for her now.

For the first recorded time in their lives Charlotte, Emily and Anne rose in open rebellion against Aunt in consequence of Tabby's accident, and by the sheer force of surprise and persistence carried the day.

Aunt's appreciation of Tabby was, understandably, of a less ardent nature than theirs. She did no violence that she could see to the rule of Christian charity if she advocated that Tabby be sent to her sister's to be nursed ; the sister lived at no distance, in Haworth, and Tabby's savings, should they prove inadequate to the strain of a long illness, could always be supplemented by little gifts from Mr Brontë.

Aunt Branwell was reckoning without her nieces. Mrs Gaskell, who had the details from a villager, tells how Aunt's decision was communicated to the three girls. "There were symptoms of a quiet, but sturdy rebellion, that winter afternoon, in the small precincts of Haworth Parsonage. They made one unanimous and stiff remonstrance. Tabby had tended them in their childhood ; they, and none other, should tend her in her infirmity and age. At tea-time, they were sad and silent, and the meal went away

untouched by any of the three. So it was at breakfast ; they did
not waste many words on the subject, but each word they did utter
was weighty. They "struck" eating till the resolution was rescinded,
and Tabby was allowed to remain. . . ."

The three girls nursed her with the utmost devotion, not only
then but for years to come when Tabby's broken leg crippled her
permanently. On the subject of Tabby they would no more give
in than on the subject of pets on which in their childhood Aunt
had been so tyrannous.

They had to do all the work of the house as well as nurse Tabby
but they did not allow that to embitter life, as parting from Tabby
would have done.

They were surprisingly active these Christmas holidays. While
Charlotte and Branwell dreamt of achieving a reputation in the
great outside world as writers, Emily and Anne, clinging more
closely than ever to the secluded life which was all they asked—
provided it were accompanied by liberty—set about collecting their
verse.

Since the previous summer Emily had been writing hers down.
In one instance it was accompanied by a note so illuminating as to
merit quoting in full : "I am more terrifically and idiotically and
brutally STUPID than ever I was in the whole course of my
incarnate existence. The above precious lines are the fruits of one
hour's most agonising labour between ½ past 6 and ½ past 7 in the
evening of July—1836." Divine discontent, ever the hallmark of
genius, could not be wanting in Emily Brontë, even at eighteen.
Reading that note we are made to realise as never before why so
little of Emily's and Anne's juvenilia has come down to us : it was
summarily destroyed.

From those Christmas holidays of 1836 date the first verses of
Anne's to be transcribed : the "Verses by Lady Geralda", whose
nostalgic contents belonged, as discussed above, unmistakably to the
previous year, when she first found herself deprived of the company
of Emily. Obviously the poem was composed at varying times for
it lacks a central unity and reflects almost contradictory states of
mind. But the feeling for nature is intense and its power over her
mind irresistible, the music of the lines impetuous and persuasive,
and as a revelation of what the free life of the moors meant to her
it serves as an illuminating contrast to the religious crisis through
which she had just passed.

Why, when I hear the stormy breath
Of the wild winter wind,
Rushing o'er the mountain heath,
Does sadness fill my mind ?

For long ago I loved to lie
Upon the pathless moor,
To hear the wild wind rushing by
With never ceasing roar ;

Its sound was music then to me,
Its wild and lofty voice
Made my heart beat exultingly
And my whole soul rejoice.

But now, how different is the sound. . . .
.   .   .   .   .   .
O why are things so changed for me ?
What gave me joy before
Now fills my heart with misery
And nature smiles no more.
And why are all the beauties gone
From this my native hill ?
Alas ! my heart is changed alone
Nature is constant still. . . .

The poem, for all its intensely personal feeling, was given a
Gondalan title by its young author, as though all composition were,
as yet, only a transposition of experience, and a contribution to a
general imaginative scheme. For a short while longer, indeed,
both Gondal and Angria were to belong to all four young people ;
the latest news and events of both kingdoms continuing to be of
interest to both camps, even if no longer directed by all four "genii".

This is made quite plain by the "diary paper" written by Emily
and Anne on Branwell's birthday in the following June, where
latest news of events in Angria are reported side by side with
reports from the Gondalan and Gaaldine capitals as of equal moment
—and we must add—equal *reality* with historical events of the
contemporary scene such as the accession of the young Queen
Victoria to the British throne !

The text of this diary paper, written in minute italic script on
a sheet of paper three and a half by four and a half inches and further
enhanced by a drawing of Emily and Anne in the act of writing, is
as follows:

                                                                Monday evening June 26th 1837.
   A bit past 4 o'clock Charlotte working in Aunt's room, Branwell reading
Eugene Aram to her—Anne and I writing in the drawing-room [sic]—Anne a
poem beginning "Fair was the evening and brightly the sun"—I Augustus-
Almeda's life 1st v, 1–4th page from the last. Fine rather coolish then grey cloudy
but sunny day. Aunt working in the little room [the old Nursery] Papa gone
out Tabby in the kitchen The Emperors and Empresses of Gondal and Gaaldine
preparing to depart from Gaaldine to Gondal to prepare for the coronation which
will be on the 12th of July Queen Vittoria [sic] ascended the throne this month.
Northangerland in Monkeys Isle—Zamorna at Eversham. All tight and right in
which condition it is to be hoped we shall all be on this day 4 years at which time
Charlotte will be 25 and 2 months—Branwell just 24 it being his birthday—myself
22 and 10 months and a peice [sic] Anne 21 and nearly a half I wonder where
we shall be and how we shall be and what kind of a day it will be then let us
hope for the best
                                           Emily Jane Bronte—Anne Bronte

I guess that this day 4 years we shall all be in this drawing-room comfortable I
hope it may be so. Anne guesses we shall all be gone somewhere together
comfortable. We hope it may be so indeed . . .

   No diary paper of Emily or Anne's was ever complete without
the inroad of drama. Interruption in the person of Aunt usually
breaks the spell cast by their musings and restores us to a sense of
realities. Like a ghost in some old play Aunt speaks without her
cue. Probably she has put her head round the door.

Aunt : "Come Emily, it's past 4 o'clock."
Emily : "Yes Aunt." [Obviously Aunt shuts the door and goes]
Anne : "Well, do you intend to write in the evening."
Emily : "Well, what think you.
(We agreed to go out 1st to make sure if we got into the humour. We may
stay in——")

   Suspended between these two alternatives the paper ends ; not
before furnishing us with the clue (if clue we needed) to their
manner of composition. We might have guessed that to "get into
the humour" for writing they would go out first on the moors.
   By rare good fortune the manuscript of Anne's poem, mentioned by Emily in the diary paper, "Fair was the evening and
brightly the sun . . .", has been preserved. Begun on this 26th June
it was finished on 1st July, when Anne signed and dated it (in her
own and not in any assumed Gondal name) and gave it the definitive
title "Alexander and Zenobia". Thus we possess the very first
document relating to this Byronic pair of lovers whose names and

fortunes were to dominate Anne's Gondal verse. They were the protagonists of her sections of the drama, as distinct from Emily's own heroes and heroines, although the families to which they belonged were to be incidental to both girls' writings. "Alexander Hybernia" and "Alexandrina Zenobia Hybernia" were to be Anne's pen-names for the majority of her Gondal verse.

In this first poem of the cycle the two young people are in adolescence still.

> One was a boy of just fourteen,
> Bold beautiful and bright,
> Soft raven curls hung clustering\round
> A brow of marble white. . . .
>
> The other was a slender girl,
> Blooming young and fair
> The snowy neck was shaded with
> The long bright sunny hair. . . .

The theme of this poem is separation, a topic very close to Anne's heart in this period of her schooldays. It is, indeed, about a *double* separation, with a flash-back to a former period when the two devoted friends—as the young people then are—were previously torn apart. Their present meeting gives them hope for a future reunion to which they mutually pledge their word.

> We met on Greecia's classic plain,
> We part in Araby,
> And let us hope to meet again
> Beneath our Gondal's sky.

The point of interest about this poem is that it reflects the devotion of Emily and Anne to each other and their misery when parted. The grief at parting of the two imaginary friends, however naïvely expressed, is poignantly actual.

> "And shall we part so *soon*," he cried,
> "*Must* we be torn away?
> Shall I be left to mourn alone,
> Will you no *longer* stay?
>
> And shall we never meet again
> Hearts that have grown together . . .?"

Alexander and Zenobia give each other a promise to meet in a favourite trysting-place two years hence and the poem ends, of course, with the happy meeting.

Its other point of interest is the opportunity it affords the young poet for expressing her love of her native hills. In a lyrical passage of perfection rare in Anne's early verse she evokes the Sladen valley with its waterfall above Haworth where, we know from Ellen Nussey, Emily and Anne loved most to linger. In this setting their happiest hours, not only of childhood and adolescence but of mature womanhood, were passed. The place as here described was Emily's and Anne's abiding paradise.

> Zenobia, do you remember
> A little lonely spring
> Among Exina's woody hills
> Where blackbirds used to sing ?
>
> And when they ceased as daylight faded
> From the dusky sky,
> The pensive nightingale began
> Her matchless melody.
>
> Sweet bluebells used to flourish there
> And tall trees waved on high,
> And through their ever sounding leaves
> The soft wind used to sigh. . . .

Within a few weeks of writing that diary paper on 26th June, Emily took the extreme course—for her—of going out to earn her living as a teacher near Halifax, under conditions which Charlotte, in the first flush of her indignation, was to call "slavery".

For Charlotte and Anne the second "Half" of that year was also to bring change. During the summer vacation Miss Wooler had moved her school from Roe Head to Dewsbury Moor—no considerable distance but a change for the worse in every particular.

The house—Heald's House, as it was called, after the family of its former owner, the Rector of Birstall (whom Charlotte was to immortalise as the Rev. Cyril Hall in *Shirley*)—was altogether less imposing than Roe Head and had but a small garden. It was of considerable antiquity, the original corner-stone (still preserved today) set in the wall over the main entrance, bearing the date 1569 with the inscription "SAY GOD BE HERE" together with the original owners' initials.

It was, and is, a low rambling structure not without charm even today, composed of a main building, rebuilt in the eighteenth century, with straggling wings, out-houses and coaching stables to the rear with roofs at varying levels, which must have had an attraction for schoolgirls and offered every incentive to games of hide-and-seek.

Indoors there was a veritable network of staircases and rooms hidden away round corners with steps leading down into them, and sloping ceilings which certainly formed part of the original Elizabethan structure. One staircase window in particular made up of a maze of the smallest diamond-shaped panes with leaded-lights was set two feet deep in the wall, and witnessed to the great age of the house.

It had been used as a meeting-house by the followers of George Fox in the latter half of the seventeenth century, and acquired by the elder Heald's father—a maltster—early in the eighteenth century. Considerably after Miss Wooler's time the kilns still existed, and a fresh-water well runs under the house still today, a circumstance which may have contributed to making it damp and unwholesome for a girl with Anne's tendencies.

Mrs Gaskell, trying to account for Anne's collapse at the end of the year and Charlotte's lasting horror of the place, imputed both misfortunes to the "low and damp" situation of the house compared with the "fine, open, breezy situation of Roe Head", but, in point of fact, Heald's House stands in a very dominating position, exposed to all the winds that blow. Seen from Roe Head, two to three miles away, the Church of St John, Dewsbury Moor (just below Heald's House) seems to tower well above the whole surrounding district. At that time Dewsbury Moor really *was* moorland, completely covered with gorse and bracken and with no other buildings within sight of the school than an old farmhouse at the rear.

In all outward respects there was little change in the routine of the girls' days consequent on the removal from Roe Head. Miss Wooler continued to be the broadminded headmistress with liberal tendencies that she had always been, using her influence with the girls to widen their interests and awaken them to the social and scientific developments of the age in which they lived. There is a story related locally of her taking her young ladies to the great exhibition at Leeds. The comical ending reminds one irresistibly of Goldsmith.

It appears that Miss Wooler, always alert to investigate anything new, had arranged to take some of the senior scholars, and those esteemed most worthy of the treat, for the day to visit the notable exhibition of scientific and modern inventions at Leeds—some eight miles away. A covered cart was hired to that effect and the worthy lady and her pupils got in and drove away. A most edifying day was in prospect and it is to be hoped that the beneficiaries of the treat were duly sensible of their great good fortune. Whether too many young ladies had been crowded in to the covered cart is not related, but the fact remains that either the burden was too great or the pony's harness too worn. Certain it is that, when at some distance from Dewsbury Moor, the harness snapped, the pony bolted and the party of young and elderly ladies was left high and dry in the middle of the road with no other recourse than the ignominious one—since the pony was too sly to let himself be caught again—of pulling the cart home themselves ! Even in the latter circumstance the good sense of Miss Wooler is made to appear. What other headmistress of her day would· have encouraged her pupils to use their muscles as well as their brains ? There was no false gentility about Miss Wooler.

And yet Charlotte, for one, was to grow further and further out of sympathy with her this term until, in a quite unjust attack upon her old friend, she very nearly severed the connection.

Miss Wooler was intending to retire at Christmas, and with that end in view was leaving Charlotte increasingly in control of the school. Enjoying robust health and spirits herself she may have been blind to the fact that Charlotte was heading for an acute attack of hypochondria and may only have remarked how exceedingly short-tempered her assistant was. Looking back on that time in later years Charlotte realised the tyranny the disease had exercised over her. Writing to her old teacher she thus confessed herself : "I endured it but a year, and assuredly I can never forget the concentrated anguish of certain insufferable moments, and the heavy gloom of many long hours, besides the preternatural horrors which seemed to clothe existence and nature, and which made life a continual walking nightmare. . . . When I was at Dewsbury Moor I could have been no better company for you than a stalking ghost, and I remember I felt my incapacity to *impart* pleasure fully as much as my powerlessness to *receive* it."

Charlotte's dissatisfaction was complete. Ellen stayed away in the south of England the whole of that autumn and the remove to

Dewsbury Moor, though only two odd miles in distance, had further deprived her and Anne of the rare but refreshing intercourse on Sundays with the friends at Birstall and Gomersal. Even the godparents were at a greater distance.

Whatever the relationship with these latter had been during the girls' schooldays at Roe Head, the opportunity to know Elizabeth Franks any better than before was suddenly to be taken from them for ever. The kind godmother, one might say "fairy godmother" of the old Thornton days, Mr Brontë's admired friend, died on 11th September 1837 while staying with her life-long friend, Anne's other godmother, Fanny Outhwaite at Bradford, and was buried in the Old Bell Chapel at Thornton where all her happy girlhood had been passed. She was forty years of age and had gone into a decline in consequence of a severe attack of "the prevalent influenza" in the previous year. It is impossible not to speculate upon the difference to Anne had she lived ; had she known Anne, not as an unformed girl inevitably her inferior, but as a mature woman able to give and to receive an equal friendship. Time was against Anne, as in so many other respects. Mrs Franks was gone before she could discover that her little god-daughter and her sisters were girls of genius and, had she known, no one can assert that she would have understood their work any better than her cousin Mrs Atkinson, who was horrified to learn that Charlotte was the author of *Jane Eyre*. Yet, in a time where kindness was much needed, Elizabeth Franks had stood by the girls and it is impossible to suppose they were anything but shattered at the news of her untimely end.

The plight of Emily at her school at Law Hill, Halifax, was a further source of misery that "Half" to Charlotte, and, still more, to Anne. To Ellen, Charlotte wrote on 2nd October 1837 : "My sister Emily is gone into a situation as teacher in a large school of near 40 pupils, near Halifax. I have had one letter from her since her departure ; it gives an appalling account of her duties—hard labour from six in the morning until near eleven at night, with only one half-hour of exercise between. This is slavery . . . I fear she will never stand it."

Two poems of Anne's, "A Voice from the Dungeon" and "The Captive's Dream", written about this time, convey with hallucinating power her preoccupation at this period with imprisonment and separation and, above all, with the vicarious suffering for others' griefs which was such a characteristic subject with her.

Under the Gondal names and situations one senses her predicament and Emily's only slightly disguised. Both poems recount the dream of a prisoner who thinks she sees for a moment the loved one who is equally a captive, and removed from her. In the lines :

> Methought I saw him, but I knew him not,
> He was so changed from what he used to be . . .

the transposition of her situation and Emily's is patently apparent. The helplessness of the sleeper's condition, the wish to cry out and reach the loved one who is suffering equally on her account was Anne's condition at that time.

> O how I longed to clasp him to my heart . . .
> And speak one word of comfort to his mind . . .
> I could not rise from my dark dungeon floor ;
> And the dear name I vainly strove to speak
> Died in a voiceless whisper on my tongue.
> Then I awoke, and, lo, it was a dream.
> A dream ? Alas ! it was reality ;
> For well I knew, wherever he may be,
> He mourns me thus. Oh, Heaven ! I could bear
> My deadly fate with calmness if there were
> No kindred hearts to bleed and break for me.

Ellen Nussey, when she saw Emily and Anne for the first time, described their attachment to be like that of twins. The complete *fusion* of sentiment, as expressed in the above lines, would, indeed, point to such a relationship.

The fact that Emily and Anne would never suffer singly was to increase greatly their sum of suffering. Such was to be their peculiar destiny.

Throughout their schooldays together Charlotte had lived at several removes from Anne in an abstraction of mind as complete as it was painful. Suddenly, as the term wore on towards Christmas, Charlotte was awakened to a sense of realities when Anne caught a severe cold which rapidly developed alarming signs.

Charlotte might be blind to other symptoms but to the dread tokens of tuberculosis she was exquisitely sensible. In a state of near-collapse herself, she suddenly took alarm at Anne's condition and, in a flurry of remorse, terror and devotion, took every practical means of arresting her sister's illness.

If none of the authorities, including Miss Wooler, considered that Anne's condition required special nursing, there was probably no one to blame but Anne herself: she had not complained. So far as the others noticed she had caught a rather worse cold than usual, and lingering colds were the order of the day in winter and inevitable at school where one "influenza cold" could spread through a dormitory unchecked by any attempted measures of hygiene. By the time Charlotte took the alarm, Anne's hacking cough, hectic cheek and laboured breath could no longer be hidden from anyone, although, naturally, to no one but Charlotte did they strike terror. To her the dreaded signs were all too recognisable. In the panic that seized her she rounded on Miss Wooler, accusing her of being to blame for Anne's condition. Very sensibly Miss Wooler lost no time in laying the situation before Mr Brontë. She wrote telling him exactly what Charlotte had said. Mercifully for Charlotte and providentially for Anne, Mr Brontë acted quickly. He wrote ordering both his daughters home. Writing after the event to Ellen Nussey, Charlotte could afford to speak of it with all the moderation and sense lacking in her conduct at the time.

"You were right in your conjecture respecting the cause of my sudden departure," she wrote from home to Ellen Nussey on 4th January 1838. "Anne continued wretchedly ill. Neither the pain nor the difficulty of breathing left her—and how could I feel otherwise than very miserable? I looked upon her case in a different light to what I could wish or expect any uninterested person to view it in. Miss Wooler thought me a fool, and by way of proving her opinion treated me with marked coldness. We came to an éclaircissement one evening. I told her one or two rather plain truths, which set her a-crying, and the next day, unknown to me, she wrote to papa, telling him that I had reproached her bitterly—taken her severely to task, etc. etc.—Papa sent for us the day after he had received her letter. Meantime, I had formed a firm resolution to quit Miss Wooler and her concerns for ever, but just before I went away she took me into her room, and giving way to her feelings, which in general she restrains far too rigidly, gave me to understand that in spite of her cold repulsive manners she had a considerable regard for me and would be very sorry to part with me. If anybody likes me I can't help liking them, and remembering that in general she had been very kind to me, I gave in and said I would come back if she wished me—so we're settled again for the present; but I am not satisfied. I should have

(2,056)

respected her far more if she had turned me out of doors instead of crying for two days and two nights together. I was in a regular passion ; my 'warm temper' quite got the better of me—of which I don't boast, for it was a weakness ; nor am I ashamed of it, for I had reason to be angry. Anne is now much better, though she still requires a great deal of care. However, I am relieved from my worst fears respecting her."

In Charlotte's blame of Miss Wooler there was a measure of self-condemnation for her own long neglect of her young sister. Anne had lived at her side in an isolation as complete as, Charlotte now realised, it had been uncomplaining ; in that endurance, as she now understood it, lay her sister's deepest reproach. Charlotte could not then do enough for Anne, whose illness she had, in sheer self-condemnation, to lay at Miss Wooler's door. She could not bear to have done Anne harm herself. Miss Wooler, whose tears were not a sign of conscience or of repentance but of shock—as her nephew writing of the event many years later so astutely divined —of shock, "as only a tender-hearted woman can be shocked if she is thought to be lacking in understanding of other people's sufferings. . . ." Miss Wooler bore Charlotte no ill-will for an outburst which she was psychologist enough to recognise as natural in a highly strung girl, terrified for a sister's life which only then had she realised was so precious to her.

So ended Anne's schooldays on a warning note that all but she were for ever after to remember. Altogether she had been at school two years and three months ; enough to equip her for the career of governess which, contrary to all her family's entreaties, she was resolutely to adopt in the coming days.

As it turned out, her training at Roe Head and Dewsbury Moor was to be something more than a time of preparation for a post as governess : it had tempered her character to a capacity of endurance which, to a rare degree, she would exercise throughout her life.

Chapter Eleven

MODERN CHILDREN

ANNE remained at home from Christmas 1837 to the spring of 1839. Singularly little evidence remains of the family's activities for that period, and it is not even certain how many of the young people were at home together during it.

The lack of exact information respecting Emily's stay at Law Hill—reckoned by some to have lasted six months, and by others eighteen months—makes it impossible to say with any certainty whether she was at home with Anne, for longer periods than school holidays, or not.

From the evidence of her poetry, however, which is all we have to go on, it would look as though she stayed at Law Hill throughout the year 1838. Never at any period before or after was its tone so consistently despondent, so little transposed upon the Gondal plane, so poignantly personal. The autumn of 1837 and the whole of the year 1838 was to be a time of profoundly felt but little sustained poetic expression. Fragments of haunting beauty, such as

"I'll come when thou art saddest"
"Far away is the land of rest"
"The Old Church tower and garden wall"

never escape from the dual themes of homesickness and captivity. They would, indeed, suggest that her stay at Law Hill was prolonged over another year, both by the bitterness and despondency of their tone and by their very brevity. On duty from 6 a.m. to 11 p.m. it is hardly surprising that it was in snatches only that she could set down her thoughts. All too seldom the propitious pause presented itself.

A little while, a little while,
The noisy crowd are barred away ;
And I can sing and I can smile
A little while I've holyday !

Only towards the end of the year 1838 did the pent-up feelings burst into sustained utterance. Then the great poems "Light up thy halls !", "Loud without the wind was roaring" and the above quoted "A little while" tolled out with a magnificence of expression that was at once a dirge for all the suffering of the year and a triumph-song for the poet who felt herself at last in complete mastery of her medium.

For Branwell the year brought a welcome change. Either in the autumn of 1837 or in the New Year 1838 he set up for himself as a portrait painter in Bradford, sharing a studio with a fellow-artist and lodging with a highly respectable family named Kirby in Fountain Street.

They had living with them at the time a young niece who later married a Mr John Ingham of Dewsbury, and whose evidence regarding Branwell comes as a refreshing corrective to the legendary picture which would represent him, even at this time, as "lounging for the most part in the bar of the George Hotel" among his artistic cronies Wilson Anderson, the landscape painter ; Geller, the mezzotint-engraver ; Richard Waller, the portrait painter ; and Leyland the sculptor. Mrs Ingham spoke of him, on the other hand, as "steady, industrious and self-respecting", adjectives all the more valuable for their rarity in application to Branwell. Altogether her account, for its detailed description of his life at this time, is of peculiar interest : it shows Branwell as a beloved brother still and Charlotte's close confidant as of yore.

"From my girlhood," wrote Mrs Ingham, "for several years I resided with my uncle and aunt Mr and Mrs Kirby, of Fountain Street, Manningham Lane, Bradford. At a time when Patrick Branwell Brontë was about twenty-two or twenty-three years of age, he came to lodge with us and had one room as his studio, and there painted many portraits. He was low in stature, about five feet three inches high, and slight in build, though well proportioned. Very few people, except sitters, came to visit him ; but I remember one, a Mr Thompson, a painter also. I recollect his sister Charlotte coming, and I remember her sisterly ways. She stayed a day, and I believe that was her only visit. They left the house together, and he saw her off by the Keighley coach. I am not aware that his other sisters or that his father . . . ever came to Mr Kirby's. It was young Mr Brontë's practice to go home at each week-end, and I remember that while sometimes he took the coach for Keighley, he on other occasions walked to Haworth across the moors. He was a very steady young gentleman, his conduct was exemplary, and we liked him very much. He stayed with us about two years and left, he said, to go to a situation as book-keeper [with the Railway Company at Luddenfoot]. Whilst lodging with us he painted my portrait and those of my uncle and aunt, and all three were accounted good likenesses."

For Charlotte the year was also to bring beneficial changes and a restoration to health and liberty. After a return to Dewsbury Moor in the New Year, she was advised by the doctor "as she valued her life" to go home and left Miss Wooler's school for good on 23rd May. She thought she had parted from Miss Wooler for good also, but happily for both this was not to be the case. The coming years would bring them together again and Charlotte to a growing appreciation of her former teacher. "Miss Wooler," she would write in later years, "is like good wine ; I think time improves her. . . ."

Liberated from what had become an intolerable burden, Charlotte blossomed out at home and spent a singularly happy and productive year, as the considerable fragments of her writing—thousands of words and lines of epic verse—attest.

With Branwell and Charlotte—and probably Emily as well—coming and going to and from the parsonage, Anne's year was not entirely solitary. For her it was essentially a period of recuperation ; intellectually and physically she was recovering the strength put out at school and lost in two serious illnesses. Under the eye of anxious elders she was kept close at home.

She was writing a considerable amount of poetry ; collecting some of the pieces written at school (like "The North Wind") and launching out into long narrative compositions bearing on the story of her Gondal heroine Alexandrina Zenobia.

In "The Parting", a poem divided into two sections to denote a passage of three years, Zenobia relates the departure from his home and his lady of the Lord of Alzerno. Vainly his abandoned partner waits his return, for, as Zenobia confesses :

> . . . all the while I knew so well
> The time and nature of his death ;
> For while he drew his parting breath
> His head was pillowed on my knee,
> And his dark eyes were turned to me
> With an agonised heart-breaking glance
> Until they saw me not. . . .

In "Verses to a Child" it is Zenobia's turn to lament desertion by her lover Florian to whose child, Flora, she recounts her past passion and in whose features she finds the lost image of the man she will never cease to love.

The striking contrast between these poems and those written the previous year are that the *personal* note is quite absent from them. The themes of imprisonment and separation do not recur. In Anne's treatment of the highly romantic loves of her Gondal heroes and heroines there is no trace of a mind burdened by the problems of real life. On her hills of home one feels that Anne had regained not only health but happiness. The religious crisis of the previous year is quite resolved.

The few glimpses afforded of the family at Haworth convey a cheerful tone. Firstly there is the portrait of his sisters painted by Branwell which, together with one other now disappeared, is the only likeness we possess of them together. For the biographer of Anne it is of supreme importance : it is the only one of her painted after she grew up. The inspired Emily of the mutilated fragment of an earlier group and Charlotte in the noble likeness drawn by Richmond in after years have each been elsewhere immortalised ; but of Anne's face in her late teens this is the only likeness we have. We see her here with all her soul looking out of her eyes.

For financial reasons the Brontë girls were never able, at this period of their lives, to live at home all together ; if one—at most two—of them came home to roost, the others felt it their duty to be gone.

Emily, who, in all probability, had remained at Law Hill throughout 1838, had to admit herself beaten by the end of the year. She came home at Christmas for good. With the exception of her nine months' schooling in 1842 at Brussels she would not leave home again.

Something more than a sense of duty or necessity prompted Charlotte in the New Year to seek fresh employment : the proposal from Henry Nussey—to which she had replied a decided negative—had shaken her out of the complacent mood induced by her restored freedom and health, and seems to have galvanised her into action again. The period of hibernation was over. She had been nearly a year at home and conscience suddenly awoke and decreed that she must go back to what she—sadly enough for a girl of twenty-two—called the "old weary round". Imperatively she felt the need of trying to earn her own living again.

She was not the only one to feel so. To the utter amazement of the family Anne announced her resolution to go out too and make her way in the world.

The alarm and opposition raised by the bare idea of Anne roughing it like her sisters was not entirely due—as she would have us believe in the autobiographical *Agnes Grey*—to their indulgence towards the baby of the house, although such a sentiment may have prompted them : it was before all else due to their fear for Anne's health. Of the four young people who had survived childhood Anne was the only one to be considered chronically delicate. The alert of the previous year at Dewsbury Moor was all too recent for the loving and anxious elders to believe in any dramatic improvement in her general condition. Anne at nineteen could not be declared grown out of her weakness. She was still subject to chronic attacks of asthma and in nothing—but in one particular— stronger than of old. But in that one particular they were to find that she had grown to her full stature.

No arguments they could bring forward, no coaxing, no tempting, no teasing, would alter her fixed intention. If Charlotte could go out and earn her living, so could she. If one of the girls were needed at home that one should not be she but Emily, for whom domesticity had no terrors provided it meant working within the four walls of Haworth Parsonage.

Quite rightly Anne was convinced of her own capacity for "going out into the world". Her difficulty was to persuade the others of her fitness.

At home, during the past year, it had become only too evident that they would never really let her pull her weight. She has described the situation exactly in *Agnes Grey*. "There was always plenty of sewing on hand ; but I had not been taught to cut out a single garment and except plain hemming and seaming, there was little I could do, even in that line ; for they all asserted that it was far easier to do the work themselves than to prepare it for me : and, besides, they liked better to see me prosecuting my studies, or amusing myself—it was time enough, they said, for me to sit bending over my work, like a grave matron, when my favourite little pussy was become a steady old cat."

"Papa," she said one day, "I should like to be a governess."
One can imagine the scene, the exclamations, the dismay, the
amusement even. "What ! My little Agnes a governess !" cried
Mr Grey, and, in spite of his dejection, he laughed at the idea.
And the maternal figure who replaces Aunt Branwell in the story
exclaims, "Why, my love, you haven't learned to take care of
yourself yet. . . . Only think . . . with a parcel of children to
attend to—and no one to look to for advice. You would not even
know what clothes to put on."

Their incredulity was complete. "But I should like it *so* much,"
she insisted. "I am sure I could manage delightfully."

One of the charms of Agnes Grey—and of Anne Brontë—was
her simple truthfulness. Her motives for wishing to go out into
the world are the true motives of any young creature curious of
novelty and keenly aware of her own capacity. She really *did* think
that she would manage "delightfully" and she genuinely thought
she would enjoy being a governess, and did not act as she did merely
to immolate herself on the altar of duty. She was far too honest
not to make this plain.

The fact that in the end she won the day is proof of the
genuineness of her intention. In spite of the chorus of opposition
she never wholly relinquished her "darling scheme". "How
delightful," she thought, "it would be to be a governess ! To go
out into the world ; to enter upon a new life ; to act for myself ;
to exercise my unused faculties ; to try my unknown powers ; to
earn my own maintenance and something to comfort and help
[those at home] besides exonerating them from the provision of my
food and clothing ; to show papa what his little Agnes could
do. . . ." Did he but know it, papa was not at the end of his
surprises with "little Anne".

How Anne's first post was obtained can be guessed easily
enough : obviously it was through Miss Wooler. It happens that
the family to whom she went, the Ingham family of Blake Hall,
the virtual lords of the manor of Mirfield—a place already well
known to Anne—were intimately acquainted both with Miss
Wooler's brother-in-law, the Rev. Edward Carter, and with Anne's
old acquaintance, the Rev. James La Trobe. The former gentleman
had christened all the little Inghams and, in his turn, could
recommend Anne. Both gentlemen, indeed, could do so whole-
heartedly.

Inghams had resided in the district of Mirfield for centuries, and at Blake Hall itself since the time of Charles I. It was the great-grandfather of Anne's employer who rebuilt part of the house in 1740. As a family they had made themselves conspicuous by their support of the Nonconformist movement throughout the Civil Wars and the eighteenth century ; the name of Benjamin Ingham indeed would most probably be known to Anne from childhood for his association with Wesley and the great part he had taken in the Evangelical Revival. In his lifetime (1712–72) Blake Hall became a regular centre for the Methodist preachers on the York-shire circuit. Here Wesley came repeatedly, over a number of years, and here also Grimshaw of Haworth—of whom Anne must have heard so much at home—preached and in turn invited Ingham not only to Haworth but to Colne in Lancashire for the regular open-air services he inaugurated there. Ingham was one of the early distributors of hymns and it is said he persuaded Grimshaw from their first meeting to introduce hymns into his services—a circumstance that could not fail to have attracted Anne, the exquisite hymn-writer, in his favour. It was to Benjamin Ingham, of course, that Mirfield owed its settlement of Moravian brothers—a connec-tion with her prospective employers that can have inspired Anne with nothing but the completest confidence.

Miss Wooler's recommendation, giving her to understand that her employer was "a very nice woman", must fully have reassured not only Anne but the whole family at home. It was not felt that she was going among total strangers. No interview seems to have been required and early in March 1839 Anne's appointment was confirmed. Even the over-anxious elders at Haworth must, excusably, have opined that Anne was in luck's way.

The children's ages were very reassuring : they ranged from six and a quarter years to seven months, and Anne was informed she would, to begin with at least, have the care of the two elder children only. Her powers, it was evident, would not be strained to impossible limits. She had nothing to apprehend. After all, her acquirements made quite impressive reading and, as the mamma of Agnes Grey declared, could not be offered by *every* poor clergyman's daughter.

The exact price at which these talents were assessed by her prospective employer was £25 per annum. The gentleman, "though possessed of a very comfortable fortune," as Anne tells us, "could not be prevailed on to give a greater salary to the instructress of his children."

Anne left home on 8th April 1839 to take up her new post at Blake Hall. How she felt on the occasion she has fully described in the opening of *Agnes Grey*. In the resilience of its tone, its buoyancy and pleasurable excitement it differs essentially from Charlotte's letter to Ellen Nussey a week later. The tone of anxiety and doubt struck at once by Charlotte—its elder-sisterly attitude—fully confirms Anne's picture in *Agnes Grey* of the childish and helpless creature her seniors still considered her to be, and explains better than she herself can do her need to prove herself something more.

"Poor child !" wrote Charlotte on 15th April to Ellen Nussey, "she left us last Monday ; no one went with her ; it was her own wish that she might be allowed to go alone, as she thought she could manage better and summon more courage if thrown entirely upon her own resources. We have had one letter from her since she went. She expresses herself very well satisfied and says that Mrs Ingham is extremely kind. . . ." How Charlotte saw Anne she never more unwittingly betrayed than in this letter. "You would be astonished," she continues to Ellen Nussey, "what a sensible, clever letter she writes ; it is only the talking part that I fear. But I do seriously apprehend that Mrs Ingham will sometimes conclude that she has a natural impediment in her speech." Somehow the evidence that Anne stuttered when afraid—like Goldsmith again and Charles Lamb—does not detract but rather adds to the charm. It very certainly is an added proof of her courage.

In her own account of leaving home Anne allows no place to courage. On the contrary, she emphasised nothing but the alluring aspects of the change.

Until the last evening before leaving home her anticipations were "full of bright hopes and ardent expectations" ; only then "a sudden anguish" seemed to swell her heart. The parting of Agnes Grey from her family brings us too close to the details of life at the parsonage not to cherish every word : it is the prettiest —and certainly the truest—picture ever to be presented of it.

"When all was ready for my departure on the morrow, and the last night at home approached—a sudden anguish seemed to swell my heart. My dear friends looked so sad, and spoke so very kindly, that I could scarce keep my eyes from overflowing ; but I still affected to be gay. I had taken my last ramble with Mary on the moors [for Mary read Emily], my last walk in the garden, and round the house ; I had fed, with her, our pet pigeons for the last time—the pretty creatures that we had tamed to peck their food from our hands : I had given a farewell stroke to all their silky backs as they crowded in my lap. I had tenderly kissed my own peculiar favourites, the pair of snow-white fantails ; I had played my last tune on the old familiar piano, and sung my last song to papa. . . . When I did these things again . . . circumstances might be changed. . . .

"My dear little friend, the kitten, would certainly be changed ; she was already growing a fine cat ; and when I returned, even for a hasty visit at Christmas, would, most likely, have forgotten both her playmate and her merry pranks. I had romped with her for the last time ; and when I stroked her soft bright fur, while she lay purring herself to sleep in my lap, it was with a feeling of sadness I could not easily disguise. Then, at bedtime, when I retired with Mary to our quiet little chamber, where already my drawers were cleared out and my share of the bookcase was empty . . . my heart sank more than ever. . . ."

It is Anne with such simple touches as these who makes us understand better than anyone what their home meant to the Brontë girls.

The next morning she was off. It was a journey of some seventeen miles, and so that Mr Smith "the draper, grocer, and tea-dealer", who hired out the one and only gig the village possessed, might get back the same day, an early start had to be made. It was early April and a Monday morning.

"I rose, washed, dressed, swallowed a hasty breakfast," she tells us, "received the fond embraces of my father, etc., kissed the cat—to the great scandal of Sally, the maid [for Sally read Tabby], shook hands with her, mounted the gig, drew my veil over my face, and then, but not till then, burst into a flood of tears."

The lane which turns *up* towards Haworth Parsonage, or *down* into Main Street, according as the traveller faces, is cobbled yet today and sharply winding as it was on that morning when Anne Brontë left home for her first post. In the high stone wall that divides the parsonage garden from the lane is a deep-set gate. Here the loved ones stood waving her farewell. "The gig rolled on," she tells us ; "I looked back ; my dear mother and sister [for mother and sister read Charlotte and Emily] were still standing at the door, looking after me, and waving their adieux. I returned their salute, and prayed God to bless them from my heart : we descended the hill, and I could see them no more."

Down the steep cobbled hill, across the valley and up the other side. From the opposite brow Anne looked back once again. "There was the village spire," she writes, "and the old grey parsonage beyond it, basking in a slanting beam of sunshine—it was but a sickly ray, but the village and surrounding hills were all in sombre shade, and I hailed the wandering beam as a propitious omen to my home."

The road to Bradford is a succession of such switch-back falls and rises, with extensive views of undulating pastureland and heath and moor on either side. Under a capricious April sky, with the light flickering over the hills and hollows, the colouring is as of a canvas by Old Chrome. Progress was necessarily slow, both from the nature of the ground and the surface of the roads which, as Smith observed, were "very heavy". His horse, Anne tells us, "was very heavy too ; it crawled up the hills, and crept down them, and only condescended to shake its sides to a trot where the road was at a dead level or a very gentle slope, which was rarely the case in those rugged regions."

Thornton, with its one village street, was still a place of ancient stone houses, of woods and gardens and, if not of childish memories, of echoes of memories repeated by her elders. The smoke of Bradford, out of which rose the roofs, spires and factory chimneys of a growing industrial centre, heralded an end to the first part of her journey—not the longer part, unfortunately. But beyond Bradford, the ground is level by comparison to the ground already covered. Anne tells us that they arrived at Blake Hall by one o'clock. They had been driving for a good five hours and she was stiff with cold.

She was, of course, back on familiar ground. Blake Hall, situated three miles from Dewsbury and five from Huddersfield, lay in its own extensive parklands, just below the rising ground on which Mirfield Church was built, and must very often have been glimpsed by Anne.

As she approached it now, from the main Huddersfield to Dewsbury road, it lay invisible in its deep belt of trees, and was approached by a winding carriage-drive. How her heart sank as the gig passed through the lodge-gates she has told us in *Agnes Grey*. In the avenue of chestnut and beech trees spring branches were already hazed with buds. Lawns lay on either hand and though she thought them beautiful she dreaded at every moment to see them cease and a clear space ahead reveal the house. The drive emerged suddenly from the overhanging boughs and swept round at right angles, bringing her up short before the wide front of Blake Hall.

Contrary to her expectations, it seems, the house had little architectural distinction. It was three-storeyed, flat-fronted and its main entrance had but two shallow steps up to it. The truth was that the south aspect had very much less character and style than the east front, which, with its bow-windowed dining-room and galleried balcony projecting from the first-floor library presented an altogether more pleasing aspect.

But to Anne, alighting from Mr Smith's hired gig, the left wing and any other palliative aspects of the house were invisible and non-existent in the flurry of being admitted and having to cross the wide hall and suffer admittance to Mrs Ingham's presence.

She was stiff from fright and cold, acutely sensible of her dishevelled appearance and, literally, could not use her hands ; they were "red and swelled", she tells us, and her face was pale and purple from the wind. Her hair was uncurled, her collar horridly crumpled, her frock splashed with mud, her feet frozen in her stout new boots. It was a predicament peculiarly galling to a young girl who prided herself on her neatness, who must have known that, given a chance, she could look distinguished if not smart. Moving to meet her new employer now, she felt she was not only clumsy but a frump.

In the person of Agnes Grey she tells us how she felt.

" 'Be calm, be calm, whatever happens,' I said to myself ; and truly I kept this resolution so well, and was so fully occupied in steadying my nerves and stilling the rebellious flutter of my heart, that when I was admitted into the hall, and ushered into the presence of Mrs Bloomfield, I almost forgot to answer her polite salutation ; and it afterwards struck me, that the little I did say was spoken in the tone of one half-dead or half-asleep."

She was received by Mrs Ingham. Mrs Bloomfield, her employer in *Agnes Grey*, she described thus : "She was a tall, spare, stately woman, with thick black hair, cold grey eyes and extremely sallow complexion."

The question here arises : how literally is the reader to interpret the descriptions of characters and incidents in *Agnes Grey* ? How closely may we consider them to adhere to fact ?

Concerning the incidents of *Agnes Grey*, we have Anne's own statement regarding their veracity : we can entertain no doubt of their absolute truth.

". . . the story of *Agnes Grey*," she wrote in her Preface to the second edition of *The Tenant of Wildfell Hall*, "was accused of extravagant over-colouring in those very parts that were carefully copied from life, with a most scrupulous avoidance of all exaggeration. . . ." Both in that passage and in the opening phrases of *Agnes Grey* itself she vouches for what she wrote. Had the novel *not* been all too revealing of the truth, she need not have taken the precautions she did. "Shielded by my own obscurity," she tells us, "and the lapse of years, and a few fictitious names, I do not fear to venture ; and will candidly lay before the public what I would not disclose to the most intimate friend."

Much as the modern reader would prefer to discredit such scenes as the destruction of the fledglings, their truth has, alas, been vouched for by Anne herself—and by Charlotte Brontë, as readers of Mrs Gaskell will remember.

When it comes to the fictitious characters in the novel some differences, if only in their social background, are at once discernible. Anne described "Mr Bloomfield" as a retired tradesman whereas Mr Ingham, although he made his money in wool and coal, belonged to the squirearchy. He was, perhaps, more typical of his district than of his class : a Yorkshireman of the West Riding, with little use for intellectual and artistic acquirements, a sportsman before all else, inconsiderate to women and subordinates, uncontrolled in temper, yet a "gentleman" in the conventional sense of the period. Unlike his immediate forbears he was a staunch adherent of the Anglican Church and a J.P. at the time Anne knew him.

Mrs Ingham was a Cunliffe Lister, her father, Ellis Cunliffe Lister of Farfield Hall and Manningham Park, being M.P. for Bradford.

At the time Anne was engaged as governess the couple had five children : a boy, Joshua Cunliffe, aged six years and four months ; and four girls : Mary, aged five ; Martha, aged three years and five months ; Emily, aged two years and one month ; and a baby, Harriette, aged eight months. The family ultimately numbered thirteen children. It was, therefore, to a young household that Anne came—a young household but not necessarily a cheerful one.

It is a point of special interest to note the exact ages of her pupils because in *Agnes Grey* she has represented them all as older than they really were. The boy is seven, "Mary Ann" (Mary) six, "Fanny" (Martha) four, and "Harriette" (Emily) "a little broad, fat, merry, playful thing of scarcely two, that I coveted more than all the rest—but with her I had nothing to do."

If Anne thought it necessary to alter the ages of her pupils she had, doubtless, sufficient reason for doing so. It was, simply, to forestall the imputation of wild exaggeration.

The little Bloomfields have been hailed with incredulity by successive Brontë critics, as little monsters overstepping the bounds of probability. Had Anne related the incidents of younger children still, she would have met with still greater disbelief. That truth is sometimes more improbable than fiction, her readers do not pause to reflect.

The boy is by far the worst ; he is revoltingly cruel as well as boastful and lying. The very excess of his inventive cruelty bears the ring of truth. Anne, who cherished all animals, and shrank from all suffering for them, could not have imagined, had she not in fact experienced, incidents like those of the young fledglings. Her anger, over the years, had hardly cooled when she wrote that scene in recollection.

The little girls are entirely credible. There is something cosy and animal in their malicious glee ; their gestures are as futile and inconsequent as their brother's are purposeful. They can be perfectly complacent—so long as no one gainsays them—in paddling through mud and puddles out of doors, rumpling their pretty frocks and grinding egg-shells, leaves, dirt, dust and twigs into the carpet at home. They have a classic dislike of being washed and dressed, and wriggle and wrestle with their unfortunate governess every time she attempts to make them presentable. Lessons which they could easily assimilate they totally refuse to repeat, for the sheer delight of watching her lose all patience. To "torment the governess" becomes the best game of the day and till bedtime—and beyond—the huge joke is prolonged. Seeing she suffers from headache, there is enormous relish to be derived from emitting steam-whistle shrieks until she has to cover her ears to save her head from splitting. Best of all delights is to spit into her handbag, raid her writing-desk and finally attempt, in a combined operation of imposing conception, to throw the one on the fire and the other out of the window.

There is nothing in all this either particularly wicked or particularly original. Scores of other children have done as much. But *not* unreproved. The trouble about the little Inghams was that their parents had new-fangled notions on discipline. They had possibly read Thomas Day and Maria Edgeworth. The fact remains that the dear little things were not to be coerced, and it was on this rock that Anne Brontë and the parents split.

She found herself in an impossible situation. On the one hand she had to face mutiny and on the other had nothing with which to reinforce her authority. She had never imagined such a situation possible. The little Inghams were not only the naughtiest children she had ever met, they were a *revelation* in naughtiness. Indeed they were so novel in her experience of childhood that she could explain them only—like many subsequent pedagogues in her shoes —by attributing their peculiar brand of wickedness to the age in which they lived. Writing some time after the event to Ellen Nussey, Charlotte defied her friend to be able, in her turn, to live "in an unruly, violent family of *modern children*, such, for instance, as those at Blake Hall." Therein lay Anne's dilemma. Her own standards of upbringing were hopelessly outmoded in this modern home.

Writing to Ellen Nussey a week after Anne had left home, Charlotte said : "We have had one letter from her since she went. She expresses herself very well satisfied, and says that Mrs Ingham is extremely kind ; the two eldest children alone are under her care, the rest are confined to the nursery, with which and its occupants she has nothing to do. Both her pupils are desperate little dunces ; neither of them can read, and sometimes they profess a profound ignorance of their alphabet. The worst of it is they are excessively indulged, and she is not empowered to inflict any punishment. She is requested, when they misbehave themselves, to inform their mamma, which she says is utterly out of the question, as in that case she might be making complaints from morning till night. So she alternately scolds, coaxes, and threatens, sticks always to her first word, and gets on as well as she can. I hope she'll do."

Agnes Grey echoes the self-same principles. "I determined always strictly to fulfil the threats and promises I made, and, to that end, I must be cautious to threaten and promise nothing that I could not perform. . . . I would carefully refrain from all useless irritability and indulgence of my own ill-temper : when they behaved tolerably I would be as kind and obliging as it was in my power to be, to make the widest possible distinction between good and bad conduct. . . ."

At nineteen she could give some hints to her elders on controlling children !

The mistake she made was to look for a sensibility equal to her own in these children. She judged that they must be stirred to better things by direct appeals to their emotions and could not, at the outset, credit that they were made of so much tougher stuff than herself.

Agnes Grey relates how, after a wearisome day of vainly trying to get Mary Ann to repeat a lesson after her, she makes a last attempt at bedtime to appeal to her better nature. "I pretended to forget the whole affair, and talked and played with her as usual," she wrote, "till night, when I put her to bed ; then bending over her, while she lay all smiles and good humour, just before departing, I said, as cheerfully and kindly as before,

" 'Now, Mary Ann, just tell me that word before I kiss you good-night : you are a good girl now, and, of course, you will say it.'

" 'No, I won't.'

" 'Then I can't kiss you.'

" 'Well, I don't care.'

"In vain I expressed my sorrow ; in vain I lingered for some symptom of contrition ; she really 'didn't care' and I left her alone, and in darkness, wondering most of all at this last proof of insensate stubbornness. In *my* childhood I could not imagine a more afflictive punishment than for my mother to refuse to kiss me at night ; the very idea was terrible. More than the idea I never felt, for, happily, I never committed a fault that was deemed worthy of such a penalty. . . ." And elsewhere she says, "With me, at her age, or under, neglect and disgrace were the most dreadful of punishments ; but on her they made no impression. . . ."

The schoolroom was upon the second floor. Here the greater part of the morning was spent in lessons until half an hour before dinner when she took the children out for a walk in the grounds.

Anne and the children *dined* at midday, while the lady and gentleman of the house took their luncheon at the same table. *They* dined at six o'clock in the evening. If the gentleman was away from home the lady joined Anne and the children at their midday dinner. Anne was, of course, required to cut up the children's meat and her meals were hardly a respite from the long day's strain. The children had lessons all the afternoon again and took a walk before tea. This was taken in the schoolroom and was the occasion for scenes of libation when "they would spill their milk over the table and themselves, plunge their fingers into their own and each other's mugs" and "quarrel over their victuals like a set of tiger's cubs".

The elder children joined their parents at dessert every evening and Anne had to dress the little girl for the occasion. After this—at about 7 p.m.—she was put to bed but the boy was allowed to remain up until 8, until which time Anne was expected to amuse him with a game. After that—and only after that, could she have any time to herself. A "frugal supper of cold meat and bread" was served her in the schoolroom at 9.30, and then she would use the blessed hour of leisure that remained for reading, letter-writing or "working", as sewing of all kinds was called.

Anne was resolved on keeping her post and on making the best of her situation to those at home. She therefore bent all her energies on rendering it as tolerable as circumstances could allow. Without illusions, she looked for amelioration where, rationally, it might be sought. With no little humour she reflected that if she could "struggle on with unremitting firmness and integrity, the children would in time become more humanised ; every month would contribute to make them some little wiser, and, consequently, more manageable, for a child of nine or ten as frantic and ungovernable as these at six and seven would be a maniac."

From home she heard that Charlotte had, at last, got a situation with a family at Stonegappe, near Skipton, and if there had been moments of weakening when she had doubted her powers to endure the sheer physical exhaustion of her post, this news confirmed her resolution. It was unthinkable to give in when Charlotte was taking up the hated burden again. As much from pride as from a genuine conviction of the necessity of her undertaking, Anne could

not afford to fail. "I flattered myself," writes Agnes Grey, "I was
benefitting my parents and sister by my continuance here ; for
small as the salary was, I still was earning something and with strict
economy I could manage to have something to spare for them, if
they would favour me by taking it. Then it was by my own will
that I had got the place ; I had brought all this tribulation on
myself, and I was determined to bear it ; nay, more than that, I
did not even regret the step I had taken. I longed to show my
friends that, even now, I was competent to undertake the charge
and able to acquit myself honourably to the end. . . ."

The sheer physical fatigue, quite apart from the vexation of
spirit, was something she had not reckoned with. "The task of
instruction," Agnes Grey found, "was as arduous for the body as
the mind. I had to run after my pupils to catch them, to carry or
drag them to the table, and often forcibly to hold them there till
the lesson was done. . . . Mary Ann," she pursues, "preferred
rolling on the floor to any other amusement ; down she would
drop like a leaden weight ; and when I, with great difficulty, had
succeeded in rooting her thence, I had still to hold her up with one
arm, while with the other I held the book from which she was to
read or spell her lesson. As the dead weight of the big girl of six
became too heavy for one arm to bear, I transferred it to the other ;
or, if both were weary of the burden, I carried her into a corner,
and told her she might come out when she should find the use of
her feet, and stand up : but she generally preferred lying there like
a log till dinner or tea time, when, as I could not deprive her of her
meals, she must be liberated, and would come crawling out, with a
grin of triumph on her round, red face. . . ."

Out of doors, on the wide lawns and shady walks, where the
serenity of early summer lay like a benison on every leaf and flower,
the same frenzied disorder reigned. The children, writes Agnes
Grey, "had no notion of going with *me* ; I must go with *them*
wherever they chose to lead me. I must run, walk, or stand,
exactly as it suited their fancy. This, I thought, was reversing the
order of things ; and I found it doubly disagreeable, as . . . they
seemed to prefer the dirtiest places, the most dismal occupations.
. . . They manifested a particular attachment to a well at the
bottom of the lawn, where they persisted in dabbling with sticks
and pebbles for above half an hour. I was in constant fear that
their mother would see them from the window, and blame me for

allowing them thus to draggle their clothes and wet their feet and hands, instead of taking exercise ; but no arguments, commands or entreaties could draw them away."

Such was life at Blake Hall for Anne. In fairness to both sides, how her employers viewed her must also be considered. Years later Mrs Ingham told one of her grandchildren that she "had once employed a very unsuitable governess called Miss Brontë who had actually tied the two children to a table leg in order to get on with her own writing." What scenes the governess had gone through before resorting to such extreme action Mrs Ingham did not relate —and most probably preferred to ignore.

Early in June Anne was visited by Mr Carter, no longer Curate of Mirfield but Vicar of Heckmondwike now, and so far succeeded in putting a good face on things that he was able to report well of her to Charlotte. Charlotte wrote home to Emily on 8th June : "Mr Carter was at Mirfield yesterday and saw Anne. He says she was looking uncommonly well. Poor girl, she must indeed wish to be at home."

Charlotte herself had hardly settled in her post before she was writing, "I could like to be at home. I could like to work in a mill. I could like to feel mental liberty. I could like this weight of restraint to be taken off. But the holidays will come. Corragio." [sic] When in July the holidays came she had already resolved not to return to her post. She had been in it two and a half months.

Incredible to relate, Papa and Aunt had formed a very unusual project for the young people's holidays. Contrary to an almost unbroken rule, they planned to go away to the seaside for a fortnight and to take Charlotte, Emily and Anne with them. Much to Charlotte's irritation it was to be Liverpool (she was burning to accept an invitation from Ellen Nussey to go away alone with her to the east coast).

The Liverpool journey remained for many days, as Charlotte wrote, "a matter of talk, a sort of castle in the air, unlikely ever to assume a more solid shape. Aunt," she wrote, "like many other elderly people likes to talk of such things ; but when it comes to putting them into practice, she rather falls off. . . ." For Anne the project would not materialise in time. She had to return to her post before the family were at liberty to put it into execution.

Writing to Ellen Nussey about the Liverpool journey on

26th July Charlotte said : "We shall not go for a fortnight or three weeks because till that time papa's expected assistant will not be ready to undertake his duties." Papa's expected assistant was his new curate, the Rev. William Weightman, who took up his duties at Haworth Church on 19th August 1839.

Of Anne's second term at Blake Hall very little is known. Evidence from Charlotte is meagre because for a whole month of that autumn she was with Ellen Nussey (her chief correspondent) at the sea from where she returned enraptured and, happily, "as well as need be, and very fat".

A domestic crisis was very shortly to call on her reserves of courage. Tabby, whose broken leg had never properly mended, became so lame in November as to have—temporarily, it was hoped —to leave the parsonage. As always in an emergency, the girls rose superbly to the occasion ; not only did Charlotte and Emily shoulder Tabby's work but they resisted all Aunt's efforts to replace her. "Emily and I are sufficiently busy," she writes to Ellen, "as you may suppose : I manage the ironing and keep the rooms clean ; Emily does the baking and attends to the kitchen. We are such odd animals that we prefer this mode of contrivance to having a new face amongst us. Besides, we do not despair of Tabby's return, and she shall not be supplanted by a stranger in her absence. I excited Aunt's wrath very much by burning the clothes, the first time I attempted to iron ; but I do better now. . . ."

This was written just before Christmas, and it was to a home already deprived of its main comfort in the person of Tabby and to sisters more than usually harassed by disputes with Aunt, that Anne returned in bitterness of heart bearing further bad news. To her deep humiliation she had been dismissed.

In the person of Agnes Grey she has told her chagrin at this totally unexpected and unjust decision. It found her utterly unprepared, at a moment when she was "rejoicing in the near approach of the holidays and congratulating myself upon having made some progress with my pupils (as far as their learning went at least), for I *had* instilled *something* into their heads, and I had at length brought them to be a little—a very little—more rational about getting their lessons done in time to leave some space for recreation, instead of tormenting themselves and me all day long to no purpose." Just then she was sent for by "Mrs Bloomfield" and calmly told her services would no longer be required after the holidays. It was no palliation of the blow to her pride to be told that her character and general conduct were unexceptionable ; every Brontë knew as much of herself in her heart of hearts. Where she had most striven to succeed, she was told she had failed : the children, according to their mother, "had made so little improvement" since Anne's arrival that their father and herself "felt it their duty to seek some other mode of instruction" for them. "Though superior to most children of their years in abilities," their mother declared, "they were decidedly behind them in attainments ; their manners were uncultivated, and their tempers unruly." And this their mother attributed to a want of sufficient firmness and diligent, persevering care on the part of their governess.

The wound was all the more hurtful since "firmness, devoted diligence, unwearied perseverance, unceasing care" were the very qualifications on which Anne had secretly prided herself. She knew the accusations of weakness and incompetence were wholly un-merited and that her employers, by their failure to support her authority and to maintain consistent discipline, were primarily to blame for their children's unteachableness. She was near to bursting into tears of vexation and shame but, rather than show any weakness or how deeply she had been hurt, she chose to say nothing in her own defence.

To have failed in her own eyes after so sustained an effort was bad enough. But to have failed in the eyes of her family was what affected Anne most. Feelingly she writes of her humiliation in *Agnes Grey*. "Thus I was dismissed, and thus I sought my home. Alas ! What would they think of me ? Unable, after all my boasting, to keep my place, even for a single year, as governess to three small children whose mother was asserted by my own aunt to be a 'very nice woman'. Having been thus weighed in the balance and found wanting, I need not hope they would be willing to try me again. And this was an unwelcome thought ; for vexed, harassed, disappointed as I had been, and greatly as I had learned to love and value my home, I was not yet weary of adventure, nor willing to relax my efforts. I knew that all parents were not like Mr and Mrs Bloomfield, and I was certain all children were not like theirs. The next family must be different, and any change must be for the better. I had been seasoned by adversity, and tutored by experience, and I longed to redeem my lost honour in

the eyes of those whose opinion was more than that of all the
world to me."

There are several points in this passage that reveal what sort of
a girl Anne Brontë had become. Contrary to the generally accepted
portrait of her as a gentle and weak nature, what emerges in this
crisis is her courage and her pride. She is a fighter and her very
language is the language immemorially spoken by soldiers. "I
longed to redeem my lost honour in the eyes of those whose opinion
was more than that of all the world to me." She did not leave
Blake Hall defeated but full of mettle for another day. The
"modern child" had *not* got the better of Anne.

Chapter Twelve

WILLY WEIGHTMAN

MUCH has been written about Anne Brontë and Willy Weightman. An impression has been created—quite contrary to the evidence at hand—that their love for each other was the central circumstance of his curacy at Haworth. Willy Weightman was at Haworth for three years, from August 1839 to September 1842, of which time Anne was at home for one year and two months only from January 1840 to March 1841. Not until January 1842, when he had been at Haworth for nearly two and a half years, is there the slightest evidence that Willy Weightman was attracted to Anne. Whereas, from his first coming up to that very time, every mention of him by Charlotte—the close observer of his slightest doings—is coupled with accounts of his multiple flirtations elsewhere. Taking into consideration Charlotte's proven blindness where her sister Anne was concerned, and Anne's own "close dissembling" of the secret in her heart, even so it is evident that Anne came late upon the scene of Willy Weightman's adventures at Haworth, drawing, as ever, very little attention to herself.

Willy Weightman was born in 1814 at Appleby in Westmorland where his father was a brewer and where he attended the Grammar School, proceeding to Durham University to read Classics. When he first arrived at Haworth after taking his M.A. degree he was twenty-five years old, fresh-complexioned, curly-haired and kind. He was, according to Mr Brontë, who ought to be able to judge of such matters, a fine scholar with "classical attainments of the first order". What was more important to the inmates of Haworth Parsonage, he was excellent company. He had a knack for getting straight at the heart of a matter ; for cutting through convention ; for ignoring barriers ; for walking directly into people's lives.

No other stranger in the whole course of the Brontë story ever succeeded, as Willy Weightman succeeded, in invading the domestic privacy of Haworth Parsonage. His is the only outside influence, with the possible exception of Ellen Nussey's, not only tolerated but allowed full sway by all the members of the family, Aunt included. Mr Brontë, whose estimate of his curate far more resembled Anne's than Charlotte's, said of him eventually that their relationship had been like that of father and son. Everyone, in short, liked Willy Weightman.

According to Charlotte, when Willy Weightman first came to Haworth, he was "lonely and rather melancholy" and she had "a great pleasure in cheering and amusing him". He arrived, moreover, declaredly in love. Charlotte was not to know, at that early stage, that the objects of Mr Weightman's passion varied as the hues of the rainbow and were, moreover, quite as evanescent as that natural phenomenon. She sympathised, she listened, she advised. Mr Weightman's flame was a young lady of his native Appleby, Miss Agnes Walton by name. What more natural than that the enforced separation should evoke sighs from the desponding swain ? His sighs and pallid cheeks were much commented on and consolation extended in "frequent and agreeable visits" to the parsonage. Even when "lonely and rather melancholy" Mr Weightman was not a tedious lover. There was, evidently, something irresistibly comic even in his most pathetic manner. Soon his glowing descriptions of Agnes Walton's charms had spurred Charlotte to paint her portrait. "I have been painting a portrait of Agnes Walton," she writes to Ellen, "for our friend. . . . You would laugh to see how his eyes sparkle with delight when he looks at it, like a pretty child pleased with a new play-thing."

The fact was that, lulled by the security of Agnes Walton's existence in not-so-far-off Appleby, Charlotte had been taken off her guard. "At home," as she told Ellen on a different occasion, "I talk with ease and am never shy, never weighed down and oppressed by that miserable *mauvaise honte*, which torments and constrains me elsewhere." Charlotte, in short, showed herself to Willy Weightman at the first as a "cheerful, chatty kind of body" (as she was contemptuously to remember later) and got on like a house on fire with him.

Taken off their guard, not only Charlotte Brontë but Ellen Nussey and, in a different manner, Emily Brontë had all admitted Willy Weightman to a degree of friendship which the conventions of the day would hardly have allowed had he been considered unattached. As counsellors and consoling angels they were immediately caught up into Willy Weightman's orbit. Agnes Walton or no Agnes Walton, by the time Anne returned from Blake Hall at the Christmas of 1839, Willy Weightman was so far the acknow-

ledged *cavaliere servante* of her sisters and the "suitor" of several
other young ladies in the district that what she thought of him or
he of her could be of only secondary interest. Willy Weightman
and his "love affairs" were the talk of Haworth and were taken
seriously by no one, or so Charlotte would have us believe. If
Anne felt differently towards him from the first, she not only hid
her feelings but was obliged to hide them, for Willy Weightman
was to philander with all those nearest and dearest to her before
ever he looked at her with the eyes of love.

It is a pity that most of our information regarding Willy
Weightman comes from Charlotte, because she was not an
unbiased witness. After a "radiant morning" their friendship
suffered an eclipse, all too obviously, on Charlotte's part, from
motives of pique.

Before a year was out she declared herself fully convinced that
he was "a thorough male flirt" who had "scattered his impressions
far and wide", and expressed it as her considered opinion that "he
ought not to have been a parson. Certainly he ought not." Even
at the time of making this rather serious charge—which eventually
she revoked—she added that she was not at all surprised the local
young women found him irresistible : "it is perfectly natural," she
agreed, "a handsome, clean, prepossessing, good-humoured young
man, will never want troops of victims amongst young ladies" ;
adding to her friend Ellen Nussey, "So long as *you* are not among
the number it is all right."

Having felt something of the "irresistible" attraction herself,
Charlotte was bent on safeguarding her best friend from a like
experience and, in doing so, remained blind to what might be
happening to her own sister Anne.

The sum of Anne's references to Willy Weightman is contained
in ten poems and in the portrait of Mr Weston in her *Agnes Grey*.
Ambiguous so long as he lived, these references became outspoken
only in the poems written some years after his death. On this scant
evidence and upon the one reference of Charlotte's to Willy
Weightman "looking out of the corners of his eyes to win [Anne's]
attention" in church, the story of their love affair reposes. Yet, of
Anne's feelings there can be no shadow of doubt ; the experience,
occupying so short a period in time, left its mark on her spirit for
ever.

It was not all tragedy ; for a fleeting period her sky was

brightened by so health-giving and warming a light that it kindled her to a new sense of being.

The year 1840 will ever stand out as the blithest in the whole Brontë story. The three girls were all at home and Branwell, who in January took up a post as tutor with a family at Broughton-in-Furness, was apparently doing quite creditably for himself. With Papa and Aunt in tolerable health and the problem of Tabby's successor again shelved, the young ladies of Haworth Parsonage would appear to have given themselves over to a mode of existence more in accord with that of other young ladies of their age and time than ever before. Temporarily at least they abandoned the pursuit of "situations". They allowed themselves the luxury of a respite at home, where the chronicle of their doings reads more like a novel by Jane Austen than a Brontë biography.

We hear of mornings spent in painting water-colour portraits under the admiring gaze of the curate (did not Emma Woodhouse do the same ?) ; afternoons in walking out under his reverence's escort ; evenings in attending his lectures at Keighley ; and returns home under the stars at the unthinkable hour of midnight. In short, had their name been Bennet instead of Brontë they could hardly have spent their days in a more social, pleasure-seeking and predominantly frivolous round. And all this because of Mr Brontë's "bonny-faced, pleasant, light-hearted, good-tempered, generous, careless, fickle and unclerical" new curate, the Rev. William Weightman.

This was the agreeable position when in February 1840 Ellen Nussey paid a visit to Haworth. It was a long time since Charlotte, Emily and Anne had all been at home together and, after some initial grumbles on Aunt's part, as always, the visit was the occasion for unwonted liveliness.

The inevitable happened. Willy Weightman, so recently sighing for distant Agnes Walton, was immediately smitten with the charms of Ellen Nussey which, as we know, were not inconsiderable. According to Charlotte he paid quite "pointed attention" to Ellen, so that for several months afterwards Charlotte considered it her duty to warn her friend not to succumb to his blandishments. "I am glad you continue so heart-whole," Charlotte wrote four months after Ellen's visit, "I rather feared our mutual nonsense might have made a deeper impression on you than was safe. . . ." As far as Ellen was concerned she seems never to have admitted the soft impeachment. Rather she rallied Charlotte on being the party most implicated. "Let me have no more of your humbug about Cupid, etc.," retorts Charlotte to Ellen's very next letter. "You know as well as I do, it is all groundless trash."

The fact was that *both* girls seem for a time to have had their heads turned and to have indulged in a great deal of flirtatious folly. For a time Charlotte could shield behind Agnes Walton and when Agnes Walton's powers waned, behind Ellen, but the truth is that when it came to Ellen asking if she might confide the whole story to their mutual friend Mary Taylor, Charlotte forbade her to do so. It was a mistake, as she very quickly realised. Mary Taylor, the most direct of human beings, was up in arms at the mystification and immediately suspected much more than there was to tell. Charlotte had quickly to order Ellen to make no more fuss and to tell Mary forthwith "every individual occurrence, including Valentines . . . and all".

The famous incident of the valentines, which redounds entirely to Willy Weightman's credit, poses the whole question of his sincerity. How much did all this flirtation mean to him ? Was he quite as naïve as Charlotte took him to be, or was it not she, rather, who was behaving with astounding naïveté ? Was Willy Weightman not simply humouring the girls when he found two of them, at least, so disposed to play his game ? Certain it is that there was more of kindness—and who knows ?—of compassion, in this gesture than of amorousness.

Ellen Nussey tells us how, learning that none of the girls had ever in her life received a valentine, he composed verses for each one of them and walked ten miles to post them so that Mr Brontë should never suspect his own curate of being the sender. Of course the girls never had any doubts at all. The impact upon them was tremendous. A whole year later Charlotte, then cynically awakened to all "the dodges and artifices of his lordship's character", could still write to Ellen : "I dare say you have received a Valentine this year from our bonny-faced friend the Curate of Haworth. I got a precious specimen a few days before I left home, but I knew better how to treat it than I did those we received a year ago."

The truth was that "those we received a year ago" created a veritable stir round the parsonage fireside. One would much like to know which set of verses was addressed to Anne. The titles of three out of the four valentines are known. Obviously the lines

"Fair Ellen, Fair Ellen" were addressed to Miss Nussey. The two other known titles are : "Away fond love" and "Soul divine". It would be pure surmise to suggest which, if either, was addressed to Anne.

It cannot, indeed, be too strongly emphasised at this period that the last name to be coupled with Willy Weightman's was that of Anne Brontë. Never for a moment is there any question of Anne being singled out for his attentions—Anne, possibly even less than Emily, who earned from the facetious curate the nickname of "the Major" for her resolute chaperoning of Ellen Nussey on their walks abroad.

On all these gay occasions Anne was but another participant, in no way a central player, in the game. As an early poem on the subject reveals, all her preoccupation at this time was to hide her love ; not only from the elders of the family but from her sisters as well. Her health had always elicited anxious comment from the members of the family : any change in colour or in spirits would be at once remarked ; the animation of joy, like the blight of disappointment, leaves treacherous traces. The poem called "Self-Congratulation" tells its own tale of what went on repeatedly at this time.

> I've noticed many a youthful form
> Upon whose changeful face
> The inmost workings of the soul
> The gazer well might trace ;
> The speaking eye, the changing lip,
> The ready blushing cheek,
> The smiling, or beclouded brow,
> Their different feelings speak.
>
> But, thank God ! You might gaze on mine
> For hours, and never know
> The secret changes of my soul
> From joy to keenest woe.
> Last night, as we sat round the fire
> Conversing merrily,
> We heard, without, approaching steps
> Of one well known to me !
>
> There was no trembling in my voice.
> No blush upon my cheek,
> No lustrous sparkle in my eyes,
> Of hope, or joy, to speak ;

But, Oh ! my spirit burned within,
My heart beat full and fast !
He came not nigh—he went away—
And then my joy was past.

And yet my comrades marked it not :
My voice was still the same ;
They saw me smile, and o'er my face
No signs of sadness came.
They little knew my hidden thoughts ;
And they will *never* know
The aching anguish of my heart,
The bitter burning woe !

Anne Brontë fell in love with Willy Weightman almost at sight.
By the date of her above-quoted poem "Self-Congratulation",
written on 1st January 1840, the lightning-like quality of her love
is revealed. She may have glimpsed him on his first arrival at
Haworth in August 1839, but all that autumn she was at her post
at Blake Hall and returned to Haworth only on her dismissal a few
days before Christmas. By New Year's Day she not only loved
him but was fully conscious of her love.

To those who ask, Was there, materially, time for her to fall in
love ? is not the sentiment implicit in this poem an imaginary sentiment, born, as in many previous poems, of poetic invention alone ?
there can be no reply. The only witness who can prove whether
the doubters or the believers are in the right is Anne Brontë herself,
and to her truth and hers alone we must incline. Whether she had
known Willy Weightman a week, a day, an hour, it had sufficed.

The very rapidity of her love conditioned its character. It was
with Willy Weightman's handsome person—his form so "angel-fair"
—that she fell in love before ever she loved the better part of him.
It was his "sunny smile" that gladdened her heart before ever she
found out that the smile emanated from "a soul so near divine".
And it could not have been otherwise. It needed time to discover
Willy Weightman's good qualities ; but it did not need many
meetings for his vivid personality to have charmed a young heart
which was, in almost every particular, Willy Weightman's exact
opposite. As she was deeply thoughtful, feeling and reflective, so
he was brilliant, mobile and optimistic. It is in no way to detract
from Willy Weightman to say that it was by the force of his animal
spirits that he won Anne Brontë's heart.

The bright curls and the rosy complexion brought on him the nickname of "Celia-Amelia" and soon the girls spoke of him as "Miss Weightman", all of which, apparently, he took in very good part.

According to Charlotte he was very vain of his person—as also of his attainments. Scribbling a letter on the back of one of his drawings, she tells Ellen how "He sketched it and one or two other little things when he happened to be here one evening, but you should have seen the vanity with which he afterwards regarded his productions. One of them represented the flying figure of Fame inscribing his own name on the clouds."

However much Charlotte might deprecate his vanity, she undertook to paint his portrait while Ellen was staying with them. This was in full academic dress and considerable mockery was aroused by Mr Weightman's particularising the various portions of silk and velvet that went to make up the imposing whole—a display of vanity that looks uncommonly like playing up to other people's preconceived ideas of what a vain man says and does rather than the genuine thing. Willy Weightman's letters are not extant to tell us how much amusement he got out of amusing the Brontë girls.

The excitements did not end there. Willy Weightman was resolved that the girls should attend a lecture he was to give at the Mechanics' Institute in Keighley. Naturally it would be in the evening and Keighley was four miles away. With Branwell away from home the girls were without their natural escort, and the convention of the day unhesitatingly pronounced Mr Weightman to represent a positive danger to four defenceless young women ! Aunt Branwell it was well known was not to be circumvented on the question of punctilio. If Willy Weightman wanted to get the girls to Keighley he must go about getting them there by devious ways.

It was at the height of winter—in February—and so many factors militated against the poor girls' prospects of an evening's pleasure. It might so easily snow, and in the space of two hours drifts up to two or three feet high could obliterate the tracks. There was no street lighting and lanterns would, naturally, have to be carried. Colds, always so prevalent in the Brontë parsonage, might incapacitate some, if not all, of the party at the last minute.

Mr Weightman, with commendable inventiveness, set about

overcoming the major obstacles. The weather, please God, might be clement when the day came.

He put his dilemma to the Vicar of Keighley, the Rev. Theodore Dury, who was not only a married man but a married man with a daughter Caroline, whom without loss of time Mr Weightman added to the list of his conquests. Mr Dury, properly primed, wrote a missive to Mr Brontë stating that he was himself attending Mr Weightman's lecture in Keighley and would esteem it an honour if the Miss Brontës and their guest, Miss Nussey, would accept to take tea with Mrs Dury and himself prior to attending Mr Weightman's lecture, to which, in due course, the whole company would repair, under suitable escort.

Mr Brontë, apparently, could find nothing exceptionable in such a proposal and acceded to Mr Dury's request.

An evening of delight thus offered itself in prospect to the least spoilt—and most intelligent—women in the West Riding of Yorkshire. There may have been moonlight, certainly it was fine, presumably no one was ill for all the girls, without a defaulter, walked down the four miles to Keighley, partook of Mrs Dury's hospitality in the old parsonage house at Keighley; after which, warmed by delicious fare and unwonted festivity, they proceeded to the Mechanics' Institute—the only source of entertainment known to them for the greater part of their lives—and sat through an evening of unadulterated enjoyment.

Mr Weightman would, obviously, be a facile speaker. He was lecturing on the Classics and was therefore primed with his subject, but the effect of his talk would very largely depend on his own humour and charm, of which there is abundant evidence. His motive in addressing a working-class audience to kindle their interest in a subject usually considered beyond their requirements was characteristic, and its kindness would not be lost upon the Brontë girls.

It was, quite obviously, a very successful evening. Speaking of it many years later Ellen Nussey recalled how, up to the last moment of their return home, Willy Weightman kept them entertained. "The Parsonage was not reached till 12 p.m.," she writes. "The two clergymen rushed in with their charges, deeply disturbing Miss Branwell, who had prepared hot coffee for the home party, which of course fell short when two more were to be supplied. Poor Miss Branwell lost her temper, Charlotte was troubled, and Mr

Weightman, who enjoyed teasing the old lady, was very thirsty. The great spirits of the walking party had a trying suppression, but twinkling fun sustained some of the party."

But in the last resort Willy Weightman cannot be judged as a playboy—which all too obviously Charlotte was disposed to do—but as a man who had chosen a profession requiring something more than charm.

The divergence between the portraits of him left by Charlotte and Anne Brontë raises the whole question of his worth and it is impossible not to ask : what was he really like ? In Charlotte's censure of Willy Weightman as "vain", "fickle" and "unclerical" there is considerable personal bitterness. This must not be forgotten when reading such a passage as the following from a letter to Ellen : ". . . for all the tricks, wiles, and insincerities of love, the gentleman has not his match for 20 miles round. He would fain persuade every woman under 30 whom he sees that he is desperately in love with her. . . ."

Anne's portrait of him, on the contrary, as Mr Weston in *Agnes Grey*, emphasises the silent worth of a deeply charitable nature. That Anne's likeness, although created with the eyes of love, was founded at least upon partial truth, Charlotte herself on one occasion bears out. Long before Mr Weston was thought of, or Anne's devotion to his memory revealed, Charlotte recorded of Willy Weightman precisely the kind of humane attention to his poor parishioners that made Mr Weston beloved of the cottagers in *Agnes Grey*.

Writing to Ellen Nussey on 29th September 1840, some months after Willy Weightman had begun to incur her condemnation, Charlotte says : "There is one little trait respecting him which lately came to my knowledge which gives a glimpse of the better side of his character. Last Saturday night he had been sitting an hour in the parlour with Papa ; and as he went away I heard Papa say to him, 'What is the matter with you ? You seem in very low spirits tonight.' 'Oh, I don't know. I've been to see a poor young girl, who, I'm afraid, is dying.' 'Indeed, what is her name ?' 'Susan Bland, the daughter of John Bland, the Superintendent.' Now Susan Bland is my oldest and best scholar in the Sunday-School ; and, when I heard that, I thought I would go as soon as I could to see her. I did go on Monday afternoon, and found her very ill and weak, and seemingly far on her way to that bourne whence no traveller returns. After sitting with her some time, I happened to ask her mother if she thought a little port wine would do her good. She replied that the doctor had recommended it, and that when Mr Weightman was last there he had sent them a bottle of wine and a jar of preserves. She added that he was always good to poor folks, and seemed to have a deal of feeling and kind-heartedness about him. . . ."

Readers of *Agnes Grey* will remember the old cottager, Nancy Brown, reporting of Mr Weston how when "poor Jem shivered wi' cold, he axed if wer stacks of coals was nearly done . . . and sent a sack o' coals next day", and how "when he comes into a poor body's house a seeing sick folks, he like notices what they most stand i' need on ; an' if he thinks they can't readily get it therseln, he never says nowt about it, but just gets it for 'em", adding that "it isn't everybody 'at 'ud do that, 'at has as little as he has ; for you know, mum, he's nowt at all to live on but what he gets fra' the rector, an' that's little enough, they say."

Not only because she loved him did Anne Brontë perceive the finer qualities in Willy Weightman ; she had to emphasise them to justify not only her choice of him as hero of her novel, but to justify her own choice to *herself*. To a point he may have been what Charlotte said of him, but to Anne those very qualities had a captivating brightness. Just because *she* was so serious-minded and he so gay, to her he would *always* be :

> The lightest heart that I have known,
> The kindest I shall ever know.

Being, as she was, deeply spiritual, she had to intellectualise her love. Time, which brought with it a fuller comprehension of his finer qualities—he proved himself loyal and generous, charitable and plucky—helped her to create an image more in accord with her ideal of manhood, which gradually she could impose upon the original, and present without a qualm of conscience to the world as the portrait of the man she loved. All this, being Anne Brontë and the most honourable of beings, she did quite unconsciously. Only so can the evolution from Willy Weightman to Mr Weston be explained.

For the modest and earnest-minded girl that she was it was necessary to find exalted qualities of heart and mind in the man

she loved—to despoil him of those obvious facile graces which, in
the person of Willy Weightman it had been "her bliss to see", and
which, all unprepared as she was, had stolen her heart. Only so
could she excuse herself to herself for loving a man who had made
her no overtures.

Thus Mr Weston could not be allowed to be handsome ; he
was not even "what was called agreeable in outward aspect. . . .
In stature he was a little, a very little, above the middle size, the
outline of his face would be pronounced too square for beauty but
to me it announced decision of character ; his dark brown hair was
not carefully curled . . . but simply brushed aside over a broad
white forehead ; the eyebrows, I suppose, were too projecting, but
from under those dark brows there gleamed an eye of singular
power, brown in colour, not large and somewhat deep set, but
strikingly brilliant, and full of expression ; there was character too,
in the mouth, something that bespoke a man of firm purpose and a
habitual thinker—a man of strong sense, firm faith, and ardent
piety, but thoughtful and stern. . . ."

Happily for Anne we possess Mr Brontë's assessment of his
curate's character which, as a confirmation of her own and a
refutation of Charlotte's, is of major importance in striking a balance
of the truth.

Astonishingly—in view of Charlotte's charge of fickleness—one
of the chief merits Mr Brontë found in his curate was stability.
"There are many," said Mr Brontë, "who for a short time can
please, and even astonish—but who soon retrograde and fall into
disrepute—Mr Weightman's character wore well ; the surest proof
of worth. He had, it is true, some peculiar advantages. Agreeable
in person and manners, and constitutionally cheerful, his first
introduction was prepossessing. But what he gained at first he did
not lose afterwards. He had those qualities which enabled him
rather to *gain* ground."

So much for his character. For his practices as a clergyman,
what Mr Brontë tells us of Willy Weightman only explains yet
further why Anne should have been so powerfully drawn to him.
Like her he eschewed the doctrine of Calvin, of "Election" and
"Reprobation" and preached a gospel of compassion and love.

"He did not see why true believers, having the promise of the
life that . . . is to come, should create unto themselves artificial

sorrows, and disfigure the garment of gospel peace with the garb of sighing and sadness. Pondering on and rejoicing in the glad tidings of salvation, he wished others to rejoice . . . evermore in the glorious liberty of the gospel. . . ."

To Anne it was, of course, of the first importance that Willy Weightman was a clergyman. In her view of life a man could not espouse a better calling. That this was so is apparent on every page of *Agnes Grey* in that section dealing with Mr Weston. Never for a moment is the reader allowed to forget Mr Weston's vocation. Not because he preaches or adopts airs of superiority over his fellow-men, but because he is shown constantly in his *functional* aspect. We find him sitting with old cottagers and rescuing their cats ; trudging distances to visit the sick ; conducting services. He comes and goes, intent on his parish duties, strangely convincing in his quiet resolute way. The fact that his work embraces a multitude of homely incidents—is, indeed, often regulated by homely incidents—shows how completely his life and work appeared integrated to Anne.

Not even in love did she lose her sense of humour. Readers of *Agnes Grey* will remember the delightful passage relative to marriage with a clergyman. It is a conversation between Rosalie Murray and her governess.

"My sister is going to be married," says Agnes.

"Is she—when ?" asks her worldly pupil.

"Not till next month."

". . . To whom is she to be married ?"

"To Mr Richardson, the vicar of a neighbouring parish."

"Is he rich ?"

"No ; only comfortable."

"Is he handsome ?"

"No ; only decent."

"Young ?"

"No ; only middling."

"O mercy ! What a wretch ! What sort of a house is it ?"

"A quiet little vicarage, with an ivy-clad porch, an old-fashioned garden——"

"Oh, stop !—You'll make me sick. How *can* she bear it ?"

The pleasant interregnum of the year 1840 was over. It has left singularly few traces. The whole of Anne's poetic output for that

year, if we may judge by what survives, was three poems only ;
yet it was a year of profound experience from which she issued
strengthened, as well as matured.

In considering the poems, one of which is the revealing "Self-
Congratulation" already discussed, their personal note seems more
assured. Apart from the nostalgic charm of her "Bluebell", written
in August, there is a cryptic little poem written on "Sunday
December 13th 1840" called "Retirement" which speaks the language of a pent-up heart easing its burden of imposed secrecy.
One senses the weariness of keeping a constant watch upon her face,
upon her words ; her need for solitude ; her cry to God.

> O let me be alone awhile :
> No human form is nigh ;
> And I may sing and muse aloud,
> No mortal ear is nigh.
>
> Away ! ye dreams of earthly bliss,
> Ye earthly cares be gone :
> Depart ! ye restless wandering thoughts,
> And let me be alone !
>
> One hour, my spirit, stretch thy wings
> And quit this joyless sod ;
> Bask in the sunshine of the sky,
> And be alone with God !

Throughout the early spring of 1841 Charlotte and Anne were
busy trying to find themselves situations as governesses. If any
further proof were needed that no understanding existed between
Anne Brontë and Willy Weightman in those early days of his
curacy, it is supplied by this voluntary departure from home in
pursuit of that independence which, at the best, could be regarded
only as a very roundabout way to matrimony.

Chapter Thirteen

THORP GREEN HALL

THAT she was not totally without hopes of a happy issue to her love Anne herself betrayed in certain confessions to the reader in *Agnes Grey*. With the honesty that one looks for in all her confidences, she tells us of her practical motives for deciding to leave home again, and adds : ". . . finally, bright visions mingled with my hopes, with which the care of children, and the mere duties of a governess had little or nothing to do." She was to earn fifty pounds a year in her new situation, double the salary she had earned with the Inghams at Blake Hall, and after reckoning that twenty pounds would keep her in "decent clothes becoming my station" and also pay for her two annual journeys to and from home, and any other necessary expenses, she dreamed of banking thirty pounds every year, a thrilling prospect which drew from her the cry : "Oh, I *must* struggle to keep this situation, whatever it might be ! both for my own honour among my friends and for the solid services I might render them by my continuance there."

With thirty pounds laid by every year—she was just twenty-one when she set out on her second adventure from home—besides laying up stores for the comfort and support of her family, she might also hope to lay by something for herself, for that modest dowry it would be her pride and joy to bring to the poor clergyman it was her utmost ambition to marry.

Anne was very much of a realist, and if she eagerly, optimistically, set out in March 1841 to take up what she hoped would be a long-term engagement, she had faced the issues. She was not fleeing home broken-hearted because Willy Weightman paid attention to every girl but herself; she knew him to be poor, far too poor to be able to contemplate marriage for the present ; he was poor and she was very young ; she could not waste her life idling in poverty at home. It was far better to face separation now when, who knows, by her going something might be achieved towards the future.

She was going to what appeared to her "a formidable distance" from home, to a gentleman's residence in a small locality called Little Ouseburn, twelve miles from York and some seventy miles from Haworth. It was the first time any of the Brontë girls had gone to a post without personal recommendation, but both Charlotte and Anne had been such a great age that early spring trying to find situations through the usual channels (Miss Wooler or Ellen Nussey) and failing in every attempt, that Anne took the unusual course at last of advertising in the papers. She stated her qualifications : "Music, singing, drawing, French, Latin, and German", and "boldly stipulated" for a salary of £50 a year. She received only two replies and of these, as she tells us in *Agnes Grey*, only one agreed to pay her the sum she asked. Of the family she, naturally, knew nothing. Their name was Robinson ; she may, possibly, have heard that they were collaterals of the Marquis of Ripon. Their residence was Thorp Green Hall, two miles from Little Ouseburn, and the gentleman was in holy orders. There were four children, three girls and a boy whose ages ranged from fifteen and a half to nine years.

Anne set out from home in the last days of March. The exact date is not known, but Charlotte, who had gone to her new post in the family of a Mr White at Upperwood House, Rawdon, six miles from Bradford, on 2nd March, received her first letter from Anne on 1st April. She reported, characteristically, that "she was very well." Knowing Anne of old Charlotte's comment to Emily was : "I hope she speaks absolute truth."

Neither the distance she had to go nor the complete strangers among whom she was to live were formidable drawbacks in Anne's eyes. Taking into account the conventional picture of Anne Brontë as a timorous and spiritless girl, the following passage in *Agnes Grey* is of peculiar interest. Speaking of her step into the unknown she says, ". . . this rendered it only more piquant to me. I had now, in some measure, got rid of the *mauvaise honte* that had formerly oppressed me so much ; there was a pleasing excitement in the idea of entering these unknown regions, and making my way alone among its strange inhabitants. I now flattered myself I was going to see something of the world. . . ."

She saw it as a good omen that her new employers lived near York, a cultural centre very different from the manufacturing districts where she had resided before—the Huddersfields, Mirfields, Birstalls and Gomersals of the industrial West Riding of Yorkshire where money-making was the only object—and both from the style of residence and the family's connections conjectured that her new employers were "thorough-bred gentry" who would treat their governess "with due consideration as a respectable, well-educated lady . . . and not a mere upper servant." So argued Agnes Grey, with excusable optimism; adding with commendable honesty, "Thus the reader will see that I had no claim to be regarded as a martyr to filial piety, going forth to sacrifice peace and liberty for the sole purpose of laying up stores for the comfort and support of my parents. . . ." She expected to derive positive benefits from her position at Thorp Green.

The journey took about ten hours. If she left home at six o'clock in the morning the Keighley coach would deposit her in Bradford (at *The Bowling Green Inn*) by half-past eight. From there by coach to Leeds and from Leeds by the new rail-road (a double excitement, not only for its novelty but for Branwell's connection with it) to York, where Mr Robinson's phaeton awaited her.

It was March, a month that can still be in the grip of winter in those northern regions, and in *Agnes Grey* she sets her arrival at Thorp Green Hall in a bewildering storm of snow which made the twelve miles' drive to Little Ouseburn in the dark "a long and formidable passage".

Of the countryside she would see nothing, though later she was to note that it was "pleasant, as far as fertile fields, flourishing trees, quiet green lanes, and smiling hedges with wild flowers scattered along their banks, could make it." In that winter's dusk in which she arrived, neither the "quiet green lanes" nor the wild flowers in the hedgerows, which make so much of the charm of the Vale of York, nor the long lush meadows that border the sleepy Ouse were visible to Anne, "with the cold, sharp snow" drifting through her veil and filling her lap, "seeing nothing and wondering how the unfortunate horse and driver could make their way even as well as they did."

Thorp Green Hall lay two miles off the main York to Borough-bridge road, at an almost equal distance from the villages of Whixley and Little Ouseburn. Acres of cultivated land, rolling and open, sweep round it in a vast circle whose perimeter is nothing short of the horizon itself; so few woods or other landmarks interpose between to break the sky-line. In winter, as Anne Brontë first saw it, its level surface smothered under snow must have looked drearily

formless to her eyes accustomed as they were to the sharp declivities
and dramatic contrasts of Haworth moors.

Off the main road, through Whixley, the carriage turned up the
enchanting village street with its Georgian house-fronts, orchards
and old-world gardens. Anne may have glimpsed the lights in the
lattice windows of *The Bay Horse Inn* as the phaeton floundered
through. After that there were no more habitations with their
lights to point the way. The lane was an almost indistinguishable
track and the phaeton seemed to be ploughing axle-deep through
the open fields, so deep was the snow.

At length the light of the phaeton lamp fell on a copse of trees,
in front of which it was possible to discern that the track—somewhat
smoothed out here—described the wide arc of a circle. Ornamental
pillars rose up on either side "and, at the call of the driver", she
tells us, "someone unlatched and rolled back upon their creaking
hinges what appeared to be the park gates. Then we proceeded
along a smoother road, whence, occasionally, I perceived some huge
hoary mass gleaming through the darkness, which I took to be a
portion of a snow-clad tree. After a considerable time we paused
again, before the stately portico of a large house with long windows
descending to the ground."

Of the Thorp Green Hall Anne knew, only the kitchen premises
and stables remain today ; the main body of the dwelling was
burned down at the turn of the century. It was a Georgian
structure, the third to stand on this site which has been occupied
since Plantagenet times.

Formerly there had been a monastery at Thorpe Underwood
(as the locality was then called) which, at the confiscation of Church
property under Henry VIII, had passed into civil hands. But in
the grounds there stands yet the "Monks' House", dating back to
the mid-fourteenth century, its timbered frame, brick and wattle
walls and diamond-paned windows still being in a state of perfect
preservation today. A romantic history attaches to the place.
Originally it was used as a "Resting House" for monks on their
frequent journeyings between Fountains Abbey and York and it is
said to have had a secret passage running many miles underground.
Not the least of its romantic attraction for present-day visitors is
the fact that when Branwell Brontë came to join Anne as tutor in
the Robinson family he was put to lodge there, in this most
genuinely Gothic portion of the estate, set in deep trees as in an

enchanted zone, yet within sight of the main "New Hall", as the one Anne inhabited was then called.

The property had been in the Robinson family only since 1795, when the father of Anne's employer had acquired it from the family of the original Tudor owners. Very nearly on the same site today there stands a new house. The old carriage-drive up which Anne drove that March evening and on so many subsequent days has been reorientated. But the whole estate, deeply shadowed in its belt of giant firs, would seem successfully to have remained hidden from the modifying hand of time and to sleep out the remainder of its days on that forgotten turning in the lane.

Her preconceived notions of the agreeable cultured family in whose midst she had come to live were soon dispelled. The Robinsons, though neither vulgar nor *nouveaux riches*, had little regard for culture. Their interests, so far as the ladies were concerned, were purely worldly and, as for the gentleman, clerk in holy orders though he might be, his chief activities were confined to the hunting-field. To poor Anne with her strict sense of values, both moral and intellectual, their superficial view of life came as an unpleasant shock at first, and later, as the situation took its darkly dramatic turn, as a profoundly depressing revelation of human nature.

The Rev. Edmund Robinson, as Anne's employer was called, had inherited the estate from his father, almost at birth one might say, since his father had died at the premature age of thirty-three when his heir was just three months old. He was now, at the time of Anne's arrival in his family, just forty-one years old, not at all the elderly invalid successive Brontë biographers from Mrs Gaskell on have made him out to be. (It is a notable fact, however, that the male Robinsons were not a long-lived race. Mr Robinson's father, as we have seen, died at the age of thirty-three ; he, himself, soon to become a premature valetudinarian, died at the age of forty-six, and the line became extinct by the tragic death of his only son at the age of thirty-seven.)

A matter of greater moment still when reviewing the evidence of Mrs Robinson's subsequent conduct, is the fact that husband and wife were of almost the same age, which dispels for ever the legend of a young and neglected wife tied to an old and sick husband.

Mr Robinson, though ordained into the Church, does not seem

to have taken up a living at any time. He was definitely *not*, either at this or any previous time, incumbent of Little Ouseburn Church as has also erroneously been stated. He did, however, officiate at the christenings of his five children, but throughout his life the livings of Little and Great Ouseburn Churches were in the hands of colleagues. The incumbent throughout Anne's period at Thorp Green was the Rev. E. R. Lascelles.

All reports agree in describing Mrs Robinson as extremely handsome. We know something of how she appeared to Anne for the first time in the description of Mrs Murray in *Agnes Grey*.

"Mrs Murray was a handsome, dashing lady of forty, who certainly required neither rouge nor padding to add to her charms ; and whose chief enjoyments were, or seemed to be, in giving or frequenting parties, and in dressing at the very top of the fashion."

Lydia Robinson was, indeed, exactly forty when Anne first went to Thorp Green. She was the daughter of a Canon of Durham, the Rev. Thomas Gisborne, of Yoxall Lodge, Staffordshire, and was, until her marriage, a brilliant ornament of Lichfield society. Canon Gisborne had considerable private means ; over and above the personal fortunes he left his daughters at his death he was able to make generous benefactions to the Church. Lydia's sister Mary married the M.P. for North Derbyshire—William Evans—and, as Branwell liked subsequently to boast, Mr Robinson was first-cousin to the Marquis of Ripon—a social setting, in which the worldly and clerical aspects were equally blended and which eloquently recalls the world of Antony Trollope.

How Mrs Robinson treated her governess, Anne herself has humorously related, in the person of Agnes Grey. "I did not see her [Mrs Murray] till eleven o'clock on the morning after my arrival ; when she honoured me with a visit, just as my mother might step into the kitchen to see a new servant girl ; yet not so, either, for my mother would have seen her immediately after her arrival, and not waited till the next day ; and, moreover, she would have addressed her in a more kind and friendly manner and given her some words of comfort as well as a plain exposition of her duties ; but Mrs Murray did neither the one nor the other." She was not very certain what she required of the governess. So long as she put a polish on her daughters' acquirements and gave her, personally, no trouble at all, she would do. If we may judge of her by the portrait of Mrs Murray in *Agnes Grey*—and there is no doubt she was that lady's prototype—she was one of those women accustomed to flattery and an easy success, who express themselves as vaguely as they think ; too used to having their desires met half-way even to express them clearly. She was very fond of misquoting scripture at Anne in explanation of her wants, opining that "as a clergyman's daughter" Anne should know what she meant.

Nothing in her supercilious behaviour would have affected Anne —except perhaps to make her smile in secret—had her influence upon her children not proved itself so wholly bad.

To Anne's profound shock and incredulity, she found the children had not been taught a proper "distinction between right and wrong". Their moral training—in Anne's eyes the most important factor in education—had been not so much neglected as perverted. The standards of conduct their mother had set them were all so false that Anne had to spend the best part of her time in trying to rectify them.

The girls were not naturally bad. After four years of continuous struggle she was partially to achieve a change of heart in them. They learned to respect and eventually to love her as the one being in whose rectitude they could lay implicit trust. But their mundane outlook, want of consideration for others, indolence, vanity and folly wore down her strength in the prolonged battle for their improvement.

There were three girls : Lydia aged fifteen and a half when Anne arrived, Elizabeth aged fourteen and Mary aged almost eleven. There was one son, called Edmund after his father, and aged just nine. In *Agnes Grey* Anne represented that there were two girls and two boys (the reason, apparently, why Brontë biographers have always assumed that there were only two Miss Robinsons). She described in the more pleasant character of John the elder boy, the characteristics of Mary, her youngest girl pupil, whom from the first she had liked best and entertained the best hopes of improving. Edmund, whom Anne taught for two years before Branwell took over his education, was a sore trial to her. "It was a trial of patience to live with him peaceably," she writes in *Agnes Grey*, "to watch over him was worse ; and to teach him, or to pretend to teach him, was inconceivable." She was expected to cram him with Latin in preparation for his going to a public school. Either immediately preceding Anne's arrival or just afterwards, the family suffered a bereavement in the person of the youngest little girl, Georgiana Jane, who died on 15th March, aged two years and eight months. Knowing how Anne, like Charlotte, had always a preference for babies over older children, one cannot help reflecting how her loveless task at Thorp Green might have been lightened by the presence of the little baby girl whose death darkened her first days in her new post.

Where all was new it was naturally with the people before the place that she was forced to come to terms. Her life was entirely spent in the company of her pupils (even her meals were taken in the schoolroom), and it is doubtful if she ever entered the other parts of the house, the drawing-room or library, until her elder pupils "came out" and her attendance upon them was sometimes required when there was company. They were outdoor children, loving to ride and hunt, with no taste for intellectual or artistic pursuits and very little sensitivity of heart. Lydia Robinson, in particular, appears to have resembled her mother in caring above all things for social success. Her mother wanted nothing more for her than superficial acquirements—music, dancing, singing—in which accomplishments the young lady was perfectly prepared to meet her mother half-way—but no further. In attempting to ground her in any further knowledge, Anne was wasting her time.

Of the other two girls, Elizabeth and Mary, we have been given some indications, both in *Agnes Grey* and *Wildfell Hall*. Miss Matilda, as Agnes Grey's second pupil was called, is described as "a strapping hoyden of about fourteen, with a short frock and trousers. . . . As an animal Matilda was all right, full of life, vigour, and activity ; as an intelligent being, she was barbarously ignorant, indocile, careless and irrational." The young lady's main interest in life was "riding her spirited pony, or romping with the dogs. . . ." Her chosen companions were the stable-boys and her only gift, so far as her distracted governess could discover, was at assimilating stable-language and rivalling her father in swearing "like a trooper".

Of Anne's relationship with the youngest Miss Robinson, Mary, we cannot help seeing an echo in the sympathetic understanding described in *Wildfell Hall* as existing between the married Helen Huntingdon and young Esther Hargrave, the "little merry romp" with the "guileless, simple", yet "fearless spirit", which Anne early predicted her mother would have some difficulty in "bending to her purposes". Long after Lydia and Elizabeth had made their "entries" into society, Mary's life remained confined to the school-room and the company of her earnest, kind and spirited young governess, Miss Brontë. Upon Mary, therefore, more than upon the other girls, the imprint of Anne's integrity left its mark.

In this worldly atmosphere it is not surprising that Anne suffered from acute loneliness. From snobbery—though not for any personal dissatisfaction—the parents ignored her ; and the servants, so different from the loyal and outspoken friends of the family to whom she was accustomed at home, took their cues from their masters and treated her with scant respect.

Her only comfort could—and did—come from the world outside, the natural world, one of the earliest and deepest sources of delight on which she ever drew. As the spring advanced and the days lengthened and brightened, much of her time could be spent in discovering the new world at her gates.

Her capricious pupils, always altering their hours for lessons, sometimes demanding, as she tells us in *Agnes Grey*, "to get the plaguey business over before breakfast", and having her roused at half-past five for the purpose, were very partial to doing their lessons out of doors—a scheme of which she cordially approved so long as the weather was suitable. But the children were utterly inconsiderate, and whether damp or fine would expect her to sit on the grass and remain out late of an evening irrespective of whether she caught cold or not. And she was constantly catching cold.

The country round Thorp Green as it was gradually revealed to her was lush and open—with tall poplars marking the boundaries of the fields, and the willowed Ouse winding lazily through the broad meadows—and very different from home. But though it lacked the grandeur and the strength to which she had been accustomed, it had a lyric charm to which her soul responded.

Except for a straggle of cottages up the lane, there were no habitations for two miles and no residents from whom Anne could seek companionship. Her employers were on calling terms with the other landowners in the district whose estates touched theirs ; but for the governess there was not even a village shop within walking distance where she could occasionally exchange a word with a fellow human being.

It was two miles from the Hall to the church at Little Ouseburn where the family worshipped, a distance she would much prefer to have gone on foot but was mostly obliged to drive with her employers, sitting back to the horses, a position which invariably made her sick and often spoiled the only hours in the week when her soul might be at peace.

In the little church of the Holy Trinity at Little Ouseburn she worshipped for over four years. One of the oldest in the country —portions of the tower date from Saxon times—it stands almost completely encircled by its hedge of yews, in the flat meadows bordering the stream which, rising as a tiny trickle only a mile away, has given its name not only to the place but to the River Ure, ten times its breadth, into which it flows, and which from there onwards is called the Ouse.

An indefinable atmosphere of antiquity pervades the little church, with its deep chancel window-recesses, narrow as arrow-slits, its Norman arch and unadorned stone walls, its homely proportions and sturdy character. It is the very antithesis of artifice, and beautiful with the beauty of simplicity. Within its walls, if any-where, Anne would find consolation for her lot.

As she settled down in her first term at Thorp Green Hall she discovered that not only was she *not* considered, as she had naïvely supposed, a "respectable, well-educated lady" by her employers, but she was excluded from the life of the family circle and from the circle of all their acquaintances as well. She was introduced to none of their neighbours and visitors, and, incredible as it may seem, was not even spoken to by any of the girls' acquaintances. Her task was to trail behind them when they walked with their friends ; to sit back to the horses, as we have seen, when they drove to church ; never to expect to be "handed in", as her much younger charges were by gentlemen wishing to make themselves agreeable, and, indeed, to be ignored as though she did not exist.

She has feelingly described her situation in *Agnes Grey*. On the occasions that her pupils chose to walk to and from church and she attended them "As none of the ladies and gentlemen [with whom they walked] ever noticed me, it was disagreeable to walk beside them, as if listening to what they said, or wishing to be thought one of them, while they talked over me, or across ; and if their eyes, in speaking, chanced to fall on me, it seemed as if they looked on vacancy—as if they either did not see me, or were very desirous to make it appear so."

It is impossible not to ask oneself what made her bear it. In the diary paper written on Emily's birthday at the end of July (in pursuance of the old childish pact to record chief family events every four years) she wrote : "I dislike my situation and wish to change it." She would very likely have done so then had not two considerations stayed her.

She got home for the holidays on Wednesday, 2nd June (Charlotte was still away at her post with the Whites) and was met by Emily with the news of a project then "hatching" at Haworth Parsonage, which was to fill her and Charlotte and Emily with great hopes for their immediate future. It was nothing less than the idea that they three should set up a school of their own. What gave the idea a solid basis was the fact that it originated with Miss Branwell and Mr Brontë, and that Miss Branwell declared herself disposed to lend them a little capital for a start.

Such a prospect—little glamorous as it might appear to young women today—filled the girls with rapture, for it would obviate once and for all the necessity of earning their living in other people's houses. Hard work it assuredly meant (they had the example of the Miss Woolers before their eyes), but work had never yet frightened them.

Throughout the summer and autumn of the year 1841 the mirage of the school project dazzled the eyes of the three sisters. "It is our Polar Star," wrote Charlotte, "and we look to it under all circumstances of despondency. . . ." Pending its realisation, what was to be gained by throwing up a situation which, however uncongenial, Anne argued with herself, was *certain* and, at the worst, need only be temporary ?

It brought with it, moreover, two very real compensations which she would have to seek in vain in another post. Thorp Green Hall was within easy distance of York Minster and the sea. To a girl with Anne's tastes there could not exist attractions superior to these ; indeed, nowhere away from home and its beloved inmates could she hope for stimuli more completely in accord with her temperament.

Returning home on 1st July from her post at the Whites, Charlotte found, to her keen disappointment, that Anne had come and gone and that all chance of seeing her that summer was over.

Charlotte would not have been Charlotte had she not protested at the tyranny of the Robinsons, who were curtailing Anne's legitimate holidays in order that she might accompany their children to the sea. Bitterly she wrote to Ellen Nussey : "I came home last night. . . . I have lost the chance of seeing Anne. She is gone back to 'the land of Egypt and the house of bondage'. . . ."

Charlotte need not have grieved. What Anne had gone back to was York Minster and the sea. No impact could, more completely, have suited her then predicament ; no impact was to have more lasting effects on her life.

We know that it was the vastness of York Minster—as it was the unbounded vista of ocean—which ravished her at the very first encounter. The sheer scale and magnitude of these works of God and man suited her needs as nothing less could, at that time, have done. They released her imprisoned spirit, suffering not *greatly* in a grand cause, but *meanly* under a succession of petty restrictions which she felt with intense alarm were gradually reducing all her faculties of heart and mind to a contemptible narrowness.

"I seemed to feel my intellect deteriorating," she writes in *Agnes Grey*. "My heart petrifying, my soul contracting : and I trembled lest my very moral perceptions should become deadened, my distinctions of right and wrong confounded, and all my better faculties be sunk . . . beneath the baleful influence of such a life."

At this identical juncture she saw the sea for the first time. It was high summer and the resort to which her employers annually repaired was Scarborough, then, far more than now, a place of incomparable natural beauty.

She saw, unencumbered by the accretions of a century of bad taste, the twin bays set in the clasp of almost perpendicular cliffs running in dramatic headlands out to sea; the scattered rocks covered with glistening weeds that seem lost on the horizon's verge in summer's haze ; the Castle, with its almost unbroken battlemented walls, towering above the promontory that divides the North Bay from the South ; the irregular huddled roofs of the old fishing village tumbling sheerly down the cliff-side like a succession of steep stone steps, their chimneys askew, their tarred and tilted sides an eloquent record of their great antiquity ; for Scarborough proudly boasts that it dates back in time before the Norman Conquest and owns still in a state of admirable preservation houses dating back to Richard III.

(2,056)

The Robinsons took furnished rooms in "the best part of the town", which in those days was considered to be that overlooking the South Bay—St Nicholas Cliff. This had been laid out during the Regency and had an air not only of architectural distinction but of social gaiety. Ever since the mid-seventeenth century, when a mineral spring had been discovered under the cliffs, this quarter of the town had been called "the Spa" and had been the resort of elegant society. "Assembly Rooms", providing concerts and balls throughout the season, a lending library and beautifully laid-out walks zig-zagging up and down the cliff-side—access to which was had by the relatively new "Toll" suspension bridge opened in 1828 and considered a feat of engineering—were so many features which made St Nicholas Cliff the very centre of attraction in Scarborough. The Cliff houses had, moreover, the advantage of commanding the very finest view of the sea that the town afforded. Built around a terrace high up on the cliff-side, at the very centre of the bay, at an equal distance from the Castle Hill to the north and the green headland that shuts in the bay from the south—sunshine flooded their windows all day long, and the unending pageant of the sea, lying far below, moved on from dawn to dusk and from dusk to dawn, for the delight of those who had the eyes to see.

Anne Brontë saw. Never, sufficiently, could she fill her eyes, her ears, her nostrils, all her senses, her heart, her mind, with the scintillating splendour of the scene. She saw the sea for the first time, lying beneath her like a living creature ; heaving, shifting, stirring, sighing, in endless motion and with endless murmur. Cerulean, roseate, pearly, opal—all the jewels of the New Jerusalem were in its shades. The sheer beauty of it was a revelation ; but how much more, its mystery and power ! The mere sight of the sea lifted her, bodily, out of the Slough of Despond into which she had fallen at Thorp Green.

She saw it now, looking down from the sitting-room window of their lodgings at the Cliff—and could no more regard it as an "element" than Emily could look on the hills of Haworth merely as heath and rock. She felt her whole being burst open by the onrush of an inexpressible emotion. It swept over her, filled her and flooded her as the oncoming tide floods the dual bays of Scarborough. Whatever she saw, she saw with the eyes of the spirit that bore through the superficial simulacra of things.

The heightened sense of being, the tingling excitement that

remained even after the first shock of encounter, told her how near atrophy all her powers had come in that first period at Thorp Green. The sea became the great restorative, physical and spiritual, towards which, in the darkest hours of her life, she looked as towards salvation. Following her pupils along the sands, accompanying them on their donkey-rides, she felt as she had not felt since the days of her care-free childhood. "Refreshed, delighted, invigorated," she writes, "I walked along, forgetting all my cares, feeling as if I had wings on my feet, and could go at least forty miles without fatigue, and experiencing a sense of exhilaration to which I had been an entire stranger since the days of early youth."

She loved the sea best when it was at its wildest, for hers was one of those still, quiet natures that quickens most to a powerful stimulus. ". . . the sea was my delight," she writes in *Agnes Grey*, "and I would often gladly pierce the town to obtain the pleasure of a walk beside it, whether with the pupils or alone. . . . It was delightful to me at all times and seasons, but especially in the wild commotion of a rough sea-breeze, and in the brilliant freshness of a summer morning."

In one of the best poems she ever wrote, where experience and expression were more truly matched than elsewhere in her unequal output, in the glorious "Lines Composed in a Wood on a Windy Day" written in the following year, she evokes that vision of the sea as the great liberator.

> My soul is awakened, my spirit is soaring
> And carried aloft on the wings of the breeze ;
> For above and around me the wild wind is roaring,
> Arousing to rapture the earth and the seas.
>
> The long withered grass in the sunshine is glancing,
> The bare trees are tossing their branches on high ;
> The dead leaves beneath them are merrily dancing,
> The white clouds are scudding across the blue sky.
>
> I wish I could see how the ocean is lashing
> The foam of its billows to whirlwinds of spray ;
> I wish I could see how its proud waves are dashing,
> And hear the wild roar of their thunder to-day !

There is no evidence to show that either her employers or her pupils revealed themselves in a more sympathetic light for the change of scene ; the contrary seems to have been the case. The tone of her diary paper written on Emily's birthday (30th July) in haste, and, one senses, in jaded spirits, betrays more than a little bitterness towards her employers. Its lack of hope strikes all the more forcibly by contrast with the buoyant tone of Emily's, written at the identical hour. The two letters are, moreover, almost identical in content.

EMILY BRONTË'S BIRTHDAY NOTE

A PAPER to be opened
when Anne is
25 years old,
or my next birthday after
if
all be well.

Emily Jane Brontë. July the 30th, 1841.

It is Friday evening—near 9 o'clock—wild rainy weather. I am seated in the dining-room, after having just concluded tidying our desk boxes—writing this document. Papa is in the parlour. Aunt upstairs in her room. She has been reading *Blackwood's Magazine* to papa. Victoria and Adelaide are ensconced in the peat-house. Keeper is in the kitchen. Hero in his cage. We are all stout and hearty, as I hope is the case with Charlotte, Branwell, and Anne, of whom the first is at John White, Esq., Upperwood House, Rawdon ; the second is at Luddenden Foot ; and the third is, I believe, at Scarborough, inditing perhaps a paper corresponding to this.

A scheme is at present in agitation for setting us up in a school of our own ; as yet nothing is determined, but I hope and trust it may go on and prosper and answer our highest expectations. This day four years I wonder whether we shall still be dragging on in our present condition or established to our hearts' content. Time will show—

I guess that at the time appointed for the opening of this paper—We, i.e. Charlotte, Anne, and I—shall be all merrily seated in our own sitting-room in some pleasant and flourishing seminary, having just gathered in for the mid-summer holidays. Our debts will be paid off and we shall have cash in hand to a considerable amount. Papa, aunt, and Branwell will either have been, or be coming—to visit us—It will be a fine warm summer evening, very different from this bleak look-out. Anne and I will perchance slip out into the garden for a few minutes to piruse [*sic*] our papers. I hope either this or something better will be the case—

The Gondalians are at present in a threatening state but there is no open rupture as yet—all the princes and princesses of the royaltys are at the Palace of Instruction. I have a good many books on hand, but I am sorry to say that—as usual I make small progress with any—however, I have just made a new regularity paper ! and I will *verb sap* to do great things—and now I close, sending from far an exhortation of courage, boys, courage, to exiled and harrassed [*sic*] Anne, wishing she was here.

ANNE BRONTË'S BIRTHDAY NOTE

July the 30th, A.D.1841

This is Emily's birthday. She has now completed her 23rd year, and is, I believe, at home. Charlotte is a governess in the family of Mr. White. Branwell is a clerk in the railroad station at Luddenden Foot, and I am a governess in the family of Mr. Robinson. I dislike the situation and wish to change it for another. I am now at Scarborough. My pupils are gone to bed and I am hastening to finish this before I follow them.

We are thinking of setting up a school of our own, but nothing definite is settled about it yet, and we do not know whether we shall be able to or not. I hope we shall. And I wonder what will be our condition and how or where we shall all be on this day four years hence ; at which time, if all be well, I shall be 25 years and 6 months old, Emily will be 27 years old, Branwell 28 years and 1 month, and Charlotte 29 years and a quarter. We are now all separate and not likely to meet again for many a weary week, but we are none of us ill that I know of, and all are doing something for our own livelihood except Emily, who, however, is as busy as any of us, and in reality earns her food and raiment as much as we do.

> How little know we what we are
> How less what we may be !

Four years ago I was at school. Since then I have been a governess at Blake Hall, left it, come to Thorp Green, and seen the sea and York Minster. Emily has been a teacher at Miss Patchet's school, and left it. Charlotte has left Miss Wooler's, been a governess at Mrs. Sidgwick's, left her, and gone to Mrs. White's. Branwell has given up painting, been a tutor in Cumberland, left it, and become a clerk on the railroad. Tabby has left us, Martha Brown has come in her place. We have got Keeper, got a sweet little cat and lost it, and also got a hawk. Got a wild goose which has flown away, and three tame ones, one of which has been killed. All these diversities, with many others, are things we did not expect or foresee in the July of 1837. What will the next four years bring forth ? Providence only knows. But we ourselves have sustained very little alteration since that time. I have the same faults that I had then, only I have more wisdom and experience, and a little more self-possession than I then enjoyed. How will it be when we open this paper and the one Emily has written ? I wonder whether the Gondaliand [sic] will still be flourishing, and what will be their condition. I am now engaged in writing the fourth volume of *Solala Vernon's Life*.

For some time I have looked upon 25 as a sort of era in my existence. It may prove a true presentiment, or it may be only a superstitious fancy ; the latter seems most likely, but time will show.

Anne Brontë

By the first week in August the family were back again at Thorp Green. Christmas was five months off, and until Christmas Anne must remain at her post—or forfeit a half-year's pay. She could neither hope for a visit from any of those she loved nor even for a free day in which to go home, as other governesses could do. It was too far and too expensive a journey for her to contemplate. No wonder reaction set in and that, after the elation of spirits she had known at Scarborough, a deep dejection should invade her. The only confidant she had was her own imagination ; the only relief she could find was in writing. "When we are harassed by sorrows or anxieties," she tells us in *Agnes Grey*, "or long oppressed by any powerful feelings, which we must keep to ourselves, for which we can obtain and seek no sympathy from any living creature, and which yet we cannot, or will not wholly crush, we often naturally seek relief in poetry . . . I still preserve those relics of past sufferings and experience, like pillars of witness set up in travelling through the vale of life, to mark particular occurrences. The footsteps are obliterated now ; the face of the country may be changed ; but the pillar is still there to remind me how all things were when it was reared."

The following two poems, written in this month of August, may, indeed, be classed among these "pillars of witness" to which Anne alludes.

For neither did she find other titles than "Lines Written at Thorp Green". The first was written on 19th August 1841.

> That summer sun, whose genial glow
> Now cheers my drooping spirit so,
> Must cold and silent be,
> And only light our northern clime
> With feeble ray, before the time
> I long so much to see. . . .
>
>   .   .   .   .   .   .
>
> And those bright flowers I love so well,
> Verbena, rose, and sweet bluebell,
> Must droop and die away ;
> Those thick, green leaves, with all their shade
> And rustling music, they must fade,
> And every one decay.
>
> But if the sunny summer time,
> And woods and meadows in their prime
> Are sweet to them that roam ;
> Far sweeter is the winter bare,
> With long, dark nights, and landscape drear,
> To them that are at Home !
>
> (Signed : A.B., August 19, 1841)

In the second, written nine days later, she does not hide that
there was a particular as well as a general cause for her dejection.
Signed with her own name, the poem is quite obviously not one
of the Gondal sequence and unmistakably refers to the secret buried
in her heart since the beginning of that year. Posthumously, this
poem was published under the title "Appeal".

> O ! I am very weary
> Though tears no longer flow ;
> My eyes are tired of weeping,
> My heart is sick of woe ;
>
> My life is very lonely,
> My days pass heavily,
> I'm weary of repining,
> Wilt thou not come to me ?
>
> Oh, didst thou know my longings
> For thee, from day to day,
> My hopes, so often blighted,
> Thou wouldst not thus delay !
>
> Signed : Anne Brontë, August 28, 1841

While Anne was looking towards Christmas as the longed-for
period of her release, a similar though far less passive impatience
was agitating Charlotte throughout the autumn of that year. Could
Anne but have suspected what the upshot of it was to be, her
dejection would have degenerated into despair. For Charlotte was
planning nothing less than for herself and Emily to go abroad.

The school-project, first launched by Papa and Aunt, had, within
a very few weeks of its inception, passed through a number of
modifications. From a vague idea it had taken concrete shape.
Miss Wooler, advised of it, had offered Dewsbury Moor (already
abandoned by Miss Eliza), complete with furniture, as a starting-
ground for the novice schoolmistresses. Charlotte, from her head-
quarters at the Whites' at Rawdon, had written of this offer to her
sisters. However much she was to turn against it shortly afterwards
("Dewsbury Moor . . . is an obscure and dreary place—not
adapted for a school") she accepted it now. It was, she considered,
"a decent, friendly proposal on Miss Wooler's part", and one that
cancelled "all or most of her little foibles in my estimation".
(Charlotte had not yet forgotten or forgiven Miss Wooler's obtuse-
ness in the matter of Anne's health.) But before any definite

conclusion could be reached between the Miss Woolers on the one
hand and the Miss Brontës on the other, a prospect opened before
Charlotte which rendered all others insignificant by comparison.

The Taylor girls, who had lost their father in January, had gone
to Belgium, where they had relations, Martha to a school in Brussels
and Mary, during the summer holidays, to join her in a tour of the
Continent. On Mary's return she wrote Charlotte a letter of such
rousing advice that Charlotte knew no rest until she followed it.
It was to the effect that if Charlotte and her sisters planned to open
a school of their own, they had far better begin by qualifying themselves adequately for the part. The first requisite to any boarding-
school was a Principal well furnished in languages. Let Charlotte
first of all perfect herself in French, Italian and German ; to which
end Brussels, as a cultural centre of exceptional distinction (and
cheapness), was the very best place she could go to and one,
moreover, where Mary and Martha Taylor could shepherd her and
facilitate both her studies and her stay. Charlotte had always
respected Mary Taylor's practical good sense ; in this particular it
coincided with that of her present employers, Mr and Mrs White,
who interested themselves in her plans to set up school and warmly
seconded the suggestion to study abroad.

But it was not Mary Taylor's good sense nor the Whites' that
really influenced Charlotte. In a poignant letter to Ellen Nussey
she confessed what were the true motives directing her course.
Only a creative artist could have felt or understood these ; only a
genius could have followed them with so unfaltering a flair.

"I have had a long letter from Mary," she wrote to Ellen on
7th August. ". . . Mary's letter spoke of some of the pictures and
cathedrals she had seen—pictures the most exquisite and cathedrals
the most venerable. I hardly know what swelled in my throat as
I read her letter ; such a vehement impatience of restraint and
steady work ; such a strong wish for wings—wings such as wealth
can furnish ; such an earnest thirst to see, to know, to learn ;
something internal seemed to expand boldly for a minute. I was
tantalised with the consciousness of faculties unexercised ; then all
collapsed and I despaired. . . . These rebellious and absurd
emotions were only momentary ; I quelled them in five minutes.
I hope they will not revive, for they were acutely painful."

They did, of course, revive, as they were bound to do, and gave
Charlotte no respite from their promptings either night or day.

How quickly the small seed stirred, shot up and flowered can be judged by the following letter she wrote to her aunt on 29th September. By then, it is quite clear, she had made up her mind.

After referring to the plan to take over Miss Wooler's school, she proceeds : "Meantime a plan has been suggested and approved by Mr and Mrs White [Charlotte's then employers] and others, which I wish now to impart to you. My friends recommend me, if I desire to secure permanent success, to delay commencing the school for six months longer, and by all means to contrive . . . to spend the intervening time in some school on the Continent. They say schools in England are so numerous, competition so great, that without some such step towards attaining superiority we shall probably have a very hard struggle, and may fail in the end. They say, moreover, that the loan of £100, which you have been so kind as to offer us, will, perhaps, not be all required now, as Miss Wooler will lend us the furniture ; and that, if the speculation is intended to be a good and successful one, half the sum, at least, ought to be laid out in the manner I have mentioned. . . . I would not go to France or to Paris. I would go to Brussels in Belgium. The cost of the journey there, at the dearest rate of travelling, would be £5 ; living is there little more than half as dear as it is in England, and the facilities of education are equal or superior to any other place in Europe. In half a year, I could acquire a thorough familiarity with French. I could improve greatly in Italian, and even get a dash of German. . . . Martha Taylor is now staying in Brussels . . . if I wrote to her, she, with the assistance of Mrs Jenkins [wife of the British Chaplain in Brussels] would be able to secure me a cheap and decent residence and respectable protection . . . and, with the assistance of her cousins, I should . . . be introduced to connections far more improving, polished, and cultivated, than any I have yet known.

"These are advantages which would turn to vast account when we actually commenced school—and, if Emily could share them with me, only for a single half-year, we could take a footing in the world afterwards which we can never do now. I say Emily instead of Anne ; for Anne might take her turn at some future period. . . . I feel certain . . . that you will see the propriety of what I say ; you always like to use your money to the best advantage ; you are not fond of making shabby purchases ; when you do confer a favour, it is often done in style ; and depend upon it £50, or £100, thus laid out, would be well employed. . . . Papa will perhaps think it a wild and ambitious scheme ; but who ever rose in the world without ambition ? When he left Ireland to go to Cambridge University, he was as ambitious as I am now. I want us *all* to go on. I know we have talents, and I want them to be turned to account. I look to you, aunt, to help us. I think you will not refuse. I know, if you consent, it shall not be my fault if you ever repent your kindness. . . ."

She was certain of Aunt's support. Those allusions to "connections far more improving, polished and cultivated" were calculated, she knew, to appeal to the maiden lady from Penzance who had always deplored the uncouth society in which the death of her sister had obliged her to live and her nieces to grow up. Charlotte never wrote a more diplomatic letter in her life. Even Mr Brontë's objections were neutralised from the outset by a reminder of the feelings with which he had left his native Ireland to go to Cambridge.

The plan could not appeal to either Emily or Anne. To Emily it meant exile, with all that that entailed of misery, sickness, frustration ; to Anne it meant a loneliness even greater than that under which she was sinking now. Yet, evidently, neither girl complained. Charlotte went ahead with her plans for Brussels, communicated the results when they were achieved, "exhorting all to hope", as though her dearest wish were that of her sisters too.

On 7th November Charlotte wrote to Emily from Rawdon : "Dear E-J. You are not to suppose that this note is written with a view of communicating any information on the subject we both have considerably at heart. I have written letters [re schools and accommodation in Brussels] but I have received no letters in reply yet. Belgium is a long way off, and people are everywhere hard to spur up to the proper speed. Mary Taylor says we can scarcely expect to get off before January. . . ."

By the New Year she intended them to be gone. Quite obviously Emily had pointed out how the scheme, as outlined by Charlotte, seemed to ignore Anne.

"Anne seems omitted in the present plan," Charlotte goes on to explain to Emily, "but if all goes right I trust she will derive her full share of benefit from it in the end. I exhort all to hope. . . ."

Emily had, moreover, also pointed out that, of the various plans in agitation from the outset, that of taking over Miss Wooler's school would have had the great advantage of uniting instead of separating them. "Grieve not over Dewsbury Moor," Charlotte urges her. "You were cut out there to all intents and purposes, so in fact was Anne ; Miss Wooler would hear of neither for the first half-year."

Strangely enough, at the very time when first Charlotte was inflamed with the desire to go to Brussels, she was acutely sensible of Anne's predicament. In the very letter in which she opened her heart to Ellen about her longing for "wings" she wrote : "I have one aching feeling at my heart ; it is about Anne. She has so much to endure ; far, far more than I have. When my thoughts turn to her they always see her as a patient, persecuted stranger. I know what concealed susceptibility is in her nature when her feelings are wounded. I wish I could be with her to administer a little balm. She is more lonely, less gifted with the power of making friends, even than I am."

The whole summer of 1841 her concern for Anne had been intense. Defrauded of a sight of her at the outset of the holidays she had written to Ellen : "I should like to see her to judge for myself of the state of her health. . . . I cannot trust anyone else's report, no one seems minute enough in their observations. I should also very much have liked you to see her. . . ." Yet, in the letter of 7th November to Emily, Charlotte made her intention plain. "Before our half-year in Brussels is completed, you and I will have to seek employment abroad. It is not my intention to retrace my steps home till twelve months, if all continues well and we and those at home retain good health."

As Christmas approached and the time drew near for Anne's return and her own and Emily's departure for the Continent, the sense of having done her duty by all was uppermost in her excited mind. "I believe in my heart," she wrote to Emily, concluding her arrangements for going abroad, "that this is acting for the best."

Chapter Fourteen

MR WESTON

DURING her absence Charlotte counted that Anne would remain at home, but was well aware how inadequate to help her was little Martha Brown, aged thirteen, the family's only servant in Tabby's prolonged absence. "How will Anne get on with Martha?" Charlotte had anxiously written Emily before returning home for the holidays. Anne could not do as Emily had done all the past year : take on herself all the most arduous duties—baking, washing and ironing—no sinecures, these, in days when no bread was bought and not an article of linen laundered outside the house. Charlotte well knew that Anne's physical strength had never been equal to such tasks. For some time Anne had known it also, and that was one of the reasons why she imposed on herself the less congenial task of going out to work.

Charlotte got home from Rawdon on Christmas Eve and found Anne there. The last impedimenta to the Brussels journey had now been cleared away. She and Emily were going to a school, the Pensionnat Heger, recommended by the British Chaplain in Brussels, which was the most economical and certain way of advancing their studies in languages and music.

Mr Brontë was to accompany his daughters as far as Brussels and the whole party would be travelling with Mary and Joe Taylor, who knew the ropes. Bliss unbounded seemed to attend the whole enterprise. Only the date of departure remained to be fixed. In the end they did not start till 8th February. The intervening holidays were not too long for all Charlotte and Emily had to do.

Branwell was expected home over the Christmas holidays, a circumstance delightful in itself to Charlotte, who refused an invitation to Ellen Nussey's to ensure seeing him. He had "never been at home for the last five months," Charlotte wrote, and she could not tell when she would see him again. As it turned out he only came for a week-end in the middle of January. How much he told and how much he suppressed of his miserable existence at Luddendenfoot does not appear. To Charlotte and Emily his transfer from Sowerby Bridge to Luddendenfoot in the previous

autumn had appeared like a promotion ; it would seem that he
did not disillusion them on the eve of their journey to Brussels.
No one at home could have a true idea of the conditions in which
he lived and under which he was supposed to work. His only
confidant at that time, his new friend Francis Grundy, the railway
engineer, has thus described them. "Had a position been chosen
for this strange creature for the express purpose of driving him
several steps to the bad, this must have been it. Alone, in the wilds
of Yorkshire, with few books, little to do, no prospects, and
wretched pay, with no society congenial to his better tastes, but
plenty of wild, rollicking, hard-headed, half-educated manufacturers,
who would welcome him to their houses, and drink with him as
often as he chose to come, what was this morbid man, who couldn't
bear to be alone, to do ?"

Branwell's plight, in which Anne was to intervene with such
momentous consequences to herself and her brother, was not recognised this Christmas of 1841 to be the desperate thing it was. He
seems to have returned to his post at Luddendenfoot, leaving his
sisters unenlightened as to his true situation and free to enjoy the
remainder of their holidays at home.

Charlotte, urging Ellen Nussey to spend a few days with them
at Haworth, added, as an irresistible bait : "Mr Weightman is still
here, just the same as ever. I have a curiosity to see a meeting
between you and him. He will be again desperately in love, I am
convinced. . . .

"His 'young reverence', as you tenderly call him," she continues, "is looking delicate and pale ; poor thing, don't you pity
him ? I do, from my heart ! When he is well and fat and jovial,
I never think of him but when anything ails him I am always sorry.
He sits opposite to Anne at Church, sighing softly, and looking out
of the corners of his eyes to win her attention, and Anne is so quiet,
her look so downcast, they are a picture."

The fact that Charlotte could draw this "picture" for her friend's
amusement is evidence enough that she saw nothing in Anne's
downcast look either now or earlier to give her any insight into
her feelings. Willy Weightman, even when openly sighing for
Anne, was no different from what he had ever been, in Charlotte's
opinion ; if his volatile fancy had any object, it was Ellen Nussey,
with whom, she still stoutly declared, he would again be
"desperately in love".

With no evidence surviving other than that left by Charlotte, whose blindness to what was going on around her was thus complete, how is one to understand the resolution taken by Anne at this identical juncture to return to her position at Thorp Green ?

Everything seemed to militate against it. Her own firm resolution on leaving the Robinsons at Christmas ; her sisters' departure for Brussels, leaving Aunt and Papa in need of her at home ; on the face of it Anne's duty seemed to lie in Haworth.

If Charlotte's "picture" of Willy Weightman in church was correct, not only Anne's duty but her pleasure lay in Haworth. On no previous occasion had Willy Weightman been reported to have turned his attentions so openly to her.

The lines in *Agnes Grey* which Anne says "owed their being to a passion of grief" would seem to suggest that she had felt a positive opposition at work.

> Oh, they have robbed me of the hope
> My spirit held so dear ;
> They will not let me hear that voice
> My soul delights to hear.
>
> They will not let me see that face
> I so delight to see ;
> And they have taken all thy smiles
> And all thy love from me.
>
> Well, let them seize on all they can :
> One treasure still is mine—
> A heart that loves to think on thee
> And feels the worth of thine.

Who, one would like to know, were the "they" of this poem ? Papa, Aunt, Charlotte ?

The one certainty we have is that her motive in fleeing Willy Weightman was not doubt of his integrity. In whatever light Charlotte may have seen him, Anne believed him to have been worthy not only of the world's esteem but of her love. This thought was the only consolation she could lay to her wounded heart. "Yes, at least, they could not deprive me of that," she says in *Agnes Grey*. "I could think of him day and night ; and I could feel that he was worthy to be thought of. Nobody knew him as I did ; nobody could appreciate him as I did ; nobody could love him as I—could, if I might : but there was the evil. What business had I to think so much of one that never thought of me? Was it not foolish? was it not wrong? Yet, if I found such deep delight in thinking of him, and if I kept these thoughts to myself, and troubled no one else with them, where was the harm of it?"

Since Willy Weightman did not declare himself—or could not declare himself—there was no help for it but to mask "the secret changes" of her soul (as she had written earlier that year) and behave as though she felt nothing. "I was a close and resolute dissembler," she writes in *Agnes Grey*, "—in this one case at least. My prayers, my tears, my wishes, fears and lamentations, were witnessed by myself and Heaven alone."

To Charlotte and the rest of the family, Anne gave as a reason for her return to Thorp Green that the Robinsons had overpersuaded her. "Anne has rendered herself so valuable in her difficult situation," wrote Charlotte to Ellen just before going to Brussels, "that they have entreated her to return to them if it be but for a short time. I almost think she will go back, if we can get a good servant who will do all our work."

What Anne felt about that return to Thorp Green she only fully confessed three years later. Writing in 1845 and looking back over the last four years, she says: ". . . I was then at Thorp Green, and now I am only just escaped from it. I was wishing to leave it then, and if I had known that I had four years longer to stay how wretched I should have been. . . ." Luckily the future into which she and Emily guilelessly peered with every diary paper remained hidden from her; she could not guess that after 1842 there would no longer be any powerful reason why she should not remain at Thorp Green, nor that there should exist one valid one, at least, why she should do so.

She returned to Thorp Green just before Charlotte and Emily and Papa set out for Brussels on 8th February 1842. The services of Martha's younger sister Hannah, a little girl of ten, had been secured as auxiliary at the parsonage, where she remained until the following year.

Anne could not hope to hear much from Brussels or write often herself; letter postage cost eighteenpence. On 26th March Charlotte wrote home that they had "got into a good school and were considerably comfortable," hard at work, as they had meant to be,

and making progress. As far as Anne could foresee, no change in
their several situations could be hoped for a year. The long
monotonous weeks stretched unrelieved ahead.

The only outlet she had was in her writing. However scant her
hours of leisure she had obviously, from her first year at Thorp
Green, spent them in composition, as the diary paper of the previous
July showed ; she had just finished writing the "fourth volume of
the life of Solala Vernon". The only definite thing we know
about Solala Vernon is that she belonged to "Gondaliand". The
four volumes of her "life" have not come down to us but,
presumably, they were, like all the rest of the Gondal Saga, written
in verse.

To Anne's return to Thorp Green in the new year, 1842, we can
fairly confidently ascribe the beginnings of a prose story which was
to mark a complete change from all her preceding work, not only
in medium but in style and character, substituting realism for
romance, fact for fiction. Called "Passages in the Life of an
Individual"—the new work was nothing short of an attempt at
autobiography—it was a faithful and minutely exact account of her
experiences as governess at Blake Hall to begin with, followed by
an account of her years at Thorp Green. Interrupted as its composition would be by the successive events of the next three years, its
character would suffer several changes—its liveliness, alas, be subdued by sorrow—and even its name be altered before it was finally
given to the world as *Agnes Grey*. By the inner evidence of this
"mirror of the author's mind" (as Charlotte was to call it later) we
can learn a very great deal about Anne's inner life at that time, as
well as about the outward circumstances that shaped it.

She was twenty-two, deeply feeling, yearning not only to receive
but to give affection and cut off from all the sources of happiness
that she prized. Driven within herself there was nothing left for
her but to observe the little world in which she moved. She was
naturally observant, penetrating beyond her years ; what she now
saw would serve not only in the present book but essentially in
The Tenant of Wildfell Hall when the time came, to portray with
absolute verisimilitude the country-house life with its intrigues,
monotonies, meannesses and snobberies that were so alien to her
soul. Charlotte might later say that such themes were strangers to
her nature, yet for over four years they were the daily diet on which
she had to subsist.

1 (*left*). Haworth Parsonage

2 (*below*). Miss Elizabeth Branwell

3 (*left*). Anne and Emily Brontë,
from the painting by Branwell Brontë

4 (*above*). Anne Brontë,
from the water-colour by Charlotte Brontë

5. Drawing by Anne Brontë, signed and dated 13th November 1839

6 (*above*). Thorp Green Hall, rear view

7 (*opposite*). Sladen Valley Waterfall

8. St Nicholas Cliff, Scarborough

9. The Museum, Cliff Bridge and Wood's Lodgings, Scarborough

What she lacked most of all in the absence of all human sympathy was the stimulus of minds akin to hers. "Never, from month to month, from year to year, except during my brief intervals of rest at home, did I see one creature to whom I could open my heart," she writes in *Agnes Grey*, "or freely speak my thoughts with any hope of sympathy, or even comprehension. . . . Never a new idea or stirring thought came to me from without ; and such as rose within me were, for the most part, miserably crushed at once, or doomed to sicken and fade away, because they could not see the light." The longing for companionship, had it just been of a general abstract nature as formerly, would have been bad enough but it was aggravated now by the enforced separation from the man she loved. In a poem written at this time, which she called "The Captive Dove", she describes how even confinement and loneliness could be made bearable were they shared by a loved companion. Her situation was aggravated by the sense of "wasted faculties"—not as Charlotte had understood the term at the time—but in the sense that irrevocably, in her case :

> The heart that Nature formed to love
> Must pine, neglected and alone.

It was inevitable that the result of so introspective a life should deepen the despondency into which her adverse circumstances cast her.

A depression akin to that out of which the Moravian minister at Roe Head had argued her weighed down upon that "concealed susceptibility" of which Charlotte had written, and bore her spirit to the ground. The morbid sense of sin, too deeply instilled in childhood to be entirely eradicated, returned to trouble the serenity of her faith in God. She suffered the double onslaught now of doubt of her own worthiness and doubt of divine compassion.

The following poems, written at the time of her return to Thorp Green, are very representative of these dual states. In "Despondency" she arraigns herself at the bar of her conscience with all her sins mustered against her and not one mitigating circumstance in her favour. It is a cry out of the deep.

> I have gone backward in the work,
> The labour has not sped ;
> Drowsy and dark my spirit lies,
> Heavy and dull as lead.

How can I rouse my sinking soul
From such a lethargy ?
How can I break these iron chains
And set my spirit free ?

.   .   .   .   .

My sins increase, my love grows cold,
And Hope within me dies ;
And Faith itself is wavering now ;
Oh, how shall I arise ?

I cannot weep, but I can pray,
Then let me not despair ;
Lord Jesus, save me, lest I die ;
Christ, hear my humble prayer !

In the lines written "In Memory of a Happy Day in February"
the rapture poured into her soul by the beauty of an early spring
day was suddenly transformed into a knowledge of God—of His
meaning and of His purpose—which completely lifted from her all
sense of fear, all sense of remoteness. In that moment of revelation
she knew that God was hers, and she His in a union that nothing
could sever.

In Memory of a Happy Day in February

Blessed be Thou for all the joy
My soul has felt to-day !
O let its memory stay with me
And never pass away !

I was alone, for those I loved
Were far away from me ;
The sun shone on the withered grass,
The wind blew fresh and free.

Was it the smile of early spring
That made my bosom glow ?
'Twas sweet, but neither sun nor wind
Could raise my spirit so.

.   .   .   .   .

It was a glimpse of truths divine
Unto my Spirit given,
Illumined by a ray of light
That shone direct from Heaven !

I felt there was a God on high
By whom all things were made ;
I saw His wisdom and His power
In all His works displayed.

.   .   .   .

Deep secrets of His providence
In darkness long concealed,
Unto the vision of my soul
Were graciously revealed.

And while I wondered and adored
His majesty divine,
I did not tremble at His power,
I felt that God was mine. . . .

When Anne got home in the midsummer of 1842 for the vacation she found Branwell there. Whether letters had prepared her for the fact or no, she found that he had been dismissed from his post. In all the chances and changes of Branwell's chequered life, so far he had never been subjected to the ignominy of dismissal. He had invariably "dismissed" himself. The fact in itself was wounding to the family pride, but the circumstances attending it were incomparably worse. The Railway Company had discovered that they were being defrauded at Luddendenfoot Station, and though investigation exonerated Branwell from the main charge, as stationmaster he was held responsible for his subordinate's offence. As his friend Grundy reported later, "Brontë was not suspected of the theft himself, but was convicted of constant carelessness. . . ." The fact was that Branwell was constantly leaving his post for days together and going off "carousing with congenial drinkers" while the one and only porter at Luddendenfoot Station was left in charge of the office and helped himself liberally out of the Company's till. The result was that not only was Branwell dismissed but he could never again hope for a job with the railways.

He had, now, successively tried his hand at four careers : as a painter, an author, a teacher and a clerk ; and had failed in all four of them. The only one for which he was truly fitted—that of portrait painter—he had thrown away as carelessly as all the rest. No work seemed congenial to him, although his vanity inclined him most to the career of letters. He arrived home in May 1842 a disgraced and a profoundly miserable man.

It was at this juncture that the friendship of Willy Weightman, begun nearly three years ago, came to his rescue. With Willy Weightman, at least, he need not play a part. With only his father and Miss Branwell at home his loneliness would have been complete, since to neither of them could he confide his wretchedness. Willy Weightman, as he said afterwards, was to prove one of the best friends he ever had. The other one was Anne.

Branwell, who has found such scant sympathy among the biographers of his sisters, was yet, it is too often overlooked, adored by them all. Even at his most degraded he was cast off only by Charlotte, who, having loved him best from early childhood, was the most disillusioned by his failure. His vivid personality, so different from all the girls, made him loved in spite of everything. There was, even at his most dissolute, a childish side to his nature, a warmth of affection, a naïve hankering after goodness, which was very appealing. "Poor, brilliant, gay, moody, moping, wildly excitable, miserable Brontë !" wrote his friend Grundy in after years. "No History records your many struggles after the Good. Your wit, brilliance, attractiveness, eagerness for excitement . . ."

No one would have been more touched than Anne by his "many struggles after the Good" ; no one would have helped him to reach after it more than she. No one, unless it were Willy Weightman.

For a short time, during those summer weeks, Anne Brontë and Willy Weightman worked side by side with a common purpose. At most Anne can have been at home a month ; possibly it was only three weeks, since the Robinsons would, as always, have exacted her attendance at Scarborough for a portion of the holidays.

Long or short, the period of growing familiarity with Willy Weightman must be measured by results, not by the calendar. It sufficed to feed her emotional life to the end.

If she had loved Willy Weightman before for his general goodness to the poor and tiresome, she had an excuse now for loving him still more for his goodness to Branwell. Branwell, in his one person, was more tiresome than the whole village of Haworth put together. He fluctuated between collapse and bravado ; between despair and truculence. In the one mood, he refused to make any effort at all and went about unshaven and unwashed, looking like a scarecrow; in the other, his pretensions were still colossal and he considered no post good enough for him. The only career still possible for him would have been to " go for a soldier ". He toyed with the idea for a few weeks that summer, but never seriously entertained it ; the hardships were rather too real for this dreamer.

In this plight Willy Weightman was the ideal companion for him. His sanguine temperament acted like a tonic upon Branwell ; his goodness was not of that overbearing kind that widens the gulf between the good and the unfortunate ; he could take his stand with the latter and not be lowered. Willy Weightman was hardy, too, and with him Branwell could walk on the moors, take a shot at the grouse, drink a few pints without being made to feel inferior as when he did these same things with some of his shadier village cronies. With Willy Weightman, Branwell could talk as with an intellectual equal, for Willy Weightman knew what good was in him and brought it out, so that Branwell would leave him not diminished in his own esteem but raised. Had Willy Weightman remained curate of Haworth over the next crucial years, Branwell's fate would have been very different.

When Anne left her brother to return to her post at Thorp Green it need have been with no forebodings of disaster. Thanks to Willy Weightman, Branwell's mental balance was in as fair a way to being restored as it could ever be again, and it is more than probable that she already saw a clear way ahead for helping Branwell in the immediate future. If all else failed and no way of earning his living offered, she thought she could secure a post for him with the Robinsons at Thorp Green as tutor to young Edmund.

That Anne contemplated recommending her brother for the post and, in the event, carried his nomination through, is a measure of her lasting belief in him. For, if one thing is more certain than another, Anne's integrity would not have allowed her to push Branwell if she had doubted either his capacity or his moral rectitude.

Charlotte and Emily had decided against returning home at the end of their first "half" abroad. "Madame Heger has made a proposal for both me and Emily to stay another half-year," Charlotte wrote home in July, "offering to dismiss her English master and to take me as English teacher ; also to employ Emily some part of each day in teaching music. . . . For these services we are to be allowed to continue our studies in French and German, and to have board, etc. without paying for it. . . . The proposal is kind and . . . I am inclined to accept it. . . ." Mary Taylor, commenting on the girls' decision to stay abroad, wrote herself from Brussels : "Charlotte and Emily are well, not only in health, but in mind and hope. They are content in their present position and even gay and I think they do quite right not to return to England."

Papa and Aunt, apparently, thought so also and gave their authorisation. When Anne returned to her post at Thorp Green the prospect of seeing either Charlotte or Emily had receded for another six months at least. But, in six months, who knows what might not happen ?

At this particular juncture Anne Brontë's prospects might be said to be brighter than at any period since her childhood : and not fallaciously so. If we may—and we must—believe the evidence of *Agnes Grey*, Willy Weightman had allowed a subtle change to appear even in his outward bearing towards her during those last weeks in Haworth. Whatever it had been in the past, it was no self-delusion now. She felt the approach of love as unerringly as birds feel spring in the air. Impalpable, untraceable as the portents might be to any sense, yet they were unmistakable to her soul. She allowed herself, those sunny days of August by the sea, the sweet solace of day-dreaming ; of believing in what she wished ; of living, in anticipation, the happiness of which she felt her heart so truly capable. She was twenty-two years old ; if not at that age, when is it permissible to hope ? "Who can tell," said Agnes Grey within herself, "Who can tell what this one month may bring forth ? I have lived nearly three and twenty years, and I have suffered much, and tasted little pleasure yet ; is it likely my life *all* through will be so clouded ? is it possible that God may hear my prayers, disperse those gloomy shadows, and grant me some beams of heaven's sunshine yet ?"

At parting from her, Willy Weightman had " not breathed a word of love" or "dropped one hint of tenderness or affection"— as in the person of Agnes Grey she acknowledges—and yet she had been "supremely happy". He had had to speak low to prevent the bystanders from overhearing what he said, but the pressure of his hand had seemed to say "Trust me." There had been "other things besides—too delightful, almost too flattering, to be repeated even to one's self. . . ." She checked these fancies with a tart reminder of how her "unamiable reserve" and her "foolish diffidence" must make her appear "cold, dull, awkward and perhaps ill-tempered too" to the man she loved. With a touching naïveté she set about trying to improve her looks. "I may as well acknowledge," she writes in *Agnes Grey*, "that about this time, I paid more attention to dress than ever I had done before. This is not saying much ; for hitherto I had been a little neglectful in that particular ; but now, also, it was no uncommon thing to spend as much as two minutes in the contemplation of my own image in the glass ; though I never could derive any consolation from such a study. I could discover no beauty in those marked features, that pale hollow cheek, and ordinary dark brown hair ; there might be intellect in the forehead, there might be expression in the dark grey eyes : but what of that ?"

The sands of Scarborough which, on all idle occasions, she sought out to exercise her eager mind and body, were the only confidant she knew. Early morning and late into the sunset, whenever her duties allowed, she hurried down to the shore, certain to find in its serene expanse a reassurance for her boundless love.

With early September the family returned to Thorp Green. In the absence of Charlotte and Emily, prolonged now of a certainty to the next summer, Anne had greater need than ever before of a sustaining comfort. She lived upon the promise of her love. Four months stretched before her to Christmas and the next holiday at home, and that encounter which she looked on now as the realisation of her fondest dreams.

As with all dreams, the awakening was as sudden as it was cruel. Early in September a letter from home told her that Willy Weightman had died on the sixth after exactly a fortnight's illness ; of that scourge only too prevalent at Haworth, cholera.

It is very improbable that Anne received any warning letter to tell her even that he was ill. Branwell, her most likely correspondent, was himself so taken up with watching by his friend's bedside that he probably never had the time to prepare her for what might happen. He had no inkling, any more than the other members of the family, of Anne's feelings for Willy Weightman.

Mr Brontë visited his curate twice a day during his illness. In the sermon which he preached at his funeral service he spoke with judgment and regard of his character, and with some little feeling of his end. The sermon which he had printed for the benefit of his parishioners would tell Anne all she was likely to hear for many weeks to come of that end about which she did not trust herself to inquire. "Notwithstanding all that medical skill, the prayers and good wishes of friends, the tender affections of relations and the careful attention of nurses could do," said Mr Brontë, "our friend is gone the way of all flesh, and the people and places which knew him once, shall know him no more."

Mr Brontë was present at his death, and "saw him in tranquillity close his eyes on this bustling, vain, selfish world ; so that," he added, he "could truly say his end was peace and his hope glory."

Willy Weightman had, in the words of Mr Brontë, "run a bright but short career". He was but twenty-eight years old when he died.

Not a word of Anne's sorrow has reached us either in letter or verse of that time. Not for two years would she be able to find her voice, to face her grief and express it, as finally she did, in the truest poetry she ever wrote. It would take years to attain that percipience by which the greatest loss may yet be turned to gain, and to wring from a blinding sorrow the faith to see and the courage to endure. Not for five years would she be able to accept what had befallen her and in regained serenity declare :

> Life seems more sweet that thou didst live,
> And men more true that thou wert one ;
> Nothing is lost that thou didst give,
> Nothing destroyed that thou hast done.

But the intervening silence was not, for all that, any the less charged with intensest suffering. In great grief the mind is not alert enough to register what the heart feels ; a lethargy lies over all ; a frost, as of blighting winter, petrifies the sense. But the thaw, when it comes overnight, releases the emotions as mountain torrents are released by spring. Either a rare and beautiful flowering follows—as in Anne's case—or the very impetuosity of the flood obliterates the land. "Severed and gone, so many years," she would come to write, "And art thou still so dear to me . . . ?"

> . . . For ever gone ! for I, by night
> Have prayed within my silent room
> That Heaven would grant a burst of light
> Its cheerless darkness to illume,
> And give thee to my longing eyes,
> A moment, as thou shinest now,
> Fresh from thy mansion in the skies
> With all its glory on thy brow. . . .

The intolerable longing, the unanswered prayer of those silent years would find no other appeasement but in being voiced—at last.

In that first October her suffering was mute. The bald facts of his illness and death and burial were all she knew. Branwell may have expatiated in a second letter, for his grief was genuine, his sense of loss entire. It is reported that sitting in the old family pew in Haworth Church, from which he had been absent for so long, he sobbed throughout the funeral of his friend.

Even so, on that 10th September, when they buried Willy Weightman, Branwell could not have imagined how soon he was to sustain another loss. With a strange recurrence death never came to the Brontë family in "single spies, but in battalions". When Maria had died, Elizabeth had shortly followed after. Willy Weightman was scarcely buried under the flagstones of the old church when Miss Branwell fell mortally sick, not of the same contagion but of an "intestinal obstruction" which, in the course of a fortnight, ended fatally too.

Branwell, reeling under the double blow, wrote distractedly to his friend Grundy : "I have had a long attendance at the death-bed of the Rev. Mr Weightman, one of my dearest friends, and now I am attending at the death-bed of my aunt, who has been for twenty years as my mother. I expect her to die in a few hours." Four days later he wrote : "I am incoherent, I fear, but I have been waking two nights witnessing such agonising suffering as I would not wish my worst enemy to endure ; and I have now lost the guide and director of all the happy days connected with my childhood. . . ."

As an excuse for not having written earlier to his friend, Branwell mentioned that "all his sisters being from home" everything in connection with his aunt's death had devolved on him.

In the case of Miss Branwell, Anne had been advised of her illness and her immediate presence at home had been requested. Mrs Robinson at first withheld her consent ; what was worse, she withheld the news of Miss Branwell's illness for several hours, so that, when Anne finally received it, and acted upon it with energy it was too late. By the time she reached Haworth Miss Branwell was already dead.

An echo of the scene played out between employer and

governess on this occasion can be found in *Agnes Grey* where news
of the illness of the heroine's father caused her, like Anne, to ask
for immediate permission to go home. ". . . immediately I sought
permission to anticipate the vacation and go without delay. Mrs
Murray stared, and wondered at the unwonted energy and boldness
with which I urged the request, and thought there was no occasion
to hurry ; but finally gave me leave, stating, however, that there
was 'no need to be in such agitation about the matter—it might
prove a false alarm after all ; and if not—why, it was only in the
common course of nature ; we must all die some time ; and I was
not to suppose myself the only afflicted person in the world'." The
lady concluded ungraciously enough by saying that she could have
the phaeton to take her to York, and added, as a parting shot, that
she ought to be *thankful* for the privileges she enjoyed, and not
repine.

That same evening Anne was travelling home to Haworth.

It was less than a month since she had heard of the death of
Willy Weightman. However blunted her perceptions must have
been to the fresh blow, yet it *was* a blow. To Branwell and herself,
far more than to their sisters, Aunt had been "as a mother". Anne
had never known any other. Of the girls she had always been
Aunt's favourite. Aunt's moral impress had been more deeply
stamped on her youth than on any of her sisters. However far
Anne had progressed away from Aunt's narrow code, the rift had
not affected their feelings towards each other. How the younger's
independent findings on religious matters had startled the elder—
without alienating her love—Anne later described in her own
Tenant of Wildfell Hall. In the scenes between Helen and her Aunt
Maxwell, where worldly wisdom and religious convention are
routed by the logic and common sense of the heroine, we find an
echo of those arguments that were once hotly debated between Miss
Branwell and Anne. There is a ring of authenticity about that scene,
in particular, in which Mrs Maxwell exhorts her niece to give up
the idea of marrying a man so predestined as Arthur Huntingdon
to burn in hell-fire for ever. " Not for ever," the niece retorts, and
quotes scripture at the astonished lady in refutation of the dogma of
damnation and in support of her own pet theories of salvation. "Oh,
Helen !" cries the scandalised Calvinist, "where did you learn all
this ?"

"In the Bible, Aunt," says the naughty girl, much as Anne had answered Miss Branwell years ago when asked, "Where are your feet, Anne ?" "On the floor, Aunt."

Anne arrived home for the funeral, an occasion charged with double meaning for her, mourning already for that previous loss sustained barely a month before. She could shed tears without having to conceal them now, since there was a natural cause for grieving and none need know exactly for which of the departed they were shed. The mourning she ordered for Aunt suited her feelings far better than any of the clothes she had worn for the past few weeks.

By the terms of Miss Branwell's will, made on 30th April 1833, her property was to be equally divided between her three Brontë nieces and her Kingston niece at Penzance. Because the Deed of Probate valued her whole estate at "less than £1500", successive Brontë biographers have assumed that Charlotte, Emily and Anne each received a legacy of approximately £350, but there is no proof of this : the sum may have been considerably less. What is speci- fied in the will is Miss Branwell's bequest of personal mementos to be left not only to the girls but to Branwell as well. By this Anne received her aunt's watch and chain as well as her share of her aunt's jewellery and personal effects, comprising "my eye-glass and its chain, my rings, silver-spoons, books, clothes, etc . . . .".

Anne's walks on returning home would constantly take her to the church under whose flagstones Willy Weightman and Miss Branwell had so lately been laid. The following lines, written two years later, relate very certainly to this and every subsequent return to the place that had known him once and would know him no more. That he had been *as he had been*, that was her truest comfort.

> Yes, thou art gone ! and never more
> Thy sunny smile shall gladden me :
> But I may pass the old Church door,
> And pace the floor that covers thee.
>
> May stand upon the cold, damp stone,
> And think that, frozen, lies below
> The lightest heart that I have known,
> The kindest I shall ever know. . . .

The others had been able to take their leave of him ; she who had loved him best had been far away. In her valediction now there was more of promise than of parting. Standing in the obscurity in old Haworth Church, where a green light fell from heavy-leaded windows, Anne Brontë pronounced her vows of everlasting faith over the dead body of her love.

> Farewell to thee ! but not farewell
> To all my fondest thoughts of thee :
> Within my heart they still shall dwell
> And they shall cheer and comfort me. . . .

The years would pass but neither love nor faith would fade. In the watches of the night she would remember him :

> Cold in the grave for years has lain
> The form it was my bliss to see ;
> And only dreams can bring again
> The darling of my heart to me.

In language very different from this his official memorial—a marble tablet—was erected in old Haworth Church. It reads :

> This Monument
> was erected by the inhabitants
> In Memory of the Late
> WILLIAM WEIGHTMAN
> Who died September 6th, 1842, aged 26 years [sic]
> And was buried in this church
> On the tenth of the same month.
> He was three years Curate of Haworth
> And by the congregation and parishioners
> In general was greatly respected
> For his orthodox principles, active zeal,
> moral habits, learning,
> mildness and affability.

In dying Willy Weightman had not only cast off his earthly seeming, but was to assume in the coming years, with the finer, purified traits of Mr Weston new attributes bestowed by a deathless love.

Two practical considerations occupied Anne in the first days of her return to Haworth : how best to help Branwell, whose loss, she realised, though of a different stamp, was as irreparable as her own ; and how completely to hide her feelings from the others. More than ever, now, she must be a "close and resolute dissembler". Charlotte and Emily had been sent for from Brussels.

After a hurried journey they arrived home on Tuesday morning, 8th November. "Of course," as Charlotte wrote to Ellen, "the funeral and all was over. . . . Papa is pretty well. We found Anne at home ; she is pretty well also."

Charlotte and Emily had had their share of shock and mourning in Brussels also. Martha Taylor, Mary's brilliant and merry-hearted young sister, "died of exactly the same illness as Mr Weightman," Charlotte said, only a week or two before the death of Aunt. The girls had felt intensely the burying of Martha Taylor in foreign ground—the youngest and blithest of the quartette that had set out with such high hopes only ten months before. The glamour had gone out of the Brussels sky.

Miss Branwell's death raised several questions needing immediate solution. One of the girls must stay permanently at home now to look after Mr Brontë. They would have to decide among themselves which it should be.

Charlotte had brought with her from Brussels a letter from Monsieur Heger for Mr Brontë. It combined all the formality of a French letter of condolence, with the kindness and consideration due to a friend. He deplored the interruption the girls' studies must suffer and considered both merited a further chance. He then made a definite and generous offer to take back both, or either, in the capacity of pupil-teacher. A salary was named and the advantages to either Charlotte or Emily enumerated at length. They were too obvious to need underlining.

There can never have existed a moment's doubt which of the girls, Charlotte or Emily, would wish Mr Brontë to accept Monsieur Heger's offer for herself. Emily had no intention of returning to Brussels. She had "worked like a horse", as Charlotte said, to learn all she could, and had borne the ordeal with much greater courage than that of Roe Head or Law Hill ; but never again. She was finished with Brussels. Her one hesitation in declaring she would stay at home with Papa and keep house for him must have arisen out of consideration for Anne. If she elected to stay at the parsonage, would Anne feel obliged to go out again to earn her living ? All three girls on receipt of Aunt's legacy—the first money that had ever come to them apart from what they had earned—resolutely refused to touch it yet ; it might fulfil a greater need some day. Anne, as resolutely, decided to return to Thorp Green. She did so, though by now she had few illusions left as to the humanity of her

employers. Her chief incentive lay in the prospect of getting
Branwell work. The Robinsons had agreed to take him as tutor
to their son. In default of anything better turning up for Branwell,
she was not going to throw away this chance for him.

At this particular juncture Branwell was, probably, closer to
Anne's heart than either of her sisters, intensely as she loved Emily.
Branwell had shared the friendship of the man she loved ; he had
nursed him in his last illness ; he bore to his memory an almost
exaggerated devotion ; with Branwell, though she could not fully
open her heart, she could, at least, ease some of the intolerable
burden of loneliness.

She knew that, if she now agreed to go back to Thorp Green,
she would probably have to remain there for years. What would
have seemed like signing her own death-warrant a few months
back had no very great importance now. She was in no state to
consider her own advantage ; if she could serve Branwell, it was
all that mattered now.

Mrs Robinson, having let her governess go home to attend her
aunt's funeral, had no intention of giving her indefinite leave.
Anne was requested to return to her post on 29th November, the
more especially since the Christmas vacation was so near !

With Emily's and Anne's—and even Branwell's immediate
future settled, nothing need prevent Charlotte from accepting
Monsieur Heger's proposal now.

In the same coach from Keighley that bore Anne to Bradford
on her way to York, Charlotte travelled to spend a few days with
Ellen, happier than she let herself acknowledge that so soon she
was to be in Brussels again.

Chapter Fifteen

BRANWELL

"WE often pity the poor," writes Anne in *Agnes Grey*, "because they have no leisure to mourn their departed relatives, and necessity obliges them to labour through their severest afflictions ; but is not active employment the best remedy for overwhelming sorrow—the surest antidote to despair ?"

The summons back to Thorp Green had this of good in it, that it forced her mind into another channel than that fretted by grief.

By the Christmas holidays, when she was allowed home again, she had found a *modus vivendi* for herself which made it easier to face the assembled family. She could be certain now that no trace of that inner strife appeared. Charlotte, inviting Ellen Nussey to stay at Haworth, was able to assure her that she "need not fear to find us melancholy or depressed. We are all much as usual. You will see no difference from our former demeanour."

Branwell, in particular, would appear to have regained his spirits. During Ellen's visit he accompanied the young ladies on the moors, and after she had returned home sent her facetious messages which Charlotte, the liveliest of the party that Christmas, had no hesitation in transmitting.

There is no doubt that his prospective post at Thorp Green appealed to him. It appealed, above all, to the snob in him. The Robinsons' style of living was very different from that of the Postlethwaites (his Cumberland employers) whom he had held in open contempt. Mr Robinson, for all he had taken holy orders, was a hunting squire ; the beautiful Mrs Robinson a leader in York society ; the eldest daughter was beginning to frequent balls and parties. In the strange mixture that was Branwell—composed of panic fear of society and personal presumption—it was precisely the Robinsons' position which first attracted him. It was Mrs Robinson's birth and standing which captivated his imagination long before her personal charms took their fatal hold on his susceptible heart. If the truth be told, Branwell had probably never, or very seldom, found himself in the company of a lady of such distinction as Mrs Robinson. Apart from the virtuous women of his own family and connections—the Mrs Firths, and Franks, Atkinsons and Outhwaites of their immediate circle—Branwell had known a few respectable women, like those of the Kirby family at Bradford ; he knew a number of publicans' wives, like Mrs Sugden of the *Talbot* at Halifax—kind, motherly women who looked after him when he was drunk—but a society woman, polished, cultured and beautiful, he had probably never met in his life. His tragedy was to be heightened by the fact that the language and manner of such a woman was to elude his understanding. He was to acknowledge that she "was vastly above" him in rank, but what he never realised was that she was also vastly beyond him in subtlety and wit. Branwell took the lady's protestations for good currency ; he was not qualified to distinguish gold from counterfeit coin.

In January 1843, when he first set out with Anne on the road to Thorp Green, his hopes were sanguine. He was determined to shine ; he trusted that his gifts of eloquence (some would call it Irish blarney) which had so deeply impressed his tap-room acquaintances might, freely interspersed with Latin, ingratiate him with the scholarly Mr Robinson. To charm the ladies of the family he felt completely confident.

Leyland described Branwell as being of a "gentlemanlike appearance ; in stature a little below middle height ; slim and agile in figure, and with a clear and ruddy complexion and a voice of ringing sweetness, whose utterance and use of English was perfect". Certainly the bas-relief head that Leyland's brother, the sculptor, executed of Branwell shows a head of considerable charm. The eyes may have been blinking, but the forehead was impressive and the mop of auburn hair had a flourish which accorded well with the owner's extravagant temperament. On first sight Branwell appears always to have pleased. From the sequel it is certain that he started by pleasing the Robinsons even better than his sister had done.

Branwell was not lodged in Thorp Green Hall itself ; he was given rooms in the old "Monks' House" which lay at a stone's throw across the park and whose gabled roof, ornate chimney-stacks, subterranean passage and long romantic history cannot have failed to captivate the Byronic hero hidden in his breast. In the "Old Hall", as Branwell called it, the timbered rooms ran the whole depth of the house and were as sound in his time as in the fourteenth

century when they were built, and as they are still today. In
Stuart times some restoration must have been effected for, sending
a drawing of it home (so accurate in detail as to make the building
recognisable today) he said it dated from the sixteen-eighties.

For Anne his presence must have brought comfort to begin
with. Of an evening, after their tasks were done for the day, and
if their presence were not required in the drawing-room, they could
sit together and read or write or indulge in hopeful talk over the
schoolroom fire, and almost imagine themselves home at the
parsonage. To Anne, at least, such quiet evenings were a boon
after her two searing years of solitude. To Branwell their charm
would soon have been exhausted. He would greatly have preferred
those evenings when, in the absence of visitors, Mr and Mrs
Robinson required the attendance of the tutor and governess in the
drawing-room. There, when Anne had performed a piece on the
piano, and one or other of the young ladies had followed it up with
a song or a duet, he felt himself in his true element when asked to
read aloud to the assembled company. Branwell read well ; it
was an outlet for his histrionic temperament ; long practice in
reading aloud to Aunt and to his sisters had given him confidence.
With the light of the oil-lamp falling on his auburn hair and
illuminating features that changed with every emotion of the text,
he may have presented a sufficiently arresting picture for Mrs
Robinson to raise her eyes from her embroidery-frame and look
across at him from time to time. Anne, bent over her stitchery,
may not have noticed the effect her rather striking brother was
creating. She tells us in *Agnes Grey* how her pupils, soon tiring of
any tedious hand-work, shifted it all on to her shoulders : "Such
as stretching the frames, stitching the canvas, sorting the wools and
silks, putting in the grounds, counting the stitches, rectifying mistakes", and finishing those pieces they were tired of. Thus absorbed
she may not, at once, have been conscious of what was going on.

By the time he had been there three months it would appear
that some inkling of it, however, was reaching Branwell himself.
In all fairness to him it must be said that it brought with it rather a
sense of foreboding than of satisfied vanity.

He had brought with him the battered notebook used at
Luddendenfoot, in which he jotted down the rough drafts of poems,
and on 30th March wrote the following lines which, for want of a
better title, he called "Thorp Green" :

(2,056)

> I sit this evening, far away
> From all I used to know,
> And nought reminds my soul to-day
> Of happy long ago.
>
> Unwelcome cares, unthought-of fears
> Around my room arise ;
> I seek for suns of former years,
> But clouds o'ercast my skies. . . .

To ward off the "unwelcome cares, the unthought-of fears" with which his present circumstances threatened him, he invoked the innocence and happiness of his childhood and, in particular, the beloved ghost of his sister Maria. Branwell, on the brink of disaster, was sending out a cry for help to the forces that had protected his childhood. That he still believed in their efficacy is some proof of a heart as yet unhardened by the world.

Mr Robinson, like Mrs Robinson, seems to have been satisfied with Branwell at the start. This satisfaction, indeed, even redounded to the credit of Anne. At this time she received a degree of consideration at the hands of her employers notably lacking in the treatment of her in the past. What must not have been her surprise when an invitation was extended to Mr Brontë to visit Thorp Green ! The surprise can have been equalled only by that which Mr Brontë himself gave his children in accepting the invitation forthwith.

He came towards the end of April. The country round Thorp Green at that time would be at its most attractive, the lanes and meadows redolent of spring and moist with early flowers. Nature here, seen in its softest aspect, could not afford a greater contrast to the primeval grandeur of the Haworth hills. So it must have seemed to Mr Brontë. Without the deep spiritual beauty of his moorland home, it yet was pleasant country. Walking the winding lanes to the nearby villages of Whixley and Little and Great Ouseburn, he must have come continuously on such a setting as Anne in the pages of *Agnes Grey* was later to describe. "It was a lovely afternoon about the close of March. . . . I presently fell back and began to botanise and entomologise along the green banks and budding hedges, till the company was considerably in advance of me, and I could hear the sweet song of the happy lark ; then my spirit of misanthropy began to melt away beneath the soft pure air

and genial sunshine. . . . As my eyes wandered over the steep
banks covered with young grass and green-leaved plants, and sur-
mounted by budding hedges, I longed intensely for some familiar
flower that might recall the woody dales or green hillsides of home.
The brown moorlands, of course, were out of the question. . . .
At length I descried, high up between the twisted roots of an oak,
three lovely primroses, peeping so sweetly from their hiding-place
. . . but they grew so high above me that I tried in vain to gather
one or two, to dream over and carry with me. . . ."

It is to be hoped that Anne Brontë enjoyed such a walk in the
warm spring days of her father's visit. He evidently returned home
well satisfied with all he had seen, for he wrote to Charlotte in
Brussels, giving her "a general assurance that Branwell was doing
well and was in good odour . . .".

Charlotte, hungry for news of home in far-off Brussels, was not
satisfied with "general assurances". She wrote to Branwell asking
for "particulars. . . . Give me a detailed account as to how you
get on with your pupil and the rest of the family. . . . Are you
in better health and spirits ? and does Anne continue to be pretty
well ? . . . I understand Papa has been to see you. Did he seem
cheerful and well ? Mind when you write to me you answer these
questions, as I wish to know. . . . Be sure you write to me soon,
and beg of Anne to inclose a small billet in the same letter ; it will
be a real charity to do me this kindness. . . . Give my love to
Anne—Dear Anne, write to me—"

While Charlotte and Branwell, old partners in experience, were
each, unknown to the other, entering into a new uneasy dream of
passion, Anne was casting her thoughts beyond this present world.
The deaths of Aunt and of Willy Weightman had cruelly revived
the doubts and fears that, since earliest girlhood and the Roe Head
days, had troubled her. If then, as an inexperienced schoolgirl, the
thought of eternal damnation had crushed her spirit from a general
sentiment of compassion for all mankind, how much more acutely
must she have suffered now that the salvation of those she tenderly
loved hung in the balance.

Without a shadow of doubt Anne's searchings of the Bible in
quest of confirmation of her hopes referred to in those arguments
between niece and aunt in the *Tenant of Wildfell Hall* relate to this
period. Never was she to think more clearly or argue with greater
logic the point most vital to all her happiness, here and hereafter,

than in the poem "A Word to the Elect" which she completed on 28th May of this year.

All Anne's indignation with the smugly virtuous, all her compassion for the unfortunate, all her trust in the justice of God and in His all-embracing love, finds expression in the burning lines of this poem. The pity of a heart singularly kind, that was incapable of happiness if all sentient creatures could not share that happiness, is what inspired the religion of Anne Brontë and made of it, in a time of general acceptance of conventional beliefs, a new and beautiful thing.

> You may rejoice to think *yourselves* secure ;
> You may be grateful for the gift divine—
> That grace unsought, which made your black hearts pure,
> And fits your earth-born souls in Heaven to shine.
>
> But, is it sweet to look around, and view
> Thousands excluded from that happiness
> Which they deserve at least as much as you—
> Their faults not greater, nor their virtues less ?
>
> And, wherefore should you love your God the more,
> Because to you alone His smiles are given ;
> Because He chose to pass the *many* o'er,
> And only bring the favoured *few* to Heaven ?
>
> And, wherefore should your hearts more grateful prove,
> Because for ALL the Saviour did not die ?
> Is yours the God of justice and of love ?
> And are your bosoms warm with charity ?
>
> Say, does your heart expand to all mankind ?
> And, would you ever to your neighbour do—
> The weak, the strong, the enlightened, and the blind—
> As you would have your neighbour do to you ?
>
> And, when you, looking on your fellow-men,
> Behold them doomed to endless misery,
> How can you talk of joy and rapture then ?—
> May God withold such cruel joy from me !
>
> That none deserve eternal bliss I know ;
> Unmerited the grace in mercy given ;
> But none shall sink to everlasting woe,
> That have not well deserved the wrath of Heaven.

And oh ! there lives within my heart
A hope, long nursed by me ;
(And should its cheering ray depart,
How dark my soul would be !)

That as in Adam all have died,
In Christ shall all men live ;
And ever round His throne abide,
Eternal praise to give.

That even the wicked shall at last
Be fitted for the skies ;
And when their dreadful doom is past,
To life and light arise.

I ask not how remote the day,
Nor what the sinner's woe,
Before their dross is purged away ;
Enough for me to know

That when the cup of wrath is drained,
The metal purified,
They'll cling to what they once disdained,
And live by Him that died.

With the beginning of June, Anne and Branwell were expected home for the holidays. Emily, writing one of her rare letters to Ellen Nussey, reports on 12th May : "All here are in good health ; so was Anne according to her last account. The holidays will be here in a week or two, and then, if she be willing, I will get her to write you a proper letter, a feat that I have never performed. . . ."

It was probably on the occasion of these summer holidays of 1843 that Anne brought home from Thorp Green the adorable spaniel bitch, Flossy, who was to become in her way almost as important a member of the Brontë household as Emily's Keeper. By the next summer Flossy was a mother herself; her advent would then, at latest, have occurred this summer.

Ellen Nussey has described Flossy—"long, silky-haired, black and white Flossy". Charlotte painted her portrait twice and in the letters and diaries she figures regularly over a period of eleven years.

She was one of those curly-coated spaniels with black-and-tan head and back, white legs and plumy tails, who worm their way immediately into the hearts of their owners. Fat, comfort-loving, faithful, yet in old age still relishing a sheep-hunt, Flossy's destiny was singularly favoured ; she became the darling of Anne Brontë, lived to be over eleven and only died of old age "without a pang". Charlotte, writing of that death in after years, was able to say : "No dog ever had a happier life or an easier death."

Charlotte, homesick in Brussels, picturing them all at home together those holidays, wrote to Emily to "walk often on the moors". With Flossy bounding before them, and Keeper at their side, very certainly Emily, Anne and Branwell walked early and late on the moors that radiant summer which Charlotte, in her stony exile, found so "Asiatically hot".

How acutely Charlotte was suffering from loneliness those summer weeks of the long vacation in Brussels, those at home could only partially guess from her wistful letters. They would not know the true cause of her wretchedness until much later.

Branwell remained for two and a half years at Thorp Green, from January 1843 to 17th July 1845. The questions that naturally spring to everybody's mind are : how much did Anne see of what was going on between him and Mrs Robinson, how soon did she see it and what did she do to prevent it ?

The evidence of Branwell's *story* (as later confided to his friends Leyland and Grundy) and of his behaviour does not agree. Branwell told his friends that Mrs Robinson made him overtures soon after his first arrival at Thorp Green. These led to "reciprocations" he had little looked for and resulted in a relationship which he thus, ambiguously, described to Grundy : "During nearly three years I had daily troubled pleasure soon chastised by fear." He would, in more simple language, have had his friends believe that he and Mrs Robinson had had some sort of an understanding for nearly three years ; that is, for the whole of his stay at Thorp Green.

The evidence of his own behaviour shows that he did not fall deeply in love with Mrs Robinson until the spring, or early summer, of his second year at Thorp Green. Then, in June 1844, his conduct at home during the holidays was such as to dismay everyone at the parsonage and rouse their anxious suspicions. He was in a fevered condition of excitement, fluctuating between exaltation and despair and chafing only to get back to Thorp Green again.

By January 1845, when next at home, his conduct showed a marked contrast to that of the preceding year ; he was so cool and collected as to give the impression of a man very sure of success, if not in possession of it already.

Branwell never specifically claimed to have been Mrs Robinson's lover, but he absolutely counted on making her his wife when her husband should die. He was too naïve to see that, whatever the lady's conduct, it was no *guarantee* of her intention to marry him. The tragedy lay in his conviction that this must be so.

In the absence of any proof of Mrs Robinson's misconduct, what remains certain is that whether she were in earnest, or whether she played a dangerous game out of boredom, she led Branwell on. But, at the same time, she would be excessively circumspect to hide it from the candid eyes of her governess—as well as from the jealous eyes of her husband—and reserve whatever insinuations she wished to convey for moments when she found herself *tête-à-tête* with the tutor. We recall the "Unwelcome cares, unthought-of fears" of Branwell's verses, written only a few months after his arrival.

One such incident Branwell has described. Mr Robinson, who, apparently, could be very wounding, and took pleasure in taking Branwell down a peg or two, had been particularly insulting that day in the presence of his wife. Upon which she showed Branwell "a degree of kindness which . . . ripened into declarations of more than ordinary feeling. My admiration of her mental and personal attractions," he wrote to Grundy, "my knowledge of her unselfish sincerity, her sweet temper, and unwearied care for others, with but unrequited return where most should have been given . . . although she is seventeen years my senior, all combined to an attachment on my part, and led to reciprocations which I had little looked for."

According to Branwell, Mr Robinson derided his claims to literary ambition and achievements, and, on one occasion, "had a day's sickness after hearing that Macaulay had sent [Branwell] a complimentary letter." Mr Robinson altogether detested Branwell before the end, but Mr Brontë, it will be remembered, when invited to Thorp Green in the spring of 1843, had found Branwell's employers excessively satisfied with his services. As late as January 1844 when Charlotte returned from Brussels and found Branwell and Anne at home for the holidays, the report she sends Ellen Nussey is still : "Anne and Branwell . . . are both wondrously valued in their situation. . . . They have just left us to return to York. . . ."

Obviously the real trouble did not begin at Thorp Green until Branwell fell seriously in love with Mrs Robinson, and this, the evidence shows, was not until the early summer of 1844. Then when he and Anne came home for the holidays his feverish behaviour disquieted the whole household.

The holidays were short enough as it was. Writing to Ellen Nussey on 9th June Charlotte says : "Anne and Branwell are now at home, and they, and Emily, add their request to mine that you will join us at the beginning of next week. . . . Do not let your visit be later than the beginning of next week, or you will see little of Anne and Branwell as their holidays are very short. They will soon have to join the family at Scarborough. . . ."

From that time on, presumably, Anne must have known that Branwell was in love with Mrs Robinson. What she could not know then, of a certainty, was the nature of Mrs Robinson's feelings, if any, for him. Having the worst possible opinion of her character, Anne would be inclined to suspect her and from then on never relax her watch upon them both.

But what an intolerable situation for a girl of her integrity ! No wonder she wrote in her diary on her return home : ". . . During my stay [at Thorp Green] I have had some very unpleasant and undreamt-of experiences of human nature. . . ."

A more withering condemnation, which may well date from this time, pencilled into the back of her Prayer Book, makes us enter more deeply still into the nature of her wounded feelings. "Sick of mankind and their disgusting ways," she wrote, in the most minute italic script. It was meant for no eyes but hers, to ease her swelling heart of who knows what fresh revelation ? The fact that the line is scribbled in her Prayer Book seems to show that an overmastering emotion possessed her when no other piece of paper was to hand. Was it in church ?

It would have been in Anne's character to speak out to Branwell and declare that they had both better throw up their posts. He would naturally refuse to do so. And then, what course remained open to Anne ? To give Mrs Robinson notice and leave him alone at Thorp Green was but a useless gesture. It would have been to court instant disaster. Without her vigilance, to what lengths of folly might not Branwell proceed ?

It appears that Mr Robinson's health deteriorated fast during the last year of the young Brontës' stay at Thorp Green. He was much confined to bed and Anne might, indeed, hesitate to leave Branwell in virtual *tête-à-tête* with the woman he now madly loved, and of whose morality Anne had the worst possible opinion.

Viewing the situation in this light, there remains little doubt open
to us that it was always in the hope of preventing disaster from
befalling Branwell that Anne remained as long as she did with the
Robinsons.

Her perplexity of spirit at this time is brought home to us in
the following lines, where, as usual with Anne, the chief head of her
discontent is levelled rather at herself than at the outside causes of
her unhappiness. Like her own Helen Huntingdon hereafter, she
was to be more angered at the deterioration she saw in herself than
in the wrongs committed against her by others.

> Not only for the past I grieve,
> The future fills me with dismay ;
> Unless Thou hasten to relieve,
> I know my heart will fall away.
>
> I cannot say my faith is strong,
> I dare not hope my love is great,
> But strength and love to Thee belong,
> Oh ! do not leave me desolate.
>
> I know I owe my all to Thee,
> Oh ! take the heart I cannot give,
> Do Thou my strength and Saviour be,
> And make me to Thy glory live.

There was yet another aspect to the case which must not be
forgotten either. Charlotte's return from Brussels, in January 1844,
was bringing the girls one step nearer to the realisation of their plan
to set up a school of their own. Throughout that year and as late
as the autumn of 1845 the school plan, in varying shapes and forms,
was busily occupying the minds of Charlotte, Emily and Anne.
Its realisation at any moment was an objective towards which Anne
in particular—the only one from home—could look as to a certain
deliverance from her present drudgery. She it was, originally, who
suggested for its site Scarborough where, it will be remembered
Agnes Grey and her mother eventually set up their school. Anne
held herself in readiness through most of the year 1844 to join her
sisters in their new school when it should be established.

The school plan, as originally conceived, had to undergo a
radical modification on Charlotte's return from Brussels. She
found her father in grievous danger of losing his sight. She realised
at once that it was out of the question to leave him. At that

identical moment nothing was more needful to Charlotte than an
absorbing occupation ; nothing less than hard work could damp
down the fires of her frustrated love for M. Heger. In a letter,
dated 24th July 1844, she confided to him her plan of opening a
school at the parsonage itself. Mr Brontë's consent had, no doubt,
been forthcoming, workmen were to be brought in before the
autumn, circulars advertising the school printed and pupils diligently
sought up and down the Dales.

The printing of the circular during Anne's and Branwell's
holidays at home was like the laying of the foundation-stone of the
enterprise they all had so much at heart. Modelled, inevitably, on
the prospectus of the Pensionnat Heger in Brussels, it announced :
"The Misses Brontë's Establishment for the Board and Education
of a Limited Number of Young Ladies, The Parsonage, Haworth,
near Bradford." For an inclusive fee of £35 a year the Young
Ladies would be boarded and receive instruction in the usual
branches : Writing, Arithmetic, History, Grammar, Geography
and Needlework. The following extras could be supplied at one
guinea per Quarter, each : French, German, Latin, Music and
Drawing ; the "Use of the Pianoforte" would be charged 5/- a
Quarter and each Young Lady's washing at 15/-. The usual bed-
linen and cutlery would have to be supplied by prospective pupils ;
a Quarter's Notice, or a Quarter's Board, would be required
previous to the removal of any pupil. The Misses Brontë had
thought of everything—save the contingency that arose : not one
parent applied, not one pupil was forthcoming to convert an ideal
prospect into solid fact. The Misses Brontë's Establishment
remained a castle in the air with its foundations on paper ; luckily
no alterations had been started on the old parsonage. Before
eighteen months were out all three girls were busy erecting edifices
of a very different nature.

But the Prospectus shows what they were qualified to teach,
and it also explains, somewhat, why during the year 1844 Anne
was obviously studying for herself, as well as for her pupils, at
Thorp Green.

She bought a number of books at that time which, as her
pencilled annotations show, she closely studied. They show, in
particular, that she was working hard at Latin, German and music.
Obviously the teaching of Latin at the Misses Brontë's Establishment would have devolved on Anne, who had several years'

experience of the subject, as the French and German would have devolved on Charlotte. Nevertheless, since both Emily and Anne might have been called on to supplement Charlotte's teaching of German, so Anne slaved at her German during this period and bought herself a brand new "Reader" containing extracts from the best authors, and a new issue of Rabenhorst's *Pocket Dictionary* on 14th September 1843.

The teaching of music which Emily had so hated at Brussels would also, presumably, have fallen to Anne's share. During 1843–4 she bought a quantity of new music, partially, no doubt, for the benefit of the Robinson girls, but also with an eye to the new school and its prospective boarders. Anne's music, as one might expect, included albums of sacred airs drawn from the classical oratorios, arias from the fashionable secular composers of her day —Weber, Rossini, Donizetti, Adam, Auber—traditional English airs and some bravura pieces, both vocal and for the keyboard, by Haydn and Mozart.

Certainly it is not too much to say that throughout the latter period of Anne's stay at Thorp Green, even when alarm over Branwell was relegating most personal considerations into the background of her thoughts, the chance which the opening of a school afforded of regaining her liberty was the one bright prospect in an otherwise darkening world.

It has always been assumed that a discovery of a very unpleasant nature prompted Anne's sudden decision to leave her post in the mid-summer of 1845. A certain amount of oral tradition, still being repeated to Mme. Duclaux in the eighteen-eighties, had it that the disruption of family life at the Robinsons had reached such a pitch that not even Anne, with her exalted sense of duty towards her pupils, could hope to remedy things any more. With Mr Robinson increasingly confined to bed, and Mrs Robinson and Branwell growing daily more imprudent in their disregard of appearances, the young people of the family got completely out of hand and had reached a degree of insubordination where their mother had but to correct them for them to threaten : "Unless you do as we wish we shall tell Papa about Mr Brontë." It would not need such a scene to be repeated often for Anne to make up her mind that the limit of her endurance had been reached. If she had borne with a detestable situation all this time, it had been, after serving Branwell, from a sense of duty and compassion towards her pupils.

In that summer of 1845 both the unworthiness of the mother and the insubordination of the daughters came to a head. Lydia, the eldest, demonstrated by an act of unparalleled imprudence for a girl of her time that she set the wishes of parents and guardian alike at defiance. On 20th October 1845, five days before her twentieth birthday and four months after the departure of Anne, she made a runaway match to Gretna Green with a gentleman from Scarborough and was "cut off with a shilling" for her pains.

The gesture does not surprise in Lydia, but her choice of husband does, when we remember how worldly a young lady she had ever shown herself. For the name of the gentleman with whom she ran away to Gretna Green was Henry Roxby, a name all too well known in Scarborough circles and, whatever his individual merits, a connection which could not be regarded by the Robinsons in any other light than exceptionable in the highest degree. For Mr Roxby was an actor, a member of a large and most distinguished family of actors, actor-managers and scene-painters whose most illustrious member was William Roxby-Beverley, the scene-painter, easily the finest artist in that style of the nineteenth century. The Roxbys owned the Theatre Royal at Scarborough, situated in St Thomas Street, which was in its heyday at the time Anne and the Robinsons visited there. Their private house was in Huntriss Row within a stone's throw of the Cliff lodgings where the Robinsons always stayed. Lydia's opportunities, therefore, for seeing Henry on the stage, or in private life, were numerous. An echo of eighteenth-century comedy seems to attach to the whole of this romance of a wealthy young lady of the highest society eloping with an actor to Gretna Green, when it is recalled that *her* name was Lydia and *his* stage-name Beverley (an addition to their family name which all members of the family assumed in honour of the old capital of the East Riding of Yorkshire).

Whatever the rights and wrongs of the case, and Anne may have sympathised with Lydia for marrying the man she loved, yet her manner of doing so and defying her parents could not but have aroused in Anne both disapproval and anxiety. Throughout that early summer she must have been a harassed confidante of the rebellious girl, and seen with growing dismay the utter futility of preaching and precept where example was so lamentably lacking.

The elopement of Lydia Robinson must have been foreseen by Anne in the weeks immediately preceding it and during her last visit with her pupils to Scarborough. Whatever her secret sympathies for Lydia, she would have counselled moderation and self-control. But it was too late.

The foundations of family life had been undermined and, however much Anne might preach, the filial respect she strove to evoke in the daughters was dead long ago. It seems very probable that the anticipation of Lydia's irrevocable folly was a contributing factor in Anne's decision to endure no more from the Robinsons and their concerns. The conduct of one and all disgusted her equally, and if her brother could not and would not extricate himself from an ignoble situation she was powerless to help any further. When she went home for the holidays on 18th June 1845 she delighted her sisters by telling them that she had given Mrs Robinson notice for good.

Quite obviously she did not give them her reasons. They knew enough of the unpleasantness of her life at Thorp Green not to need any special reasons for her quitting it at last. To Charlotte, who knew all about the loneliness and humiliation of the governess's life in a large household, the only marvel had been that Anne had borne with the Robinsons for so long.

Branwell came home with Anne. Suspecting nothing, Charlotte, in announcing their return to Ellen Nussey, said he was only to have a week's holiday now as he had to return to his post until the family went to Scarborough. Charlotte herself, happy in Anne's return which permitted her to accept an invitation to go to Derbyshire with Ellen, saw nothing in Branwell's behaviour to rouse her suspicions ; it was not Anne who would have opened her eyes. Charlotte had been so despondent since her return from Brussels that Anne was the last person to spoil what little pleasure came her way. Charlotte stayed away three weeks ; Emily and Anne remained at home ; Branwell returned to Thorp Green.

What passed between Branwell and Anne never transpired. She knew that if he went back it would be to certain disaster. Whatever pleas she brought forward at the last were useless to move him from his fixed resolution. When Branwell jumped into the chaise on the first lap of his journey back to Mrs Robinson, Anne knew that she had failed in the biggest undertaking of her life. She had failed to save Branwell. But it is noticeable that her anger and chagrin were never, now or later, turned against him. She was always to consider him the victim—not the instigator—of a wicked deed. Above all, she turned against herself in contempt and scorn : she had failed where she most needed to succeed. The sense of failure which informs all her subsequent writings was to leave her little peace from this time on.

Before the storm broke there was a strange hush. Branwell away, Charlotte away, Emily and Anne were alone at home together for the first time for many years. Emily was in festive mood ; she, at least, had no reason for wretchedness. The long summer days, in spite of wild, squally weather, were a time of freedom in which to range afar. She and Anne decided on a "first long journey together", as Emily afterwards proudly spoke of it. They went to York and spent two nights away. It was as though Anne, aware that in leaving Thorp Green she was losing two of the purest pleasures life had afforded her so far, the sea at Scarborough and the Minster at York, were seizing a last occasion to see one of them at least once again. The Robinsons were at Scarborough ; no fear of encountering them at York.

To Emily it was a rapturous expedition, still filling her imagination a month later when she wrote her customary diary paper. To Anne the outing which should have brought a deep delight found her too preoccupied to raise her spirits. She was still bearing the weight of her wretched secret alone, and would doubtless have done so for years had the truth not broken of itself.

Charlotte reached home on Saturday, 19th July after a pleasant visit to Hathersage. "It was ten o'clock at night when I got home," she wrote to her late hostess, "I found Branwell ill [Charlotte's euphemistic expression for "drunk"]. He is so often owing to his own fault. I was not therefore shocked at first, but when Anne informed me of the immediate cause of his present illness I was greatly shocked. He had last Thursday received a note from Mr Robinson sternly dismissing him, intimating that he had discovered his proceedings, which he characterised as bad beyond expression, and charging him on pain of exposure to break off instantly and for ever all communication with every member of his family. We have had sad work with Branwell since. He thought of nothing but stunning or drowning his distress of mind. No one in the house could have rest."

"Last Thursday" would be 17th July. Mr Robinson wrote from

Scarborough where the family, with the exception of Edmund, had been since 5th July (see *Scarborough Gazette* for that date). It may be worth noticing that Edmund joined his parents and three sisters, according to the *Scarborough Herald* on that very 17th July. Was it on some revelation of his that his father acted in dismissing Branwell ?

Branwell's frenzy of grief and rage was more than his father, aged nearly seventy, could stand. He packed Branwell off with the sexton, John Brown, for a week to the sea. Mr Brontë and Miss Branwell had always favoured the Lancashire coast and Branwell was now sent to Liverpool at as great a distance as Mr Brontë could afford to send him from Scarborough, where the lady of his adoration was then residing.

On Anne devolved the task of telling the shattered family what had led up to this ; she herself could not know what had precipitated the final catastrophe. Branwell, to the end, defended Mrs Robinson. It was not from him that they received the indelible impression of Mrs Robinson's chief responsibility in the affair ; that was from Anne. It only went to confirm the rumours which afterwards were current that Mrs Robinson, tired of Branwell's extravagant pretensions, herself informed her husband, in true Potiphar's wife style, of the young tutor's displeasing attentions, and asked for his dismissal.

Branwell had counted on marrying Mrs Robinson after her husband's death, an event which was expected at any moment and which, without doubt, had helped to bolster up his illusions. Mrs Robinson, as the event was to show, had no such intention whatever. The nearer and the more certainly her husband's death approached, the more necessary for her ultimate plans was the removal of the tutor. With some consideration for Anne's feelings perhaps, Mrs Robinson waited for Anne to leave Thorp Green (possibly hoping Branwell would accompany her) before dealing him his *coup de grâce*.

If Branwell was not altogether guiltless in what followed, he certainly showed how completely unworldly he was. He still firmly believed that Mrs Robinson would marry him after her husband's death and totally refused to see in any of her conduct the actions of a heartless worldling. Maddened as he was at his dismissal, he was not totally bereft of hope. There is a great difference between the grief he experienced at this juncture and the total collapse, mental and physical, which followed the next year's events. Between this month of July and the following May, when Mr Robinson's death did in fact occur, Branwell, though drunken and trying in the extreme to his relations, still remained capable of a certain amount of intellectual effort, kept in close touch with his friends Leyland and Grundy : was, in short, biding his time. He made a few attempts to communicate with Mrs Robinson, but even when they failed was confident that her husband's death would restore him to the lady of his dreams.

Infinitely worse as Branwell's case was to become later, his present collapse seems to have surprised those at home. They were, very certainly, not prepared for it as Anne had been. A month after the blow had fallen Charlotte wrote to Ellen : "My hopes ebb low indeed about Branwell. I sometimes fear he will never be fit for much. His bad habits seem more deeply rooted than I thought. The late blow to his prospects and feelings has quite made him reckless. . . . One ought, indeed, to hope to the very last ; and I try to do so, but occasionally, hope, in his case, seems a fallacy. . . ."

It became glaringly obvious in a little while to his sisters that the plan of opening a school in a home disordered by his presence was an impossibility which no optimism could overcome or disregard. Branwell never again succeeded in getting work. He made a few ineffectual and ill-written attempts to apply for posts, but he was naturally passed over in favour of better men.

Neither want of money nor "insufficient qualifications" could more effectively have wrecked the girls' long-cherished plan of setting up school than the perpetual presence in the home of their drunken brother.

Chapter Sixteen

ACTON BELL

EVERYTHING they had been working for was brought to nothing by the disaster overtaking Branwell. It found Anne and Charlotte, each for her own uncommunicated reasons, weakened by a long term of cankering grief. Emily alone of the household could meet the challenge with undiminished vigour. While Charlotte had been in Brussels, and Branwell and Anne at Thorp Green, Emily had gained from the precious months of solitude and freedom at home an expansion of spirit which was to support her through every mortal trial that lay ahead. She had attained to a contentment of mind beyond the reach of any of the others.

Alone on the illimitable moors Emily had found a *modus vivendi* with misfortune which, for all its appearance of detachment, was certainly *not* the result of indifference or callousness. Quite the reverse. Out of an over-sensitive heart she had raised her philosophy, her protective shield against the knocks of life. A clear-sighted recognition of the unpleasant conditions life imposes on the living ; the courage to *accept*, not to *resist* its hardest terms ; these were the only safeguards against suffering she had discovered.

No more eloquent expression of the differing states of mind with which the girls entered upon this new and crucial phase of their existence can be found than in the dual diary papers Anne and Emily wrote again this year on the anniversary of Emily's birthday.

As in the preceding ones there are some astonishing similarities of thought and even of expression, but how resilient is Emily's state of mind, how despondent Anne's !

The text of Anne's birthday note runs :

Thursday, July the 31st, 1845. Yesterday was Emily's birthday, and the time when we should have opened our 1841 paper, but by mistake we opened it today instead. How many things have happened since it was written—some pleasant, some far otherwise. Yet I was then at Thorp Green, and now I am only just escaped from it. I was wishing to leave it then, and if I had known that I had four years longer to stay how wretched I should have been ; but during my stay I have had some very unpleasant and undreamt-of experiences of human nature. Others have seen more changes. Charlotte has left Mr White's and been twice to Brussels, where she stayed each time nearly a year. Emily has been there too, and stayed nearly a year. Branwell has left Luddenden Foot, and been a tutor at Thorp Green, and had much tribulation and ill health. He was very ill on Thursday, but he went with John Brown to Liverpool, where he now is, I suppose ; and we hope he will be better and do better in future. This is a dismal, cloudy, wet evening. We have had so far a very cold wet summer. Charlotte has lately been to Hathersage, in Derbyshire, on a visit of three weeks to Ellen Nussey. She is now sitting sewing in the dining-room. Emily is ironing upstairs. I am sitting in the dining-room in the rocking-chair before the fire with my feet on the fender. Papa is in the parlour. Tabby and Martha are, I think, in the kitchen. Keeper and Flossy are, I do not know where. Little Dick is hopping in his cage. When the last paper was written we were thinking of setting up a school. The scheme has been dropt, and long after taken up again and dropt again because we could not get pupils. Charlotte is thinking about getting another situation. She wishes to go to Paris. Will she go ? She has let Flossy in, by-the-by, and he is now lying on the sofa. Emily is engaged in writing the Emperor Julius's Life. She has read some of it, and I want very much to hear the rest. She is writing some poetry, too. I wonder what it is about ? I have begun the third volume of *Passages in the Life of an Individual*. I wish I had finished it. This afternoon I began to set about making my grey figured silk frock that was dyed at Keighley. What sort of a hand shall I make of it ? E. and I have a great deal of work to do. When shall we sensibly diminish it ? I want to get a habit of early rising. Shall I succeed ? We have not yet finished our *Gondal Chronicles* that we began three years and a half ago. When will they be done ? The Gondals are at present in a sad state. The Republicans are uppermost, but the Royalists are not quite overcome. The young sovereigns, with their brothers and sisters, are still at the Palace of Instruction. The Unique Society, about half a year ago, were wrecked on a desert island as they were returning from Gaaldine. They are still there, but we have not played at them much yet. The Gondals in general are not in first-rate playing condition. Will they improve ? I wonder how we shall all be, and where and how situated, on the thirtieth of July, 1848, when, if we are all alive, Emily will be just 30. I shall be in my 29th year, Charlotte in her 33rd, and Branwell in his 32nd ; and what changes shall we have seen and known ; and shall we be much changed ourselves ? I hope not, for the worse at least. I, for my part, cannot well be flatter or older in mind than I am now. Hoping for the best, I conclude.

In startling contrast to Anne's, Emily's diary paper reads :

My birthday—showery, breezy, cool. I am twenty-seven years old to-day This morning Anne and I opened the papers we wrote four years since, on my twenty-third birthday. This paper we intend, if all be well, to open on my thirtieth—three years hence, in 1848. Since the 1841 paper the following events have taken place. Our school scheme has been abandoned, and instead Charlotte and I went to Brussels on the 8th of February, 1842.

Branwell left his place at Luddenden Foot. C. and I returned from Brussels, November 8th, 1842, in consequence of aunt's death.

Branwell went to Thorp Green as a tutor, where Anne still continued, January, 1843.

Charlotte returned to Brussels the same month, and after staying a year, came back again on New Year's Day 1844.

Anne left her situation at Thorp Green of her own accord, June 1845.

Anne and I went our first long journey by ourselves together, leaving home on the 30th of June, Monday, sleeping at York, returning to Keighley Tuesday evening, sleeping there and walking home on Wednesday morning. Though the weather was broken we enjoyed ourselves very much, except during a few hours at Bradford. And during our excursion we were, Ronald Macalgin, Henry Angora, Juliet Angusteena, Rosabella Esmalden, Ella and Julian Egremont, Catharine Navarre, and Cordelia Fitzaphnold, escaping from the palaces of instruction to join the Royalists who are hard driven at present by the victorious Republicans. The Gondals still flourish bright as ever. I am at present writing a work on the First Wars—Anne has been writing some articles on this, and a book by Henry Sophona—We intend sticking firm by the rascals as long as they delight us which I am glad to say they do at present. I should have mentioned that last summer the School Scheme was revived in full vigour—We had prospectuses printed, despatched letters to all acquaintances imparting our plans, and did our little all but it was found no go—now I don't desire a school at all, and none of us have any great longing for it. We have cash enough for our present wants, with a prospect of accumulation—We are all in decent health, only that papa has a complaint in his eyes and with the exception of B who I hope will be better and do better, hereafter. I am quite contented for myself—not as idle as formerly, altogether as hearty and having learnt to make the most of the present and hope for the future with less fidgetiness that I cannot do all I wish—seldom or ever troubled with nothing to do, and merely desiring that everybody could be as comfortable as myself and as undesponding, and then we should have a very tolerable world of it.

By mistake I find we have opened the paper on the 31st instead of the 30th. Yesterday was much such a day as this, but the morning was divine—

Tabby who was gone in our last paper is come back and has lived with us two years and a half and is in good health—Martha, who also departed, is here too—We have got Flossy, got and lost Tiger—lost the hawk Hero, which with the geese was given away, and is doubtless dead, for when I came back from Brussels I inquired on all hands and could hear nothing of him. Tiger died early last year—Keeper and Flossy are well, also the canary acquired four years since. We are now all at home, and likely to be there some time. Branwell went to Liverpool on Tuesday to stay a week. Tabby has just been teasing me to turn as formerly to "Pilloputate". Anne and I should have picked the black currants if it had been fine and sunshiny. I must hurry off now to my turning and ironing. I have plenty of work on hands, and writing, and am altogether full of business. With best wishes for the whole house till 1848, July 30th, and as much longer as may be. I conclude.

At such a moment, with the recent events still humming, one would suppose, in everyone's minds, Emily's review of the present state of the family must ever amaze the reader, to say the least of it. The whole tone of the letter is buoyant in the extreme. Branwell's misfortunes, Papa's complaint of the eyes are noted but in no way considered in the nature of incurable ills. Nothing, indeed, is irremediably bad, if rightly considered. "I am quite content for myself : not as idle as formerly, altogether as hearty, and having learnt to make the most of the present . . . desiring that everybody could be as comfortable as myself and as undesponding, and then we should have a very tolerable world of it."

There we have in a few lines of disjointed prose the secret of Emily Brontë's contentment, the key to her unshakable courage in adversity. Her strength, both physical and moral, was drawn from the perfect integration of her daily life into the life of her dream. Between her imaginary world, and the world around her, there was no division. Effortlessly she could range from one into the other, with no barrier to stay her body and no prohibition to arrest her mind. She was one of the fortunate few for whom the worlds of reality and imagination have no frontiers, for whom the movement from one into the other demands neither passports nor passage perilous. Emily Brontë inhabited Gondal not as a *conscious* escape from the world of Haworth or the vaster world beyond, but because it was her natural world, the climate in which her thoughts most freely moved, as her active limbs moved most swiftly over the heathy moors of Haworth. She need not seek that world ; it grows inside. It is no more removed from her than the people who inhabit it are separate entities from herself. She *is* (we note from her own declaration) "Ronald Macalgin, Henry Angora, Juliet Angusteena, Rosabella Esmalden" and all the rest of that radiant company.

She is perfectly sane ; she knows the "rascals" are make-believe (who made them but herself ?), but they are not only as *real* as the members of her own family, they are as *necessary* to her.

To be not yourself, but any one of a host of vigorous men and women who carve out their own destinies with fearless resolution, is not only to *overcome* the limitations of one's lot but to be *unaware* of them—as Emily needed the unbounded horizon of the hills for her physical home, so she needed the multiple and free generation of her nursling race for the expanding of a spirit all too cramped for space.

Almost the half, certainly the most important part of Emily's poetry was written during the period of her untrammelled liberty at home. The years 1841, 1843-5, while Charlotte, Branwell and Anne were away at their various posts, were the years of fruition for Emily's genius. Then, in a state of unbroken harmony with herself and the earth about her, she was able, at one and the same time, to direct her father's home, humour an old servant and train a young one ; bake the bread (ever reputed the most delicious in Haworth), iron the vast quantities of bed and table linen laundered at home ; keep the household accounts and, during Charlotte's absence abroad, look after the few precious investments in the new railroad company that Aunt's legacy had allowed : all this, and meantime to be writing some of the acknowledged masterpieces of English verse.

One says "to write", but the *writing* is nothing compared with the spiritual experience the writing implies. In the four years of her chief poetic output Emily travelled far. From those excursions on which none could follow her she brought back echoes and flashes of eternal truths, to render which she had but the imperfect medium of words. On scraps of paper, as unobtrusive as possible, she jotted down in almost indecipherable italic script those messages from an unseen world. From time to time the scraps of paper were in danger of getting lost and she would copy some of them into a little notebook, the cheapest, meanest of the kind then used for entering washing-lists. One day late in the autumn following Branwell's dismissal from Thorp Green, Charlotte came upon one of these notebooks, with consequences that were to deflect the whole current of their lives.

Charlotte herself has told us of that discovery in a narration unforgettable to all who have once read the life-story of the Brontës. But what Charlotte did not include in her narration was some account of her own state of mind at the particular moment at which Emily's verses fell into her hand. To understand it one must have read the letter she wrote to Monsieur Heger on 18th November that same autumn. It was to be the last letter she ever wrote him. The text is self-explanatory.

Monsieur, the six months of silence have run their course. It is now the 18th of Novr. ; my last letter was dated (I think) the 18th of May. I may therefore write to you without failing in my promise.

The summer and autumn seemed very long to me ; truth to tell, it has needed painful efforts on my part to bear hitherto the self-denial which I have imposed on myself. You, Monsieur, you cannot conceive what it means ; but suppose for a moment that one of your children was separated from you, 160 leagues away, and that you had to remain six months without writing to him, without receiving news of him, without hearing him spoken of, without knowing aught of his health, then you would understand easily all the harshness of such an obligation. I tell you frankly that I have tried meanwhile to forget you, for the remembrance of a person whom one thinks never to see again, and whom, nevertheless, one greatly esteems, frets too much the mind ; and when one has suffered that kind of anxiety for a year or two, one is ready to do anything to find peace once more. I have done everything ; I have sought occupations ; I have denied myself absolutely the pleasure of speaking about you—even to Emily ; but I have been able to conquer neither my regrets nor my impatience. That, indeed, is humiliating—to be unable to control one's own thoughts, to be the slave of a regret, of a memory, the slave of a fixed and dominant idea which lords it over the mind. Why cannot I have just as much friendship for you, as you for me—neither more nor less ? Then should I be so tranquil, so free—I could keep silence then for ten years without an effort.

My father is well but his sight is almost gone. He can neither read nor write. Yet the doctors advise waiting a few months more before attempting an operation. The winter will be a long night for him. He rarely complains ; I admire his patience. If Providence wills the same calamity for me, may He at least vouchsafe me as much patience with which to bear it ! It seems to me, Monsieur, that there is nothing more galling in great physical misfortunes than to be compelled to make all those about us share in our sufferings. The ills of the soul one can hide, but those which attack the body and destroy the faculties cannot be concealed. My father allows me now to read to him and write for him ; he shows me, too, more confidence than he has ever shown before, and that is a great consolation.

Monsieur, I have a favour to ask of you : when you reply to this letter, speak to me a little of yourself, not of me ; for I know that if you speak of me it will be to scold me, and this time I would see your kindly side. Speak to me therefore of your children. Never was your brow severe when Louise and Claire and Prosper were by your side. Tell me also something of the School, of the pupils, of the Governesses. Are Mesdemoiselles Blanche, Sophie, and Justine still at Brussels ? Tell me where you travelled during the holidays—did you go to the Rhine ? Did you not visit Cologne or Coblentz ? Tell me, in short, my master, what you will, but tell me something. To write to an ex-assistant governess (No ! I refuse to remember my employment as assistant governess—I repudiate it) —anyhow, to write to an old pupil cannot be a very interesting occupation for you, I know ; but for me it is life. Your last letter was stay and prop to me— nourishment for half a year. Now I need another and you will give it me ; not because you bear me friendship—you cannot have much—but because you are compassionate of soul and you would condemn no one to prolonged suffering to save yourself a few moments' trouble. To forbid me to write to you, to refuse to answer me, would be to tear from me my only joy on earth, to deprive me of my last privilege—a privilege I never shall consent willingly to surrender. Believe me, my master, in writing to me it is a good deed that you will do. So long as I believe you are pleased with me, so long as I have hope of receiving news from you, I can be at rest and not too sad. But when a prolonged and gloomy silence seems to threaten me with the estrangement of my master—when day by day I await a letter, and when day by day disappointment comes to fling me back into overwhelming sorrow, and the sweet delight of seeing your handwriting and reading your counsel escapes me as a vision that is vain, then fever claims me— I lose appetite and sleep—I pine away.

May I write to you again next May : I would rather wait a year, but it is impossible—it is too long.

[Postscript in English.]

I must say one word to you in English. I wish I could write to you more cheerful letters, for when I read this over I find it to be somewhat gloomy—but forgive me, my dear master—do not be irritated at my sadness—according to the words of the Bible : "Out of the fulness of the heart, the mouth speaketh," and truly I find it difficult to be cheerful so long as I think I shall never see you more. You will perceive by the defects in this letter that I am forgetting the French language—yet I read all the French books I can get, and learn daily a portion by heart—but I have never heard French spoken but once since I left Brussels—and then it sounded like music in my ears—every word was most precious to me because it reminded me of you—I love French for your sake with all my heart and soul.

Farewell, my dear Master—may God protect you with special care and crown you with peculiar blessings.

This was the mood and this the enfeebled state of mind in which she discovered Emily's poetry ; no wonder it acted on her like an intoxicant.

"One day, in the autumn of 1845," she related years later, "I accidentally lighted on a MS volume of verse in my sister Emily's handwriting. Of course, I was not surprised, knowing that she could and did write verse : I looked it over, and something more than surprise seized me—a deep conviction that these were not common effusions, nor at all like the poetry women generally write. I thought them condensed and terse, vigorous and genuine. To my ear, they had also a peculiar music—wild, melancholy and elevating.

"My sister Emily was not a person of demonstrative character, nor one on to the recesses of whose mind and feelings even those nearest and dearest to her could, with impunity, intrude unlicensed ; it took hours to reconcile her to the discovery I had made, and days to persuade her that such poems merited publication. . . ."

The operational word is out ; it was the sudden realisation that writing of such quality as Emily's could be *published* that galvanised Charlotte to renewed life and action.

No matter that it took hours to reconcile Emily to the discovery—days to the idea of publication—Charlotte was resolved. She had need be, and intrepid also, to sustain the storm of anger which now burst upon her head. Emily's temper did not flare out very often, but when it did it made the household quail.

Anne, so much nearer Emily in understanding than Charlotte,

could interpret that anger without explanation. To her, Emily had read some of the chapters of her life of the (Gondal) Emperor Julius, as the recent diary papers revealed, but Emily had not read her poetry to Anne. Anne knew she was writing it, wondered much what it was about, but forbore to inquire. If Emily had meant her to read her poems she would have shown them to her.

Charlotte had broken in to Emily's secret world without leave. To look at these poems, even had they had no special significance for Emily, was an attaint on her privacy : to pore over them, to ponder their meaning, was an outrage Emily would not forgive.

In the terrible scene that followed it is evident that Emily tore from the room in a rage. Charlotte and Anne were left to face each other, and nothing is more likely than that Charlotte questioned Anne on her knowledge of Emily's writings. Anne, had she known anything, would not have told it. Instead, with the composure that always so impressed Charlotte, she got up and fetched a little notebook of her own poems and handed it to Charlotte. What she *said* was : "Since you like Emily's, you might like to look at mine" ; what she was effectually *doing* was to deflect Charlotte's purpose from probing further into Emily's secrets.

Though she realised that she was probably prejudiced, Charlotte thought Anne's verses had "a sweet, sincere pathos of their own" ; they only helped to confirm her purpose, which was nothing less than for the three of them to publish a joint volume of poetry.

There was no solution to their present predicament like authorship. It required nothing of them (as setting up school had done) but what they already had. Even should it require a little cash, there was Aunt's legacy. Charlotte was as certain as—four years before—she had been about going to Brussels. Now, as then, she believed in her heart that "she was acting for the best". The realisation that this recourse was open to them came like an answer to prayer. It was something new, and yet—it was as old as her earliest memories of childhood.

"We had very early cherished the dream of one day becoming authors," Charlotte's narrative continues. "This dream, never relinquished, even when distance divided and absorbing tasks occupied us, now suddenly acquired strength and consistency ; it took the character of a resolve."

She was so carried away by her own ardour that she could afford to disregard Emily's vehement objections. She believed Emily to be sufficiently like herself ultimately to see with her eyes. "I knew," she writes, ". . . that a mind like hers could not be without some latent spark of honourable ambition, and refused to be discouraged in my attempts to fan that spark to flame."

Emily had always respected Charlotte's judgment and had time and again let her sweep them all along in her wake when some practical resolution had to be reached. The fact that after some days Emily *did* submit to Charlotte's representations only goes to show how deeply she trusted Charlotte, and how unaware she herself was of the effect this sharing of her inmost life was, in the long run, to have.

The important thing about Emily Brontë's imaginary world had always been that it had no *separate* existence from its creator ; it lay in no sense of the word *outside* of Emily ; it grew, as we said before, *within*. There, like a pregnant mother, she carried it everywhere with her, even from York to Keighley and from Keighley to Haworth as the last diary paper revealed.

That hardy relationship, natural in origin and the source of all health and happiness to her, was essential to the well-being of Emily Brontë.

When Charlotte delivered Emily's poetry to the world, it was like the cutting of an umbilical cord ; the severance gave Emily's creation a life of its own, but it ended hers.

Authorship was *not* what Emily Brontë most needed to give her contentment ; she needed to *live* the imaginary life, not to share it. If the carefree world of her creation was to be limited to the comprehension and taste of others it was no longer a free world and her own. It may fairly be said that in direct ratio as authorship brought Emily Brontë fame, it dried up the source of her inspiration. After the autumn of 1845 she wrote only two poems worthy to be ranked with those that came before. *Wuthering Heights*, written and finished before April 1846, published in 1847, belongs in *conception* to the time before Emily's writing was discovered by Charlotte and the publication of the poems decreed. In urging her sisters on the path of fame Charlotte was ensuring their immortality —and our lasting gratitude—but all unknown she was robbing Emily of her source of life.

When the heart-burning at length died down Emily was partially won over to Charlotte's plan. She laid down her conditions. No Gondal titles or names were to be published with the poems. Deprived of their dramatic setting, of their sequence in the Gondal Chronicle, the key to their meaning would be missing and not even the most perspicacious reader would find the solution, or invade her privacy.

Let there be no mistake, the "privacy" Emily was defending so fiercely was not that of the parson's daughter of Haworth (who could entertain any curiosity about her ?) but that of the imaginary heroes and heroines into whom her own personality had been successfully projected. It was Gondal's Queen, the tremendous Augusta Almeda, and her tragic lovers whom Emily Brontë was shielding from prying eyes when she insisted on deleting the proper names from poems being prepared for the press.

This resolution applied equally to Anne. Though of late years their writing had not been in close collaboration, the Gondal Saga was the creation of them both, and Anne's poems in a very high percentage were signed by Gondal pseudonyms and related to Gondal themes. Nothing of these imaginary persons or places must appear in any of the poems about to be published, though Anne had not Emily's reasons for wishing to suppress their Gondalan origin. Indeed Anne had often used the names of "Olivia Vernon", "Alexandrina Zenobia" and "Alexander Hybernia" as a cover behind which to conceal *personal* experience. The opposite was the case with Emily ; *she* lived by her imaginary creation, not they by her.

The result, which neither could then foresee, was that the realistic and only right interpretation that could be given Anne's verse was eventually applied to Emily's ; and that when all trace of the imaginary protagonists was removed from her poems, the situations and passions were inevitably ascribed to her. For who was to tell the difference in the *nature* of the griefs which inspired the one sister to write :

> Cold in the earth, and the deep snow piled above thee !
> Far, far removed, cold in the dreary grave !
> Have I forgot, my Only Love, to love thee,
> Severed at last by Time's all-wearing wave ?

and the other :

> Cold in the grave for years has lain
> The form it was my bliss to see ;
> And only dreams can bring again
> The darling of my heart to me.

Charlotte, less convinced than her sisters, perhaps, of escaping misrepresentation, or simply less courageous, selected none of her Angrian poetry for the projected volume. Since it was by far the best of her output, she thus inflicted on herself a serious aesthetic handicap.

When the work of elimination was completed it was decided that Charlotte should contribute nineteen poems and Emily and Anne each twenty-one ; the manuscripts were neatly recopied, each in the hand of their respective authors, made up into a parcel and sent out into the world.

What most impresses the modern author in the story of the Brontës' earliest venture into print is the rapidity with which the whole plan, once conceived, was carried through. Assuming that it was some time in December that Charlotte came across those poems of Emily, from first to last it took them not quite five months.

By 28th January (1846) they had, after some rebuffs from other publishers, been recommended by Messrs Chambers of Edinburgh to try a small firm that rather specialised in verse, Messrs Aylott & Jones of Paternoster Row. To them Charlotte wrote on that day, received an answer by return of post, which encouraged the girls to despatch the manuscript of the poems on 6th February. The publication was to be at their own cost and was fixed at the sum of £31 10s. This sum they sent on 3rd March. They began correcting proof-sheets on 13th March; by late May the volume entitled *Poems, by Currer, Ellis and Acton Bell* was out !

They had, as it is seen, adopted pseudonyms, Currer, Ellis and Acton Bell, "the ambiguous choice", as Charlotte later said, "being dictated by a sort of conscientious scruple at assuming Christian names positively masculine, while we did not like to declare ourselves women, because—without at that time suspecting that our mode of writing and thinking was not what is called 'feminine'— we had a vague impression that authoresses are liable to be looked on with prejudice . . . .".

It was Charlotte, naturally, who carried out the whole correspondence with Messrs Aylott & Jones. She signed her letters "C. Brontë"—to be addressed "c/o the Rev. P. Brontë, Haworth, near Bradford" and was addressed in return as "C. Brontë, Esq" by her publishers. Mr Brontë's increasing blindness and Tabby's infirmity of foot were considered guarantees enough against discovery. All went well until 28th March, when a batch of proof-

sheets very nearly miscarried. In great agitation Charlotte wrote
to the publishers to address to "Miss Brontë" in future instead of
to "C. Brontë, Esq"—a humiliating avowal for the agent of the
Messrs Bell to have to make !

Indubitably the period of the preparation of the *Poems* for the
press was one of activity and hope. No pains were spared, no
possibilities left unexplored. Charlotte despatched sometimes four
letters a week in their anxiety to know, firstly, whether the manuscripts, forwarded in two separate parcels, had safely reached their
destination ; to discuss the choice of paper and of type (to be
modelled on nothing less than the fashionable Moxon's recent
edition of Wordsworth), to decide to what periodicals copies
should be sent for review : besides the almost daily passage to and
fro of proofs. It was a happy, busy time, falling providentially
when most it was needed to heal some of the recent scars left by a
succession of unpropitious years and fortifying them, in a measure,
against the fresh onslaughts fate held in store.

In the last week of May 1846 the *Poems of Currer, Ellis and Acton
Bell* appeared and the authors each received their six complimentary
copies. As no one in the household was taken into their confidence,
the arrival, undoing and secretion of the precious volumes must
have added the delight of mystification to the deeper contentment
of possessing at last a book wholly their own.

It was a neat, unassuming enough little volume of 165 pages,
in a clear type, on good paper, bound in dark green cloth, and a
handy size to slip into a pocket, even a lady's under-pocket, should
intruders appear.

The work of each author was designated by her pseudonym
after each poem, a rather clumsy arrangement in place of differenti-
ating their authorship in the table of contents. With a few
exceptions the poems followed in regular rotation, one by Currer,
one by Ellis, one by Acton. Occasionally only did two poems by
the same author appear together. There was thus achieved a
connection in their work which, indeed, must have made them feel
very close.

It is particularly interesting to note here that although most
critics were not deceived, the *Dublin University Magazine*, which
gave the book so encouraging a review, conjectured "that the
soi-disant 3 personnages were in reality one".

Anne's contribution to the volume was, as stated above, twenty-

one poems. To judge from the total number of her poems preserved, Anne had, in that winter of 1845-6, forty-six poems from
which to choose.

Inevitably, given the circumstances in which the volume was
sent forth, her choice could not and did not fall upon her "Gondal"
poems—they numbered up to that date fourteen, among which
some of her finest verse was undeniably to be found. Their
dramatic settings, calling for power of sentiment and forcefulness
of expression, revealed a facet of Anne's talent which, regrettably,
had to remain absent from the selection presented to the public.
Thus from her first appearance in print Anne's verse was subjected
to a muzzle, as it were, which tended to throw a false emphasis on
her achievement. From the twenty-one poems published in 1846
an impression of lyric sweetness was derived which gave little
indication either of the power and energy or of the originality
which characterised the greater part of her "Gondal" verse and
of much that was still to come. In Acton Bell's contributions
to the joint volume of verse the critics and public alike could
have found nothing presaging the ruthless realism of *The Tenant of
Wildfell Hall*.

The *almost* total exclusion of Gondal poems (three lyrics easy of
transposition were finally included) threw Anne back for her choice
upon purely personal poems, which, by their very nature, were for
the most part of recent composition. With the exception of one
early poem (the half-autobiographical "Self-Congratulation") they
were written between 1842 and 1845 and reflected essentially her
state of mind while absent from home at Thorp Green. Their
subject-matter was thus inevitably tinged with nostalgia not only
for home, as in "Home" and "The Consolation", but for all past
happiness, especially that associated with recollections of childhood.
To disassociate her happiest impressions of childhood from the
natural surroundings that provoked them was an impossibility, thus
in the poems "Remorse", "Past Days" and "The Arbour", all the
freshness and loveliness of her moorland home is inextricably woven
into her recollections.

Poems descriptive of the power of nature—the most compelling
influence in youth as in her maturity—rank, as might be expected,
among her highest achievements. The perfect "Lines Composed
in a Wood on a Windy Day", where emotion and expression have
achieved a fusion as felicitous as it is rare in Anne's writing, is

probably the best poem she ever wrote, though not the most characteristic. [Quoted in Chapter Thirteen, p. 163.]

The period 1842–5 from which all these poems were drawn was that of her lost love as well as of her prolonged absence from home. The memory of Willy Weightman inspired such elegiac pieces as : "A Reminiscence", "Appeal", "The Captive Dove" and "Self-Congratulation".

Her deeply thoughtful nature could not dissociate the problem of death from that of the destiny of the soul, and a large section of these poems, eight in all, dealt with religious and philosophical subjects. In these, the most ambitious of the collection, in "Vanitas Vanitatum", "Views of Life" and the dialectical "Word to the Elect" especially, the power of Anne's logic was never more compelling. Her argument is lucid and probing, her attack sometimes disconcertingly pungent. What a challenge rings out in the opening lines of her "Word to the Elect" :

> You may rejoice to think *yourselves* secure ;
> You may be grateful for the gift divine—
> That grace unsought, which made your black hearts pure,
> And fits your earth-born souls in Heaven to shine.
>
> But, is it sweet to look around, and view
> Thousands excluded from that happiness
> Which they deserve at least as much as you—
> Their faults not greater, nor their virtues less ?

There is a fire and force in these poems all too seldom associated with her writing, which point, as *The Tenant of Wildfell Hall* was in turn to do, to latent powers which needed only time to release them. These were themes on which she felt intensely.

Though excluding some of her most original verse, the selection of her poems that appeared in the 1846 edition showed Anne Brontë to be unmistakably a poet. Though technically she may seldom have reached perfection, there is music in every line she wrote. Some of her openings are hauntingly memorable :

> Oh, weep not, love ! each tear that springs
> In those dear eyes of thine . . .
>
> I mourn with thee, and yet rejoice
> That thou shouldst sorrow so ;

Yes, thou art gone ! and never more
Thy sunny smile shall gladden me . . .

O God ! If this indeed be all
That Life can show to me . . .

In the simple rhythms she chose there is something singularly poignant and touching that was not always in keeping with the subject. She sought not only to express a truth but an *exact shade* of truth, and had not always the ability to achieve it. Her full measure as a poet could not be judged either by this first selection nor in the meagre posthumous edition put out by Charlotte, excluding as they both did her earliest and most lyrical Gondal poems and her later philosophic and religious verse. Even today, when the last manuscript poem seems to have come in, we may be very certain that we have not seen the whole of Anne Brontë's poetic potential.

Of those periodicals which reviewed the book, the notices in the July issues of *The Critic* and *The Athenaeum* and the October issue of the *Dublin University Magazine* gave the greatest pleasure to the authors. Charlotte wrote to the editor of the latter journal and thanked him in her own name and that of her "brothers Ellis and Acton" for the indulgent notice which their book had received ; the review she considered had exactly fulfilled the "right end of criticism—without absolutely crushing, it corrects and rouses".

The *Athenaeum* critic, in an article called "Poetry for the Million", had the insight to see that Ellis Bell possessed a "fine quaint spirit and an evident power of wing that may reach heights not here attempted", and that his poems conveyed an impression of originality "beyond what his contributions to these volumes embody". But it was the notice in *The Critic* which heartened them most. It ran : "They in whose hearts are chords strung by Nature to sympathise with the beautiful and the true, will recognise in these compositions the presence of more genius than it was supposed this utilitarian age had devoted to the loftier exercises of the intellect." Here was understanding indeed.

Understanding, coupled with a sentiment akin to hero-worship, greeted the authors from another source. A letter addressed to their publishers and forwarded by them to Haworth requested the Messrs Bell to favour a certain Mr F. Enoch, a song writer, with their signatures. He had "read and admired their poems" and was sufficiently carried away to *say* so. This first contact with their reading public agitated as much as it cheered the Messrs Bell. They wrote to their publishers, enclosing specimens of their signatures but requesting that the letter might be posted from London in order to avoid giving any clue to residence or identity by post-mark.

In such expressions of sympathy and understanding the girls found justification enough for their temerity. Even without them they would not now have turned back.

Before ever the slim volume of their poems had appeared from the press, as early as 6th April of that exciting spring, C. Brontë, the agent for the Messrs Bell, was writing to Messrs Aylott & Jones regarding a fresh literary venture.

"Gentlemen," she wrote, "C., E. and A. Bell are now preparing for the press a work of fiction, consisting of three distinct and unconnected tales, which may be published either together, as a work of three volumes of the ordinary novel size, or separately as single volumes, as shall be deemed most advisable. . . ."

This is the first intimation we possess of the existence of *The Professor*, *Wuthering Heights* and *Agnes Grey*, for the "three distinct and unconnected tales" were no other than these.

Messrs Aylott & Jones did not deal in works of fiction. By return of post they intimated as much, but added that if they could be useful in supplying the Messrs Bell with a list of those firms which made a feature of such publications they would be pleased to do so.

The kind offer was accepted, a list of the principal publishing firms in England and Scotland was received and a letter drawn up, a type-letter, which Charlotte, as the amanuensis of the trio, began sending out upon the weary rounds ; for this time well over a year was to pass before a single publisher agreed to consider any one of the novels.

One such type-letter still exists today and is preserved in the Memorial Library of Princeton University. Addressed to the publisher, Henry Colburn of London, and dated 4th July 1846, it effectually dispels the theory, hitherto generally accepted, that the Brontës' first novels were only written *after* the publication of the *Poems* in 1846 and in direct consequence of their authors' decision from now on to write professionally.

On examination the facts show that quite the contrary was the case. The girls had each begun and *advanced* "a work of prose fiction" by 6th April 1846 when Charlotte first mentioned the matter to Messrs Aylott & Jones. There is reason to believe that Henry Colburn, to whom Charlotte's extant letter is addressed, on 4th July 1846, was the first publisher after Aylott & Jones to whom the manuscripts were offered. Furthermore, the evidence of Charlotte herself in the biographical memoir to her sisters' works, tells us that the novels went the publishers' rounds "for the space of a year and a half" and, since these were all finally accepted for publication by the July-August of 1847, they were in existence and indeed near completion *at least* as early as April 1846 when we first hear of them.

Of *Agnes Grey* there had already been a previous mention in the diary paper of 30th July 1845, when Anne wrote : "I have begun the third volume of *Passages in the Life of an Individual*." Since that July evening the book had been finished and the title changed to the definitive *Agnes Grey*.

Together with *Wuthering Heights* and *The Professor* it was now sent out to six publishing firms in turn, preceded by the following letter :

"Sir, I request permission to send for your inspection the M.S. of a work of fiction in 3 vols. It consists of three tales, each occupying a volume and capable of being published together or separately, as thought most advisable. The authors of these tales have already appeared before the public.

"Should you consent to examine the work, would you, in your reply, state at what period, after transmission of the M.S. to you, the authors may expect to receive your decision upon its merits. I am Sir, Yours respectfully, C. Bell. Address, Mr Currer Bell, Parsonage, Haworth, Bradford, Yorkshire."

The great difference in the authors' situation, this time, was that they could claim to have "already appeared before the public" ; in consequence they were firmly resolved not to publish "on their own account".

Already the *Poems* had cost considerably more than originally agreed. An extra £5 had to be paid for paper and printing, and the modest initial £2 spent on advertisement had shortly to be increased by another £10 if the Messrs Bell wished notices of their book to appear in more than a very limited number of newspapers and journals ; even so, they were made to feel that they were doing things in a very small way. They dared not, in spite of

Aunt's precious legacy, spend another penny on launching their novels ; the price for "carriage" was bad enough as each successive publisher returned the scripts with a curt refusal. It was surely not poverty which caused them to return the same worn paper wrapping with the address scored out and yet another added to every successive publisher they tried, but it was certainly want of worldly wisdom !

It was hardly surprising that, as Charlotte related afterwards, "The MSS were perseveringly obtruded upon various publishers for the space of a year and a half and usually their fate was an ignominious and abrupt dismissal."

They must all have received a shock when, in the mid summer of 1847 an answer was at last received from an unknown firm— Messrs Thomas Cautley Newby of 72 Mortimer Street, Cavendish Square—agreeing to publish the two novels by Ellis and Acton Bell but *declining* to handle that of Currer Bell !

Never in the whole course of their lives had Charlotte not played a leading part in their enterprises ; for Charlotte to be passed over in their favour was an experience as new as it was unpleasant—we may be sure—to Charlotte's loyal sisters. They were so little used to pushing themselves forward, that the answer must have left them for a time at least sorely perplexed.

There was another proviso attached to Newby's offer ; he asked the authors to share the risk of the cost of publication. He mentioned the sum of £50 for an edition of 350 copies. He undertook to refund it as soon as initial expenses had been defrayed.

They had resolved on spending not another penny on publication, but that was a year ago when the comparatively easy launching of their book of poems made them unduly sanguine. For Charlotte to advise them one way or the other now was awkward ; her own manuscript had been refused, her sisters' accepted ; it was not for her to say to them, "You cannot accept these terms." Even if that had been her opinion she would have hesitated to express it. As she said later of Emily : "It is usually best to leave her to form her own judgement, and *especially* not to advocate the side you wish her to favour ; if you do, she is sure to lean in the opposite direction, and ten to one will argue herself into non-compliance."

However the case may have been debated, Emily and Anne decided on accepting Newby's terms. It was a big sum to part with (as already stated they had only about £300 each from Aunt's legacy and whatever savings Anne had been able to make at Thorp Green). There is something dashing about this decision that savours of Gondal. It was a gesture of either excess of hope or defiance, for at that identical moment the complete failure of the *Poems* to sell had resulted in their giving away the surplus copies of the edition for which they had so proudly paid the previous year. To Wordsworth, Tennyson, Lockhart and De Quincey copies were sent with the accompanying wryly humorous letter :

> Sir—My relatives Ellis and Acton Bell, and myself heedless of the repeated warnings of various respectable publishers, have committed the rash act of printing a volume of poems.
>
> The consequences predicted have, of course, overtaken us : our book is found to be a drug ; no man needs it or heeds it. In the space of a year our publisher has disposed but of two copies, and by what painful efforts he succeeded in getting rid of these two, himself only knows.
>
> Before transferring the edition to the trunkmakers, we have decided on distributing as presents a few copies of what we cannot sell ; and we beg to offer you one in acknowledgment of the pleasure and profit we have often and long derived from your works. I am, Sir, Yours very respectfully,
>
> Currer Bell
>
> June 16th 1847

It was in this identical month of June that Emily and Anne concluded the business with Newby. In accepting his terms it was agreed that *Wuthering Heights* and *Agnes Grey* should be published together as a three-volume novel, *Wuthering Heights* taking up the first two volumes and *Agnes Grey* the third.

Meanwhile the rejected *Professor* continued on his rounds. Separated from its companion novels, it was found to be too short to fall into any of the categories in which fiction was being presented at the time. So Charlotte was told, with greater courtesy than usual, by the firm of Smith, Elder & Co. of Cornhill, who returned the much-travelled manuscript to her yet once again in the following July. But this time the rejection was accompanied with a healing balm ; if Currer Bell had *another* work of sufficient length to make a "three-decker" novel, Messrs Smith, Elder & Co. would be interested to consider it.

The story is world-famed how Charlotte, having by her the manuscript of her just-finished novel *Jane Eyre*, despatched it to Cornhill on 24th August, had it instantly accepted and published within the space of eight weeks (16th October 1847) ! By 19th October she was in possession of her six complimentary copies and by 26th October the press reviews were beginning to pour in. There was never a dissentient voice : as the *Westminster Review* said, *Jane Eyre* was "decidedly the best novel of the season".

And meanwhile Emily and Anne, whose works had found a publisher before Charlotte's, were still waiting for news of *Wuthering Heights* and *Agnes Grey*.

All through July they had been correcting the proofs ; by the first week in August the last sheets were in the publishers' hands and ready for the press ; and then they heard nothing more. The tremendous excitement over the lightning career of *Jane Eyre*—its acceptance, its publication, its immediate success—seethed through the parsonage (even Mr Brontë this time could not be kept in the dark and retired with a copy of the novel to the parlour, opining, after a perusal of the first chapters, that it was "more than likely"). All this was going on and still nothing more was heard from Newby regarding the publication of *Wuthering Heights* and *Agnes Grey*.

Impatience gave place to anxiety ; who and what was this Newby, of whom no one knew anything ? He had pocketed the girls' £50 and thereafter had given not a sign of life. Letters were doubtless written to him, but they have not been preserved. Charlotte, from her very first contacts with her publishers, had been made aware how singularly fortunate she was in dealing with gentlemen in every sense of the word, and sought through Smith, Elder & Co. to find out something more about her sisters' unsatisfactory publishers. Writing to Mr Williams (of the firm of Smith, Elder & Co.) on 10th November she said : "A prose work by Ellis and Acton will soon appear ; it should have been out, indeed, long since ; for the first proof-sheets were already in the press at the commencement of last August, before Currer Bell had placed the manuscript of *Jane Eyre* in your hands. Mr Newby, however, does not do business like Messrs Smith & Elder [*sic*] ; a different spirit seems to preside at Mortimer Street to that which guides the helm at 65, Cornhill. . . . My relations have suffered from exhausting delay and procrastination. . . . I should like to know if Mr Newby often acts as he has done to my relations, or whether this is an exceptional instance of his method. Do you know, and can you tell me anything about him ? You must excuse me for going to the point at once, when I want to learn anything ; if my questions are impertinent you are, of course, at liberty to decline answering them. . . ."

Messrs Smith, Elder & Co. were to learn more of Mr Newby's proceedings in the future ; however unfavourable their judgment may have been now, it was to be increased a hundredfold when Anne came to publish her second novel.

Newby, of course, was just biding his time. Seeing the enormous success of *Jane Eyre* he was waiting to cash in on it. Whether further representations from the incensed authors stirred him or no, by December, with the second edition of *Jane Eyre* going through the press, he seemed to think the time sufficiently ripe. Before 14th December Emily and Anne were each in possession of their six complimentary copies.

Much of their first delight was dashed by the very unsatisfactory presentation of the books. Charlotte, writing to her own publishers, said the volumes were "not at all well got up and abounded in errors of the press. . . . The orthography and punctuation of the books are mortifying to a degree : almost all the errors that were corrected in the proof-sheets appear intact in what should have been the fair copies." Increasingly happy in her relations with her own publishers and very certainly regretting that her sisters had not bided their time to share her own good fortune, she added : "If Mr Newby always does business in this way, few authors would like to have him for their publishers a second time."

The books were bound in deep claret-coloured, fine-ribbed cloth. As agreed, *Wuthering Heights* took up the first two volumes, *Agnes Grey* the third. In spite of past vexation and present disappointment with the slovenly printing of Mr Newby's presses, such as they were, we may be very certain the volumes brought a glow of happiness to the thin cheeks of their authors.

Anne Brontë's own copy of *Agnes Grey* (it was a compact volume of 363 pages), which is preserved in Princeton University Library, is full of the author's corrections of these numerous errors. One can imagine her sitting, with bowed head, the light of the lamp falling on her pretty hair, absorbed in her task. *Agnes Grey* was published in one volume ; it had not the breadth to take up two like Emily's *Wuthering Heights*, far less three, like Charlotte's *Jane Eyre*. Yet it held in its modest dimensions a perfection of its own.

"*Agnes Grey*," wrote Charlotte a week after the book had come out, "is the mirror of the mind of the writer." She could not have more exactly defined its worth.

Though *Agnes Grey* may have fallen into relative obscurity nowadays it must not be forgotten that in George Moore's opinion it was "the most perfect prose narrative in English literature. . . . As simple and beautiful as a muslin dress . . . the one story in English literature in which style, characters and subject are in perfect keeping."

These are high claims indeed and worth recalling in any attempt to assess the book's lasting worth.

Agnes Grey, as its original title shows, had been begun as an autobiography. Its value today is still permanently enhanced by the fact that it relates, with startling adherence to truth, the circumstances of Anne's two experiences as governess.

For good or for ill, Anne did not leave it there. The artist within her took charge and the book, begun with one intention, had very soon far exceeded it and become a full-scale work of fiction.

Not full-scale in the sense of bulk ; one of *Agnes Grey's* chief merits is its exquisite proportions. It is well proportioned as a French interior is well proportioned, with each article of furniture on so small yet perfect a scale that no object appears crowded or overwhelmed by its fellows.

Yet it was inevitable that the dual purpose of the book should emerge ; that those portions which were derived from fact should be more vividly realised and that the purely fictitious incidents should be slurred over, as inappropriate, as it were, to the fuller treatment. Thus the happy ending to which, as fiction, Anne had not the heart to deny her heroine, is written in so low and subdued a key that it saddens rather than elates the reader. Judged from the standpoint of art this is a mistake ; the story of *Agnes Grey* begun in such buoyant style, with so much wit and sparkle, should not modulate into a minor key and close in solemnity since, in spite of some tribulations, the heroine's happiness is assured.

So the author, at least, would have us believe. But the sadness of Anne's own experience in love broods over the tale and makes us rather doubt the ordering of the facts at the story's close. They are so very lightly sketched in, with none of the bite and incision of outline in which the exposition and middle of the book are etched, that one sees them as through a mist, only partially discernible.

That does not diminish their charm. There is, indeed, an elegiac charm pervading the whole of the latter half of the book, from Chapter 13 to the end, which fully makes up for the loss of the vivacity and humour of the opening. But the difference is there. *Agnes Grey* is a book that falls in two, not only because it is part-autobiographical and part-fictional, but because, written over a period of probably at least three years, it reflects the tragic change in Anne's circumstances.

It seems likely that she began writing *Passages in the Life of an Individual* in her second year at Thorp Green, in 1842. She may even have begun it much earlier, during the interregnum at home following her dismissal from the Inghams. Whenever it was, she could still view her experiences at Blake Hall with enough humour to derive an artistic satisfaction from their narration. The opening chapters of the book, all those relating to Blake Hall indeed, are instinct with satirical observation and, what is rarer far, with a sense of humour as regards her own failures and distresses. The style is elastic and reveals a cheerful mind "full of bright hopes and ardent expectations".

It is this section of the book, the first six chapters in particular, in which Anne showed herself, to quote George Moore again, to have not only all Jane Austen's qualities but some others as well. (Her true literary progenitors, one is tempted to suggest, were Goldsmith and Maria Edgeworth; for she probably never read Jane Austen any more than Charlotte had done.)

Her time for writing would be very limited once she was fully engaged in teaching at Thorp Green. With the tragic autumn of 1842 and the death of Willy Weightman, a burden so great was added to her already flagging spirits that the zest and animation went out of her writing, however much she needed writing of some sort to absorb her. But all the delight was gone. There is observation as sharp of the Murray family as of the Bloomfields, but bitterness has replaced the good humour, and disappointment effectually dimmed the youthful ardour. The opening chapters of *Agnes Grey* are the work of a young person, still full of sanguine hopes ; the latter half betrays the effort of a stricken heart.

An identical circumstance attended the composition of *Shirley* and left similar indelible traces of the conflicting states of mind in

which it was written, but Charlotte, unlike Anne, had by the time
she was writing her third novel achieved a greater mastery of her
medium. Time which militated in favour of Charlotte was to be
so cruelly lacking for the development of Anne. There is tantalising
promise in both her books of the masterpiece that should have come
thereafter.

Agnes Grey is as different from *Wildfell Hall* as two books by
one and the same author can well be, yet unmistakably they are
from the same pen : an uncompromising honesty invests both tales.
This quality it is which gives *Agnes Grey* its distinctive value.
It is the honesty of the author which insists upon that self-analysis
of the heroine's feelings and motives which constitutes not only the
book's originality but its truth. Character described from *without*
is one thing—and Anne was to show herself a mistress at tersely
satirical portraiture—but that which is revealed to us, by growing
degrees, from *within*, is far more rare and nearer the movement of
life. Though the plot of *Agnes Grey* is too static to arouse keen
excitement in the reader, there is nothing static in the characters.
The flux of feeling, the uncertainty of temper, the deteriorating
effect of time, it is *these* considerations that hold our attention and
make us wonder right to the very end *how* the characters will finally
resolve their problems.

The literary qualities of the book are best judged by their
appropriateness ; the style suits the matter, and though Anne always
excelled in purely descriptive passages—her loving eye for all aspects
of the natural scene being perfectly matched by her fastidious choice
of language—there is no writing for the sake of writing.

The book is rich in such observation of character as the
following :

"Mr Bloomfield," she writes of her first employer, "was a
retired tradesman who had realised a very comfortable fortune, but
could not be prevailed upon to give a greater salary than £25 to
the instructress of his children."

Here is the grandmother of the Bloomfield family—"Hitherto,
though I saw the old lady had her defects (of which one was a
proneness to proclaim her perfections) I had always been wishful
to excuse them, and to give her credit for all the virtues she pro-
fessed, and even imagine others yet untold."

For a parson's daughter the following sketch of a worldly cleric
is full of savour. "Mr Hatfield would come sailing up the aisle,

or rather sweeping along like a whirlwind, with his rich silk gown flying behind him and rustling against the pew doors, mount the pulpit like a conqueror ascending his triumphal car ; then, sinking on the velvet cushion in an attitude of studied grace, remain in silent prostration for a certain time. . . ."

So much of the psychological interest of *Agnes Grey* derives from the personal experience of the author that the tendency is to consider it rather in its autobiographical than in its literary connection. It is part of Anne's quality, however, that though she told nothing but the truth, by the force of imagination she seemed to be inventing, and it is Agnes Grey with whom readers are concerned, not Anne Brontë.

Its essential truthfulness no competent critic has ever doubted. Charlotte Brontë, stung by Lewes's accusations of extravagance and improbability in her own *Jane Eyre*, wrote of *Agnes Grey* to her publishers : "*Agnes Grey* should please such critics as Mr Lewes for it is 'true' and 'unexaggerated' enough." As the reviewer in *Douglas Jerrolds' Weekly* wrote : "The author, if not a governess, must have bribed some governess very largely, either with love or money, to reveal to him the secrets of her prison house . . .," so convincingly did Acton Bell set forth "the minute torments and incessant tediums" of her situation.

In this respect one near-contemporary reader's views are peculiarly worth recording. Lady Amberley noted in her diary for 1868 : "read *Agnes Grey*, one of the Brontës, and should like to give it to every family with a governess and shall read it through again when I have a governess to remind me to be human."

In due course the professional reviews arrived at the parsonage, regularly forwarded to the authors by Mr Newby. The discerning critic on *Douglas Jerrolds' Weekly* was of opinion that *Agnes Grey* was a tale "well worth the writing and the reading" ; that on *Britannia* (who had a mind to discern sublimity in *Wuthering Heights*) found nothing to call for special notice in *Agnes Grey*, but conceded that "some characters and scenes" were nicely sketched in.

It was the writer on *The Atlas* who gave Emily's and Anne's novels the most exhaustive review. As was inevitable, he compared the two productions. *Agnes Grey* he found "more level and more sunny. Perhaps", he added, "we should best describe it as a somewhat coarse imitation of Miss Austin's [sic] charming stories". It did not offend "by any startling improbabilities", and he found the incidents relating to the governess's life "such as might happen to anyone in that situation of life and, doubtless, have happened to many. The story, though lacking the power and originality of *Wuthering Heights*, is infinitely more agreeable. It leaves no painful impression on the mind—some may think it leaves no impression at all. *We are not quite sure that the next novel will not efface it.*"

In the last line Anne may have read a challenge which strangely accorded with her then intentions, for, by the time she was reading the *Atlas* critic's review, she was already engaged on writing her second novel.

The *Atlas* reviewer had elsewhere declared it his opinion that Currer, Ellis and Acton Bell (whose *Poems* he now well remembered having noted some two years before) had all come before the public now ". . . with so much success as to make their future career a matter of interesting speculation in the literary world."

What the publishers and critics who foretold their future successes could not imagine was against what present odds their authors worked. Not until the sad tale was eventually told by Charlotte and Mrs Gaskell was the truth even partially suspected.

Chapter Seventeen

THE TENANT OF WILDFELL HALL

EXACTLY two years elapsed between the *completion* of *Agnes Grey* and that of *Wildfell Hall*, but an interval of more like four years separated the *beginning* of the earlier book from that of the second. Otherwise the mark of maturity that distinguishes *Wildfell Hall* could hardly be explained.

A wealth of experience divides their two worlds—which is not to say that the advance is one of unadulterated gain. What *Wildfell Hall* has acquired in worldly knowledge it has lost in freshness.

The buoyancy of the opening chapters, in particular, of *Agnes Grey*, the caustic wit—the Jane Austen-like sparkle and sheer enjoyment of human folly—is nowhere to be found in the later novel. In their place is a depth of insight, an awareness of the shabbiness and shadiness in human relationships never attempted by the sunny enchantress of Chawton. Above all, in *Wildfell Hall* Anne is demonstrating, like an impartial anatomist before a class of students, the corroding effect on character not only of self-indulgence, vice and profligacy, but of virtue itself if too long and too painfully exposed to a consciousness of superiority over hostile and degrading influences. A love of perfection, she would seem to say, is no guarantee against temptation ; deterioration is at work on the good just as much as on the evil and its effect, when felt, is a more intolerable suffering than any inflicted from without. What makes *Wildfell Hall* telling still today is the character of Helen Huntingdon, the heroine, whose peculiar admixture of qualities is the cause of so much of her own suffering, and in whom Anne mirrored with that unflinching honesty which is the hall-mark of all her work the impatient and imperfect nature, with its fierce temper, passionate affections and inflexible honesty, which she knew to be her own. The evolution from Agnes Grey to Helen Huntingdon is indeed a sad one. "Here," Anne seems to say, "is the counterfeit presentment of two sisters—nay, of one and the same girl, seen at the dawn of life and in maturity—intrepid both, young and ardent, with faith and feelings of the very finest order destined to part company at the outset of life. For Agnes, after a succession of moderate trials, destiny will be kind ; on Helen, the ordeal, even when survived, will leave its mark for ever."

This was a theme very close to Anne's heart ; in her own life she had, unhappily, proved its veracity : people are not so nice nor so good after great tribulation ; the heart, more especially the sensitive heart, can survive certain experiences only by becoming hardened. It is a deplorable condition of existence which, to be honest with oneself, one had better face with what courage one may.

In the autobiographical poem "Self-Communion", a long work contemporary with *Wildfell Hall*, Anne has memorably described the inevitable trend.

> God alters not ; but Time on me,
> A wide and wondrous change has wrought :
> And in these parted years I see
> Cause for grave care and saddening thought.
> I see that time, and toil, and truth
> An inward hardness can impart—
> Can freeze the generous blood of youth,
> And steel full fast the tender heart.

This was one of the themes attempted in *Wildfell Hall*, a book possibly too full of challenges against conventional complacency ever to be much liked, and because of this, far more than because of the sensational delineation of a profligate society, it must for ever ring true.

Less than any other of the Brontë novels can *The Tenant of Wildfell Hall* be separated from the circumstances in which it was composed.

It can be truly said that the Brontës were never to know what it was to work in peace. The periods of even their most moderate successes were always to be marked with sudden stress, when not completely darkened by tragedy. At almost every phase of their literary achievement when a modicum of enjoyment might have been theirs, their tranquillity was shattered by Branwell's misdemeanours and the burden of responsibility increasingly laid on them by their father's decline.

"What family hasn't its trials ?" as Charlotte repeatedly asked of her friend Ellen, but trials so extreme as theirs, combining every degree of illness and of vice, of misfortune and disappointment, of conscious genius and frustrated talents, have rarely, if ever, been borne by one and the same family ; a family singularly bound by love and temperament to form an indestructible whole. Much as we may wonder that their literary output was as considerable as it was, it is impossible not to reflect how far greater it might have been had they *not* been afflicted with circumstances so adverse and unkind.

Fate decreed that the period of their main literary achievement was to correspond exactly with the period of Branwell's residence at home—from the summer of 1845 to 1848—from which infliction there was to be no reprieve but death. Shut up in a small house with their drunken drug-addict of a brother, how could it be otherwise than that the stamp of Branwell is on so much of what they wrote ? The wonder is he is not in everything.

After the initial frenzy following his dismissal from Thorp Green, Branwell was tolerably quiet that winter of 1845. Charlotte accused him chiefly of idleness, not so much of incapacity, in his failure to find any work. He still had some money left from his last salary and was drinking it steadily. The attitude of Charlotte was fast hardening into that rooted aversion which his spineless self-indulgence was to rouse in her far more than in either of his other sisters. "You say well," she wrote to Ellen at the end of the year, "in speaking of Branwell, that no sufferings are so awful as those brought on by dissipation. . . . Alas ! I see the truth of this observation daily proved."

By March he seems to have run through his money ; during an absence of Charlotte's at the Nusseys, he managed to borrow a pound from his father on the plea of an urgent debt to pay, and drank himself silly for three days. Emily, reporting the matter to Charlotte on her return, said "he was a hopeless being"—a statement of fact, doubtless unaccompanied by anything more than a shrug of the shoulders. By April Charlotte sees in him a permanent incubus. ". . . how can we be more comfortable so long as Branwell remains at home and degenerates instead of improving. It has lately been intimated to him that he would be received again on the railroad where he was formerly stationed, if he would but behave more steadily, but he refuses to make an effort—he will not work—and at home he is a drain on every resource, an impediment to all happiness."

Nothing could be clearer. Charlotte was writing on 14th April

1846, by which date the *Poems of Currer, Ellis and Acton Bell* were not only in the press, but the question of the "three distinct and unconnected tales" was actually being debated with Messrs Aylott & Jones. Branwell at home was "a drain on every resource and an impediment to all happiness". But Branwell was far from being at his worst, as his family was very soon to experience. However Charlotte might judge his present behaviour, he was actually at that moment attempting to do something for himself. On 28th April he wrote to his friend Leyland at Halifax : "I am presenting enquiries about situations suitable to me whereby I could have a voyage abroad. The quietude of home and the inability to make my family aware of the nature of most of my sufferings makes me write." On 2nd May he was again writing, this time to his friend Grundy, stating that he was in better health than for years past and anxious for employment now.

What Branwell's destiny might have been had Mrs Robinson left him in the relative peace he had now attained is a tantalising question ; but Mrs Robinson was not to leave him in peace.

Within a few days of the publication of the *Poems of Currer, Ellis and Acton Bell*—an event, incidentally, which they never communicated to their brother—the Rev. Edmund Robinson died at Thorp Green, on 26th May 1846. Whatever her motives, Mrs Robinson immediately despatched to Haworth the family coachman, George Gooch, with messages for Branwell whose gist was : to keep away at all costs.

Gooch arrived on horseback, alighted at the *Black Bull* and sent a message up to the parsonage for Branwell, and the two men were closeted together for a long time in the saloon bar. The facts Gooch had been primed to impress on Branwell were that Mr Robinson had made a codicil to his will with a view to preventing all prospect of a marriage between Mrs Robinson and Branwell. The property was tied up on his children and was to be administered by trustees. One of these was Mr Robinson's York solicitor and the other his brother-in-law, the Venerable Charles Thorpe. This gentleman (according to Branwell's subsequent narration) had declared that if Branwell showed himself at Thorp Green he would shoot him on sight. In case such deterrents and threats were not enough to keep Branwell away, Gooch expatiated on the sufferings and grief of Mrs Robinson who had worn herself out nursing her husband, and who could not now be persuaded out of her bedroom or off her knees, so intense were her remorse and shame. In short, "it was a pity to see her," the servant said, while strongly intimating that it would be *impossible* to see her.

The hint was broad enough even for Branwell to understand : his presence at Thorp Green was not only *forbidden* by the lady's relatives, it was not desired by her.

His mission accomplished and a meal devoured, Mr Gooch called for his horse and rode off down the hill. No one noticed that Branwell had not accompanied him to the door. Only the servant girl, more than an hour later, hearing strange sounds coming from the saloon bar—which she tried later to describe and said were like the bleating of a calf—pushed open the door, went in and found Branwell in a fit upon the floor.

Relating the bare facts in a letter to Ellen, Charlotte wrote : "Of course, he then became intolerable. To Papa he allows rest neither day nor night, and he is continually screwing money out of him, sometimes threatening that he will kill himself if it is withheld from him. He says that Mrs Robinson is now insane ; that her mind is a complete wreck owing to remorse for her conduct towards Mr Robinson and grief for having lost him. I do not know how much to believe—Branwell declares that he neither can nor will do anything for himself . . . he will do nothing, except drink and make us all wretched."

The money he "screwed" out of Papa was not all now being spent on drink ; he needed it for opium as well—opium which, at that time, could be openly bought across the counter of any chemist's shop and to which Branwell had already taken out of bravado years ago, and from which he had successfully weaned himself in the intervening years.

From this time on there is no further talk of applying for jobs or of attempting to keep up appearances. It is a steady decline. Mrs Robinson's intermediaries, with what motive it is indeed difficult to decide, cannot leave him alone. At intervals he receives letters from her physician, Dr Crosby, her lady's maid (Ann Marshall) and also again from the coachman, all depicting in the most lurid colours her state of mind and the impossibility of receiving either communications or visits from Branwell. It is as though the lady had seriously feared he would make a rash attempt to visit her. He did send her a letter which was inevitably intercepted by her brother-in-law, another of Branwell's avowed enemies, the M.P. for North Derbyshire, Mr Evans, and which was sent back to him by Dr Crosby. According to Branwell this gentleman knew him well and "pitied his case most sincerely", but the upshot of the doctor's diplomatic letters was to debar Branwell effectively from all hope of the future. Mrs Robinson was represented as being now insane, now repentant and now decided upon entering a nunnery : whatever else the lady was prepared to be it was in *no* eventuality to become the wife of Mr Branwell Brontë.

Whatever was the truth behind this fantastic "Gothic" romance, Branwell told his friends, as he had told his sisters, that he had firmly believed the lady would marry him. "I had reason to hope," he wrote Leyland nearly a year after the death of Mr Robinson, "that ere very long I should be the husband of a lady whom I loved best in the world and with whom, in more than competence, I might live at leisure to try to make myself a name in the world of posterity." A more genuine and disinterested grief is echoed in the words of another letter to his friend : "I never cared one bit about the property. I cared about herself, and always shall do. May God bless her, but I wish I had never known her !"

One cannot help thinking what Anne must have felt when he said this and similar things to her. It was so true and so reasonable ; if only he had never met Mrs Robinson. And he never *would* have met her if it had not been for Anne.

This reflection which, in his saner moments, Branwell could make must not be overlooked in assessing the part that self-accusation played in Anne's resolve to write *The Tenant of Wildfell Hall.* Her motive in doing so, which was to point to others a moral—as she declares in her Preface to the second edition—was quite as much to impose a penance on herself for her presumption and for her failure in saving her brother.

According to Charlotte, to Mrs Gaskell, and to local tradition as well, Branwell was to remain in some sort of correspondence with Mrs Robinson for at least another year. According to his own statements he was in correspondence with Dr Crosby to within two months of his death. Incredible though it may seem, Branwell declared to his creditors that Dr Crosby was the means of procuring him money from Mrs Robinson. To this mysterious "source" of supply Charlotte referred more than once in her letters, attributing to its means each fresh bout of drunkenness in which Branwell indulged.

He had no further hope of anything at all—sometimes he saw his case with pathetic clarity. "I would bear it," he writes to his friend, "but my health is so bad that the body seems as if it could not bear the mental shock. . . . My appetite is lost ; my nights are dreadful, and having nothing to do makes me dwell on past scenes—on her own self, her voice, her person, her thoughts, till I could be glad if God would take me. In the next world I could not be worse than I am in this."

But the tragi-comedy did not end here. While Branwell was drinking himself to death for his hopeless love, persuading himself that Mrs Robinson's seclusion was dictated by a grief akin to his own, that lady was very busy preparing for her second marriage.

There was absolutely no truth in the report carefully conveyed to Branwell regarding the disposition of Mr Robinson's will, as a reference to the terms of that document reveal. No specification of any sort was made regarding his widow's remarrying—she was left perfectly free to do so and lost very little time in setting about it.

Mrs Robinson's chief difficulty at this time seems to have been how to dispose of her daughters. Husbands in abundance seem to have come forward for these young ladies' hands but not husbands after their own hearts. They wished to temporise ; their mother was resolved to have them settled, the sooner to leave herself free.

As though Anne and Branwell had not suffered enough already from the family, a new and hardly credible situation arose some six months after the death of Mr Robinson. Anne, to her surprise, was once more approached by her late pupils and made the unwilling confidante of their family divisions, while Branwell, necessarily kept in the dark by all, was languishing for a single word of hope.

"The Misses Robinson," wrote Charlotte on 1st March 1847, "who had entirely ceased their correspondence with Anne for half a year after their father's death, have lately recommenced it. For a fortnight they sent her a letter almost every day. . . . They speak with great affection of their mother and never make any allusion intimating acquaintance with her errors. We take special care that Branwell does not know of their writing to Anne."

The Robinsons' home-life seems to have been permanently broken up by the death of the father. Throughout the spring and summer of 1847 we find Mrs Robinson senior, the late Mr Robinson's mother, taking Elizabeth and Mary and young Edmund for long periods to Scarborough where, as formerly, they stayed at their favourite lodgings at the Cliff, and where their arrivals and departures were duly noted in the fashionable news of the day. Their mother seems rarely to have been with them during this time, either from ill-health or through an active prosecution of plans for the future of them all which absorbed her increasingly.

It is, perhaps, worth noting in this connection that the tablet erected to Mr Robinson's memory in Little Ouseburn Church makes no mention of his widow and family. It reads :

Edmund Robinson, Esq
Died May 26th 1846
Aged 46

"Precious in the sight of the Lord
is the death of his Saints."
"When the shore is won at last
who will count the billows past ?"

By the beginning of the next year (1848) Mrs Robinson's plans were taking shape and her daughters bitterly criticising her. In a letter of Charlotte's of 28th January 1848 we get the first intimation that Mrs Robinson is waiting for the death of the wife of a certain gentleman to be able to marry him. This was Sir Edward Dolman Scott, one-time M.P. for Lichfield, whom she did succeed in leading to the altar before the year was out. Lichfield had been Mrs Robinson's paternal home and the acquaintance, based on relationship, dated from her girlhood. Sir Edward Scott was seventy-five at this time, Mrs Robinson forty-eight.

"The Robinsons still amaze me," writes Charlotte, "by the continued frequency and constancy of their correspondence. Poor girls ! they still complain of their mother's proceedings ; that woman is a hopeless being ; calculated to bring a curse wherever she goes by the mixture of weakness, perversion, and deceit in her nature. . . ."

"Mrs Robinson," wrote Charlotte on 18th August 1848, "is anxious to get her daughters husbands of any kind, that they may be off her hands, and that she may be free to marry Sir Edward Scott, whose infatuated slave, it would appear, she is. . . ."

"Anne continues to hear constantly, almost daily from her old pupils, the Robinsons," Charlotte wrote on 28th July. "They are both engaged now . . . and if they do not change their minds, which they have done already two or three times, will probably be married in a few months. Not one spark of love does either of them profess for her future husband, one of them openly declares that interest alone guides her, and the other, poor thing ! is acting according to her mother's wish, and is utterly indifferent herself to the man chosen for her. . . . Anne does her best to cheer and counsel her, and she seems to cling to her quiet, former governess, as her only true friend. Of their mother I have not patience to speak ; a worse woman, I believe, hardly exists ; the more I hear of her the more deeply she revolts me ; but I do not like to talk about her in a letter."

By August the "unfortunate Lady Scott" was dead and on 8th November Mrs Robinson married her widower. The marriage was performed by special licence in the strictest privacy at Bath. But by November the news could no longer affect Branwell.

It is against the background of this sordid story that Anne conceived and wrote her *Tenant of Wildfell Hall*.

It has generally been believed that without Branwell this particular book could never have been written. That opinion must be modified to include the experience Anne gained by her residence at Thorp Green, irrespective of Branwell, and by the incursion of the Robinson family into the retirement of her Haworth home.

Wildfell Hall is not merely the study of a debauchee ; it is the representation of a debauched society. Arthur Huntingdon is no worse in degree, though he may be in kind, than the other male characters in the book : Hattersley, Grimsby, Hargrave and Lord Lowborough. They have all shared a mutual past of dissipation which has made of Huntingdon what he is, and their several rôles, as the story unfolds itself, are made to bear directly on the development of the plot. Furthermore they are not types, still less are they, in the Morality Play sense, personifications of the vices. They are individuals, extremely vital individuals, leading depraved lives, speaking a language racy, strong and terse that is as personal to each as it is admirably rendered by the author. They move before us in a succession of scenes that ring as with the very echo of their hollow lives.

" 'Is it to be the last, Lowborough ?' Huntingdon mockingly asks his friend who has just ruined himself and sworn never to gamble again. 'The last,' he answered, somewhat against my expectation. I took him home—that is, to our club—and plied him with brandy and water till he began to look rather brighter. 'Huntingdon, I'm ruined,' said he, taking the third glass from my hand. 'Not you !' said I. 'You'll find a man can live without his money as merrily as a tortoise without its head or a wasp without its body.' 'But I'm in debt,' said he, 'deep in debt ! And I can never never get out of it !' 'Well, what of that ? Many a better man than you has lived and died in debt, and they can't put you in prison, you know, because you're a peer,' and I handed him his fourth tumbler.' "

It is not that the characters in *Wildfell Hall* can be identified as portraying any particular person or any group of persons known to Anne ; but all too obviously their origins are not far to seek ; the world of Grassdale Manor is essentially the social milieu of Thorp Green Hall.

This is particularly evident in the setting of the story, which is a large country house (Grassdale Manor) supposedly at a distance of a hundred miles from London, lying in its own park and surrounded by wooded country, meadowland and streams. It does not appear to be in the immediate vicinity of any town and the only neighbours to the Huntingdons are the Hargrave family, composed of a mother, two daughters and a son. The elder of the two daughters, Millicent, is married to one of Huntingdon's boon companions, the brutal Hattersley ; the younger daughter is still in the schoolroom with a governess, and the brother, Walter Hargrave, another of Huntingdon's crew, is in love with Helen Huntingdon and pursues her with his sinister attentions.

Of particular interest, in the Thorp Green connection, is the character of the mother, Mrs Hargrave, of whom the following is a description. "I don't like Mrs Hargrave ; she is a hard, pretentious, worldly-minded woman. She has money enough to live very comfortably, if she only knew how to use it judiciously—but she is ever straining to keep up appearances, with that despicable pride that shuns the semblance of poverty as of a shameful crime. She grinds her dependants, pinches her servants and deprives even her daughters and herself of the real comforts of life. . . ." The relationship between mother and unmarried daughter are also markedly reminiscent of those which Anne had so much recent occasion to study, and in the friendship between the married Helen Huntingdon and the teen-age Esther Hargrave is more than one echo, we feel, of that which grew up between Anne Brontë and her pupils. "I am very much attached to my little friend," says Helen Huntingdon, "and so is she to me. I wonder what she can see to like in me—but she *has* no other society, save that of her uncongenial mother and her governess. I often wonder what will be her lot in life. It seems as if I should feel her disappointment even more deeply than my own. . . ." Esther's lot in life would be decided by a worldly marriage, if her mother's ambitions would prevail. "Mrs Hargrave and her daughter are come back from London," writes Helen Huntingdon. . . . "Esther is full of her first season in town. Her mother sought out an excellent match for her and even brought the gentleman to lay his heart and fortune at her feet ; but Esther had the audacity to refuse the noble gifts. He was a man of good family, and large possessions, but the naughty girl maintained he was as old as Adam, ugly as sin, and hateful as—one who shall be nameless. 'But, indeed, I had a hard time of it,' said she : 'Mamma was very greatly disappointed at the failure of her darling project and very, very angry at my obstinate resistance to her will, and is so, still. . . . You can't imagine how she lectures me—I am disobedient and ungrateful ; I am thwarting her wishes, wronging my brother, making myself a burden on her hands—I sometimes fear she'll overcome me after all. I have a strong will, but so has she——' " With such a situation, with such arguments, the letters Anne had been receiving, sometimes "almost every day" from her ex-pupils, had been filled. And it is impossible not to recognise as her own advice in real life that which she puts into the mouth of her heroine in the novel.

"Pray don't," says Helen, as her young friend threatens to give way to the maternal pressure. "Stand firm, and your mamma will soon relinquish her persecution and the gentleman himself cease to pester you with his addresses."

To Grassdale Manor every autumn Arthur Huntingdon invites a house-party to enjoy the shooting and minister to his devastating *ennui*. Its members are never chosen with any respect for his wife's feelings or inclinations ; the men are one and all avowed libertines —the boon companions of his bachelor days—and the women either scheming, immodest or stupid. Chief among the latter are Lady Lowborough, a mature and brazen beauty who becomes Huntingdon's mistress, Mrs Hargrave, the scheming mother of a young and fresh-hearted daughter, and Millicent Hattersley, a weak young wife who gives way to every evil propensity in her husband.

Very advisedly Anne sets her story back some twenty years in time ; it is supposed to cover the period 1821–8. By doing so she rendered more credible the "Regency" manners of her gentlemen. For they are nothing less than a set of Regency rakes, violent, uncontrollable debauchees the whole pack of them, with not even the thinnest veneer of respectability to cover their unashamed depravity. Very far off, yet, is the Victorian convention of morality, even of decorum, in this quite uninhibited society.

For the purposes of the plot, moreover, it was necessary that the heroine's uncle himself, in whose house she had been brought up, should be little better than a reformed *roué*, for it is owing to his intimacy with a very dissolute sort of man that Helen is first brought to the notice of Huntingdon, whose father was one of her uncle's intimates.

That genial old gentleman's views on matrimony are, naturally, more lax than those of his bigoted wife and he despatched the matter of his niece's engagement with unhoped-for celerity. "Now, Nell," says he, "this young Huntingdon has been asking for you. What must I say about it ? Your aunt would answer 'No'—but what say you ?" "I say yes, Uncle," says Helen. . . . "Very good," cried he. "Now that's a good, honest answer. Wonderful for a girl ! Well, I'll write to your father tomorrow. He's sure to give his consent, so you may look on the matter as settled." And so it was.

Huntingdon's associates, as he himself had done in the past, derive their chief amusement from getting drunk and making love to each other's wives. They are men of rank and fortune who consider marriage only as the last desperate resource of those whose fortunes cannot stand the strain of years of riotous living. Woe betide any member of the confraternity who takes that extreme measure for any other motive than a purely mercenary one. For one of them to marry for love is a treachery which is pursued by the relentless venom of the others. What are the gaming-houses for but to "repair" a dwindling fortune ? With the savagery of a pack of wolves they set on any member of their band who tries to reform and withdraw ; if he can no longer minister to their pleasures it is time for him to rot !

Lord Lowborough, whose character is of prime importance to the plot and assembles a number of traits reminiscent of Branwell (indeed, if Branwell stood as the model for anyone in the book, it was for Lord Lowborough and not for Huntingdon as has always been declared)—Lord Lowborough brings down on his head the double weight of their contempt and anger by marrying for love and resolutely giving up drink. There is something satanic in the force of their hatred for him and the callousness with which they try to precipitate his ruin. His desperate struggles to free himself from the devil of drink and of drugs is described in masterly fashion in a succession of scenes rendered all the more shameful for their being related by Huntingdon to his young and innocent fiancée.

"One evening, as we were sitting over our wine," relates Huntingdon, "Lowborough suddenly relapsed into silence, sinking his head on his hand and never lifting his glass to his lips, till he interrupted us in the middle of a roar of laughter by exclaiming : 'Gentlemen, where is all this to end ? Will you just tell me that now ? Where is it all to end ?' He rose. 'A speech ! A speech !' shouted we. 'Hear ! Hear ! Lowborough's going to give us a speech !' He waited calmly till the thunder of applause and jingling of glasses had ceased, and then proceeded : 'It's only this, gentlemen, that I think we had better go no further. We'd better stop while we can.' "

His proposal is, of course, met with an uproar of contumely. He sticks to his guns, however, but his wretchedness and loneliness (a woman he had genuinely loved has just jilted him) drive him continually back to the old haunts and Huntingdon is always at hand to egg him on. He takes to laudanum instead of drink. ". . . For some time he continued to look in upon us pretty regularly of an evening, still abstaining, with wonderful perseverance, from the 'rank poison'. But some of our members protested. They did not like to have him there sitting like a skeleton at a feast, instead of contributing his quota to the general amusement . . . and watching, with greedy eyes, every drop they carried to their lips. We went on with our merry carousals as before, till he startled us all by suddenly drawing up his chair and leaning forward with his elbows on the table and exclaiming with portentous solemnity :

" 'Well, it puzzles me what you can find to be so merry about. What you see in life I don't know—I see only the blackness of darkness, and a fearful looking for judgement and fiery indignation !'

"All the company simultaneously pushed up their glasses to him and I set them before him in a semi-circle and tenderly patting him on the back, bid him drink." They finally put him into such a frenzy that he snatched up a bottle of brandy "and sucked away, till he suddenly dropped from his chair, disappearing under the table amid a tempest of applause. The consequence of this imprudence was something like an apoplectic fit." And so on and so forth in a like vein.

Such, then, is the background and these the subsidiary characters against which the main drama, that between Arthur Huntingdon and his wife Helen, is played out.

The contest between them—and this is its chief claim on our interest—is of a dual nature : it is presented both on a physical and on a spiritual level. In the former, inevitably, the man triumphs ; in the latter, the woman.

But the interest, and the justice, of the story reside in the fact that *both* parties are to blame, that both, in very different respects, at one time or another, are the authors of their own misfortunes.

There is what may be called the "Huntingdon Plot" and there is the "Helen Plot". In the first Anne is showing us to what inevitable ruin unbridled self-indulgence leads ; in the second the disastrous consequences of presumption in young and ignorant girls like Helen who, in their inexperience, imagine they can overcome and convert the very forces of nature itself. In the resultant clash between passion and purity, it is, inevitably, purity that goes to the wall.

But, here, the final balance is retrieved by an appeal to the eternal values.

On the spiritual plane Helen, through suffering and experience, attains finally to a self-knowledge which is, of itself, the condemnation of her early facile virtue. "Fool that I was," she cries, as the realisation of her hopeless lot closes in on her, "to dream that I had strength and purity enough to save myself and him ! Such vain presumption would be rightly served, if I should perish with him in the gulf . . . !" Her married life has taught her how hard it is to preserve one's own integrity, let alone improve another's ! When she has learned how completely she has failed her wretched husband, and in all her sanguine aims at reforming him, then only, when she has touched the nadir of suffering, does she find the strength and the humility to help him in the end.

That she *does* save his soul—and her own—is the whole point of the story. But it had to be at this price ; at the price of defeat, humiliation, despair. Anne is not prepared to give a facile answer to the problem of how to combat evil. She had tried it herself in the case of Branwell and had failed. Nothing easier—and nothing further from the truth—than to place all the winning cards in Helen Huntingdon's hands and give her a bloodless victory over her wicked husband. Had *The Tenant of Wildfell Hall* been a tract, this is what its author would have done. But in default of great artistry, of the genius which a Thackeray would have brought to this tale and made of it a second *Vanity Fair*, Anne had a great integrity and it was the truth she set out to tell. She had learned the truth of just such a situation at first hand and it left her, not self-righteous, but overwhelmed with a sense of failure, defeat and humiliation. It is out of such self-probing that *The Tenant of Wildfell Hall* was born, not, as has generally been maintained, uniquely out of a desire to point the moral of Branwell's fall.

The characters are firmly set before us. The youth and freshness of Helen, her eagerness, merriment and spirit—the strong wilfulness that is the outcome not of spoiling but of an independent mind, convincingly she comes before us as a young girl never doubting her happiness. Arthur Huntingdon is self-indulgent and vain. All his vices derive from the initial one of vanity ; he must be flattered and indulged ; any contradiction, any opposition rouses a temper, naturally jovial but dangerously heated by years of debauchery. He is neither a confirmed drunkard nor continually ill-tempered when she first marries him ; one of the finest touches in Anne's most convincing likeness of this florid, self-satisfied blackguard is the gusto with which he enjoys all the good things of life. His cheerful impudence, his chuckling good-humour, so long as no one and nothing crosses his will, make him extremely popular with both men and women alike. Anne is always at her best in describing him and everything appertaining to him, by which, obliquely, she builds up the character. All his assurance of address is conveyed in the description of his arrival at Helen's home, bowling merrily across the lawn in the light phaeton, "from which he sprang out over the side onto the portico steps and disappeared into the house."

What makes *The Tenant of Wildfell Hall* something more than a novel with a purpose is its sense of life. The characters develop ; they grow, they deteriorate, they age ; they do not remain untouched by experience. They learn not by any theorising of the author's but from the lessons of life itself.

It is not enough to know that Helen is virtuous ; it is only when her virtue is put to the proof, when the sinister Hargrave, making capital out of her husband's infidelity, is perpetually trying to wear down her resistance, that there is any meaning in the attribute. To his persevering plea "Try me and see," she answers superbly : "I have nothing left me but the solace of a good conscience and a hopeful trust in Heaven and you labour continually to rob me of these. If you persist, I shall regard you as my deadliest foe."

Our sympathy for Helen is maintained, *not* only by her great qualities of courage, truthfulness, pride (all Brontë qualities, these) but by her bad temper, her jealousy and finally her strong, fierce hatred of the man she once so deeply loved. All these alterations in her once romantic and fervent temperament are admirably graduated ; from the first appalled query within herself, "Surely that man will make me dislike him at last ?" to the dreadful cry, "I hate him for having brought me to this !" there is the slow, corrosive action of years.

The time-factor in *The Tenant of Wildfell Hall* is indeed of the first importance because, without the passage of years, the effect after which the author is reaching throughout could not be achieved : that effect is nothing less than to show the deterioration of the good by contact with the wicked. Helen Huntingdon's tragedy is not simply that she has a bad husband, but that *he makes her bad*, or, at least, sufficiently fallen in her own esteem to break her spirit. The depth of her misery is sounded when she cries : "Instead of being humbled and purified by affliction, I feel they are turning my nature into gall."

She is *not* a patient Griselda—if she were, the whole moral of the book would be different. She is "sick with passion and cannot trust herself to speak" when her husband and his mistress, Annabella Lowborough, flaunt their mutual infatuation before her eyes. She will *not* forgive and subscribe to his vices, and her indignation at his ingratitude is quite as fierce as her shock at his immorality. The whole point about Helen is that she, who had believed her love for her husband to be so great as to be able to save him from falling into his old vices, when he deceives her, is as naturally furious and unforgiving as any less virtuous and high-minded woman would be. Once assured of his infidelity she makes no attempt whatever to regain his love or to turn him away from his paramour. "He may drink himself dead now," she says, "it is not my fault."

She firmly resolves to leave him and lives only in anticipation of the moment when she can best effect her escape. In the interval, as she squarely tells him, she will from that day and hour be a wife to him only in name. He has to accept her terms to prevent the scandal spreading. For a Victorian lady they are bold terms indeed.

In a period when the divorce laws operated one way only and married women had no property of their own—save what was conceded to them by "settlements"—Helen Huntingdon is thinking and acting like a woman of the twentieth century. She is, in effect, demanding equal legal rights with men ; since they are naturally refused her by a husband wishing at all costs to avoid a scandal, she proclaims her will—and her capacity—to earn her own living.

She is, surely, one of the very first married women in fiction who is both competent and resolved to keep herself not by any of the accepted means of employment open to women of birth and education such as housekeeper, companion, governess, but as a painter selling her canvasses to dealers.

What is more, Anne shows her as succeeding in doing so. After one abortive attempt to escape from her husband with her little boy, whose systematic perversion is attempted by the now besotted Huntingdon, she ultimately does so, reaches Wildfell Hall, a decaying property formerly belonging to her parents and near which a brother still resides, and lives for several months in seclusion —and security—on the successful sale of her pictures. Two developments in her situation alone prevent her continuing to live there in comparative ease. She falls in love with Gilbert Markham—one of the few neighbours whose acquaintance she has made—and she hears that Huntingdon is dying. He has fallen from his horse and gangrene has set in. It is now, having survived all feeling for the husband who did his best to break her heart, and only now, that she can attempt, with any hope of success, to do for him what she set out in her ignorant girlhood to achieve : not his reformation, not even his recovery, since his life is despaired of, but simply the salvation of his soul.

The book has to be read and the intolerable conduct of Huntingdon witnessed to give its full value to the decision Helen takes to flee the new friend whose love she in her inmost heart returns, and to go back to the revolting husband who has now been abandoned by his latest mistress, the sinister Miss Myers.

Arthur Huntingdon is never less than convincing ; he is never anything but a living creature—boastful, hearty, vulgar when best pleased, self-pitying, despicable, cowardly when ill. "What's the matter with you ?" Helen in her ignorance asked him once when he came home sapped of all vitality. "Well !" cried he, "that passes everything ! After all the wear and tear that I've had, when I come home sick and weary, longing for comfort, and expecting to find attention and kindness, at least, from my wife, she calmly asks me what is the matter with me !"

The trouble with Huntingdon, his wife declares, is that he has "never had an idea of exerting himself to overcome obstacles" any more than he has "of restraining his natural appetites", and these two things are the ruin of him. "I lay them both to the charge of his harsh yet careless father, and his madly-indulgent mother. If ever I am a mother," the young Helen reflects, "I will zealously strive against this crime of over-indulgence. I can hardly give it a milder name when I think of the evils it brings."

Here we have the crux of the matter, according to Anne. It is by the defective education given to boys that the vices of men are implanted. It is a subject on which both she and Charlotte can be eloquent ; a subject on which, alas ! their experience with Branwell had made them very wise.

They both resented the distinction made in the bringing up of girls and of boys in their time ; the girls hemmed inside a protective barrier keeping them from both sight and knowledge of all evil, the boys turned out to prove themselves by trial and error and, more often than not, proving nothing but disastrous failures. "You would have us encourage our sons," says Helen Huntingdon, "to prove all things by their own experience, while our daughters must not even profit by the experience of others. Now I would have both so to benefit by the experience of others . . . that they should know beforehand to refuse the evil and choose the good, and require no experimental proofs to teach them the evil of transgression. I would not send a poor girl into the world unarmed against her foes and ignorant of the snares that beset her path ; nor would I watch and guard her till . . . she lost the power or will to protect herself ; and as for my son—if I thought he would grow up to be what you call 'a man of the world'—one that has 'seen life' and glories in his experience, even though he should so far profit by it as to sober down—I would rather that he died tomorrow— rather a thousand times !"

There is a direct echo—or precursor was it?—of this passage in a letter Charlotte wrote Miss Wooler at the height of the trouble with Branwell. "You ask me if I do not think men are strange beings. I do indeed—and I think too that the mode of bringing them up is strange—they are not half sufficiently guarded from temptations. Girls are protected as if they were something very frail and silly indeed, while boys are turned loose on the world as if they, of all beings in existence, were the wisest and the least liable to be led astray."

It must be concluded that the education Branwell himself had received at home at the hands of his father and aunt appeared to his sisters to have been directly responsible for the disasters that overtook him. Their contention seems to have been that he was over-indulged on the one hand and insufficiently protected and prepared for the battle of life on the other.

The subject, it is apparent, is a source of exquisite pain to both of Branwell's sisters. Charlotte was still haunted by it when, years later, she heard Thackeray lecture on Fielding. "Had Thackeray owned a son grown or growing up," she wrote then to Mrs Gaskell, "would he have spoken in that light way of courses that lead to disgrace and the grave? . . . as if he had never stood by and seen the issue, the final result of it all. I believe, if only once the prospect of a promising life blasted at the outset by wild ways had passed close under his eyes, he never *could* have spoken with such levity of what led to its piteous destruction. Had I a brother yet living, I should tremble to let him read Thackeray's lecture. I should hide it away from him. . . ."

To Anne the subject was of such paramount importance in the year immediately following the final disgrace of Branwell that it left her no peace. Instead of fleeing it, as she might well have done, in her book she deliberately chose it as the subject. Many of her critics, her sister Charlotte among them, deplored both her theme and her manner of treating it. She might have written something far more pleasant than *The Tenant of Wildfell Hall*, but that was not what she set herself to do. She was not seeking an escapist's heaven : it was Heaven itself to which this dauntless young woman aspired —not for herself alone but for as many as her feeble voice could reach.

She was attempting something that not even the great Thackeray dared do—man of the world and famous author as he was. He might protest against the conventions binding Victorian fiction, as in his Preface to *Pendennis*, but he submitted to them, all the same. "Even the gentlemen of our age," he wrote, "we cannot show as they are, with the notorious foibles and selfishnesses of their lives and education. Since the author of *Tom Jones* was buried, no writer of fiction among us has been permitted to depict . . . a man."

He overlooked the fact that two years before he wrote those words, to depict a man, and an immoral man, was precisely what Anne Brontë—twenty-eight, unmarried and unknown—had the temerity to do. And because she was more unadvised and innocent than Thackeray she did so unflinchingly.

Huntingdon claims a man's rights to succumb to temptation, invoking the age-old excuse of the differences of the sexes and the two moral codes ruling their conduct. "It is a woman's nature to be constant," Huntingdon argues, "but you must have some commiseration *for us*, Helen ; you must give us a little more licence . . . remember, *I'm* a poor, fallible mortal." Anne Brontë, in advance of her time, denied this right to Huntingdon, or to any other man, and made it one of the capital issues of her book to proclaim that one equal moral law was binding for men and women alike.

With the legal position of women still supporting the immoral favouritism accorded men, Anne was not likely to engage the sympathy of her hearers unless she used strong measures. Strong measures alone would do. By the very nature of the task she set herself she was bound to be uncompromising. She had to present at first hand, not in reported narration, a series of scenes exhibiting men and women at their most bestial, else the revulsion she needed to create would be too adulterated to take effect.

Very rightly, since such was her objective, Anne renders her debauchees both repulsive and alarming, but, if that was a fault, she committed a fault also in making them hideously menacing and alive.

"Lord Lowborough had entered a minute or two before," (this is on the evening of the "jollification") "and had been standing before the door grimly surveying the company. He now stepped up to Annabella [his wife] who sat with her back towards him with Hattersley still beside her . . . 'Well, Annabella,' said her husband, 'which of these bold, manly spirits, would you have me resemble ?'

" 'By heaven and earth, you shall resemble us all!' cried Hattersley, starting up and rudely seizing him by the arm. 'Hallo, Huntingdon! he shouted—'I've got him! Come, man, and help me! And d——n me if I don't make him drunk before I let go! He shall make up for past delinquencies as sure as I'm a living soul.' There followed a disgraceful contest ; Lord Lowborough, in desperate earnest and pale with anger, silently struggling to release himself from the powerful madman that was striving to drag him from the room. I attempted to urge Arthur to interfere on behalf of his outraged guest but he could do nothing but laugh. 'Huntingdon, you fool, come and help me, can't you!' cried Hattersley, himself somewhat weakened by his excesses. 'I'm wishing you god-speed, Hattersley,' cried Arthur, 'and aiding you with my prayers : I can't do anything else, if my life depended on it! I'm quite used up. . . .' 'Annabella, give me a candle!' said Lord Lowborough, whose antagonist had now got him round the waist and was endeavouring to root him from the door-post to which he madly clung with all the energy of desperation. 'I shall take no part in your rude sport,' replied his lady, coldly drawing back, 'I wonder you can expect it.' But I snatched up a candle and brought it to him. He took it and held the flame to Hattersley's hands till, roaring like a wild beast, the latter unclasped them and let him go."

It is by the frequent renewal of such scenes in her home that Helen Huntingdon is brought to say : "Things that formerly shocked and disgusted me, now seem only natural. I know them to be wrong, because reason and God's Word declare them to be so : but I am gradually losing that instinctive horror and repulsion which were given me by nature and instilled in me by the precepts and example of my aunt." On herself and in her own home had Anne been able all too often to prove the truth of the assertion : "Things that formerly shocked and disgusted me now seem only natural." She knew indeed what she was writing about.

There is a generally accepted notion that Arthur Huntingdon is an embodiment of Branwell. The points of resemblance are so few and the dissimilarities so numerous, that it is worth while to confront the two men and examine afresh the validity of the claim.

Branwell, with all his weaknesses, was an artist—*though* an artist *manqué*. From earliest childhood literature had been a passion with him, and all his ineffectual life he had striven after fame. Byron, Wordsworth, Coleridge, De Quincey, Scott, Ossian, Chateaubriand

—he had adulated them all in turn and aped their style and manner in a hope of catching something of the contagion of their genius. Set against this genuine enthusiasm for letters the intellectual inertia of Huntingdon. "He is getting tired," notes his wife in the early days of their marriage, "not of me, I trust, but of the idle quiet life he leads—and no wonder, for he has so few sources of amusement ; he never reads anything but newspapers and sporting magazines ; and when he sees me with a book he won't let me rest till I close it."

There is a fundamental want of heart in Huntingdon which cannot, for all his contemptible qualities, be imputed to Branwell. When Helen Huntingdon's father dies she relates how her husband is "vexed to hear of it, because he saw that I was shocked and grieved and he feared the circumstance would mar his comfort." When his wife spoke of ordering her mourning, he cried, "Oh, I hate black ! . . . I hope, Helen, you won't think it your bounden duty to compose your face and manners into conformity with your funeral garb. . . . Why should you sigh and groan, and I be made uncomfortable because an old gentleman in ——shire . . . has thought proper to drink himself to death ?" Branwell could speak in this style, but not when it concerned a death in the family, as he sufficiently showed when Aunt Branwell died.

Huntingdon is hateful to the servants, and to all whom he considers his inferiors. Branwell was never so genial as when in company with the villagers, and was generally liked. The Haworth villagers are shrewd observers and nothing meets with their contempt more certainly than insincere and patronising ways. Long after poor Branwell was gone, the young woman who served at the *Bull* remembered the beautiful bow and sweep of his lifted hat and his courteous smile and ready "Good-morning, Anne" with which, invariably, he greeted her.

Where Huntingdon and Branwell are alike is in their genius for hypocrisy and their equal *enjoyment* of that genius.

The person Branwell does strikingly resemble in *Wildfell Hall* is Lord Lowborough, with his pale face and stooping dazed appearance, his pitiful efforts at reform, his genuine longing after better things, his desperate capacity for suffering, even to his drug-taking and tragic love affair and the betrayal of him by the woman he loves.

Lord Lowborough has the character to give up successively gambling, drugs and drink, because initially he is a decent man, with a mind capable of higher aspirations and a heart susceptible to kindness. It is Annabella, his wife, who deals him the deadliest blow, and in this circumstance it would seem as though Anne were stressing the peculiar cruelty and power of love to shatter a man who has hitherto resisted and overcome so many other foes. Nothing was to shake her conviction, which she communicated to her sisters, that it was Branwell's experience at Thorp Green—and after—which was directly responsible for his downfall.

The Tenant of Wildfell Hall would have failed in its initial purpose if Anne had ended it with the escape of Helen from her husband. On the material plane the story can be said to end here (except for the epilogue of her eventual marriage to Gilbert Markham) but spiritually it had to be pushed one step beyond the grave—as Emily in Wuthering Heights threw down the barriers between life and death, and followed the souls of her protagonists into their further state, for which this existence had been but a preparation.

The death of Arthur Huntingdon could not, given Anne's belief, be the end of him or of the book. It had to be the justification, through her heroine, of her chief article of faith : even the wicked will not be *eternally* damned.

From the very beginning the question had been debated between the Evangelical aunt and the unorthodox niece, in a dialogue which cannot fail to evoke for readers similar arguments that must often have taken place between Aunt Branwell and Anne.

Helen's aunt, before ever the engagement between Arthur Huntingdon and Helen had been concluded, earnestly besought her to consider the result of binding herself to a man whose known dissipations would probably lead him straight to Hell. "Suppose even," argued the severe matron, "that he should continue to love you and you him, and that you should pass through life together with tolerable comfort—how will it be in the end, when you see yourselves parted for ever, you, perhaps, taken to eternal bliss and he cast into the lake that burneth with unquenchable fire—there for ever to——" "Not for ever !" interjects Helen—"only till he has paid the uttermost farthing !" and substantiates her belief by an imposing array of texts. "Oh, Helen !" cries her horrified aunt, "where did you learn all this ?" "In the Bible, Aunt," answers the young theologian.

The passage, so strongly reminiscent of Anne's earlier verses,

"A Word to the Elect", would have no value in the context of the book did they not, as it were, sound a *leit motif* which would not find its full and triumphant development until the death of Arthur Huntingdon.

It is as though Anne wished to weight the scales with every conceivable argument against herself, so patent a challenge does the death of Arthur Huntingdon oppose to her beliefs. He is then utterly unregenerate, more odious even than at any moment in his odious past. His self-commiseration is abject ; his disregard of his wife's feelings, complete ; his terror of death devoid of a single element of nobility.

A more repulsive invalid cannot be imagined, a more horrible death-bed evoked by which to watch. And yet, in spite of her unfailing honesty towards herself—the clear-eyed disillusionment with which she notes all his selfishness and her own deadened feelings—when he is dead, she has no doubt whatever that he will be forgiven.

"None can imagine the miseries, bodily and mental, of that death-bed ! How would I endure to think that that poor trembling soul was hurried away to everlasting torment ? It would drive me mad. But thank God I have hope—not only from a vague dependence on the possibility that penitence and pardon might have reached him at the last, but from the blessed confidence that, through whatever purging fires the spirit may be doomed to pass, . . . it is not lost, and God, who hateth nothing that he hath made, will bless it in the end !"

This is the message of *The Tenant of Wildfell Hall*, without which the rest of the story would be meaningless. All her life Anne Brontë had been moving towards this justification of the tenet nearest to her heart : the doctrine of pardon and atonement by the love of God.

By writing *The Tenant of Wildfell Hall* she had not only placated the Dark Deity of her childhood, but proclaimed the new and risen faith which had emerged from her suffering, of eternal pardon and eternal love.

Chapter Eighteen

BEST-SELLER

WHEN Anne had finished writing *The Tenant of Wildfell Hall* she did not offer the manuscript to Charlotte's publishers—as Charlotte expected her to do—but sent it to Newby. Something of Newby's satisfaction and Charlotte's pique can be heard in the latter's report to Mr Williams—of Smith, Elder & Co.—dated 5th February 1848 —in which, commenting on the excellent sales of *Wuthering Heights* and *Agnes Grey*, she says that Mr Newby is, consequently, "getting into marvellously good tune with his authors".

To judge by a letter written by Mr Newby to "Ellis Bell, Esq." on 15th February, he had hopes of receiving not merely *one* but *two* new works from the authors of *Wuthering Heights* and *Agnes Grey*. Ellis, as well as Acton, had apparently been in communication with him, for he writes : "Dear Sir, I am much obliged by your kind note and shall have great pleasure in making arrangements for your next novel. I would not hurry its completion for I think you are quite right not to let it go before the world until well satisfied with it, for much depends on your next work, if it be an improvement on your first you will have established yourself as a first-rate novelist, but if it fall short the critics will be too apt to say that you have expended your talent in your first novel. I shall therefore have pleasure in accepting it upon the understanding that its completion be at your own time, etc."

Wuthering Heights and *Agnes Grey* were selling well, and Newby was confidently awaiting two new novels by their successful authors. The tone of Newby's letter, moreover, is reasonable and co-operative and not of a nature to arouse either Ellis or Acton Bell's suspicion of any sharp practice.

It was Currer Bell who first took the alarm. Her publishers (Smith, Elder & Co.) informed her that Newby was sedulously spreading the rumour that *Jane Eyre* was the work of Ellis Bell and, to Charlotte's confusion, *The Athenaeum* and other literary periodicals were repeating the error. Hitherto she had understood that the boot was on the other foot, that *Wuthering Heights* had been ascribed to the author of *Jane Eyre*, and, truth to tell, Charlotte had received the news with a certain complacency. She had written to her publishers that she was far from being ashamed at having *Wuthering Heights* and *Agnes Grey* attributed to her pen, but must in all truthfulness deny the honour.

Now the astute Newby, faced with the overwhelming success of *Jane Eyre*, was using similar tactics and ascribing his publications to the same pen and sending up the sales of *Wuthering Heights* and *Agnes Grey* to a most satisfying extent.

The Messrs Bell, if they were to expose either the publisher's deceit or the reviewers' mistakes, had no recourse short of revealing their identity. This was so extreme a contingency and so wholly repugnant to Ellis that Charlotte dare not urge it, although the horrid thought presented itself to her that Smith, Elder & Co. might think she was playing a double game.

"Ellis, Acton and Currer care nothing for the matter personally," she wrote her publishers, "the public and the critics are welcome to confuse our identities as much as they choose ; my only fear is lest Messrs Smith, Elder & Co. should in any way be annoyed by it."

Anne's contract with Newby over *The Tenant* was on a very different basis to that for *Agnes Grey*. Anne received £25 on the day of publication and was to receive another £25 on the sale of the first 250 copies. *The Tenant* was a full-length three-volume novel and was sold at the usual price of £1 11s 6d the set.

It came out early in June and was an immediate and sensational success. In view of the present eclipse into which the book has fallen, it is well to remember that, of all the Brontë novels, it had the greatest contemporary sale, with the one exception of *Jane Eyre*.

The success however was not by any means due to a concensus of praise from the critics. Opinions were sharply divided into attacks on the book's "coarseness", "brutality" and "morbid revelling in scenes of debauchery" on the one hand, and praise for its thrilling excitement and startling incident on the other. The very fact that the book presented a challenge to convention ensured it a *succès de scandale*. It was daring in subject, bold in execution, exciting in incident ; in short, a boon to circulating libraries, on whose support the success or failure of any novel depended.

Within a month of publication Newby was preparing a second edition. To any author such news must bring a thrill of satisfaction, but in Anne it aroused very mingled feelings. She realised that on many of her readers the whole purport of her book had been lost.

Her object in describing so vividly the spiritual and physical deterioration of a human being had been taken by some for capital fun and lively entertainment and by others as a scandalous insistence on scenes and situations which public decency usually forbids. To tickle the palate of the one order of readers had been as far from Anne's intention as to offend the other. She was quite unaware, it seems, that what she had attempted was an outrage to conventional morality, whichever way it was looked at.

Nor was this to be her only concern. Not only her readers but her publisher was soon to involve her in undreamt-of mortifications. Mr Newby, seeing fresh profit to be derived from the confusion in the identity of the Bell brothers, boldly offered the American rights of *The Tenant* to a New York firm alleging it to be a new work by Currer Bell, whose *Jane Eyre* was already a hot favourite in the States. He further assured them that, to the best of his belief, all the Bell novels—*Jane Eyre*, *Wuthering Heights*, *Agnes Grey* and *The Tenant of Wildfell Hall* were in reality by one and the same person, who chose to use the three pseudonyms according as he published later or earlier works. In offering his American correspondent what was, in effect, a scoop, Newby declared it to be his opinion that *The Tenant of Wildfell Hall* was distinctly the best so far of any of the Bell novels. The American firm naturally jumped at the offer and, what was more natural still, bragged of their good luck to their less fortunate colleagues. But among these happened to be the firm with whom Smith, Elder & Co. always dealt and who, having already published *Jane Eyre* by arrangement with him, had offered a high price for and been promised the first sheets of whatever new work Currer Bell might write. Conceiving themselves to be extremely shabbily used by Smith, Elder in the matter, they wrote Cornhill a pretty stiff complaint.

When George Smith read this letter he was as irate as ever his American correspondent could be. Writing of this incident in after years, he said he did not positively suspect Currer Bell of giving his new book to Newby—although to all appearances it looked like it—but he did strongly suspect that *someone* was fooling him. He wrote immediately to Haworth and told Currer Bell that his firm would be glad to be in a position to contradict the statement (advanced by Newby that all the Bell novels were by the same writer), "adding at the same time that we were quite sure Mr Newby's assertion was untrue". Not only was the American edition of Currer Bell's next novel—for which a high price had already been offered to Smith, Elder & Co.—at stake, but the whole course of their future relations with this highly successful novelist who, they might justly opine, was only now at the very beginning of his career. Well might Smith, Elder & Co. feel very anxious at this threat to a most hopeful collaboration.

Whatever of anxiety or annoyance it cost Smith, Elder & Co., the effect on Charlotte and Anne was like a bombshell. For all the diplomatic wording of Mr Smith's letter, it left the girls in no doubt that their very integrity was in question—Currer Bell had the appearance of having played up two publishers against each other and in flagrant breach of good faith, of giving the manuscript of a work promised one publisher to another. The very fear that had seized Charlotte in January, when Newby spread the rumour that *Jane Eyre* was by Ellis Bell, returned in far greater force now : Messrs Smith, Elder & Co. *must* suspect Currer Bell of duplicity.

It did not take Charlotte and Anne many hours to come to the inescapable conclusion that the era of mystification must end. Their cherished anonymity was no longer providing an effective screen to their modesty, but rather, casting a dubious light upon their honour. It must immediately be laid aside, the true identities of Currer and Acton Bell, those two best-selling novelists, be revealed. Ellis Bell, smiling his enigmatic smile at the folly and perversity of man, listened to their debates with amused detachment, and gave them his blessing to get out of the scrape as they best might—so long as they didn't mention him.

The question was : *how* to get out of the scrape ? A letter could no longer convey the absolute proof that Messrs Smith, Elder & Co. required ; only ocular demonstration would do. Before mid-afternoon was reached Charlotte and Anne had taken their resolution : they would go to London, show themselves to Currer Bell's publishers in proof of their separate identities and then call on Acton Bell's unscrupulous publisher and confound him personally.

The letter from Smith, Elder & Co. had reached Charlotte on a Friday morning—Friday, 7th July 1848. Not for a moment did the girls hesitate to put their plan into action there and then. It meant travelling all night and reaching Cornhill in the morning, but the idea that the directors of the firm might possibly not be at the office on a Saturday morning never entered their innocent heads. They thought only of clearing their fair names.

From the moment they had taken the decision to go they moved at lightning speed and in a state, as Charlotte later recalled, of "constant excitement". A small trunk was packed containing, besides necessities, a change of dresses ; a village lad, passing with his cart, was hailed to convey it down to the station at Keighley and was given eighteenpence for his pains ; for the two excited girls the four miles' walk would be some relief to their wrought-up energies. For it *was* exciting, thrillingly exciting, to be going to London to see their publishers. Much as they might have shrunk from such a necessity, had they been given time or the choice to consider it in advance, now that it could not be avoided, there was, in the unusual cause for such an action, something singularly satisfying and stimulating to the two modest women that they were. For the inference was inescapable that it was by reason of their outstanding success as writers that this contingency had arisen. They were best-sellers, and publishers on both sides of the Atlantic were fighting over their books.

It was July and the walk should have been a joy, cutting by way of the fields as the girls generally did, across Oakworth down into Keighley. But half-way a storm burst which soaked them to the skin and there was no help for it but to travel all night in their wet clothes. They were very extravagant ; joining the London train at Leeds they took first-class tickets ; it cost them £2 5s 6d each for a single fare. But the comfort and relative privacy of a first-class carriage were well worth the price to such inexperienced and timid travellers. They never slept a wink all night ; who can wonder ? The train got into Euston Square at seven o'clock in the morning, a cab was hailed and Charlotte gave the direction : "To the Chapter Coffee House, Ivy Lane, Paternoster Row." It was the only place she knew of in London ; it was where Papa had brought her and Emily on their first journey to Brussels and it held memories, singularly hopeful and disassociated from all the heartache that followed.

The cab-hire cost them three shillings, but what a wealth of entertainment they got for their money ! London on a summer's morning, with the streets empty save for market drays and the beautiful buildings rising unimpeded to the view, before ever the shifting, spreading tide of humanity turned which, later, would block from sight so much that was singular and lovely in the architecture of the house-fronts and doorways.

To Anne it was a raree-show indeed. Never, excepting at York, had she had a chance to see noble architecture, buildings on a grandiose scale, antiquity perfectly preserved.

The profile of the City, silhouetted against the sky, as Anne craned her neck to look out of the cab, was of a multitudinous huddle of chimney-stacks and roofs, steep, slanting and darkly smoke-begrimed and only miraculously lightened here and there by the steeples of Wren's churches, looking pallid and frail in the early day, and melting into the air like wisps of smoke.

Poor Branwell, in the past, had told her about St Paul's—how the sheer weight of it had seemed to bear him down. Charlotte, Papa, Emily, they had all told her about it and it was what she most wished to see in London.

Happily for her the Chapter Coffee House lay in its shade and the impossibility of seeing anything but a section of its colonnades from the cab was soon repaired by their arrival. Even then, standing on the pavement of Paternoster Row, it was impossible to distinguish anything more than an impact of power. The cab had to be paid, the inn entered, a room engaged, and not until they had been shown to it and the door shut could she stand at the window and take in the whole huge presence of the church that seemed to fill not only that portion of the town but a vast segment of the sky.

There was no time to stand enraptured there. It was eight o'clock and they needed to tidy themselves and to have some breakfast before engaging on the business of the day. When they saw themselves in the glass they looked very pale and their curls were sadly tumbled. They effaced as best they could the ravages of the journey, went down to the Coffee Room and ordered some breakfast, and when they had finished it sallied forth into the sun. The tide of humanity had turned with a vengeance now and beat against them as they tried to pursue their way. They thought they would have to take a cab to drive to Cornhill ; they had no idea they were so close to it ; but the sight of the shops, mostly stationers and book-shops, was too tempting to be utterly disregarded. They started walking and finally, by strangely devious routes, having quite lost their way, they arrived at the door of No. 65 Cornhill, having taken an hour to cover the distance from Paternoster Row.

Charlotte, recounting the whole adventure to Mary Taylor later, said with what "queer inward excitement" they approached their goal. "We found 65 to be a large bookseller's shop," she wrote, "in a street almost as bustling as the Strand. We went in, walked up to the counter. There were a great many young men and lads here and there ; I said to the first I could accost : 'May I see Mr Smith ?' He hesitated, looked a little surprised. We sat down and waited a while, looking at some books on the counter, publications of theirs well known to us, of many of which they had sent us copies as presents. At last we were shown up to Mr Smith."

It happens that Mr Smith has related his recollections of that morning as well as Charlotte, and that we know from him that he was busy in his office when the clerk announced that two ladies wished to see him. He was *very* busy and sent out to know their names. When the clerk returned, to Mr Smith's equal surprise and annoyance, as he frankly owns, he reported that the ladies declined to give their names but asked to see him on a private matter.

George Smith, in his early twenties at the time, had only recently been promoted head of the firm by the death of his father. He was a handsome, rather spoilt and very sophisticated young man, with suave manners and a temper under control ; but in spite of perfect poise he was rather taken aback by so much intransigence. He hesitated a moment before he decided to have the ladies in.

When they entered, his expert eye saw they were very provincial ; he describes them as "two rather quaintly-dressed little ladies". They were exceedingly pale and anxious-looking ; one of them was very small and wore spectacles. It was she who came forward and, without a word, laid his own letter, addressed to "Currer Bell, Esq.", into his hand. George Smith noticed that it had been opened and he relates how he asked them, with some sharpness, "Where did you get this from ?" "From the post-office," was the reply. "It was addressed to me. We both came that you might have ocular proof that there are at least two of us."

By this time Charlotte was plucking up courage and obviously beginning to enjoy herself. It was George Smith's turn to look confounded and to feel a fool.

"I laughed at his perplexity," Charlotte told Mary Taylor. "I gave my real name : Miss Brontë. We were in a small room— and there explanations were rapidly gone into : Mr Newby anathematised, I fear, with undue vehemence. Mr Smith hurried out and returned quickly with . . . Mr Williams [the firm's Reader who had instantly recognised the hand of genius in *Jane Eyre*] a pale, mild, stooping man of 50.   Then followed talk—talk—talk —Mr Williams being silent, Mr Smith loquacious."

But though he flowed in talk, George Smith's eyes were none the less active and his appraisal of the appearance of the girls is valuable—since it is the only one we possess which may be said to come from a man of the world.   George Smith saw the Miss Brontës with the eyes of a young man about town.   Their provincialism must inevitably strike him, but there was in this prototype of "Dr John" a finer fibre which could penetrate below surface impressions and 'discern where singularity ceased and originality began.   "This was the only occasion," he writes, "on which I saw Anne Brontë.   She was a gentle, quiet, rather subdued person, by no means pretty, yet of a pleasing appearance. . . .   Her manner was curiously expressive of a wish for protection and encouragement, a kind of constant appeal, which invited sympathy.   I must confess that my first impression of Charlotte Brontë's appearance was that it was interesting rather than attractive. . . .   There was but little feminine charm about her and of this fact she was herself uneasily and perpetually conscious. . . ."   George Smith, whose acquaintance with Charlotte was to deepen over the next five years, could certainly not have discovered the latter circumstance on this first meeting nor have made the pathetic discovery which he goes on to relate—that he believed "she would have given all her genius and fame to have been beautiful."

Mr Smith lived with his mother and sisters in Westbourne Terrace and he immediately invited Charlotte and Anne to stay with them during their London visit.   They of course declined ; their stay must be very short and they had not come prepared to make visits.   A compromise was reached by which George would bring his sisters to call on them that evening and take them all to the opera.

So it was left.   Poor Charlotte paid for the morning's excitement with headache and sickness, and the prospect of the evening's social obligations only added to her nausea.

The visit to Newby, of which nothing more is recorded than that it took place, was presumably deferred until after the week-end. It is a thousand pities that the encounter between the shifty publisher and his best-selling author has been passed over in silence.   Acton

Bell, as we know, was not to be put off speaking "unpalatable truths" if he felt it his duty, and if we may judge by the tone of the Preface to the second edition of *The Tenant* which Anne was to write on her return to Haworth, Mr Newby was told off with some asperity.

To return to the momentous Saturday. It may be doubted whether their morning's ordeal did not appear trivial by comparison with what lay ahead of them that evening. Poor Charlotte's "thundering headache" only partially gave way to a strong dose of sal volatile, but she did not lose her sense of the fitness of things. In the afternoon they went out and bought themselves a pair of gloves and a parasol each, by which it may perhaps be augured that after the previous day's storm the sun shone brightly and the prospect of two days' visiting and sight-seeing in London made those elegant appendages necessary.

They had neither of them brought anything suitable to wear for such an occasion as the opera ; they had a change of frocks, but alas ! they were high-necked, and when Mr Smith and his sisters arrived at the Chapter Coffee House in the evening Charlotte's worst fears were confirmed : "the gentlemen were in evening costume, white gloves, etc. and the ladies—'two elegant young ladies', were in full dress. . . ."

George Smith had shown considerable insight when he guessed that Charlotte would have "given all her genius and her fame to have been beautiful". To her the evening, so gratifying in all other respects, was marred by the consciousness of her own lack not only of beauty but of elegance. It is this thought that recurs continually in her recollection of the event. "They must have thought us queer, quizzical-looking beings, especially me with my spectacles. I smiled inwardly at the contrast, which must have been apparent, between me and Mr Smith as I walked with him up the crimson-carpeted staircase of the Opera House and stood among a brilliant throng at the box-door, which was not yet open. Fine ladies and gentlemen glanced at us with a slight, graceful superciliousness quite warranted by the circumstances. Still, I felt pleasantly excited in spite of headache and sickness and conscious clownishness." It is sad to reflect that such thoughts could beset Currer Bell on one of the very rare occasions when homage was being paid her genius.

She tells us that she glanced across at her sister and was surprised to see that Anne was "calm and gentle", as always. Anne, with

Mr Williams for her cavalier, was not only outwardly at ease but
inwardly tranquil. She was not persecuted with the sense of her
plainness, as Charlotte was ; she had no need to be ; George Smith,
who was hard to please and said she was not pretty, found her
"very pleasing" nevertheless ; her portraits confirm this, and the
witness of Ellen Nussey, Bell Nicholls and all the parsonage servants
is unanimous : they all declared her colouring to be lovely. However that might be, no *mauvaise honte* weighed heavily on her spirits
and prevented her looking about her at the absorbing scene. The
setting, with its crystal lustres, lighted candles and moving crowd
was calculated to engross her completely and make her forget herself
in the greater interest afforded by what to her was such an unusual
spectacle.

But what, above all, must have made the evening one of delight
was the opportunity, unique in the whole course of her life, of
hearing music performed by first-class executants. Anne knew
enough about singing to find *any* opera sung by top-ranking artists
of absorbing interest, even should the music not be particularly to
her taste. It was *The Barber of Seville*, and though Charlotte said
she fancied there were things she would have liked better, Rossini's
music is among the scores Anne possessed and studied, and it is not
necessary she should share Charlotte's opinion. The supreme grace,
wit, elegance of the music could not be lost on such a musical ear.

It would not rank with York Minster, far less would it compare
to the sea, but that evening at the opera was one of the few high-
lights in a life passed almost exclusively in the shade.

"The next day, Sunday," Charlotte continued her account to
Mary Taylor, "Mr Williams came early and took us to church."
They asked to be taken to St Stephen's, Walbrook, in the hope of
hearing a famous preacher, Dr Croly. Unfortunately he did not
preach that Sunday. "In the afternoon Mr Smith came in his
carriage with his mother, to take us to his house to dine. Mr
Smith's residence is at Bayswater, six miles from Cornhill ; the
rooms, the drawing-room especially, looked splendid to us. There
was no company—only his mother, his two grown-up sisters, and
his brother, a lad of twelve or thirteen, and a little sister. . . . We
had a fine dinner, which neither Anne nor I had appetite to eat,
and were glad when it was over. . . .

"On Monday we went to the Exhibition of the Royal Academy
and the National Gallery, dined again at Mr Smith's, then went

home with Mr Williams to tea and saw his comparatively humble but neat residence and his fine family of eight children. A daughter of Leigh Hunt's was there. She sang some little Italian airs which she had picked up among the peasants in Tuscany, in a manner that charmed me . . ." and very certainly Anne as well.

In addition to this considerable programme they walked in Kensington Gardens on the Sunday and were struck with the beauty of the scene, the fresh verdure of the turf and the soft rich masses of foliage. The weather was fine and it is to be hoped the new parasols gave to their owners pleasure as well as protection from the sun.

They were resolved on returning home on the Tuesday for a reason they would not have chosen to confide in Mr Smith or his mother ; they simply could not afford to stay longer in London. Their bill at the Chapter Coffee House for the three days and nights was £2 5s ; there were daily cab-fares and such little expenses as the entrance to Burlington House. And neither of them would have thought of returning home without presents for those they had left behind. They bought Tabby and Martha a book each (which cost them 4s 6d). How dearly one would like to know what the titles were ; would they be "improving" or "light" literature ? We shall never know.

But another purchase whose title we *do* know and which cost them 12s was a volume of Tennyson's poems. We do not need to be *told* that this was for Emily, to feel certain that it was so— Tennyson was much admired at the parsonage and a copy of the ill-fated volume of Currer, Ellis and Acton Bell's *Poems* had been addressed to him the previous year. Tennyson's latest volume had just appeared : it was *The Princess,* and one cannot think of a subject more likely to appeal to Emily Brontë in all contemporary literature.

Charlotte and Anne themselves were laden with presents of books from Mr Smith when they returned to Haworth on the Tuesday. They took the day train and were less extravagant than on their journey down, travelling second class. Even so the tickets cost them £1 12s each and, what with a late tea at Leeds and tips to porters to convey their luggage home, the expense of the whole trip cost them over £7 each. It is very unlikely that either of them had ever before spent such a sum of money over one week-end— but that was the price they had to pay for being best-sellers now !

Chapter Nineteen

CUP OF WRATH

AN overwhelming lassitude followed on the five days of unrelieved excitement. Charlotte, looking at herself in the glass on their return home, saw that she looked grey and very old; "a more jaded wretch . . . it would be difficult to conceive. I was thin when I went, but was meagre indeed when I returned. . . ." Thanking Mr Williams on Anne's behalf and her own for "his kind attention to them while in town", she said that in a day or two, no doubt, they would get the better of the fatigues of their journey. Charlotte, however "weak and restless" she declared herself to be for a day or two, had returned strangely elated by her London visit. She had now seen her publishers, taken the measure of their honour and judgment, and brought away with her the conviction that with men like that to sponsor and promote her writing she could enter with a new confidence and a new relish into the lists of literature. She was writing *Shirley* and took up the manuscript, laid aside for her journey to London, more light-heartedly than she had approached any task in her life before. It was a period of hope for Charlotte, sweet by reason of its novelty and unclouded by any foreknowledge of its brevity.

For Anne there were no anticipations, pleasurable or distressful. She felt now only that she wanted rest. Her task was almost done. Her second book—a child of so much trouble to her—needed but a Preface to its second edition (which she must furnish at once) to go from her for good. She would then have done her best by it and her public, and could do no more.

The soaking she and Charlotte had received on their walk down to Keighley at the outset of their journey had left her even more than habitually of late with a constriction of the chest, a breathlessness that sometimes crushed her cruelly. But, as usual, she did not mention these things. Charlotte, watching every change in her since their schooldays at Roe Head with lynx eyes, had written the previous year to Ellen Nussey: "She has an extraordinary heroism of endurance. I admire, but I certainly could not imitate her."

In the space of the last eighteen months Anne had been seriously ill three times. In December 1846 she had the worst attack of asthma since childhood. "Poor Anne has suffered greatly from asthma," Charlotte had written to Ellen, "but is now, I am glad to say, rather better. She had two nights last week when her cough and difficulty of breathing were painful indeed to hear and witness, and must have been most distressing to suffer ; she bore it, as she does all affliction, without one complaint, only sighing now and then when nearly worn out."

From January to March of this very year 1848, Anne had been ill almost without intermission with what had been diagnosed as successive attacks of "influenza, attended with distressing cough and fever" which, Charlotte had reported to Miss Wooler, had "left her chest very weak".

One of Anne's rare letters to be preserved, that of 26th January 1848 to Ellen Nussey, mentions this bout of illness with the usual understatement that characterised any discussion of her health. In its reticence, also, regarding the sole purpose and interest of her life at that time, the writing of *The Tenant of Wildfell Hall*, it is also characteristic. (The edge of this letter has been cut, probably by Ellen Nussey before lending it to Mrs Gaskell ; hence the words in brackets have to be assumed from the text.)

Haworth
January 26th, 1848

My dear Miss Nussy [*sic*]

I am not going to give you a " nice *long* epistle "—on the contrary I mean to content myself with a shabby little note to be ingulfed in a letter of Charlotte's which will, of course, be infinitely more acceptable to you than any production of mine, though I do not question your friendly regard for me, or the indulgent welcome you would accord to a missive of mine even without a more aggreeable companion to back it, but you must know there is a lamentable deficiency in my organ of language which makes me almost as bad a hand at writing as talking unless [I] have something particular to say. I have now however to [thank] you and your friend Miss Ri[ng]rose for your kind letter an[d] her pretty watch guards, whi[ch] I am sure we shall all [of] us value the more for [being] the work of her own han[d] for she is no stranger [to] any of us. I am glad she still [con]tinues with you for both [your] sake and hers, and I [hope] Mr. Ringrose will be [per]suaded to let her stay some [ti]me longer, for I am sure it [wo]uld do you both good. [I] fear your sister must [ha]ve suffered a good deal [fro]m the cut in her hand, [b]ut, bad as the accident was, it is a mercy it was attended with no worse results. It is dreadful to think of what *might* have occurred and in all probability *would*, if the game had been kept a few days longer. You do not tell us how *you* bear the present unfavourable weather. We are all cut up by this cruel east wind, most of us e.i. [*sic*] Charlotte, Emily, and I, have had the infueza [*sic*] or a bad cold instead, twice over within the space of a few weeks ; Papa has had it once, Tabby has hitherto escaped it altogether—I have no news to tell you, for we have been nowhere, seen no one, and done nothing (to *speak* of) since you were here—and yet we contrive to be busy from morning to night. Flossy is fatter than ever, but still active enough to relish a sheep hunt—I hope you and your circle have been more fortunate in the matter of colds than we have. With kind regards to all, I remain, dear Miss—

The edge of the paper is again cut here and there is no signature. In a different hand and ink someone has added overleaf :

Nussey, Yours ever affectly Anne Bronte [*sic*]

It was these recurrent attacks of illness that made the writing of *The Tenant of Wildfell Hall* like a rearguard action fought against tremendous odds. She had been engaged on it since the previous summer (since the very time that Newby had accepted the manuscripts of *Wuthering Heights* and *Agnes Grey*), driving herself to the task during every available interlude of good health to the exclusion of all other occupations. Throughout the radiant summer of 1847 she had been "sitting stooping over her desk", as Charlotte complained to Ellen (without divulging what it was Anne was doing at her desk), adding : "I would fain hope she is a little stronger than she was, and her spirits a little better, but she leads much too sedentary a life. . . . It is with difficulty we can prevail on her to take a walk or induce her to converse. . . ."

How "close and resolute a dissembler" Anne could on occasion be, appears in another of her letters to Ellen Nussey that relates also to this period of her complete absorption in her book and whose evasion of all the subjects of interest is almost masterly. Written in the previous autumn, on 4th October 1847, it reads like the most conventional of little notes exchanged between Victorian ladies suffering rather from too few than from too many calls upon their time.

Haworth
October 4th –47

My dear Miss Ellen,
Many thanks to you for your unexpected and welcome epistle. Charlotte is well, and meditates writing to you. Happily for all parties the east wind no longer prevails—during its continuance she complained of its influence as usual. I too

suffered from it, in some degree, as I always do, more or less ; but this time, it brought me no reinforcement of colds and coughs which is what I dread the most. Emily considers it a " dry uninteresting wind ", but it does not affect her nervous system. Charlotte agrees with me in thinking the note about Mr. Jenkin's a very provoking affair. You are quite mistaken about her parasol ; she affirms she brought it back, and I can bear witness to the fact, having seen it yesterday in her possession. The one you have discovered may possibly have been left by Miss Ringrose. As for my book, you are welcome to keep it as long as you or your friends can derive any benefit from its perusal, I have no wish to see it again, till I see you along with it, and then it will be welcome enough for the sake of the bearer. We are all here much as you left us ; I have no news to tell you, except that Mr. Nicholl's begged a holiday and went to Ireland three or four weeks ago, and is not expected back till Saturday—but that I dare say is no news at all. We were all severally pleased and grateful for your kind and judiciously selected presents—from papa down to Tabby,—or down to myself, perhaps I ought rather to say. The crab cheese is excellent, and likely to be very useful, but I don't intend to need it. It is not choice, but necessity that has induced me to choose such a tiny sheet of paper for my letter, having none more suitable at hand ; but perhaps it will contain as much as you need wish to read or I to write, for I find I have nothing more to say except that your little Tabby must be a charming creature, and when the wedding fever reaches *you* I hope it will be to some good purpose and give you no cause to regret its advent, and— that is all, for as Charlotte is writing or about to write to you herself I need not send any message from her. therefore accept my best love and I must not omit the Major's compliments [the family nickname for Emily] believe me to be your affectionate friend,

ANNE BRONTË.

To Ellen, Charlotte could confide her distress at Anne's visible decline, but she could not say what added bitterness to that distress : the conviction that Anne was making herself ill over something that was not worth-while. To Mr Williams, alone, after the event, could she speak her mind and say how "unfortunately chosen" she considered the subject of her sister's book and how little qualified she thought her to handle it. It was an opinion on which Charlotte never went back. Years later she still said : "The choice of subject was an entire mistake. Nothing less congruous with the writer's nature could be conceived." From this she deduced that Anne "hated her work, but would pursue it. When reasoned with on the subject, she regarded such reasonings as a temptation to self-indulgence . . ." and would listen to none of them.

For all her vigilance, what Charlotte did not see was that her attitude to her sister's work was adding, immeasurably, to her sister's burden.

(2,056)

There can be little doubt at all that Charlotte's disapproval was known and keenly felt by Anne. The sisters were too honest with each other ever to hide their true sentiments regarding each other's work : such criticism had always been freely and fairly exchanged between them since childhood and they looked to each other never to say less than the truth, as it appeared to them.

Before ever *Wildfell Hall* was published and the censure of some sections of the press reached Anne, she wrote the poem, "The Narrow Way" (27th April 1848), which though ostensibly an exhortation to the Good Pilgrim not to flag in his progress, reflects all too evidently the deep hurt and disappointment she suffered at the incomprehension with which her own struggle upward had been received.

> Believe not those who say
> The upward path is smooth,
> Lest thou shouldst stumble in the way,
> And faint before the truth. . . .

On the merits of its religious sentiments it is one of the poems which has ultimately found its way into hymnals and is, from time to time, sung on special occasions in churches. The quality which makes it so perennially touching, however, is surely that of wounded susceptibility, that "kind of constant appeal" for protection and encouragement which George Smith found so compelling of sympathy, and which Anne, where most she might look for it, was not to receive. Unmistakable is the application of the lines :

> Seek not thine honour here ;
> Waive pleasures and renown ;
> The world's dread scoff undaunted bear,
> And face its deadliest frown.
>
> To labour and to love,
> To pardon and endure,
> To lift thy heart to God above,
> And keep thy conscience pure ;
>
> Be this thy constant aim,
> Thy hope, thy chief delight ;
> What matter who should whisper blame,
> Or who should scorn or slight ?
>
> What matter, if thy God approve,
> And if, within thy breast,
> Thou feel the comfort of His love,
> The earnest of His rest ?

"You will have seen some of the notices of *Wildfell Hall*," Charlotte wrote to Mr Williams a bare fortnight after their return from London. "I wish my sister felt the unfavourable ones less keenly. She does *not say* much, for she is of a remarkably taciturn, still, thoughtful nature, reserved even with her nearest of kin, but I cannot avoid seeing that her spirits are depressed sometimes. . . ." What Charlotte does not appear to have seen was that the "reserve" and the "depression" were inevitably heightened by her own attitude to what she persistently regarded as her sister's failure.

As long ago as the previous autumn she had made up her mind that Anne should go to the seaside during the summer of 1848, even if only for "a brief sojourn".

Now the summer of 1848 was upon them and nothing more was said. Until the Preface for *Wildfell Hall* was written and despatched Anne for one would consider nothing else, whatever it might be. She did not tell Charlotte that this last effort required of her—this vindication of her book and of her own integrity—was out of all proportion to that which she had already furnished during a year of literary creation. She suddenly felt as though she could do no more. To make plans beyond the immediate present was beyond her.

It was mid-July and throughout the long hot days Emily and Anne sat writing in the parsonage garden. In after years Martha Brown's younger sister, Tabby, would remember seeing them carrying out their little wooden stools and desks to the bottom of the lawn where, in the shade of the currant bushes, they would sit and write undisturbed for hours.

There is no trace of feebleness in the defence Anne wrote of the work she had so much at heart. Like everything else undertaken in the name of Acton Bell it hides whatever of shrinking or timidity there may have been in the author's nature.

The Preface to the second edition of *The Tenant of Wildfell Hall*, meant to rectify her readers' errors, served above all to lay before the public Anne Brontë's claims, both as a writer and a woman, to perfect freedom of thought and execution. To temporise with accepted opinion was not in any Brontë : there is much more of defiance than of excuse in the terms of the Preface with which "dear gentle Anne" sent the second edition of her book out into the world.

The complete text of the Preface, usually omitted in reprints of *The Tenant of Wildfell Hall*, is a piece of as concise writing and clear thinking as Anne ever achieved. It is worth reading on its own account :

July 22nd 1848

While I acknowledge the success of the present work to have been greater than I anticipated, and the praises it has elicited from a few kind critics to have been greater than it deserved, I must also admit that from some other quarters it has been censured with an asperity which I was as little prepared to accept, and which my judgement, as well as my feelings, assures me is more bitter than just. It is scarcely the province of an author to refute the arguments of his censors and vindicate his own productions ; but I may be allowed to make here a few observations with which I would have prefaced the first edition, had I foreseen the necessity of such precautions against the misapprehensions of those who would read it with a prejudiced mind or be content to judge it by a hasty glance.

My object in writing the following pages was not simply to amuse the Reader ; neither was it to gratify my own taste, nor yet to ingratiate myself with the Press and the Public ; I wished to tell the truth, for truth always conveys its own moral to those who are able to receive it. But as the priceless treasure too frequently hides at the bottom of a well, it needs some courage to dive for it, especially as he that does so will be likely to incur more scorn and obloquy for the mud and water into which he has ventured to plunge, than thanks for the jewel he procures ; as, in like manner, she who undertakes the cleansing of a careless bachelor's apartment will be liable to more abuse for the dust she raises than commendation for the clearance she effects. Let it not be imagined, however, that I consider myself competent to reform the errors and abuses of society, but only that I would fain contribute my humble quota to so good an aim ; and if I can gain the public ear at all, I would rather whisper a few wholesome truths therein than much soft nonsense.

As the story of *Agnes Grey* was accused of extravagant over-colouring in those very parts that were carefully copied from the life, with a most scrupulous avoidance of all exaggeration, so, in the present work, I find myself censured for depicting con amore, with a "morbid love of the coarse, if not of the brutal" those scenes which, I will venture to say, have not been more painful for the most fastidious of my critics to read than they were for me to describe. I may have gone too far ; in which case I shall be careful not to trouble myself or my readers in the same way again ; but when we have to do with Vice and vicious characters, I maintain it is better to depict them as they really are than as they would wish to appear. To represent a bad thing in its least offensive light is, doubtless, the most agreeable course for a writer of fiction to pursue ; but is it the most honest or the safest ? Is it better to reveal the snares and pitfalls of life to the young and thoughtless traveller, or to cover them with branches and flowers ? Oh, reader ! if there were less of this delicate concealment of facts, this whispering "Peace, peace", when there is no peace, there would be less of sin and misery to the young of both sexes who are left to wring their bitter knowledge from experience.

I would not be understood to suppose that the proceedings of the unhappy scapegrace, with his few profligate companions I have here introduced, are a specimen of the common practices of society—the case is an extreme one, as I trusted none would fail to perceive ; but I know that such characters do exist, and if I have warned one rash youth from following in their steps, or prevented one thoughtless girl from falling into the very natural error of my heroine, the book has not been written in vain. But, at the same time, if any honest reader shall have derived more pain than pleasure from its perusal, and have closed the last volume with a disagreeable impression on his mind, I humbly crave his pardon, for such was far from my intention ; and I will endeavour to do better another time, for I love to give innocent pleasure. Yet, be it understood, I shall not limit my ambition to this—or even to producing "a perfect work of art" : time and talents so spent I should consider wasted and misapplied. Such humble talents as God has given me I will endeavour to put to their greatest use ; if I am able to amuse, I will try to benefit too ; and when I feel it my duty to speak an unpalatable truth, with the help of God, I *will* speak it, though it be to the prejudice of my name and to the detriment of my reader's immediate pleasure as well as my own.

One word more, and I have done. Respecting the author's identity, I would have it to be distinctly understood that Acton Bell is neither Currer nor Ellis Bell and therefore let not his faults be attributed to them. As to whether the name be real or fictitious, it cannot greatly signify to those who know him only by his works. As little, I should think, can it matter whether the writer so designated is a man, or a woman, as one or two of my critics profess to have discovered. I take the imputation in good part, as a compliment to the just delineation of my female characters ; and though I am bound to attribute much of the severity of my censure to this suspicion I make no effort to refute it, because, in my own mind, I am satisfied that if a book is a good one, it is so whatever the sex of the author may be. All novels are, or should be, written for both men and women to read, and I am at a loss to conceive how a man should permit himself to write anything that would be really disgraceful to a woman, or why a woman should be censured for writing anything that would be proper and becoming for a man.

She sent it off to Mr Newby. Her task was done. Whether she contemplated taking up her pen again in the remote future, for that day and for the succeeding days she aspired only after peace. It was not yet to be.

On that very day Mr Brontë received a letter from a publican in Halifax advising him that unless a bill owed him by Branwell were paid at once he would proceed to a summons. Mr Brontë handed the letter to his son—together with ten shillings—and ordered him to deal with it. Obviously Branwell did not dare tell him what sum was involved. He owed not only Mr Nicholson, of the *Old Cock*, Halifax, but Mrs Sugden of the *Talbot* and the landlord of the *Commercial Inn*. He sat down and dashed off a letter to his friend Leyland, vowing that John Brown would be at Halifax the following Wednesday to placate the landlord of the

Old Cock with the 10s and solemnly undertaking, meanwhile, to get the full sum with which to discharge his debt, as well as those others equally pressing at the *Talbot* and *Commercial*, from Dr Crosby.

Incredible as it may seem, Branwell still expressed himself as "morally certain" of receiving money "through" Dr Crosby, though three full years had passed since he had left Thorp Green. "The old quarter", as Charlotte called it, for getting money was still apparently functioning. In the previous January Charlotte complained of his having "by some means contrived to get more money from the old quarter" and to have led them all "a sad life" in consequence. Branwell had *then* written to the same landlord of the *Old Cock* asking him to send in his bill, expressing himself as confident of being able to settle it "through the hands of one whom I may never see again".

He was still—though Charlotte said of him in this very July that his constitution seemed shattered—getting about and going over to Halifax fairly frequently and drinking enough to stupefy himself for days, sleeping during the day-time and keeping his father, and frequently the whole household, awake at night. He was in an advanced stage of delirium tremens. "I have had five months of such utter sleeplessness, violent cough and frightful agony of mind," he wrote Leyland on this day regarding the threat to sue him, "that jail would destroy me for ever."

His creditors' threat to jail him was not an empty one. Some eighteen months before a Sheriff's Officer had arrived at the parsonage gate with a warrant of arrest. His family had had no choice but to see him led off to York, or to pay the sum due. "Of course his debts had to be paid," Charlotte, who was relating the matter, told Ellen. "It is not agreeable to lose money, time after time, in this way ; but where is the use of dwelling on such subjects. It will make him no better."

"Time after time" the debts were paid and, so as to keep the knowledge of them from Mr Brontë as much as possible, they were paid by the sisters.

It was more than two years now since Charlotte had spoken a word to him. Her disillusionment was complete ; the brother who had once been her closest and dearest companion, the only sharer of that imaginary world, "the Kingdom Below", which had enchanted their brilliant childhood—the "Young Soult" of their first excursions into rhyme, the "Captain John Flower" of Verdopolitan politics, the "Patrick Benjamin Wiggins" of Angrian high society, the Byronic "Northangerland" who epitomised in his own person all the daring and the romance of their darling creation—was reduced to a poor shattered wreck, beneath her notice now.

Emily's support of him has become legendary. The story of her nightly vigils to unbar the door to him long after all were abed, of her strength in carrying him often up the stairs to the room which he now shared with his father, has been handed down through successive generations of Haworth residents and needs no further witness to confirm its truth. Such conduct was in keeping with her character. That he was "hopeless" she had long ago remarked : it was in his nature to be so, and there was an end to it. Acceptance was her creed.

> Do I despise the timid deer
> Because his limbs are fleet with fear ?
> Or would I mock the wolf's death-howl
> Because his form is gaunt and foul ?
> Or hear with joy the leveret's cry
> Because it cannot bravely die ?
> No ! Then above his memory
> Let pity's heart as tender be. . . .

The girl who wrote those lines had no use for recrimination.

While Charlotte turned away her head to avoid seeing his ruin, and Emily lent that silent sympathy which animals show towards misfortunes beyond their questioning, Anne watched him day by day and prayed for him without intermission. Was he not her own peculiar care ? What she felt, she tried to express in the lines she called :

The Penitent

> I mourn with thee, and yet rejoice
> That thou should'st sorrow so ;
> With angel choirs I join my voice
> To bless the sinner's woe.
>
> Though friends and kindred turn away,
> And laugh thy grief to scorn ;
> I hear the great Redeemer say,
> "Blessed are ye that mourn."

Hold on thy course, nor deem it strange
That earthly cords are riven :
Man may lament the wondrous change,
But there is joy in heaven.

He spent the days now mostly sleeping. This is the only possible explanation for the report made by Charlotte later that he "never knew what his sisters had done in literature—he was not aware that they had ever published a line."

Sometimes he lay in bed incapable either of sleep or of exertion. The old habits died hard with him and he would still, occasionally, take a book or magazine to bed and try to focus his failing sight and bend his wandering mind towards the printed page. It was all a blur. The book would fall from his hand and he would sink back into supine unconsciousness. One day that he did this the candle set fire to his bed-curtains. He was stupefied rather than asleep, hearing and smelling nothing. Whether it was that she came to bring him a meal, or that she looked in as a regular routine to see how he did, Anne happened to open the door, saw the fire and rushed to his help. Her cries and struggles to move him were completely ineffectual ; he didn't hear her, he didn't see her. Such strength as she had she put out to drag him from bed, but she was not Emily. Strange as it may seem, the one preoccupation of the whole household was always to spare Papa. Instead of calling for him now, or, if he were out, rousing the whole household, she sped downstairs without a sound, fetched Emily who, directly she heard what was afoot, snatched up the water-ewer in the kitchen, rushed upstairs, caught Branwell up in her arms and cast him in a corner of the room. Then, with perfect self-possession, she tore down the flaming bed-curtains and emptied the water-jug over them. The only comment she and Anne exchanged was, "Don't alarm Papa." This was the manner of their life during those summer weeks of 1848.

With Branwell sick to death one day and riding over to Halifax another in pursuit of his old cronies and of that stimulus that only drink and drugs could give, it is unlikely that Charlotte's project of the previous year to get Anne to the sea was even mooted. Without any precise cause for alarm they lived from day to day in anticipation. It was a time of waiting, for all.

Charlotte, the only one to be deeply engaged in a book, now *Wildfell Hall* had gone out into the world, was writing *Shirley*. The moment her household duties were done she settled down in

the dining-room for the day. Emily and Anne sat in the garden
or, as the shimmering heat drained slowly from the sky, they
wended their way to the moors.

There was nothing to keep Anne now from taking those walks
of which she had deprived herself last year. By mutual consent
she and Emily sought out their favourite haunts—the Sladen valley,
Withens heights and Upper Ponden from where the kirk, their
"fairy-cave" of childhood, reared its black head against the westering
sky.

From many a walk now as they were turning home, their last
glances would rest upon those hills from which had come their life,
as much in valediction as delight. Neither need tell the other what
she felt ; between them there was complete communion. And
not between *them* only, but between them and this earth and sky
as well.

Emily and Anne, feeling within themselves strange stirrings of
an approaching severance from all they had known and loved, had
need as never before of that assurance, daily gained, of their participation with the life, unchanging and everlasting, of that scene.
From the contemplation of such eternal truths they would turn
homewards fortified against whatever the future held in store.

The correspondence between the Robinsons and Anne had been
kept secret from Branwell by everyone at the parsonage. He did
not need these reminders to keep his grief alive : he never forgot
Mrs Robinson. When Mary Duclaux visited Haworth in 1883 to
collect material for her Memoir of Emily Brontë, she met the
"Anne" who had been employed at the *Black Bull* in Branwell's day.
She still remembered how "in the early morning, pale and red-eyed,
he would come into the passage of the Inn with his beautiful bow
and sweep of the lifted hat . . . and ready 'Good-morning Anne.'
Then he would turn to the bar, and feeling in his pockets for what
small moneys he might have, sixpence, eightpence, tenpence, as the
case might be, he would order so much gin and sit there drinking
till it was all gone, then sit still there, silent ; or sometimes he would
passionately speak of the woman he loved ; of her beauty, sweetness,
of how he longed to see her again ; he loved to speak of her even
to a dog ".

"He loved to speak of her even to a dog." Branwell was fast
touching the bottom of the pit ; he had not much further to fall.

Soon the wasted intellect would be quite extinguished, the wick burned out. Life held together only by the good or ill fortune of the day, the lack or possession of a few pence with which to buy gin. "Dear John," he scrawled one Sunday morning at noon to his old crony the sexton, John Brown, "I shall feel very much obliged to you if you can contrive to get me Five pence of Gin in a proper measure. Should it be speedily got I could perhaps take it from you or Billy at the lane top, or, what would be quite as well, sent out for, to you. I anxiously ask the favour because I know the good it will do me. *Punctually* at Half-past Nine in the morning you will be paid the 5d out of a shilling given me then."

On 22nd September Grundy, who had in vain waited for Branwell to come over to Skipton where he was then working and where he had recently invited him to a meal at the *Devonshire Arms*, decided to ride over to Haworth and see for himself how matters stood with his friend. He had no sanguine expectations for, as he recorded later, he knew Branwell was "lost now, for he had taken again to opium".

Arrived at Haworth that Friday evening Grundy ordered a dinner for two at the *Bull* and sent a message up to the parsonage. ". . . The room looked cosy and warm," he remembered many years later, "the bright glass and silver pleasantly reflecting the sparkling firelight, deeply toned by the red curtains."

To his surprise Mr Brontë was shown in. "He spoke almost hopelessly" of his son, warning Grundy of the change he would find in him. Branwell was in bed when Grundy's message came— he had felt almost too weak for the last few days to leave it, but was getting up immediately and insisted on coming down to his friend. Grundy was never to forget the hallucinatory quality of that evening ; his record of it reads like a Gothic romance.

While he sat waiting for Branwell, "presently the door opened cautiously and a head appeared. It was a mass of red, unkempt uncut hair, wildly floating round a great, gaunt forehead ; the cheeks yellow and hollow, the mouth fallen, the thin white lips not trembling but shaking, the sunken eyes, once small now glaring with the light of madness—I hastened to my friend, greeted him in my gayest manner, as I knew he liked best, drew him quickly into the room and forced upon him a stiff glass of hot brandy. Under its influence, and that of the bright cheerful surroundings, he looked frightened—frightened of himself. He glanced at me for a moment, and muttered something of leaving a warm bed to come out into the cold night. Another glass of brandy, and returning warmth gradually brought him back to something like the Brontë of old. He even ate some dinner, a thing which he said that he had not done for long ; I never knew his intellect clearer. He described himself as waiting anxiously for death—indeed, longing for it, and happy, in these his sane moments, to think that it was so near. He once again declared that death would be due to the story I knew, and to nothing else.

When at last I was compelled to leave, he quietly drew from his coat sleeve a carving-knife, placed it on the table, and holding me by both hands, said that, having given up all thoughts of ever seeing me again, he imagined when my message came that it was a call from Satan. Dressing himself, he took the knife, which he had long had secreted, and came to the inn, with a full determination to rush into the room and stab the occupant. In the excited state of his mind he did not recognise me when he opened the door, but my voice and manner conquered him, and 'brought him home to himself', as he expressed it. I left him standing bare-headed in the road, with bowed form and dropping tears. . . ."

The villagers remembered, long afterwards, seeing him swaying there at the top of Haworth unable to walk the three minutes from the *Bull* to his home, and stumbling and falling and finally grovelling the last yards of the way upon his knees. When he was got into bed that night it was never to leave it again. He died on the Sunday morning after a twenty minutes' struggle.

But not before he had made his peace with God and man.

For several days a change had been coming over Branwell. All the bitterness towards his family, wrote Charlotte, seemed gone ; he spoke lovingly, kindly to them and, stranger still, scoffed no longer at old beliefs which he had shaken off for so many years. "All at once he seemed to open his heart to a conviction of the existence and worth" of that religion and those principles in which he had been brought up, but in which for so many years he no longer believed. In his dying moments Branwell prayed, and "to the last prayer his father offered up at his bedside, he added 'Amen'."

"How unusual that word appeared from his lips," Charlotte wrote to Mr Williams. "Of course you, who did not know him, cannot conceive."

The mercy of Branwell's end sustained Mr Brontë, Emily and

Anne in a manner that astonished Charlotte. She herself, once the funeral was over, collapsed. An acute attack of jaundice kept her in bed for several days. She excused herself for failing her father at such a time on the plea of it being the first death-scene she had witnessed, but what shattered her in reality was not so much Branwell's passing but the long unkindness that had preceded death.

There exists a letter of Anne's written on Charlotte's behalf to Mr Williams during those crucial days, which beneath the conventional wording is eloquent of two things : of Anne's own serenity of mind on the occasion and of her tender solicitude for Charlotte. (Charlotte, writing a week later, spoke of the "untiring care and kindness of her dear, dear sisters. . . .") Though Mr Williams was, admittedly, not Anne's but Charlotte's friend, the self-effacement of the writer is complete.

> Haworth, Sept 29th 1848
>
> Dear Sir,
>   My sister wishes me to thank you for your two letters, the receipt of which gave her much pleasure, though coming in a season of severe domestic affliction, which has so wrought upon her too delicate constitution as to induce a rather serious indisposition, that renders her unfit for the slightest exertion. Even the light task of writing to a friend is at present too much for her, though, I am happy to inform you, she is now recovering ; and I trust, ere long, she will be able to assure you herself of her complete restoration, and to give you her own sentiments upon the contents of your letters. Meantime, she desires her kindest regards to you, and participates with me in sincere pleasure at the happy effects of Mrs. Williams' seaside residence. I am, dear Sir, Yours sincerely,
>
>   A. Brontë.

Charlotte might, and did, judge her dead brother before witnesses ; but it was not in either Anne or Emily to do so. Not even to Mr Williams would Anne pass comment upon the nature of the "severe domestic affliction" the family had undergone ; she saw it with other eyes than Charlotte's. For, there can be no doubt, to Anne the death of Branwell appeared in the light of a divine mercy, in direct answer to prayer. For months past Anne had known that there was nothing more that she could do for him but pray for a change of heart and a cessation of suffering. Miraculously, both had been granted her.

Helen Huntingdon, holding the hand of her dying husband, had so longed to hear him breathe one word that might be interpreted as prayer ; but no sound had come and he had gone from her without a sign of pity or of pardon, either for herself or him. Anne had been more blessed than her heroine.

She, who had known better than any of the family the cause, and the extent, of Branwell's miseries ; who had felt so directly responsible for him ; who had tried so hard to be his guardian angel and who had felt so signally her failure, had, in the last hour, when hope, indeed, might have died, been justified in her undying faith. The divine mercy had been manifest. In that supreme hour the old Branwell they had all loved, and lost so many years before, had been restored to them ; he had asked for pardon and had gone in peace. Of his salvation she was now assured.

Since the death of Willy Weightman there was nothing that had been so near her heart. For Anne Brontë those she loved were like fledgling birds fallen from their nest, needing her kind hands to pick them up and carry them safely home. The terror of the *worst* that might befall Branwell was now removed—the "Cup of Wrath" was drained. Confidently, tranquilly, she accepted her discharge ; he had no need of a guardian angel now—faltering, ineffectual guardian that she had been—for he was safe in the bosom of his God.

Branwell had told Grundy that last night at the *Bull*, that "his death would be due to the story he knew, *and to nothing else.*"

Grundy's final comment on the event was : "P.B.B. was no domestic demon ; he was just a man moving in a mist who lost his way.   More sinned against than sinning, at least he proved the reality of his sorrows.   They killed him. . . ."

It is impossible not to wonder in what terms Anne Brontë— who had every reason to agree with Francis Grundy—conveyed to the Miss Robinsons the information of her brother's death.

Chapter Twenty

FORTITUDE FROM PAIN

THE cause of Branwell's death given by the doctor who attended him was not "consumption" (as it was to be in the case of Emily and Anne) but "chronic bronchitis and marasmus". It was not disease that killed Branwell but dissipation.

His funeral took place on the Thursday, 28th September, and was conducted by the Rev. William Morgan, Mr Brontë's oldest friend, who had come over specially from Bradford to perform the final rites as, at Thornton all those years ago when life was full of promise for the proud father, he had performed the first.

At Branwell's funeral Emily caught cold. Before a month was out Charlotte was writing to Ellen that she was "very uneasy" about both her sisters. Emily's cough and cold were "very obstinate", Charlotte suspected that she had a pain in the chest and *sometimes* thought she caught a "shortness in her breathing"; she looked "very, very thin and pale. Nor", wrote Charlotte, "can I shut my eyes to the fact of Anne's great delicacy of constitution. The late sad event has, I feel, made me more apprehensive than common." Sudden changes in temperature and the "cold, penetrating winds" were, moreover, militating against the invalids.

Looking back on this time Charlotte realised later that she was not being "more apprehensive" than the situation warranted but, quite the contrary, the situation had long been there and none of them had ever noticed it. "Since September," she wrote to Mr Williams in January, "illness has not quitted the house. It is strange it did not use to be so, but I suspect now all this has been coming on for years. Unused, any of us, to the possession of robust health, we have not noticed the gradual approaches of decay : we did not know its symptoms : the little cough, the small appetite, the tendency to take cold at every variation of atmosphere, have been regarded as things of course. I see them in another light now."

In Emily and Anne the illness ran a different though a parallel course. From the moment Charlotte took the alarm at the beginning of November, hardly a month after Branwell's funeral, it was evident that both were gravely ill. To begin with, it seemed

286

impossible to distinguish which was in greater jeopardy. The seeds of Anne's consumption had been laid so long ago, it had so evidently been with her all her life that, though its progress was slower than Emily's, its outcome was from the first a foregone conclusion. As Charlotte wrote to Mr Williams : "Anne, from childhood, seemed preparing for an early death." But no such terrible anticipation had ever entered into her thoughts of Emily. Now Emily was no sooner ill than she was dying ; in her case the disease indeed lived up to its name of "galloping" consumption. True, no attempt was made to arrest its course ; she received no treatment of any sort. This was her will, which no entreaties, no representations, no arguments put forward by her broken-hearted sisters ever weakened.

The story of that titanic struggle Charlotte has told in words unmatched for pathos and nobility ; to think of Emily's last days is to recall them. "The details of her illness," wrote Charlotte, "are deep-branded in my memory, but to dwell on them . . . is not in my power. Never in all her life had she lingered over any task that lay before her, and she did not linger now. She sank rapidly. She made haste to leave us. Yet, while physically she perished, mentally she grew stronger than we had yet known her. Day by day, when I saw with what a front she met suffering, I looked on her with an anguish of wonder and love. I have seen nothing like it ; but, indeed, I have never seen her parallel in anything. Stronger than a man, simpler than a child, her nature stood alone. The awful point was, that while full of ruth for others, on herself she had no pity ; the spirit was inexorable to the flesh ; from the trembling hand, the unnerved limbs, the faded eyes, the same service was exacted as they had rendered in health. To stand by and witness this, and not dare to remonstrate, was a pain no words can render."

Emily's strength had come from her capacity to elude the issues of real life. In the imaginary kingdom where she had lived so many years, she was not only undisputed queen but she herself and all who inhabited it with her had led a charmed life. This was *not* child's play (although it bore many resemblances to it), but Emily's defensive palisade against the pressure of human events.

Suddenly the whole structure collapsed. The world without had, with increasing clamour, drawn about and besieged the inner sanctuary. It was never, in any sense, out of cowardice that she had sought refuge there but from a distaste for what the world had

to offer. So long as the world had no need of her, she had none
for it. But now the world had come in strength against her.

For Emily it had been a moment of shameful surrender when
her secret writings had been torn from her and given to the world.
It had been the first blow struck at the root of her existence. The
depth of the wound inflicted on that occasion can fairly be measured
by the contempt under which she always sought to hide her fierce
revolt. As Charlotte had, later, to confess to Mr Williams, Emily
never alluded to her poems other than scornfully as those "rhymes" ;
for the most part she never mentioned them again after publication.

How right she had been never to wish to share her imaginative
experience (except with Anne) had been proved by the general
reception accorded *Wuthering Heights*. It was not sales that could
compensate Emily for the total incomprehension of the critics
towards her hero Heathcliff and towards her unshakable belief in
the immortality of love. The publication of her poems and novel
had brought her no compensation for the loss of her privacy. If
the artist within her recognised and claimed for her own creation
nothing short of the highest award, then only disappointment can
have followed publication. In her lifetime Emily Brontë was not
to receive any assurance, other than that of her devoted sisters, that
what she had created was truly great.

And yet, now the "dome of many-coloured glass" had been
shattered, it was no longer possible for her to write, as formerly,
for herself alone. The "white radiance" was no longer immaculate
—it was no longer about her—it was no longer visible to her
eyes.

That was the worst effect of having to share her visions—seeking
to make them comprehensible or palatable to other tastes than hers
was like mewing the sight of an audacious falcon. Poetry was no
longer an expansion of the spirit, it had become a new form of
imprisonment. From the evidence of her last poem to be preserved
("Why ask to know the date, the clime ?"), begun in September
1846 and resumed in May 1848, writing had become a laborious
exercise, out of which the impetus and joy had gone for ever. The
world within had been undermined, and that without, in all its
grief and ugliness, was pressing her hard on every side.

For two years she had been the confidante of the degradation and
decline of her only brother. If she had hoped anything for Branwell, it was buried with him now under the old church pavement.

Her sources of consolation, potent as once they had been, were not like Anne's and could not persuade her now that his loss was anything but pitiable.

And over and above all the other causes for disillusion and dismay in that tragic autumn of 1848, there was the inescapable evidence that Anne was sinking before her very eyes. Between Anne and herself from then on it would be a race against death. In a world without Anne had Emily, for all her fortitude, the courage to live ? Had disease not entered into the alliance against her, who knows how she might have risen above the challenge of fate ? But the forces now leagued against her were formidable and all she had to oppose to them was her pride.

In such an atmosphere it seems almost incredible that life crept on at the parsonage, with very little alteration on the surface. There were the household duties, the laborious sewing (a formidable task in days when all underwear was made at home and the badge of mourning was carried even on the handkerchiefs of all the members of the family), the animals to feed, the great household washing and ironing to do. In none of these accustomed tasks did Emily fail now, to the despair of Charlotte and Anne. Only by the total absence of music in that house of mourning was anything noticeably changed in the routine of life.

In the dining-room where the three girls spent the greater part of each day the writing-desks were seldom opened now.

Charlotte was supposed to be writing *Shirley*. To Mr Williams she confided on 18th October that, for the present, her book, alas ! had to be laid aside ; "both head and hand seem to have lost their cunning . . .". The greater need she felt, therefore, for some external stimulus to preserve her sanity. "Not feeling competent this evening either for study or serious composition, I will console myself with writing to you," she confessed to Mr Williams. The picture of Currer Bell that her letter conjures up, "sitting muffled at the fireside, shrinking before the east wind (which for some days has been blowing wild and keen over our cold hills), incapable of lifting a pen for any more formidable task than that of writing a few lines to an indulgent friend", is precious as setting the scene against which, with no variants now, the epilogue was being played out.

It was no longer possible for Emily or Anne to go out at all. Mr Nicholls, Mr Brontë's curate since the summer of 1845,

(2,056)

undertook to exercise the dogs ; he took Keeper and Flossy with him for long walks over the moors. By such attentions the poor man, yearning to help Charlotte in her crushing sorrow, hoped to convey a little of his love.

The last echoes of their literary achievements came in from London, Paris and New York. Smith, Elder & Co. published a new edition of the *Poems of Currer, Ellis and Acton Bell* in October. It was more attractively bound than the Aylott & Jones first edition, in French blue cloth with a design of a poet's lyre on the cover. The American firm of Lea & Blanchard, of Philadelphia, also brought out an edition of the *Poems*, and Harper Bros. of New York published a one-volume edition of *The Tenant of Wildfell Hall*, bearing on its title-page the imprint "*The Tenant of Wildfell Hall* by Acton Bell, author of *Wuthering Heights*". So the old confusions were still being exploited. Ellis and Acton Bell could afford to smile now at the disingenuous practice of publishers on both sides of the Atlantic.

Mr Williams forwarded all the reviews that the new editions provoked. *The Standard of Freedom* and *The Morning Herald* both contained notices of the poems, which the authors, in their anxiety that Mr Smith should suffer no loss by the edition, trusted would "at least serve a useful purpose . . . in attracting public attention to the volume". "As critiques," wrote Charlotte to Mr Williams, "I should have thought more of them had they more fully recognised Ellis Bell's merits ; but the lovers of abstract poetry are few in number."

The French translation of *Jane Eyre* was reviewed in the *Revue des Deux Mondes* by Eugène Forçade, who had enjoyed and understood the work, even by the author's reckoning.

Mr Newby, not to be quelled by any amount of snubbings, announced in his autumn list that he was shortly to bring out new works by both Ellis and Acton Bell. The report, duly conveyed to Haworth by Mr Williams, served at least to animate the penultimate scene.

"I am indeed much surprised," Charlotte wrote Mr Williams, "that Mr Newby should say that he is to publish another work by Ellis and Acton Bell—Acton has had quite enough of him—I think I *have* before intimated that that author never more intends to have Mr Newby for a publisher. Not only does he seem to forget that engagements made should be fulfilled, but by a system of petty and

contemptible manoeuvring he throws an air of charlatanry over the
works of which he has the management. This does not suit the
'Bells' ; they have their own rude North-country ideas of what is
delicate, honourable and gentlemanlike. Newby's conduct in no
sort corresponds with these notions. . . . Ellis is at present in no
condition to trouble himself with thoughts either of writing or
publishing. Should it please Heaven to restore his health and
strength, he reserves to himself the right of deciding whether or not
Mr Newby has forfeited every claim to his second work." Charlotte might refute Newby's claim to have the publishing of Ellis
and Acton Bell's new books, but what she could not—and did not
deny—was that new books were in the making. Newby's letter
to Emily of the previous February was evidence of Emily's being
engaged on a novel and Anne fully intended—as the sequel showed
—to write another book. How far either got with them will never
now be known, since Charlotte decided on destroying all their
unfinished work.

The American editions of the "Bell" novels were reviewed in
the *North American Review* for October 1848 under the title "Novels
of the Season". A copy was duly forwarded to Haworth. Whatever the findings of the critical faculty, their works had passed
nowhere unremarked. *Jane Eyre, Wuthering Heights, Wildfell Hall,*
had caused a sensation wherever they had been read. Remembering
the eighteen months of continuous rejection by one firm of
publishers after another, the ultimate destiny of those much-
thumbed manuscripts must have amazed the authors themselves.
Originally they may possibly have expected more courtesy, but
never the pandemonium of encomium and contumely which finally
broke about their ears. Charlotte, having first herself run through
the critique in the *North American Review,* awaited a propitious
moment, as she reckoned, for sharing its contents with her two
"ferocious" fellow-authors.

"*The North American Review* is worth reading," she wrote
to Mr Williams on 22nd November 1848, "there is no mincing the
matter there. What a bad set the Bells must be ! What appalling
books they write ! Today, as Emily appeared a little easier, I
thought the *Review* would amuse her, so I read it aloud to her and
Anne. As I sat between them at our quiet but now somewhat
melancholy fireside, I studied the two ferocious authors. Ellis, 'the
man of uncommon talents, but dogged, brutal, and morose', sat

leaning back in his easy chair drawing his impeded breath as best he could, and looking, alas ! piteously pale and wasted ; it is not his wont to laugh, but he smiled half-amused and half in scorn as he listened.   Acton was sewing, no emotion ever stirs him to loquacity, so he only smiled too, dropping at the same time a single word of calm amazement to hear his character so darkly portrayed. I wonder what the reviewer would have thought of his own sagacity could he have beheld the pair as I did. . . ."

The whole strident contention of the reviewer must have sounded out of key and false to ears made doubly sensitive of hearing now to undertones reaching them from beyond the permanently shut windows—sounds of the last leaves falling in the garden, of the robin's farewell song, of the drip of fog slowly dispersing before the pallid sun—which, although they spoke of valediction, were precious yet as holding the encroaching silence at bay.

In consequence of Newby's and Harper's persistent policy in confusing the authorship of the three novels, Acton Bell, in his capacity as author of *Wuthering Heights, The Tenant of Wildfell Hall*, "and, if we mistake not, of certain offensive portions of *Jane Eyre*", was singled out by the American critic for special contumely.

"Acton, when left altogether to his own imaginations, seems to take a morose satisfaction in developing a full and complete science of human brutality.   In *Wuthering Heights* he has succeeded in reaching the summit of this laudable ambition. . . . *The Tenant of Wildfell Hall* resembles it in the excessive clumsiness with which the plot is arranged and the prominence given to the brutal element of human nature.   The work seems a convincing proof that there is nothing kindly or genial in the author's powerful mind and that, if he continues to write novels, he will introduce into the land of romance a larger number of hateful men and women than any other writer of the day.   Gilbert, the hero, seems to be a favourite with the author, and to be intended as a specimen of manly character ; but he would serve as the ruffian of any other novelist. His nature is fierce, proud, moody, jealous, revengeful, and some-times brutal.   We can see nothing good in him except a certain rude honesty ; and that quality is seen chiefly in his bursts of hatred and his insults to women.   Helen, the heroine, is doubtless a strong-minded woman, and passes bravely through a great deal of suffering : but if there be any lovable or feminine virtues in her composition, the author has managed to conceal them. She marries a profligate, thinking to reform him ; but the gentleman, with a full knowledge of her purpose, declines reformation, goes deeper and deeper into vice, and becomes at last as fiendlike as a very limited stock of brains will allow. . . . He has almost constantly by him a choice coterie of boon companions ranging from the elegant libertine to the ferocious sensualist, and the reader is favoured with exact accounts of their drunken orgies and with numerous scraps of their profane conversation. All the characters are drawn with great power and precision of outline and the scenes are as vivid as life itself. . . . The reader of Acton Bell gains no enlarged view of mankind . . . but is confined to a narrow space of life, and held down, as it were, by main force, to witness the wolfish side of his nature literally and logically set forth. But the Criminal Courts are not the places in which to take a comprehensive view of humanity and the novelist who confines his observation to them is not likely to produce any lasting impression, except of horror and disgust."

Though Acton Bell might excusably gasp at some of the foregoing accusations, it was the American critic who would have been amazed had he been told that to create an impression of "horror and disgust" at the vices of society had been precisely the author's aim.

With *The North American Review* the last word on their novels to reach Ellis and Acton Bell had been pronounced. What their future public and critics would think, they would never know. For them their literary achievement was over ; judgment had been pronounced on the poems and novels. Contrary to all their expectations their books had penetrated across the Channel, across the Atlantic and at home had sold out in successive editions. They were being read by more people than they had imagined possible in those now remote-seeming days of two and a half years ago when they had ventured forth before the public, but, of all that great number, no one in the world seemed to have understood them. More surprised than distressed, they silently registered the world's rebuke and accounted themselves failures.

Writing was beyond the powers of any of them now. Mr Williams, sensing the heartache behind those signals for help which were Charlotte's letters, began sending parcels of books to beguile the monotony of those days.

Many months later Charlotte confessed to him that she had not had the heart, herself, to get immersed in any reading, but remembered thankfully "how the opening of the parcel and the examination of the books had cheered Emily and how their perusal had occupied her for many a weary day."

In the first week of December another chapter of the past was finally closed for Anne. The Miss Robinsons came to Haworth to see her. Strictly speaking, only one of them was a "Miss Robinson" any longer, Mary having been married on 19th October to Mr Henry Clapham of Keighley, from where she came now accompanied by her sister Elizabeth. Charlotte, prodigiously interested to see these much-talked-of young ladies at last, reported on the visit to Ellen Nussey. "They are attractive, stylish-looking girls. They seemed overjoyed to see Anne ; when I went into the room they were clinging round her like two children—she, meantime, looking perfectly quiet and passive."

Mary's marriage had taken place at Allestree in Derbyshire among her mother's kinsfolk, her bridegroom being a young man of twenty, son of a notable Keighley family. He was to die less than seven years after the marriage.

The marriage of Mrs Robinson to Sir Edward Scott had been very privately celebrated at Bath on 8th November in the presence of only her own sister and brother-in-law. The latest news the girls brought of their mother was that "she was in the highest spirits." On that description of her the curtain rings down on the drama that cost Branwell Brontë his life. The Miss Robinsons, evidently attached to their one-time governess, "clinging about her" in their youth and exuberance, would not have doubted, by the marks of death on her, that they were now seeing her for the last time. They had no idea, of course, that she had ever published anything.

With Emily growing daily weaker, the condition of Anne was all too evident to Charlotte also. Reporting to Ellen Nussey on 10th December, she wrote : "I am thankful to say, that my own health at present is tolerable. It is well such is the case ; for Anne, with the best will in the world to be useful, is really too delicate to do or bear much. She, too, at present, has frequent pains in the side. . . ."

In secret Charlotte had written to Dr Epps, a famous homeopa-

thist, a statement of Emily's case, clinging in last hope to the belief
that from someone who could not be classed as "a poisoning doctor"
Emily might consent to take advice. The attempt, like all the
others, was in vain. Emily continued to disregard every opinion,
to neglect every recognised method of arresting the disease. She
was, of course, far beyond all help by the time Charlotte consulted
Dr Epps. It was the second week of December and the cold was
intense.

The east wind had not ceased to rage for days. The opening of
the front and kitchen doors let in a piercing air which, Madame
Duclaux was told by the parsonage servants in after years, literally
staggered Emily as she crossed the stone-flagged passage, and made
her reel against the wall. She was trying to feed the dogs—a duty
and a pleasure which nothing would make her abandon to any of
the others. Charlotte and Anne, witnessing the scene, dared not
stretch out helping hands ; it would have been to acknowledge
that they thought her beaten. And this neither of them, to the
bitter end, ever let her see.

The evening came when Emily could no longer read to herself.
One of the new volumes sent by Mr Williams was Emerson's *Essays*.
Hoping to give her a last pleasure, Charlotte took up the book and
began reading aloud. She read on till she found that Emily was
not listening. She thought to take up the book again next day,
but the day had come when, for the author of *Wuthering Heights*,
the reading—and making—of books was at an end. "The first
glance at her face told me," wrote Charlotte later, "what would
happen before night-fall."

To bring her in some token of that world outside, towards
which all her being strained, Charlotte rose early in the December
day and hurried away to the moors. The ling was withered and
the long, waving grasses were stiffened with frost. The bilberry
clumps were pale, their hectic colour faded ; the moss was dun.
The very earth seemed to be sick to death in communion with
Emily. In despair of finding one blade of living growth to cheer
her dying sister, Charlotte ran far up the valley where, in a sheltered
flank of the hillside, a few bells of heather yet blew.

When she reached home and hurried upstairs it was still early
day : Emily was not yet up. (She was still getting up at seven
every morning and not going to bed till ten p.m.) Charlotte laid

the sprig of heather on her pillow. She had hoped for a flicker of recognition for what had all her life been Emily's favourite flower ; but Charlotte had left it a day too late : Emily could no longer see ; every object was equally blurred to her fading eyes. Yet there was no question of her staying in bed. If her sisters had dared suggest it she would not have heard them.

Downstairs Charlotte was writing a letter to Ellen. It was dated Tuesday, 19th December 1848. "Dear Ellen," she wrote, "I should have written to you before, if I had one word of hope to say ; but I had not. She grows daily weaker. . . . The physician's [Dr Epps] opinion was expressed too obscurely to be of use. He sent some medicine which she would not take. Moments so dark as these I have never known. . . ."

Emily came downstairs. They heard her foot shuffle on every tread ; her breathing could be heard all over the house. She came in, sat down and took up some sewing. Anne, Charlotte and the dogs were there. Keeper laid his massive head against her knee. Nobody spoke.

It was late in the morning when Emily said, "You can send for a doctor now, if you like." In what spirit those words were spoken Charlotte never told. Was it, in that proudest of mortals, a declaration of defeat ? A cry for help ? Or, rather, was it not a signal of victory ? The ultimate concession to the feelings of others of one who, at last, was assured of her own escape ? Before ever the doctor could be brought, she was gone—not easily, not painlessly, but ecstatically, of that we must be assured, for all her life she had aspired after liberty.

Well might Anne cry out of the deeps of that awful day :

> O Thou hast taken my delight
> And hope of life away !—

Existence without Emily, even had she been lent the physical strength, was a spiritual impossibility. She could not remember a time, so far back into the dawn of their days had the presence of Emily made itself felt, when she had not looked to that beloved sister, as to the air she breathed and the food she ate, as a source of life. Of far more, indeed ; as of the source of all "delight and hope". The death of Emily struck at the very principle of life itself and left Anne dying.

Yet, outwardly, she showed no sign of giving in. (Capitulation, indeed, was not a word in the Brontë vocabulary.) For Emily she need have no fears : the destination of that incomparable soul left her without a doubt. All her remaining powers must be employed in rendering herself equal to that exalted destiny. How could she in the little time accorded her yet hope to reach so high ? By some act of service, by some fresh dedication of her powers. It was not love of life, but a straining after the highest immortality that made Anne fight for existence to the bitter end.

No one was left alive who understood her any more. The love of her father and sister, materially expressed as it was every day, could not penetrate to her as Emily's did even from beyond the grave. That gulf which few mortals span was easier to cross than that dividing her from her living relations. Anne, as Charlotte had once complained to Mr Williams, had all her life been "of a remarkably taciturn, still, thoughtful nature, reserved even with her nearest of kin . . ." except with Emily. How impenetrable the wall was to become between the living and the living, the sequel was soon to show.

Emily was buried on Friday, 22nd December, Mr Brontë's curate, the Rev. Arthur Bell Nicholls, officiating.

Mr Brontë, proving himself a true father of his children in his love of animals, allowed Keeper to follow the coffin. They walked across from the parsonage into the churchyard, through the gate in the wall in procession, Mr Brontë and Keeper leading the way, Charlotte and Anne following, Tabby and Martha in the rear. In church throughout the service Keeper sat in the family pew with the others. When all was over and the return had to be made— the unthinkable return without Emily—Keeper tried to stay behind in the church and had to be led home.

"I now look to Anne," wrote Charlotte the day after the funeral, "and wish she were well and strong ; but she is neither." "My father and sister Anne," she wrote Mr Williams two days later, "are far from well. . . . I am not ill ; I can get through daily duties and do something towards keeping hope and energy alive in our mourning household. My father says to me almost hourly, 'Charlotte, you must bear up, I shall sink if you fail me' ; these words, you can conceive, are a stimulus to nature. The sight, too, of my sister Anne's very still but deep sorrow wakens in me such

fear for her that I dare not falter. Somebody must cheer the rest."
That was written on Christmas Day. Before ten days were out
Mr Brontë had sent for a specialist to see Anne.

It happens that we have an eye-witness account of what took
place on the occasion of Dr Teale's visit. He was a lung specialist
from Leeds, highly esteemed of the Faculty and of the great
Dr Forbes himself, the foremost consultant of the day in cases of
consumption. Mr Brontë could not have done better.

The eye-witness was Ellen Nussey who had come to Haworth
in answer to an urgent call from Charlotte. "I never so much
needed the consolation of a friend's presence. . . . Try to come.
Pleasure, of course, there would be none for you in the visit, except
what your kind heart would teach you to find in doing good to
others." Ellen, deeply attached to all at the parsonage—most of
all to Emily—had not hesitated to come.

She was, therefore, in the house when Dr Teale paid his visit to
Anne (apparently this took place 5th January) and in all good faith
set down what she remembered of that day many years later. She
could not guess that Anne, also, was to leave her record of it, and
unwittingly to expose the strange insensitivity of the witness's story.
It conveys better than any more informed evidence could do, the
incomprehension of the healthy for the dying, an incomprehension
not unobserved of Anne.

"Anne was looking sweetly pretty and flushed and in capital
spirits for an invalid," wrote Ellen. "While consultations were
going on in Mr Brontë's study, Anne was very lively in conversation, walking round the room supported by me. Mr Brontë
joined us after Dr Teale's departure and, seating himself on the
couch, he drew Anne towards him and said, 'My *dear* little Anne.'
That was all—but it was understood."

Dr Teale had told Mr Brontë that Anne's case was too far
advanced for any hope to be entertained. Both lungs were deeply
affected. The only treatment he could prescribe was to alleviate
suffering, and to retard the rapid progress of disease ; but cure, at
this stage, there was none.

There was no question, of course, of withholding the verdict
from Anne. Laconically, as Ellen had witnessed, the truth was told.
By a singular fortune which has preserved her thoughts for us,
when so much else was destroyed, we know exactly what Anne
went through. It hardly concurs with Ellen's account of "sweetly

pretty looks and capital spirits", but it *does* confirm Charlotte's evidence of "a remarkably taciturn . . . and reserved" nature. In her darkest hour Anne stood alone, opening her heart only to her God.

Two days after Dr Teale's visit to Haworth she began the important poem that was to be her last. It speaks for itself. The first eight verses, scribbled in pencil in the old childish italic print, were written upon that day (7th January 1849) ; the rest was written in ink at later intervals, the whole being finished on 28th January. They represent for us, therefore, as nothing else can, the true state of her mind during the greatest crisis of her life. She had been told that she was to die and, characteristically, it was not fear of death but the crushing sense of having failed to do anything worth-while with her life that overwhelmed her now. The pathos of hopes unfulfilled was never more simply or more poignantly expressed.

Anne's manuscript reads :

Jan 7th

A dreadful darkness closes in
On my bewildered mind ;
O let me suffer and not sin,
Be tortured yet resigned.

Through all this world of blinding mist
Still let me look to Thee,
And give me courage to resist
The Tempter, till he flee.

Weary I am—O give me strength,
And leave me not to faint ;
Say Thou wilt comfort me at length
And pity my complaint.

I've begged to serve Thee heart and soul,
To sacrifice to Thee
No niggard portion, but the whole
Of my identity.

I hoped amid the brave and strong
My portioned task might lie,
To toil amid the labouring throng
With purpose keen and high ;

But Thou hast fixed another part,
And Thou hast fixed it well ;
I said so with my bleeding heart
When first the anguish fell.

O Thou hast taken my delight
And hope of life away,
And bid me watch the painful night
And wait the weary day.

The hope and the delight were Thine :
I bless Thee for their loan ;
I gave Thee while I deemed them mine
Too little thanks, I own.

Shall I with joy Thy blessings share
And not endure their loss ;
Or hope the martyr's crown to wear
And cast away the cross ?

These weary hours will not be lost,
These days of passive misery,
These nights of darkness, anguish-tost,
If I can fix my heart on Thee.

Weak and weary though I lie
Crushed with sorrow, worn with pain,
I may lift to Heaven mine eye
And strive and labour not in vain ;

That inward strife against the sins
That ever wait on suffering
To strike wherever first begins
Each ill that would corruption bring ;

That secret labour to sustain
With humble patience every blow ;
To gather fortitude from pain
And hope and holiness from wo.   [sic]

Thus let me serve Thee from my heart
Whate'er may be my written fate,
Whether thus early to depart
Or yet a while to wait.

If Thou shouldst bring me back to life,
More humbled I should be,
More wise, more strengthened for the strife,
More apt to lean on Thee.

Should death be standing at the gate,
Thus should I keep my vow ;
But hard whate'er my future fate,
So let me serve Thee now.

                              Finished. Jan. 28, 1849.

These lines represent a month of spiritual struggle ; of growth, of understanding, and finally of acceptance whatever the decree,

Whether thus early to depart
Or yet a while to wait.

which represents a far, far journey from the baffled outcry of the opening lines.

With acceptance came strength ; with the will to live there came the courage to die.

From then on, having tested the worth of her endurance, of her capacity to face death unflinchingly, and knowing that it must be soon, she began to mend and set herself to live to some purpose yet. Though not in *her* sense was she ever to accomplish her purpose, she was, in the short reprieve afforded her, fully to earn the right to be ranked, as long as her name is remembered, among "the brave and strong".

An incident, reported by Ellen Nussey to Mrs Gaskell years later, would seem to relate to this time, in spite of initial errors and incongruities.

Mrs Gaskell, describing how Ellen was kept in complete ignorance of her friends' literary activities—though she suspected that they wrote for magazines—relates how she was finally confirmed in this idea when "on one of her visits to Haworth, she saw Anne with a number of *Chamber's Journal* [*sic*], and a gentle smile of pleasure stealing over her placid face as she read. 'What is the matter ?' asked Ellen. 'Why do you smile ?' 'Only because I see they have inserted one of my poems,' was the quiet reply ; and not a word more was said on the subject."

No poem of Anne Brontë's (or of any of the girls) appeared in *Chamber's Journal* at any time. But in the August 1848 issue of *Fraser's Magazine* there was published Anne's poem "The Three Guides" (written 11th August 1847). Ellen Nussey's story could but relate to this publication and moreover to this particular visit to Haworth in January 1849. She had not been there at any other time since the month of August, and did not again visit Haworth in the lifetime of Anne.

With Emily's death the embargo on any reference to the sisters' publications was raised, since it was she rather than the others who had insisted on secrecy. On this very visit of Ellen's to Haworth, Charlotte gave her a copy of *Wuthering Heights*—as a present, not as a loan, as she later wrote to explain, and from then on the truth was no longer hidden from Ellen. Hence Anne's ready response to her inquiry.

Chapter Twenty-One

THE LAST WORD

THE virulence of Anne's disease had been impressed on the family by Dr Teale and precautions insisted upon that had been totally neglected in the case of Emily. He had urged the immediate departure of Ellen Nussey and, indeed, felt so strongly on this head that he communicated directly with Brookroyd to procure her recall.

She left Haworth on 9th January. Charlotte, writing to her the next day (to apologise for Martha's forgetting to put her box into the gig and not discovering the omission until an hour after Ellen was gone), reported that "Anne had a very tolerable day yesterday, and a pretty quiet night last night, though she did not sleep much . . . ."

The doctor had forbidden Charlotte to continue sharing a bed with Anne. They must sleep in separate beds though they might still continue to share a room. It was the old haunted room, filled with the ghosts of Anne's childhood ; the room in which her mother and aunt had died and in which she had slept, in that same double bed, as far back as she could remember.

Sleeplessness was one of the conditions of their new suffering. "The days," wrote Charlotte, "pass in a slow, dark, march ; the nights are the test ; the sudden wakings from restless sleep, the revived knowledge that one lies in her grave, and another not at my side, but in a separate sick bed."

Such was the material condition of their lives. Of the serenity of Anne's mind ever since she had faced and subdued the imminent fear of death, Charlotte was constantly made aware : she could not but remark on it in her letters to Ellen and Mr Williams : "Anne is very patient in her illness, as patient as Emily was unflinching. I recall one sister and look at the other with a sort of reverence as well as affection—under the test of suffering neither has faltered. . . ." ". . . Anne seems so tranquil this morning, so free from pain and fever, and looks and speaks so like herself in health that I too feel relieved. . . ." ". . . Her mind seems generally serene, and her sufferings hitherto are nothing like Emily's. . . ." ". . . Her state of mind is usually placid. . . ."

Like a refrain such comments recur in almost all Charlotte's letters of the early months of 1849. Anne's outward calm—a reflection only of that inner strength which the spiritual victory had brought—created not only the semblance but, in some small measure, the actual reality of improvement ; the malady, at least, was held at bay. Watching her, listening to her night and day, trembling between hope and disillusionment, Charlotte noted every sign and clung to it as a drowning man clutches at straws.

In those first three months of the year there *was* a slight improvement. In January Anne had been at her worst. Shortly after Dr Teale's visit Charlotte reported : "Anne and I sit alone and in seclusion as you fancy us, but we do not study. Anne cannot study now, she can scarcely read ; she occupies Emily's chair ; she does not get well. . . ." By 2nd March Charlotte could write to Mr Williams : "My sister still continues better ; she has less languor and weakness ; her spirits are improved. This change gives cause, I think, both for gratitude and hope. . . ." Yet Charlotte can never trust the illusory signs again. "At times I hear the renewal of hope's whisper, but I dare not listen too fondly ; she deceived me cruelly before."

The difference—the whole difference—between Anne's case and Emily's was that Anne was given the best treatment available at the time ; she herself did everything she could to get better. Comparing the progress of her illness with "the fearful, rapid symptoms which appalled in Emily's case", Charlotte made the distinction clear. "There is some feeble consolation in thinking we are doing the very best that can be done. The agony of forced, total neglect, is not now felt, as during Emily's illness. Never may we be doomed to feel such agony again. It was terrible."

Dr Teale had prescribed cod-liver oil and carbonate of iron as a basic treatment, with applications of blisters for emergencies. The cod-liver oil "smelt and tasted like train oil," but Anne took them as long as she could (three months). "At last," wrote Charlotte, "she was obliged to give them up ; the oil yielded her no nutriment, it did not arrest the progress of emaciation, and as it kept her always sick, she was prevented from taking food of any sort."

Yet cod-liver oil was considered, even by one of the foremost lung specialists of the day, Dr Forbes, to whom Charlotte wrote in April for further light on Anne's case, to be "a peculiarly efficacious medicine". Dr Forbes, who was editor of the *Medical Review*, endorsed all Dr Teale's findings and declared that the remedies prescribed by his Leeds colleague were just what he would have recommended himself. But he added a warning against "entertaining sanguine hopes of recovery".

"Sanguine hopes" neither of the girls had, but an indomitable fighting spirit. Anne had a great desire to try hydropathy—then much in vogue—and took "Gobold's Vegetable Balsam", as prescribed, and said she thought it did her good. "As it is the first medicine which has had that effect," wrote Charlotte, "she would wish to persevere with it for a time."

Mr Williams, as in Emily's case, urged homeopathy. Charlotte had tactfully to decline the offer of his help which conflicted with the treatment Anne was already following. But they were prepared to try anything.

The one cure both invalid and nurse most eagerly wished to try —a change of air—had been banned by Dr Teale. Charlotte had no sooner heard him declare Anne's case hopeless than her "first impulse" had been to hasten her away to a warmer climate. But this was forbidden ; Anne was not to travel ; not to stir from the house this winter ; the temperature of her room was to be kept constantly equal. They had but to await the coming of spring. "Spring lies before us, and then summer—surely we may hope a little !" Charlotte cried, early in February, to Mr Williams.

Meanwhile each sad day had to be got through as best it might. Mr Williams continued to send parcels of books from London, and as Anne's illness "assumed a less alarming character" she took pleasure in reading again. "The choice of books is perfect," Charlotte wrote of a parcel just received on 1st February. "Papa is at this moment reading Macaulay's *History*, which he had wished to see. Anne is engaged with one of Frederika Bremer's tales." "The Cornhill books are still our welcome and congenial resource when Anne is well enough to enjoy reading." The titles of some of the volumes dispatched by Cornhill we know : there were Borrow's works, Carlyle's *Miscellanies*, Thackeray's *Journey from Cornhill*, Frederika Bremer's *Tales* (mentioned above) and Alexander Harris's *The Emigrant Family*, which Anne was reading when Charlotte wrote to thank Mr Williams for a parcel received on 5th April. "Do not ask me," she adds, "to mention what books I should like to read. Half the pleasure of receiving a parcel from Cornhill consists in having its contents chosen for us."

Charlotte, for the first time since Emily's death, had sufficient interest to copy out the first volume of *Shirley* and suggest sending it to Mr Williams to read. The occupation, and the encouragement which all the directors at Smith, Elder & Co. gave the opening chapters of her eagerly expected book, restored her to a partial tranquillity. The sense of what she *yet* might achieve, were the bitterness of her present lot only removed, finds an echo in many a letter of this time. "Oh ! if Anne were well, if the void Death has left were a little closed up, if the dreary word *nevermore* would cease sounding in my ears, I think I could yet do something."

That was the supreme suffering of both sisters alike : the longing to do that which they knew themselves competent to do, yet were debarred from doing by sorrow, sickness and death.

It was the resolve to achieve something yet which kept Anne alive. "I have no horror of death," she wrote to Ellen Nussey on 5th April, "if I thought it inevitable, I think I could quietly resign myself to the prospect, in the hope that you, dear Miss Nussy, would give as much of your company as you possibly could to Charlotte and be a sister to her in my stead. But I wish it would please God to spare me not only for Papa's and Charlotte's sakes, but because I long to do some good in the world before I leave it. I have many schemes in my head for future practise—humble and limited indeed,—but still I should not like them to come to nothing, and myself to have lived to so little purpose. . . ."

Three months had passed since Dr Teale's visit in January, but the verses written then and the letter to Ellen Nussey now were instinct with the same resolution, to live to some purpose yet.

An instinct, strong as a bird's to return to last year's nest, impelled her towards the sea. If she could only get to the sea she was sure she could be saved. She so urged the point that Charlotte very reluctantly consulted Dr Teale. It was mid-April when his answer came. He did not object. What was more fortunate still, he recommended Scarborough, the place of all places where Anne longed to be.

Charlotte saw only the dangers and difficulties of such a scheme when she considered Anne's emaciated state and excessive weakness and all the fatigues of a cross-country journey. "She has sometimes been so weak, and suffered so much from pain in the side during the last few days, that I have not known what to think. She may rally again," wrote Charlotte on 1st May, "but there *must* be some improvement before I can feel justified in taking her away from home. . . . She seems herself but half conscious of the necessity of such a delay. . . ."

Anne, indeed, saw no such necessity. She already felt borne aloft as on wings, so eager was her spirit for the flight. She fixed on Scarborough all her dying desires as though that sea and sky could bring her the assuagement of her pain, the fulfilment of her hopes and the confirmation of her life-long faith. She was right in thinking so. Scarborough would be not only the consummation of every lingering wish but the gateway to Eternity for her.

It was she, and not Charlotte, who hurried forward their plans. They were all perfectly plain and easy to execute. She realised that Charlotte was going to be faced with a dilemma, torn between her two duties to her father and to her invalid sister. Anne wrote to Ellen Nussey asking her if she would accompany her to the sea. Her letter, written on black-edged note-paper, reads :

Haworth
April 5th 1849

My dear Miss Nussy [sic]
I thank you greatly for your kind letter, and your ready compliance with my proposal as far as the *will* can go at least. I see however that your friends are unwilling that you should undertake the responsibility of accompanying me under present circumstances. But I do not think there would be any great responsibility in the matter. I know, and everybody knows that you would be as kind and helpful as any one could possibly be, and I hope I should not be very troublesome. It would be as a companion not as a nurse that I should wish for your company, otherwise I should not venture to ask it. As for your kind and often repeated invitation to Brookroyd, pray give my sincere thanks to your mother and sisters, but tell them I could not think of inflicting my presence upon them as I now am. It is very kind of them to make so light of the trouble but trouble there must be, more or less—and certainly no pleasure from the society of a silent invalid stranger—I hope however that Charlotte will by some means make it possible to accompany me after all, for she is certainly very delicate and greatly needs a change of air and scene to renovate her constitution—And then your going with me before the end of May is apparently out of the question, unless you are disappointed in your visitors, but I should be. reluctant to wait till then if the weather would at all permit an earlier departure. You say May is a trying month and so say others. The earlier part is often cold enough I acknowledge, but according to my experience, we are almost certain of some fine warm days in the latter half when the laburnhams and lilacs are in bloom ; whereas June is often cold and July generally wet. But I have a more serious reason than this for my impatience of delay ; the doctors say that change of air or removal to a better climate would hardly ever fail of success in consumptive cases if the remedy were taken in *time*, but the reason why there are

so many disappointments is, that it is generally deferred till it is too late.   Now I would not commit this error ; and to say the truth, though I suffer much less from pain and fever than I did when you were with us, I am decidedly weaker and very much thinner, my cough still troubles me a good deal, especially in the night, and, what seems worse than all I am subject to great shortness of breath on going up stairs or any slight exertion.   Under these circumstances I think there is no time to be lost.   I have no horror of death : if I thought it inevitable I think I could quietly resign myself to the prospect, in the hope that you, dear Miss Nussy [sic] would give as much of your company as you possibly could to Charlotte and be a sister to her in my stead.   But I wish it would please God to spare me not only for Papa's and Charlotte's sakes, but because I long to do some good in the world before I leave it.   I have many schemes in my head for future practise—humble and limited indeed—but still I should not like them to come to nothing, and myself to have lived to so little purpose.   But God's will be done.   Remember me respectfully to your mother and sisters, and believe me, dear Miss N.

Yours most affectionately,

ANNE BRONTË.

She knew *where* she wanted to be and *what* she wanted to see once again, with an eagerness of longing that comes with a sense of the finality of all encounters.   She thought her impatience was prompted by practical considerations ; but in effect she was chafing to be gone where nothing could bind her any more.

She knew exactly where she wanted to go in Scarborough—to Wood's Lodgings on St Nicholas Cliff, overlooking the South Bay, where she had so often stayed before.   Miss Wooler, having heard of the sisters' intention and owning a house in Scarborough herself, had most kindly written to offer the use of it in her absence.   But it overlooked the North Bay, and was nowhere near those sites and scenes that Anne knew best and loved.   Under her present physical limitations she felt that to go to Miss Wooler's house would not be like going to Scarborough at all.   Charlotte had to write a diplomatic letter declining the kindly meant offer and stating that rooms had already been engaged.   "I am not myself acquainted with Scarbro'," she wrote, "but Anne knows it well, having been there three or four times.   She had a particular preference for the situation of some lodgings, we wrote about them, and finding them disengaged, took them."

It would have been much cheaper to have stayed at Miss Wooler's ; knowing something of the Brontë girls' financial situation, this would have been one of the reasons prompting the kind lady's offer, but for the first time in their lives money need not be a major consideration. Anne could afford to take the lodgings she liked best (the Cliff was in the most expensive part of town), and pay Charlotte's expenses and Ellen Nussey's as well, thanks to a bequest she had just received from her godmother, Miss Fanny Outhwaite.

With the death of Fanny Outhwaite, which had occurred on the 14th of February of that year, the last link with the old Thornton days was severed. As recently as Charlotte's going to Brussels, Miss Outhwaite was busy trying to find her a post with friends of her own. Later, at the peak of Mr Brontë's blindness, he had consulted his old friend Dr Outhwaite and noted in his medical journal the relief his prescriptions had brought. Now they were all gone and Miss Outhwaite, dying herself and informed of Anne's state, had left her £200 with which to procure, if not health, at least the last unfulfilled desire of her heart. As Charlotte wrote to Ellen : "If Anne is to get any good she must have every advantage. Miss Outhwaite left her in her Will a legacy of £200 and she cannot employ her money better than in obtaining what may prolong existence, if it does not restore health."

At Anne's request Charlotte had written to Scarborough and engaged lodgings at the famous Mr Wood's.

"Wood's Lodgings", as they were called, occupied that portion of St Nicholas Cliff now completely covered by the *Grand Hotel* and consisted of a large four-storied house—nine windows wide— and two adjacent cottages which dated from early Regency days and afforded accommodation for a great number of visitors at a time. There were fourteen sets of lodgings in the large house alone, ranging from two sitting-rooms and two or three bedrooms to four sitting-rooms (drawing-room, dining-room, breakfast-room and parlour) and sixteen to eighteen bedrooms. They were designated by numbers, thus : No. 1 The Cliff, No. 2 The Cliff, etc. Extra accommodation could be had in one of the adjoining cottages if required, and a housekeeper was in residence at each suite of lodgings with her own premises and kitchen.

Anne had frequently stayed at the Cliff with the Robinsons, though not always in the same suite of rooms. In one and the same year, sometimes, the Robinsons had stayed first on one floor and then on another. But the situation of the rooms, on whatever floor one stayed, commanded the finest view in Scarborough and was acknowledged the "very first in town".

Charlotte had written for a "good-sized sitting-room and an airy double-bedded room with a sea-view", and had received the reply that this accommodation could be furnished them at No. 2 The Cliff at the price of 30s the week. The housekeeper that year was a Mrs Jane Jefferson, and very kind she proved.

They hoped to start on their journey on 23rd May, which was a Wednesday, the weather having now set in fine and warm. Yet Charlotte's heart was full of misgivings. She wanted to give Anne her last wish, but would have welcomed any impediment that was not positively unkind. She was still so extremely ill : ". . . the journey and its consequences still continue a source of great anxiety to me ; I must try to put it off two or three weeks longer if I can. . . ."

When she looked at Anne, Charlotte doubted whether anyone so weak and emaciated could undertake a journey at all. "She is more emaciated than Emily was at the very last ; her breath scarcely serves her to mount the stairs, however slowly. She sleeps very little at night." Still, there was no question of Anne giving in. "She is up all day," Charlotte reported to Miss Wooler, a week before the journey, "and even goes out a little when it is fine . . . but," she added, "we creep rather than walk."

It was not only to Scarborough that Anne was going ; she had particularly asked that the journey, necessarily broken at York, should allow of sufficient time for her to visit the Minster once again. Charlotte, only too anxious to diminish the fatigues of the journey, urged that they spend one night at York.

Neither of the sisters had any suitable clothes for a sojourn at a fashionable watering-place and a replenishment of their wardrobes was imperative. Appealing as usual to Ellen when mundane matters were in question, Charlotte wrote asking where bonnets and dresses and shawls might best be found; at York or at Scarborough? They decided finally on spending the afternoon and night at York before going on to the coast the next morning.

In the same little notebook in which she had entered the expenses for their London trip, in the far-off July of the preceding year ("When I saw you and Mr Smith in London," Charlotte wrote to Mr Williams now, "I little thought of all that was to come between July and Spring"), Charlotte and Anne now wrote down the list of their present needs. "To be bought. Bonnet. Corsets. Stockings blk silk. Dress. Gloves. ribbon for neck."

It reads like the preparation for a happy holiday undertaken under the best auspices, rather than the prelude to so solemn a departure. Charlotte, herself, was acutely aware of this when she wrote to Ellen, three days before the journey : "I wish it seemed less like a dreary mockery in us to talk of buying bonnets, etc. Anne was very ill yesterday. She had difficulty of breathing all day, even when sitting perfectly still. To-day she seems better again. I long for the moment to come when the experiment of sea-air will be tried. Will it do her good ? I cannot tell ; I can only wish. Oh ! if it would please God to strengthen and revive Anne, how happy we might be together. His will, however, be done !"

Ellen was to meet them at Leeds to catch the afternoon train to York. The weather was radiant and she was in good time for the appointment. She waited on the platform where the Keighley trains come in, but first one and then another train arrived, and still no sign of Charlotte and Anne. Her anxiety and forebodings increased as the hours passed. She waited several hours but they never came. Afterwards she recalled how, during that nerve-racking wait, she saw two coffins carried from trains to waiting hearses outside the station.

She was profoundly disturbed at the non-appearance of her friends, but realised that they could not have got a message to her at the station. There was nothing for it but to return home for the night. Early next morning she set off for Haworth.

As she turned into the lane she saw the gig waiting outside the parsonage and flew up to the gate just in time to see Anne and Charlotte come out. Martha Brown was with them, Mr Nicholls, and the two dogs. Mr Brontë had made his last farewells and with old Tabby was withdrawn from prying eyes inside the silent house. Happily for Ellen, Charlotte had warned her in her last letter of the change she would see in Anne. "I fear you will be shocked when you see Anne," she had written, "but be on your guard, dear Ellen, not to express your feelings; indeed, I can trust your self-possession and your kindness." Anne, as Charlotte had written in a previous letter, was very much emaciated. "Her arms are no thicker than a little child's."

She had been very ill the day before and it had been impossible to start. She was reported somewhat better this morning, but to Ellen she looked dying. She helped Anne into the gig and turned to say a word to Martha. Martha spoke openly of what they had to expect, only now that Anne was safely hidden from her sight giving way to her overwhelming grief.

Did Anne, as she clasped Flossy once more in her arms and pressed a kiss upon her shining head, remember Agnes Grey's departure from home, almost exactly ten years ago, when, "to the great scandal of Sally, the maid", she had kissed her cat adieu ?

The journey proved unexpectedly easy. The initial effort over, there was a revival of spirits in Anne that amazed both Charlotte and Ellen. Everywhere they met with the greatest kindness ; burly-shouldered Yorkshiremen offered their strong arms wherever trains had to be changed, or railway lines crossed ; Anne did not have to walk at all ; she was carried from stage to stage of her journey.

Having arrived at York they took coach at once to the *George Hotel*, Coney Street, a central position from which to set out on their various errands. Here they had dinner which, Ellen recorded later, Anne enjoyed very much.

It was radiant summer weather and the charm of the old streets and alleys and the beauty of the buildings beguiled even Charlotte and Ellen to share something of Anne's delight. They hired a bath-chair for her, and she asked to go immediately to the Minster.

She had been many times before. The last time was when she came with Emily in the summer of 1845 after her return from Thorp Green. It was the only journey they had ever made together. It had been a veritable "rally" of the Gondals, Emily and herself impersonating—no, not impersonating—"*being*" in the language of Emily, Ronald Macalgin, Henry Angora, Juliet Angus-teena, Rosabella Esmalden. . . . The Gondals—oh ! wild and happy rallies of their childhood, when they had ranged the moors ! As fleet of foot, as free of mind, as light of heart as now mind and body alike were crushed under the intolerable burden !

The Minster reared its immensity before her. She would not be able to penetrate far inside now. But she could sit in one of the first rows of chairs and allow the towering columns to do their centenarian task of drawing up the souls of mortals on to another plane. She could seek out with her glance, and greet lovingly, those ennobling emblems of beauty and of faith that she had known and loved erstwhile. They were unchanged. They still spoke of the durability of worship and of the need of men for something greater and higher than themselves. With the heavy hand of death upon her no encounter could have been more salutory to her spirit than this with that supreme monument to human achievement and the divine idea.

Ellen Nussey, observing her rapt look that afternoon, wrote years later : "Her visit to York Minster was an overwhelming pleasure not for its own imposing and impressive grandeur only, but because it brought to her susceptible nature a vital sense of the greatness of our Divine Architect."

As Anne looked up at the towering ancient windows, at the fluted columns, at the almost invisible roof, so high and ethereal it soared above her head, something of what passed in her mind has reached us in the broken ejaculations overheard by Charlotte and Ellen. Over-burdened as she had been for the past months by the sense of her own failure, here, in sight of one of the greatest achievements of man, supreme consolation came to her in the realisation that, beside the work of God, even this was as nothing. To aim high was all that mattered ; even if one failed, God would recognise the intention.

Charlotte and Ellen, watching her upturned face, saw its expression of rapture, heard the whispered words : "If finite power can do this, what is the . . ." and, fearing the effects of a too great emotion, urged her away.

They went out into the city and did their shopping, Anne in a noticeably happy frame of mind. In the little account-book Charlotte entered : £2 16s 6d spent on bonnets, 1s 6d for chair-hire ; 1s for coach-hire. Their bill at the *George* cost them £2 os 6d. They spent a comfortable night and took train the next day for Scarborough. The fare for the three of them cost £1 10s.

It was something over an hour's run from York to Scarborough and all the way was familiar country to Anne. She sat forward in her seat, eagerly scanning the countryside and pointing out to Ellen and Charlotte landmarks and beauty-spots that she welcomed like old acquaintances appearing in one's dreams.

The weather again was very lovely, warm and still. The lush pastureland spreading on either side of the train presented itself to their view in its finest apparel, the fields bordering the Ouse full of meadow-sweet and buttercups in flower, and the trees, so different from the thorns and sycamores of Haworth, standing in their full panoply of summer leaf. And ever and anon, in the gardens of the great houses dotting the countryside, lilacs and laburnums in full flower.

The sea was announced many miles before Scarborough was reached or sight of it had. The low foot-hills fell away and there was a sense of going over the rim of the world that enlarged, inexpressibly, the universe. And, more eagerly than ever now, Anne leaned forward in her seat.

The air as they got out of the train had a fluttering quality in spite of the stillness of the day, and the taste of salt was immediately on their lips. They hired a coach from the station to drive to their lodgings. It was but a little after noon and they were in excellent time for the two o'clock dinner.

It was Friday, 25th May, and as Anne sat by the wide-open windows of the sitting-room looking down on the sea, the sense of having, indeed, "arrived" excluded all other considerations.

"Our lodgings are pleasant," Charlotte wrote to Mr Williams. "As Anne sits by the window she can look down on the sea, which this morning is calm as glass. She says if she could breathe more freely she would be comfortable—but she cannot breathe freely."

The bedroom was a floor higher than the sitting-room, both overlooking the sea which, with the natural elevation of the cliff, appeared to be far below ; a view which enlarged the already wide expanse of ocean and made the horizon seem to span a moiety of the world.

In front the house and its adjacent cottages gave on to a square in the centre of which was an oval-shaped garden, laid out in the formal French manner, and surrounded by wrought-iron palings. There were other—Georgian—houses opposite, but immediately to the left and beyond the square the "Spa" Bridge led to the Museum, the "Saloon", the grand "Esplanade" and all the features of the South Cliff Gardens which, since the mid-seventeenth century, had so curiously combined the attractions of a seaside resort with those of a fashionable spa.

Mrs Jefferson and her servants proved themselves truly kind, but, more accustomed to the moribund than Charlotte, they warned her not to expect Anne to last long.

Anne might be sinking fast but, in her own eyes at least, that was no reason for conceding anything to her state. She acted as though nothing were altered from the time of those previous visits whose traces she needed—with all the urgency of the dying—to rediscover again.

On the Saturday morning she insisted on going to the Baths and, as Ellen afterwards recorded, "would be left there with only the Attendant in charge." Anne walked back to their lodgings, a distance of about five hundred yards, quite alone ; Ellen and Charlotte had not dared wait outside the Bath-house and did not know what time to expect her. As she reached the garden-gate she fell down exhausted ; but, immediately picking herself up, she forbade the people of the house to say anything to her friends, and it was not for several days that they heard of the incident.

In the afternoon, the tide being out, they went down to the sands and hired a donkey-carriage for Anne. How often she had watched others in the past drive slowly to and fro along the shore and pitied their incapacity to share with her fleet young limbs the joy of motion in that exhilarating air.

Now, when the donkey-boy wanted to beat up his animal to a trot she forbade it. Ellen Nussey, after a turn on her own along the sands, found Anne in the midst of a homily to the astonished boy on kindness to animals. She took the reins from him and said she would drive herself. She chose to be alone, not only dismissing him but begging Charlotte and Ellen to go off on their own. She was anxious for them to miss nothing of the beauty of Scarborough, and earnestly begged them, on every occasion when they were out together, to leave her ; she preferred it so. They understood her need for solitude ; she had so much to absorb and so little time in which to do it.

At that early season of the year there were no crowds. She could let the donkey pick his way across the sands and rest her eyes on the sea, the rocks and the noble headland on which the castle ruins stand, and not have her thoughts diverted. It was all exactly as she had seen it last. Nothing had changed—nothing germane to the place. There were naturally fewer bathing-machines than at midsummer, and the water-carts that fetched water for the Baths would not be down before the turn of the tide. There were a few of these "elderly gentlemen of regular habits and sober Quaker ladies" she had written of in *Agnes Grey* that formerly had been such a feature of the place, but they did not advance towards the moist stretches of sand towards which she let her donkey bear her.

It was here that, for a moment of time, love had brought her a plenitude of bliss. It was here, on these sands, that she had thought of Willy Weightman. He had been nearer to her here than at Haworth, although that last summer of 1842 she had felt him draw *very* near in their common care for Branwell. Then there had been in their parting, in the pressure of his hand, in his whispered words, something like a promise which their next meeting was to fulfil. In anticipation of those Christmas holidays she had allowed herself to imagine how it would be when they met again. . . . It was here, on these sands, that she had clearly seen him coming towards her for that blessed reunion.

She had not had the heart to do to Agnes Grey what life had had the cruelty to do to her. To Agnes Grey Mr Weston had come, walking across the sands at low tide, as in this present hour.

She turned her gaze from side to side of the great circle of the bay and greeted its overhanging cliffs and shining rocks with a caressing glance. He had never come, but it was something to have awaited him. The anticipation had been enough to fill her life.

Charlotte and Ellen startled her by appearing at her side, anxious lest the little lifting breeze might chill the air. She said she was quite ready to be going now.

After tea the evening was still so bland and beautiful that they went out again. Anne was very anxious for them to walk along the Spa Bridge, that had been considered a feat of engineering in its day. Supported on high arches like a viaduct, it spanned the valley between St Nicholas Cliff and the South Cliff on which the Spa and its attendant buildings, walks and gardens were laid out. Charlotte noted among the expenses of the journey the sixpence they each paid at the toll for crossing the bridge.

The view from there dominates the whole of Scarborough, with the town huddling inland to the west and the castle rising steeply on its promontory to the north across the bay. In the little harbour at its base rocks the fishing-fleet that, for centuries, has ensured the prosperity of its population.

It was very peaceful and very beautiful. The castle alone stood illumined now in the last ray of light. Its long line of wall, bastioned at regular intervals, looked rose-pink and ethereal on its height, half-way to Heaven. At such an hour more than at any other it is the *genius loci*.

It was up there that Mr Weston had proposed to Agnes Grey. He had walked her right through the town, walked her very fast, looking grave and abstracted the while "so that vague surmises concerning what it might be" had troubled her mind, and only when they had come "within sight of the venerable old church and the castle hill, with the deep blue sea beyond it" had Mr Weston appeared cheerful again. He had wanted the right setting in which to propose ; somewhere high and noble and enduring—like that great escarpment girt by the sea, in which to speak of the noblest sentiment of all. The words had been simple and few. "You love me then ?" he had said, fervently pressing her hand ; and all she had answered had been : "Yes."

"I shall never forget that glorious summer evening," Agnes Grey had said, "and always remember with delight that steep hill, and the edge of the precipice where we stood together watching the splendid sunset mirrored in the restless world of waters at our feet."

Next day was Sunday and Anne fully expected to go to church. She was surprised at Charlotte's vehemence in opposing her. Charlotte and Ellen were acutely aware of the difficulties hemming her in on every side. She, herself, was no longer aware of the barriers ; she already thought and planned like a disembodied spirit.

Then, if she could not go to church, they at least could go in her place ? She earnestly begged them to leave her. She was not aware of the change in her appearance and was again surprised at their refusal to be parted from her even for an hour.

She proposed they should go out, since it was so beautiful a day, and it was agreed that after dinner they should do so.

She wanted to be out of doors and alone, and after dinner made an excuse, as Ellen divined, of their not having seen the "Saloon", to beg them to go so far. They complied, while she "sat half-way in a comfortable seat near the beach."

The Saloon, as the actual Spa building was called, had been considered a great marvel at the time of its erection in 1838, some three years before Anne first visited Scarborough. Built on the shore at the base of the South Cliff, where the medicinal spring had first been discovered in the previous century, it had nothing but a low sea-wall between it and the tide and presented a truly romantic aspect with its Turkish towers and spires as though just washed ashore on some Byronic isle.

Years afterwards Ellen Nussey remembered the Sunday evening that followed. "It closed in with the most glorious sunset ever witnessed. The castle on the cliff stood in proud glory gilded by the rays of the declining sun. The distant ships glittered like burnished gold ; the little boats near the beach heaved on the ebbing tide, inviting occupants. The view was grand beyond description. Anne was drawn in her easy chair to the window to enjoy the scene with us. Her face became illumined almost as much as the glorious scene she gazed upon. Little was said, for it was plain that her thoughts were driven by the imposing view before her to penetrate forwards to the region of unfading glory. . . ."

The immensity of the view as well as the transforming medium of the light contributed to the unearthliness. It was an apocalyptic hour. Never had her soul been more in need of such reassurance. Everything was moving to its appointed end.

Perhaps the sight of Charlotte's stricken face fell as a reproach upon her conscience. She had gone ahead so eagerly that she had forgotten the dreary epilogue the others must go through alone. Completely alert now, she asked Charlotte what she thought would be the most bearable to them—to papa—about burying her ? Had she better try to get home ? They obviously mistook her intention because they asked her if she would *prefer* to die at home ? Emphatically she said no ; it was only for their sakes—to spare them that return journey. They asked her what *she* would prefer —that was all they wanted to know. To die *here*, that was her ultimate desire. Charlotte, fully assured of this, could write afterwards : "I wanted her to die where she would be happiest. . . . She loved Scarborough."

The next morning she was the first dressed, refusing all help the others offered, and the earliest ready to go down to the floor below for breakfast. But here the stairs daunted her. Ellen found her standing at the head of the staircase, suddenly afraid. She could not face the descent. It was the first weakness to which she admitted and it made her very unhappy. Going ahead, half-lifting and half-supporting her, Ellen did her best to get her down, but owns that it was a miserable failure and that she only just reached the sitting-room before she dropped Anne into her chair. She was "very miserable at the fact" but Anne put out her arms to comfort her and said : "You know it couldn't be helped, you did your best."

Although they made a pretence of eating their breakfast, there was no talk of going out that morning. Anne sat in the window till eleven o'clock and then quietly said she felt a change.

The instant effect on her companions forced her to think again of their predicament : how were they going to manage ? She said she thought she had better see a doctor. One was sent for. When he came she was still sitting in the window. She turned when he entered and, after apologising for troubling him, asked him to tell her truthfully if he thought she would reach home alive if she started at once.

The poor man looked at her, unable at first to gauge with whom he had to deal, then he looked at Charlotte and Ellen. Mistaking his hesitation Anne assured him he need not be afraid to speak. . . . She did not wish to give her companions any undue trouble by dying in a boarding-house ; she thought it would be better for them if she went home ; would that be possible if they travelled today ?

He took her hand and held it while he tried to tell her that it was not a question of travelling either today or tomorrow—of trying to travel at all. His concern was so great that Anne came quickly to his rescue. She understood, she said. Thanking him for his truthfulness she courteously dismissed him. Her composure, wrote Ellen, was so complete, she looked "so serene, so reliant", that neither Charlotte nor she dared give way to their grief. They were aware how much she needed not to be detained any longer.

She still remained sitting in her arm-chair, intent on the sea. The tide had begun to turn ; the day was at noon. The radiance of a cloudless sky poured into the room. Prophetically, Anne had forecast the dual mystery of that hour months before in the lines :

> There is a rest beyond the grave,
> A lasting rest from pain and sin. . . .
> Show me that rest—I ask no more.
> Oh, drive these misty doubts away ;
> And let me see that sunny shore,
>   However far away !
> However wide this rolling sea,
> However wild my passage be,
> Howe'er my bark be tempest-tossed,
>   May it but reach that haven fair,
>   May I but land and wander there
> With those that I have loved and lost. . . .

The passage was *now*, the sea calm, the arrival certain.

The doctor, who returned two or three times to follow her condition, "wondered at her fixed tranquillity of spirit and settled longing to be gone." As Charlotte told Mr Williams later, he said that "in all his experience he had seen no such death-bed, and that it gave evidence of no common mind. . . ." To Charlotte there was "piercing pain" in the recollection of the absolute acceptance with which Anne awaited death. "Anne," she wrote to Mr Williams, "had had enough of life such as it was—in her twenty-eighth year she laid it down as a burden."

The crying of Charlotte reached her through the enveloping peace. They had moved her to the couch. It was Charlotte who needed reassurance, not she ! She found the strength to say that "she was very happy and believed she was even then passing out of earth into Heaven." She heard them pray for her. How could she let them know there was nothing to fear ? . . . It was life that needed courage, not death. Suddenly, very clearly, she said : "Take courage, Charlotte, *take courage* !"

For her not a vestige of fear remained. Death, coming in such a form to take her, so apparelled on this celestial day, forbade the veriest qualm. She made ready for him as to the happiest encounter of her life. For at last the shadow of Calvin no longer fell on Christ.

Anne Brontë died at the age of twenty-nine having, according to her own standards, done nothing "to any purpose" with her life. She had lost all the beings nearest to her heart—the incomparable sister, the lover to whom she might never confess her love, the pitiable brother. Yet the eye-witnesses of her death never doubted that they were present at a triumph of the spirit—not at a defeat. Well might the doctor say of such a passing that "it gave evidence of no common mind." "So still and so hallowed were her last hours and moments," said Ellen Nussey many years afterwards. "There was no thought of assistance or dread. The doctor came and went two or three times. The hostess knew that death was near, yet, so little was the house disturbed by the presence of the dying, and the sorrow of those so nearly bereaved, that dinner was announced as ready through the half-open door, as the living sister was closing the eyes of the dead."

It was just two o'clock in the afternoon of Monday, 28th May 1849.

It was Ellen Nussey who registered the death and to whom is due the error that Anne's age was given as twenty-eight. She had, of course, turned twenty-nine in the previous January. This error was later repeated on the gravestone and, in spite of fresh instructions from Charlotte in 1852, who found there were no less than five errors in the inscription, has not been rectified to this day. The cause of death was given as : "Consumption—6 months—not certified."

In the same issue of the *Scarborough Gazette* (for Thursday, 31st May 1849) which reported in the "Visitors' List" the arrival of "Miss Bronte" at Mrs Jefferson's rooms at No. 2 The Cliff, Anne's death was reported in the following terms : "On the 28th inst, at this place, of consumption, Miss Anne Bronte [no diaresis] of Brookroyd, Birdstal [*sic*] near Leeds." Unknown as the Miss Brontës were, for reasons best known to herself, Charlotte preferred to make use of Ellen's address and omit all mention of her own both here and in the entry for Anne's burial in the church registers.

The funeral took place on Wednesday, 30th May. It was attended only by Charlotte, Ellen and a lady visitor who, coming from Birstall and seeing from the visitors' lists that Anne was a fellow-townswoman, went in sign of respect. The doctor who had attended Anne also offered to be present, Ellen remembered years later, but his offer was declined.

The parish church of Scarborough, St Mary's, was undergoing restoration at the time of Anne's death and had been closed for services since the preceding 11th October. It was not reopened for public worship until 25th July 1850, and during the whole of that period services were conducted at the daughter church, Christ Church, Vernon Road. It was here that Anne's funeral service was held. The entry in the church registers records that the vicar, the Rev. J. W. Whiteside, officiated. Anne's age was again given as twenty-eight and her residence as "Scarboro' from near York". To Charlotte and Ellen there was some advantage in the service being held at Christ Church since Vernon Road was the next street to Wood's Lodgings. It is most likely, indeed, that Anne's coffin was carried there overnight in view of the fact that the mourners were in furnished lodgings.

The burial took place in St Mary's churchyard, at the foot of the castle, in that beautiful spot Anne must so often have passed as she climbed the hill on her former walks to the church and the castle above, and from which so radiant a prospect opens of the old town, the shining bay, the rocks and the verdant headlands running out to sea. There, in full view of the boundless main, she lies in the most fitting resting-place that could be found for her.

Charlotte was very undecided, then and later, whether to leave Anne in Scarborough or transfer her eventually to Haworth.

Much has been said about Mr Brontë's absence from his daughter's funeral. Though Charlotte sought to excuse it to conventional-minded people like Mrs Gaskell (claiming that an "annual church solemnity" at Haworth occurred on the same day), the truth was that she refused to expose her father to another such ordeal ; she had hurried on the funeral to prevent his coming. In the last six months he had buried his only son, his beloved Emily, and had now entered on his seventy-third year.

When he wrote to Charlotte it was to urge her to stay some time longer at the sea before attempting the return home. With Ellen she went down the coast to Filey and stayed there for three weeks, finally reaching Haworth on Thursday, 21st June.

Ellen had offered to go back with her, but Charlotte refused : what "was to be undergone and was not to be avoided", as she later wrote, was best endured alone. "I am now home again," she wrote to Mr Williams a few days later, "I call it home still—much as London would be called London if an earthquake should shake its streets to ruins. . . . Haworth parsonage is still a home to me, and not quite a ruined or desolate home either. . . . Papa is there, and two most affectionate and faithful servants, and two old dogs, in their way as faithful and affectionate. Emily's large house-dog . . . and Anne's little Spaniel. The ecstasy of these poor animals when I came in was something singular. At former returns from brief absences they always welcomed me warmly . . . but not in that strange, heart-touching way. I am certain they thought that, as I was returned, my sisters were not far behind. But here my sisters will come no more. Keeper may visit Emily's little bedroom, as he still does day by day, and Flossy may still look wistfully round for Anne, they will never see them again. . . ."

Nothing, no one, would ever replace them in her heart. "To me," she wrote to Mr Williams, "these two have left in their memories a noble legacy. Were I quite solitary in the world—bereft even of Papa—there is something in the past I can love intensely and honour deeply—and it is something that cannot change—which cannot decay—which immortality guarantees from corruption."

In the empty house where, henceforward, there would be only an old man to share her sorrow and her increasing fame, there was one thought that kept her alive : it was the example of her sisters. Not of their genius, not even of their love, but of that quality peculiar to both which, in dying, they had bequeathed to her. By it she taught herself to live and work and, in the heart of her desolation, to feel their presence yet. Never in the years to come would she think of either without hearing Anne's parting words, exhorting her from beyond the grave to "Courage !"

SOURCES OF EVIDENCE

The evidence on which this book is based has been derived from the following five main sources :

I ORIGINAL DOCUMENTS

Comprising original MSS of letters, diaries, poems, written by Anne Brontë and her sisters, their relatives and friends, and preserved at :

1 *The Brontë Parsonage Museum, Haworth*
   The Bonnell Collection and documents in the possession of the Brontë Society

2 *The British Museum* (Ashley Library)

3 *The United States*
   (*a*) The Bonnell Collection, Philadelphia
   (*b*) The J. Pierpont Morgan Library, New York
   (*c*) The Berg Collection, New York Public Library
   (*d*) The Henry Huntingdon Museum, San Marino, California
   (*e*) The Department of Rare Books, University of Texas Library, Austin, Texas

   In the case of doubtful readings in published texts of the poems, application has been made to the owners in the U.S.A. who have supplied transcripts from the original MSS.

II OFFICIAL DOCUMENTS

Comprising birth, death and marriage entries in the registers of the following Yorkshire churches, with texts from memorial tablets and grave-stones in their precincts : St Peter's, Hartshead ; All Saints', Dewsbury ; St James's, Thornton ; St Mary le Virgin, Mirfield ; St Peter's, Birstall ; St John's, Dewsbury Moor ; St Peter's, Huddersfield ; St John the Baptist, Kirkheaton ; St Michael and All Angels, Haworth ; Holy Trinity, Little Ouseburn ; St Mary's, Scarborough ; Christ Church, Scarborough.

   In the case of births, deaths and marriages taking place after 1837, copies of all entries have been obtained from the General Register Office, Somerset House, London.

III PERSONAL EFFECTS

Comprising drawings, copies of manuscript-music, embroidery, books belonging to or executed by Anne Brontë and her sisters.

IV LOCAL INFORMATION

Obtained on the spot at places in any way connected with Anne Brontë : Thornton, Mirfield, Dewsbury, Huddersfield, Little Ouseburn, York, Scarborough. Together with much local information obtained at Haworth from descendants of families in close contact with the Brontë family.

V WORKS ABOUT THE BRONTËS AND THE BRONTË COUNTRY

Listed separately with the editions used in quoting from the Brontë letters, poems and novels, where original MSS or transcripts are not available.

ABBREVIATIONS

AB	Anne Brontë
AG	*Agnes Grey*
CB	Charlotte Brontë
EJB	Emily Jane Brontë
EN	Ellen Nussey
Miss B	Miss Branwell
PBB	Patrick Branwell Brontë
WSW	W. S. Williams
WW	Willy Weightman
BPM	Brontë Parsonage Museum
BST	Brontë Society Transactions
DNB	Dictionary of National Biography
SBC	*The Brontës and their Circle* by C. K. Shorter
SLL	*The Brontës, Life and Letters* by C. K. Shorter
TWH	*The Tenant of Wildfell Hall*
WS/BLFC	*The Brontës : their Lives, Friendships and Correspondence* edited by T. J. Wise and J. A. Symington
WS/PEA	*Poems of Emily Jane Brontë and Anne Brontë* edited by T. J. Wise and J. A. Symington
Benson	*Selections from the Poems of Charlotte, Emily, Anne and Branwell Brontë* edited by A. C. Benson
Chadwick	*In the Footsteps of the Brontës* by Ellis Chadwick
Duclaux	*Emily Brontë* by Mary Robinson (Duclaux)
Gaskell	*The Life of Charlotte Brontë* by E. C. Gaskell
Hatfield	*The Complete Poems of Emily Jane Brontë* edited by C. W. Hatfield
Turner	*Haworth, Past and Present* by J. Horsfall Turner

In quoting from Anne Brontë's novels, *Agnes Grey* and *The Tenant of Wildfell Hall*, the text of Smith, Elder and Co's edition of 1900 has been used throughout, but the page references, for the greater convenience of modern readers, apply to the current reprints in the *Nelson Classics*.

In quoting from Mrs Gaskell's *Life of Charlotte Brontë*, the reprint in the current *Everyman Edition* has been used.

NOTES

Chapter One

GENERAL SOURCES

Particulars regarding Thornton have been ascertained on the spot. Miss Firth's Diary : edited by her grandson, Professor Moore Smith published in *The Bookman* October 1904 ; SLL II, 410–23.

Letters of Maria Branwell to Patrick Brontë ; SLL I, 33–48.

Fennells and Morgans ; SLL II, 50–2.

The Maternal Relatives of the Brontës ; Rowe, J. Hambley, BST 1922 ; Hatfield, C. W., BST 1939.

page

1 AB's birth : Miss Firth's diary, 17th January 1820.

6 Miss B : Miss Firth's diary ; BST, 1937, 103–14.

7 Parsonage servants : Chadwick, 47 ; Wm. Scruton, *Thornton and the Brontës*, 62, 83.

8 Removal to Haworth, 20th April 1820 : registers of Haworth Parish Church, St Michael and All Angels.

8 AB's christening, 25th March 1820 : registers of Thornton Parish Church, St James's.

8 Choice of AB's name : see above articles on the maternal relatives of the Brontës, BST 1922, 1939.

9 Brontës' stay at Kipping during move : Turner, 84.

Chapter Two

GENERAL SOURCES

Miss Firth's Diary, Chadwick, Gaskell, SBC, SLL, Turner.

page

10 The move to Haworth : Chadwick, 53–5 ; Turner, 84.

12 AB's early delicacy : CB to WSW, 4th June 1849, SBC, 185 ; CB to Laetitia Wheelwright, 15th March 1849, SLL II, 33.

12 AB's asthma : a life-long malady which earned her the family nick-name of "Old Asthma" : see CB to EJB, 29th May 1843, SLL I, 268 ; CB to EN, 15th December 1846, SLL I, 341.

12 Mrs Brontë's illness : see Mr Brontë's letter to Mr Buckworth, 27th November 1821, BST 1931.

12 CB's recollection of her mother : Duclaux, 23.

13 AB's childhood : Chadwick, 172.

page

14 Mr Brontë's proposals : Chadwick, 67 ; SLL I, 68 ; SBC 33–43.

15 The Brontë girls' social isolation : Gaskell, 33.

16 Isabella Dury : from original letter in BPM.

Chapter Three

GENERAL SOURCES

Miss Firth's Diary, Chadwick, Duclaux, Gaskell.

page

17 Crofton Hall School, Wakefield : Mr Brontë's letter to Mrs Gaskell, 20th June 1855, BST 1933, 89.

18 Fees at Cowan Bridge : Chadwick, 76–7 ; BST 1953, 188.

18 Cowan Bridge, general : BST 1946, 1953, 190–1 ; Chadwick, 76–7 ; Duclaux, 35 ; SLL I, 69 ; Miss Firth's Diary, September 1824.

19 Story of the Masks : Gaskell, 36.

20 Fees paid at Cowan Bridge : Chadwick, 76–7 ; Gaskell, 38–9.

21 EJB's lines : from poem beginning with those lines, written 4th December 1938, probably at Law Hill.

21 Crow Hill Bog burst : Mr Brontë's sermon on the subject. See *Complete Works of Rev. P. Brontë* by J. Horsfall Turner, 211–19.
    For a full account of the bog burst see Turner, 149–52.

22 EJB, "a darling child" : Duclaux, 35.

23 Cowan Bridge holidays : "five weeks at midsummer only". See BST 1953, 192.

23 Tabby : BST, 1941.

24 CB's recollections of Cowan Bridge : letter to Miss Wooler, 28th August 1848, SLL I, 448 ; letter to WSW, 5th November 1849, SLL II, 81.

24 Franks' visit to Cowan Bridge : *The Bookman*, October 1904, 18.

25 Elizabeth's journey : Chadwick, 76.

26 Funeral of Maria : PBB's poem "Caroline", written 1840, Benson, 386.

Chapter Four

GENERAL SOURCES

The Arminian Magazine, 1798 ; *The Wesleyan Methodist Magazine*, 1799–1812 ; Southey's *Life of Wesley*.

page

28 Miss B's age : she was born 2nd December 1776 ; Mrs Brontë, 15th April 1783. See BST 1937, 1939.

29 The Branwell family : for particulars regarding the Branwell family see BST 1923, 1937, 1939, 1946. In addition I am indebted for many inter-

esting facts to Miss Frances Branwell of Penzance, a great-grand-daughter of Thomas Branwell by his first wife.

30 Mrs Brontë and her sisters, Methodists : Thomas Percival Bunting in *The Life of Jabez Bunting*, the eminent Methodist preacher, Vol. I, note to p. 197, writes thus of Maria at the time of her marriage : "Miss Branwell belonged to the Methodist family of the Carnes of Penzance. . . . A set of the Methodist Magazines from the commencement formed part of Miss Branwell's marriage-dowry, and, doubtless, awoke Charlotte Brontë's love of the marvellous . . ."

31 Wesley's views on dress : Southey's *Life of Wesley*, 3rd edition, II, 349.

31 Miss B's will : SLL I, 244-6.

32 Miss B buried near her sister : SLL I, 244-6.

32 The religion of little Maria : see PBB's poem "Caroline", quoted on pp. 26-7 :

> "She lay, as I had seen her lie
> On many happy nights before,
> When I was humbly kneeling by—
> Whom she was teaching to adore ;
> Oh, just as when by her I prayed,
> And she to Heaven sent up my prayer——" ;

also EN's recollections of CB at Roe Head, SLL I, 89 :

> "She described Maria as a little mother among the rest, superhuman in goodness and cleverness . . ."

32 A religion of fear : see report of the Moravian minister on Anne's religious training : Wm. Scruton on "Reminiscences of the late Miss Ellen Nussey", BST 1898, 27.

33 Lines from AB's poem "Self-Communion", WS/PEA, 284 ; Benson, 310.

33 Lines, "Oppressed with sin and woe . . ." : from poem "Confidence", WS/PEA, 243 ; Benson, 356.

33 AB's crushing sense of sin : see, in particular, her poems : "Despondency" ; "To Cowper", "A word to the Elect", "Vanitas Vanitatum", "Music on Christmas Morn", "A Prayer", "If this be All", "Confidence", WS/PEA.

34 Mr Brontë's letter : *The Bookman*, October 1904.

34 Wesley on the upbringing of children : Southey's *Life of Wesley* (3rd edition).

35 AB's early delicacy : see above, chapter two, notes for p. 12.

35 Miss B's affection for AB : see EN's "Reminiscences of Charlotte Brontë" in *Scribner's Magazine* May 1871, BST 1899.

35 Miss B's discipline : see G. Elsie Harrison, *The Clue to the Brontës* 55.

page

35 PBB at Grammar school : SBC, 114.

36 Miss B's reading : see *Shirley*, chap. XXII, 388.

37 Letter to Hartley Coleridge: Gaskell, 126–7; SLL I, 184. Neither source gives
the correct text of the letter now in the Texas collection; they give the
addressee as Wordsworth whereas it was to Hartley Coleridge that Charlotte
wrote. See *TLS*, 14th May, 1970.

39 Régime of love : AG, chap. III, 29–30.

39 Miss B's favourite : Gaskell, 124.

39 EJB's religion : see her answer to Mary Taylor, SLL I, 118.

39 AB's piety : CB to Martha Brown, 5th June 1849, SLL II, 53.

Chapter Five

41 Lines ,"Brightly the sun of summer shone" : from poem "Memory"
signed and dated 29th May 1844, WS/PEA, 229 ; Benson, 333.

41 "A little girl . . ." : see AG, chap. XVII, 133.

42 Lines, "Summer days . . ." ; from poem "Past Days " signed and dated
21st November 1843, WS/PEA, 226 ; Benson, 338.

42 Lines, "A fine and subtle spirit . . ." : from poem "The Bluebell " signed
and dated 22nd August 1840, WS/PEA, 209 ; Benson, 287.

43 Lines, "There is a silent eloquence . . ." : from poem "The Bluebell"
signed and dated 22nd August 1840, WS/PEA, 209 ; Benson, 287.

43 Lines, "As in the days of infancy . . ." : from poem "Memory " signed
and dated 29th May 1844, WS/PEA, 230 ; Benson, 333.

43 The finding of primroses : AG, chap. XIII, 103.

43 Distant prospects : CB to James Taylor, SLL II, 138.

Chapter Six

45 Dinner in the kitchen : Chadwick, 69.

45 Milk puddings : SLL I, 67.

45 Tripe and onions : see John Greenwood's Diary, BST 1951, 35.

46 Miss B and animals : see EN's "Reminiscences of Charlotte Brontë" in
Scribner's Magazine, May 1871, BST 1899, 79 : "During Miss Branwell's
reign at the parsonage the love of animals had to be kept in due subjection
. . ."

46 Periodicals at the parsonage : Gaskell, 55.

47 Toys for the children : Ratchford, F. E., *The Brontës' Web of Childhood*,
6 : "A set of ninepins, a toy village, and a dancing doll he (Mr Brontë)
gave to Miss Branwell for the girls . . ."

page

49 Lines, " With grey walls . . ." : from " Home ", WS/PEA, 237 ; Benson, 329.

49 The parsonage garden : see EN's "Reminiscences of Charlotte Brontë" BST 1899.

49 Cherry tree incident : Chadwick, 87.

50 Chief Genius Branii : Ratchford, *The Brontës' Web of Childhood*, 15.

50 The Play of the Islanders : Gaskell, 53–4.

52 "Sneaky" : the original wooden soldier chosen by PBB and named "Buonaparte " by him (Ratchford, *The Brontës' Web of Childhood*, 6) was renamed "Sneaky " in CB's account of the "Twelve Young Men off the mouth of the Niger " (Ratchford, op. cit., 12) and eventually was transferred to Branwell himself as an eponymous name.

53 Glass Towns: for evidence of the direct influence of the paintings of John Martin on the conception of Glass Town, see Gérin, *Charlotte Brontë: The Evolution of Genius*, 43.

53 CB's "History of the Year 1829" : Gaskell, 55.

54 Mr Brontë's deed of gift to Martha Brown : from original text in BPM, Haworth.

55 Letter from Crosstone : CB to the Rev. P. Brontë, SLL I, 77–8.

55 Bewick : *Jane Eyre* chap. 1, 2 ; TWH, chap. LIII, 475.

56 "I see, I see appear . . ." : Ratchford, *The Brontës' Web of Childhood*, 56.

56 Offer of CB's godparents : W. W. Yates "Dewsbury and the Brontës", BST 1895, 12 : "The expense of her education there [Roe Head] was borne by her God-parents, the Rev. Tomas Atkinson and Mrs. Atkinson with whom Charlotte often stayed when the work of the week at Roe Head was over."

Chapter Seven

57 Lines, ". . . long ago I loved to lie" : from "Verses by Lady Geralda" signed and dated December 1836, quoted from transcript supplied by Miss F. E. Ratchford from original MS, WS/PEA, 185.

57 Lines, "To range the mountains wild" : from Song "Come to the banquet . . ." signed and dated 4th September 1845, WS/PEA, 252.

57 Lines, "Beneath this lone and dreary hill" : from "Verses by Lady Geralda", WS/PEA, 185.

58 PBB's sanguinary phase : "Branwell . . . always brought the Young Men's Play back to the game of destruction and war . . .", Ratchford *The Brontës' Web of Childhood*, 15. For other examples of his "taste for the gruesome" see op. cit. 7, 11, 12.

58 Lines from "The North Wind" : signed and dated 26th January 1838, WS/PEA, 200.

page

59 Destruction of AB's papers after her death : see Biographical Notice of
    Ellis and Acton Bell by CB prefixed to 1850 edition of their works. CB's
    destruction is implicit in her declaration : "It would not have been difficult
    to compile a volume out of the papers left by my sisters, had I in making the
    selection, dismissed from my consideration the scruples and wishes of those
    whose written thoughts these papers held. But this was impossible . . .
    I have, then, culled from the mass only a little poem here and there."
    See also : SBC, 132 note ; Chadwick, 288, 299. "Charlotte Brontë
    committed a grievous wrong when she destroyed the Gondal Chronicles
    and the fairy tales composed by her sisters . . ."

61 Lines, "We know where deepest . . ." : from song of same title, signed
    and dated 3rd September 1845, WS/PEA, 250.

61 Lines, "We long have known . . ." : loc. cit.

61 Lines, "I was roaming . . ." : from "I dreamt last night", 1846, from
    original MS in BPM, Haworth, WS/PEA, 267 ; Benson, 300.

61 Lines, "We had wandered . . ." : loc. cit.

61 Lines, "It may be pleasant . . ." : from Song "Come to the banquet",
    WS/PEA, 252.

62 Lines, "I'd rather listen . . ." : loc. cit.

62 Lines, "Zenobia, do you remember . . ." from "Alexander and Zenobia",
    dated 1st July 1837 from transcript of original MS, WS/PEA, 191.

62 EN's first visit to Haworth : from "Reminiscences of Charlotte Brontë"
    first published in *Scribner's Magazine*, May 1871. See also BST 1899.

64 Vocabulary of Proper Names : inserted in *Goldsmith's Grammar of General
    Geography*, copy in the BPM, Haworth.

64 Arabic names: the Spanish provenance of so many names of the Brontës'
    imaginary characters can be traced to their reading of the numerous reports
    of the Peninsula War in *Blackwood's Magazine* in the 1820s.

64 AB's list of principal Gondal characters : Ratchford, *Gondal's Queen*, 195.

66 EN'S recollections of the parsonage and of the family : BST 1899.

66 Mr Brontë : *Shirley*, chap. VII, 113.

68 Lines, "I loved . . ." : from poem "I dreamt last night" from original
    MS in BPM, Haworth, WS/PEA, 267 ; Benson, 300.

68 Diary paper : from original at BPM, Haworth.

Chapter Eight

70 CB's recommendations on literature : CB to EN, 4th July 1834, SLL I,
    111.

71 Keighley Mechanics' Institute : for catalogue of books available at the
    Keighley Mechanics' library, see BST 1950, 344–58.

page

71 Ponden Hall library : see Ratchford, *The Brontës' Web of Childhood*, 4, 19, 31, 71.

71 The collection of books: for the early influence of Scott and Byron on the Brontës, see Gérin, *Emily Brontë*, 26–8, 44.

72 AB's views on being a governess : AG, chap. I, 10

73 Lines, "While on my lonely couch . . ." : from "Dreams", written spring 1845, WS/PEA, 241 ; Benson, 295.

73 Lines, "As in the days of infancy . . ." : from "Memory", written 19th May 1844, WS/PEA, 230 ; Benson, 333.

73 Lines, "The language of my inmost heart . . ." : from "To Cowper", written 10th November 1842, WS/PEA, 216 ; Benson, 335.

73 Music : AB's music, all annotated by her hand, together with several albums of MS music copied by her, can be seen at BPM, Haworth.

74 Mary and Martha Taylor at Haworth : see CB to EN, 7th June 1838, SLL I, 151.

75 Drawing : Chadwick, 102.

76 Presents of clothing : CB to Mrs Franks, May 1831, *The Bookman*, October 1904 ; and CB to EN, 4th July 1834, SLL I, 110.

77 Branwell's fees : Mr Brontë to Mrs Franks, formerly Elizabeth Firth, 6th July 1835, *The Bookman*, October 1904. From the context it would appear that Mr Brontë's gratitude was here specifically related to the generous help given him by his children's godparents, as in the case of Charlotte.

77 Lines, "A tender heart . . ." : from poem "Self-Communion", verses 5 and 16, WS/PEA, 284 ; Benson, 310.

79 EJB and liberty : CB on EJB at Roe Head in "Biographical Notice of Ellis and Acton Bell", prefaced to 1850 posthumous edition of her sisters' works.

80 Lines, "O why are things so changed . . ." : from " Verses by Lady Geralda", WS/PEA, 186.

81 AB's drawing : the original can be seen at the BPM, Haworth ; see illustration facing p. 96.

83 Miss Wooler : for particulars regarding the Miss Woolers see Chadwick, Chap. VIII ; the registers of Birstall, Mirfield and Dewsbury churches ; the recollections of their nephew, the Rev. Max Blakeley, BST 1952, 113–14 ; and SBC, 241–3.

85 Miss Wooler's methods : Gaskell, 69.

Chapter Nine

86 AB's prize : see SBC, 164.

87 Mary Taylor's comment : SLL I, 117.

page

88 CB's Roe Head journal : quoted from original MS at BPM, Haworth, Bonnell collection.

89 CB's letters to EN from Roe Head : SLL I, 117–26.

91 Lines, "I have passed . . ." : from "The North Wind", 26th January 1838, WS/PEA, 200.

92 Lines, "Oh, Heaven ! I could bear . . ." : from "The Captive's Dream", 24th January 1838, (misnamed "The Captains Dream") WS/PEA, 199.

92 CB's friends at Birstall, etc. : for information regarding CB's Sunday evening visits see Yates, W.W., "The Brontës and Dewsbury", BST 1895, 12.

93 CB staying with godparents : SLL I, 51–2 ; Chadwick, 40.

94 Invitation from AB's godmother : see CB's letter to Mrs Franks, *The Bookman*, October 1904 ; Mr Brontë's letter to Mrs Franks, 13th June 1836, *The Bookman*, October 1904.

95 Amelia Walker of Lascelles Hall : see CB's letter to EN, SLL I, 124.

97 George Moore : see his *Conversations in Ebury Street*, 214–23.

97 Lines, "Eternal Power . . ." : from poem "The Doubter's Prayer", 10th September 1843, WS/PEA, 222.

98 Lines, "I see one kneeling . . ." : from poem "Self-Communion". WS/PEA, 285 ; Benson, 310.

98 CB on AB's religious doubt : see "Biographical Notice of Ellis and Acton Bell", prefixed to 1850 posthumous edition of her sisters' works, Smith, Elder and Co.

99 The Rev. James La Trobe : see his narrative reported by Wm. Scruton in "Reminiscences of the late Miss Ellen Nussey", BST 1898, 26–7.

102 Lines, "Oppressed with sin and woe . . ." : from poem "Confidence", WS/PEA, 243 ; Benson, 356.

Chapter Ten

103 Tabby's accident : Gaskell, 107. The accident occurred in December 1836 and not in 1837 as Mrs Gaskell erroneously dated it. CB's letter to EN is dated 29th December 1836, WS/BLFC.

104 Emily's note : see Raymond, Ernest, *In the Steps of the Brontës*, 90. He states that the note is written under a poem for July 1836. It does not appear in Hatfield which begins with four fragments, one of which is dated July 1836. But there is the unmistakable ring of authenticity in the note.

105 Lines, "Why, when I hear . . ." : from AB's poem "Verses by Lady Geralda", WS/PEA, 185.

106 Diary paper for 26th June 1837 : quoted from original text at BPM, Haworth.

page

107 Lines, "One was a boy . . ." : from poem "Alexander and Zenobia", quoted from transcript of original text supplied me by Miss F. E. Ratchford, WS/PEA, 188–91.

107 Lines, " 'We met on Greecia's classic plain . . .' " : loc. cit.

107 Lines, " 'And shall we part . . .' " : loc. cit.

108 Lines, " 'Zenobia, do you remember . . .' " : loc. cit.

108 Removal of Miss Wooler's school to Dewsbury Moor : see Stuart, Erkine, *The Brontë Country*, 109–12 for particulars regarding the school at Heald's House, Dewsbury Moor.

110 CB's health : CB to Miss Wooler, SLL I, 340.

111 EJB at Law Hill : obviously EJB did not go to Law Hill until October 1837, because she made no mention of it in her diary paper of 26th June 1837 ; and CB's letter to EN reporting her arrival at Law Hill has now definitely been dated 2nd October 1837, as EN herself dated it in the —unpublished—edition of her letters collated by J. Horsfall Turner.

112 Lines, "Methought I saw him . . ." : from poem "The Captive's Dream", 1838, WS/PEA, 199.

112 Lines, "O how I longed to clasp . . ." : loc. cit.

113 Departure from Dewsbury Moor : CB's letter to EN dated 4th January 1838, SLL I, 145–6.

Chapter Eleven

115 Law Hill: for the evidence *re* EB's stay at Law Hill, see Gérin, *Emily Brontë*, 83–4.

115 EJB's poems : quoted from text in Hatfield, "I'll come when thou art saddest . . ." : undated, fragment No. 37, p. 56, WS/PEA, 50.
"Far away is the land of rest . . ." : dated October 1837, 53, WS/PEA, 48.
"The Old Church Tower and garden wall . . ." : dated October 1837, 52, WS/PEA, 45.

115 Lines, "A little while . . ." : quoted from poem dated 4th December 1838, Hatfield, 93, WS/PEA, 75.

116 Mrs Ingham : Mrs Ingham's recollections of PBB, see BST 1895, 1945.

118 The original of the so-called " gun-group " of the sisters with Branwell, sitting round a table on which are a gun and dead game, has disappeared. An engraving of it appeared in J. Horsfall Turner's *Haworth Past and Present* from which reproductions have been made.
    A further group of Anne, Charlotte, and Emily (sitting in that order) was cut up by Mr Nicholls and only the profile figure of Emily preserved —this is now in the National Portrait Gallery.
    Tracings of all three figures were made and their names written in by John Greenwood, the Haworth stationer, before the destruction of the picture. This has permitted the identification to be confirmed.

page

119 Family's attitude to AB : AG, chap. I, 7.

120 AB wants to become a governess : AG, chap. I, 9–10.

122 CB's letter : to EN, 15th April 1839, SLL I, 155.

122 Departure from Haworth : AG, chap. I, 11–12.

124 Last sight of Haworth : AG, chap. I, 13.

124 Arrival at Blake Hall : AG, chap. II, 14.

126 Preface to 2nd edition of TWH : text quoted from Haworth Edition (1900) with Introduction by Mrs Humphrey Ward.

126 Inghams of Blake Hall : particulars regarding the Ingham family and Blake Hall have been ascertained on the spot and from the registers of Mirfield Church. Additional details have been kindly supplied by Miss Susan Brooke, M.A., F.S.A., and Miss Stancliffe of the Old Rectory, Mirfield. See also Miss Brooke's article, "Anne Brontë at Blake Hall", BST, 1958.

128 CB on "Inghams" : to EN, 24th January 1840, SLL I, 174.

129 AB on controlling children : AG, chap. III, 25.

129 Good-night kiss : AG, chap. III, 29.

130 AB's hope that children will improve : AG, chap. III, 31.

131 AB's determination to succeed : AG, chap. III, 31–2.

131 Physical fatigue : AG, chap. III, 26, 27–8.

131 Children playing at well : AG, chap. III, 21–2.

132 CB on Mr Carter's visit : letter to EN, SLL I, 159.

132 CB on new post : letter to EJB, SLL I, 162.

132 Liverpool journey ; letters to EN 26th July and 4th August 1839, SLL I, 164.

133 Domestic crisis : CB, to EN 21st December 1839, SLL I, 172.

133 AB's dismissal : AG, chap. V, 47.

134 Feeling of humiliation : AG chap. V, 47–8.

Chapter Twelve

136 AB and WW : it is significant, as Ellis Chadwick remarks (op. cit. 166), that Mrs Gaskell, the best-informed on the subject, should have omitted all reference to the intimacy existing between WW and the Brontë girls. Yet Mrs Gaskell saw all CB's letters relating to him and had, further, received the confidences of EN.

136 WW's age : reference to the registers of St Lawrence's Church, Appleby, shows that he was christened on 29th May 1814. He was 25, therefore,

when he arrived at Haworth after taking his M.A. degree at Durham. His age was erroneously given both in his death certificate and on the memorial tablet erected to him in Haworth Church.

137 CB on WW : letters to EN, 14th July 1840, SLL I, 189 ; 9th April 1840, SLL I, 177–8 ; 4th August 1839, SLL I, 165.

138 CB on WW : letters to EN, 29th September 1840, SLL I, 193 ; 14th July 1840, SLL I, 189 ; 20th August 1840, SLL I, 190–1 ; 20th January 1842, SLL I, 228.

139 Lectures at Keighley : that WW gave more than one lecture at the Mechanics' Institute is shown by CB's reference to "another lecture" in her letter of 9th April 1840. The first was in February and was that described by EN for Shorter ; see SLL I, 176.

139 CB on "mutual nonsense" : letter to EN 14th July 1840, SLL I, 189.

140 CB on "Cupid" : letter to EN, 9th April 1840, SLL I, 178.

140 The valentines : EN's account to Shorter, SLL I, 176 ; CB's letter to EN, 3rd March 1841, SLL I, 204.

141 Lines, "I've noticed many a youthful form" : from "Self-Congratulation", 1st January 1840, WS/PEA, 208 ; Benson, 348.

143 WW's vanity : CB to EN, 12th November 1840, SLL I, 194.

144 WW's lecture on the Classics : see EN's account, SLL I, 176.

145 CB on WW : letters to EN, 3rd March 1841, SLL I, 206 ; 29th September 1840, SLL I, 192.

146 Nancy Brown : AG, chap. XI, 94.

146 Lines, "The lightest heart . . ." : from "A Reminiscence", April 1844, WS/PEA, 229 ; Benson, 325.

147 Mr Weston : AG, chap. XI, 96.

147 WW's character : see Mr Brontë's funeral sermon, 2nd October 1842, printed by J. V. Walker, Halifax, WS/BLFC.

148 AB in love : AG, chap. VIII, 71.

149 "Retirement" : WS/PEA, 211 ; Benson, 143.

Chapter Thirteen

150 Thorp Green : when writing the name both AB and PBB invariably omitted the final "e". For the purposes of this book it has therefore again been omitted.

Information regarding Thorp Green and the Robinson family has been ascertained on the spot. I am particularly indebted to the Rev. F. Northorp, late Vicar of Great with Little Ouseburn Churches, who supplied copies

page

of all relevant data from the registers of his church, together with much local information respecting the antiquities of the place.

For much evidence regarding Mrs Robinson and her family the reader is particularly directed to "The Leyland MSS", transcribed by J. A. Symington, arranged with notes by C. W. Hatfield, BST 1925 (Brotherton Collection, Manchester University Library).

For PBB in particular, see BST 1925, 1927, 1938, 1945.

150 AB's hopes in new post : AG, chap. VI, 53, 54.

151 AB's qualifications : AG, chap. VI, 51.

151 AB's salary : AG, chap. VI, 52.

151 AB's excitement : AG, chap. VI, 53.

152 Arrival at Thorp Green Hall : AG, chap. VII, 54.

155 Mrs Robinson's appearance : AG, chap. VII, 58.

155 Mrs Robinson's family : T. Olsen "The Weary are at Rest", BST 1945, 276–7.

155 Treatment of governess : AG, chap. VII, 58–9.

156 Edmund Robinson : AG, chap. VII, 65.

157 The girls : AG, chap. VII, 55, 63.

158 Hours of lessons ; AG, chap. VII, 67.

159 On attending church : AG, chap. XIII, 102.

160 The school project : CB to EN, 1st July 1841, SLL I, 213.

161 York Minster : Chadwick, 382, for proof that AB visited it many times.

161 Intellect deteriorating : AG, chap. XI, 95.

161 Scarborough : for particulars regarding old Scarborough see Theakston's *Guide*, 8th edition, 1860, Rowntree's *History of Scarborough*, and *Scarborough Gazette* 1841–8.

162 The sea : AG, chap. XXIV, 181.

163 Lines, "My soul is awakened . . ." : poem "Lines Composed in a Wood on a Windy Day", written 30th December 1842, WS/PEA, 219.

164 Diary paper for 30th July 1841 : quoted from text in Ratchford, *Gondal's Queen*, 189.

165 AB's diary paper : op. cit.

166 Relief in writing : AG, chap. XVII, 141.

166 Lines, "That summer sun . . ." : from "Lines written at Thorp Green", written 9th August 1841, WS/PEA, 213 ; Benson, 290.

167 Lines, "O ! I am very weary . . ." : poem "Appeal" written 28th August 1841, WS/PEA, 214 ; Benson, 342.

page

167 The school project : CB to EN, 17th October 1841, SLL I, 221.

168 Mary Taylor's advice : CB to EN, 7th August 1841, SLL I, 218.

169 CB's letter to Miss B : 29th September 1841, SLL I, 219-20.

170 CB's letter to EJB : 7th November 1841, SLL I, 223-4.

171 CB's anxiety over AB : CB to EN, 7th August 1841, SLL I, 219 ; 10th June 1841, SLL I, 212 ; 7th November 1841, SLL I, 223.

Chapter Fourteen

172 PBB expected home : CB to EN, 17th December 1841, SLL I, 225.

173 Grundy on Luddendenfoot : F. H. Grundy, *Pictures of the Past*, 75.

173 CB on WW : letters to EN, 10th and 20th January 1842, SLL I, 227-8

174 Lines, "Oh, they have robbed me . . ." : AG, chap. XVIII, 142.

174 Thoughts of WW : AG, loc. cit.

175 "A close . . . dissembler" : AG, chap. XVII, 141.

175 AB's return to Thorp Green : CB to EN, 10th January 1842, SLL I, 226.

175 AB's diary paper : quoted from Ratchford, *Gondal's Queen*, 193.

175 Departure for Brussels : the date given by EJB in her diary paper, Ratchford, *Gondal's Queen*, 192.

177 Longing for companionship : AG, chap. XI, 94.

177 Lines, "The heart that Nature formed . . ." : from "The Captive Dove", 31st October 1843, WS/PEA, 223 ; Benson, 346.

177 Lines, "I have gone backward . . ." : poem "Despondency", 20th December 1841, WS/PEA, 214 ; Benson, 352.

178 Lines, "Blessed be Thou . . ." : poem "In Memory of a Happy Day in February", 10th November 1842, WS/PEA, 217.

179 Grundy's report : *Pictures of the Past*, 86.

179 PBB : for a further account of Branwell's career with the railways see Gérin, *Branwell Brontë*, 182-204.

180 PBB cast off by CB : Duclaux, 124, states that "after March 1846 . . . she kept an utter silence to him," and Chadwick, 361, says that "If Haworth tales are to be believed, she did not speak to him for weeks together."

181 Madame Heger : CB to EN, July 1842, SLL I, 239.

182 "Supremely happy" : AG, chap. XX, 159.

182 "Trust me" : AG, chap. XXI, 163.

183 Attention to dress : AG, chap. XVII, 133.

183 WW's death: his death certificate, entered at the General Register Office,

page

Somerset House, carries as cause of death, "Cholera and Peritonitis terminating in Ematimasis."

184 Mr Brontë's account of WW's death : funeral sermon preached 2nd October 1842, WS/BLFC I.

184 Lines, "Life seems more sweet . . ." : from poem "Severed and gone, so many years", April 1847, WS/PEA, 273–4 ; Benson, 304.

184 Lines, ". . . For ever gone ! " : loc. cit.

185 PBB at WW's funeral : Chadwick, 169.

185 Miss B's death : PBB to F. H. Grundy, 25th October 1842 and 29th October 1842, SLL I, 242–3.

185 AB arrives too late : BST 1938, 174 ; AG, chap. XVIII, 151.

186 AB's religious arguments with Miss B : TWH, chap. XX, 170.

187 Miss B's will : SLL I, 244–6.

187 Lines, "Yes, thou art gone !" : from poem "A Reminiscence", WS/PEA, 229 ; Benson, 325.

188 Lines, "Farewell to thee !" : from poem, TWH, chap. XIX, 160–1, WS/PEA, 282 ; Benson, 323.

188 Lines, "Cold in the grave . . ." : from poem "Night", unsigned, written early in 1845, WS/PEA, 241 ; Benson, 294.

189 Martha Taylor's death : CB to EN, 10th November 1842, SLL I, 246.

Chapter Fifteen

191 Pity for the poor : AG, chap. XX, 156.

191 Christmas at Haworth : CB to EN, 20th November 1842, SLL I, 251.

192 Description of PBB : F. A. Leyland, *The Brontë Family, with Special Reference to Patrick Branwell Brontë.*

192 PBB's lodgings at Thorp Green : Chadwick, 175.
      The "Old Hall" at Thorp Green, or "Monks House" as it is more generally called, still stands today, very little changed in exterior from what it was in PBB's day and easily recognisable by his drawing of it made in August 1844, the original of which can be seen at the BPM, Haworth.

193 PBB reading aloud : he was accustomed at home to reading aloud to his aunt and sisters. See EJB's diary paper for 26th June 1837, "Charlotte working in aunt's room Branwell reading *Eugene Aram* to her" (Lytton's novel published in 1832), Ratchford, *Gondal's Queen*, 187.

194 Lines, "I sit this evening . . ." : from PBB's poem "Thorp Green", written 30th March 1843 in the small notebook in which he jotted down rough

drafts of poems while at Luddendenfoot in 1841, at home in 1842 and later at Thorp Green. See BST 1927, 95.

194 Robinsons' satisfaction with AB and PBB : CB to EN, 10th January 1842, SLL I, 226, "Anne has rendered herself so valuable in her difficult situation that they have entreated her to return to them if it be but for a short time ..." Also CB to PBB, 1st May 1843, "... I have received a general assurance that you do well and are in good odour, but I want to know particulars ...", SLL I, 266. Also CB to EN, 23rd January 1844, "Anne and Branwell have just left us to return to York. They are both wondrously valued in their situations," SLL I, 277.

194 Mr Brontë's visit : CB to PBB, 1st May 1843, SLL I, 266.

194 Walks at Little Ouseburn : AG, chap. XIII, 102.

196 Lines, "You may rejoice ..." : poem originally called "A Word to the Calvinists", later "A Word to the Elect ", 28th May 1843, WS/PEA, 220.

197 Flossy : she was given to AB by one of the Misses Robinson, SBC, 141. See CB to EN, 5th April 1844, for first mention of Flossy. She here mentions a visit of EN's from which she returned to Brookroyd taking with her a bitch puppy of Flossy's, who must therefore have been acquired at least the previous year. See SLL I, 278, note.

198 PBB's account of events at Thorp Green : letter to F. H. Grundy, October 1845, SLL I, 294 6 ; Duclaux, 121 ; T. Olsen, "The Weary are at Rest", BST 1945, 277 ; also PBB's letters to J. B. Leyland, 25th November 1845, June 1846, June or July 1846, 24th (?) January 1847, BST 1925.

198 PBB's behaviour : CB to EN, 13th January 1845, "Branwell has been quieter and less irritable on the whole this time than he was in the summer," SLL I, 288 ; Duclaux, 113.

199 Mrs Robinson's insinuations : Gaskell, 196, "... she had made the criminal advances ...' ; also PBB to J.B. Leyland 24th (?) January 1847, "... she loved me even better than I did her," BST 1925, 303.
    See also PBB to J.B. Leyland, June or July 1846, describing "her horror at having been the first to delude me into wretchedness, and her agony at having been the cause of the death of her husband ...", BST 1925.
    Also CB to EN, 28th July 1848, "... a worse woman I believe hardly exists ; the more I hear of her the more deeply she revolts me ...", SLL I, 441.
    "Both Anne and Charlotte always believed Branwell had been made a sport of ...", Chadwick, 287.
    CB to EN, 28th January 1848, "... that woman is a hopeless being ; calculated to bring a curse wherever she goes by the mixture of weakness, perversion, and deceit in her nature ...", SLL I, 392.

199 Mr Robinson and PBB's claims to literary ambition : PBB to J. B. Leyland, 25th November 1845, BST 1925.

200 Mrs Robinson's feelings for PBB : CB to EN, 28th July 1845, BST 1925 ; PBB to J. B. Leyland, January 1847, BST 1925.

page

200 AB's Prayer Book : can be seen at BPM, Haworth.

201 Lines, "Not only for the past . . ." : from poem "A Prayer", dated 13th October 1844, WS/PEA, 232 ; Benson, 353.

202 Plan to open school : CB to M. Heger, 24th July 1844, WS/BLFC II, 10.

202 School Prospectus : SLL I, 275.

203 Insubordination of young Robinsons : Duclaux, 117-8 ; BST 1945, 277 ; Gaskell, 197.

204 Lydia Robinson's runaway match : see original Gretna Green marriage certificate preserved in the registers of Little Ouseburn Church.

204 Roxby family : see DNB. For information regarding the Roxby family I am indebted to the Chief Librarian of Scarborough Reference Library for his helpful researches into the careers of that eminent family of actors, producers and scene designers, and for showing me his considerable collection of Playbills for the period of the Roxbys' ownership of the Theatre Royal in St Thomas' Street, Scarborough.

206 CB's return from Hathersage : CB to EN, 23rd July 1845, SLL I, 303.

206 Mr Robinson's letter to PBB "last Thursday" : see *Scarborough Gazette* for 17th July 1845, the date on which Mr Robinson wrote to PBB. It may be worth noting that Edmund Robinson joined his parents and sisters on that very day (see *Scarborough Gazette* for visitors' list). Was it on some revelation of his that his father acted in dismissing PBB ?

207 PBB's collapse : CB to EN, 18th August 1845, SLL I, 307.

208 PBB : for more detailed information see Gérin, *Branwell Brontë*, 216-84.

Chapter Sixteen

209 AB's diary paper : Ratchford, *Gondal's Queen*, 193-4.

210 EJB's diary paper : op. cit. 191-3.

213 CB to M. Heger : 18th November 1845, WS/BLFC II, 69-71.

215 EJB's volume of verse : see Biographical Notice of Ellis and Acton Bell prefixed to the 1850 posthumous edition of their works.

215 EJB's temper : See Gaskell, 184, for the occasion when she mastered Keeper, "no one dared when Emily's eyes glowed in that manner out of the paleness of her face, and when her lips were so compressed into stone."

216 CB's narrative : Biographical Notice of Ellis and Acton Bell, see above.

218 Lines, "Cold in the earth . . ." : from EJB's poem headed "R. Alcona to J. Brenzaida", and dated 3rd March 1844, Hatfield, 222-3, WS/PEA, 6.

218 Lines, "Cold in the grave . . ." : AB's poem "Night" dated early 1845, WS/PEA, 24 ; Benson, 284.

219 Publication of poems : Duclaux, 141.

page

219 Pseudonyms : No certainty exists as to the origin of the pseudonyms chosen by the Brontës. Successive editors have pointed out why CB and EJB may have taken the names Currer and Ellis, both frequently to be found in the West Riding and in circles known to the Brontës. For AB's choice of Acton no clue exists. Apart from the family of Sir John Acton, Minister to the King of Naples with whom Nelson had many dealings during his Mediterranean campaigns, the name occurs only in the DNB in connection with the authoress Eliza Acton, 1777–1859. Her first volumes of poems appeared in 1827 and 1836, at the very time the Brontë girls were beginning to collect their scattered pieces. Eliza Acton enjoyed some reputation in her day and was the author of verses addressed to Queen Adelaide on her visit to Tunbridge Wells shortly after the death of William IV in 1837. She also wrote verses of welcome to Queen Victoria on her first visit to Scotland in 1840, and contributed to the literary journals of the day. Her career may not have escaped the notice of the Brontës, following so close on her footsteps.

219 Date of publication : Duclaux quotes 7th May 1846 as the date inscribed by EJB in her own copy of the *Poems* which Duclaux saw and handled while working on her biography of Emily Brontë in 1883, Duclaux, 141.

219 *Poems by Currer, Ellis and Acton Bell* : see copies of 1st and 2nd editions at BPM, Haworth.

222 Lines, "You may rejoice . . ." : from "A Word to the Elect", 28th May 1843, WS/PEA, 220.

222 Lines, "Oh, weep not, love ! . . . :" from "Stanzas", 1st October 1845, WS/PEA, 254.

222 Lines, "I mourn with thee . . ." : from "The Penitent", 1845, WS/PEA, 255 ; Benson, 330.

223 Lines, "Yes, thou art gone ! . . . : from "A Reminiscence", April 1844, WS/PEA, 229 ; Benson, 325.

223 Lines, "O God ! If this indeed . . ." ; from "If this be All", 20th May 1845, WS/PEA, 242 ; Benson, 331.

224 Messrs. Aylott & Jones : correspondence with CB, SLL I, 324–8.

224 Henry Colburn : for particulars of Brontë MSS, first editions etc. now in the Memorial Library, Princeton University, U.S.A., see Dr Charles A. Huguenin's article, BST 1955.

225 *The Professor*: the finished MS of *The Professor* was dated by Charlotte 27th June 1846.

226 Newby's offer : for particulars regarding Newby's agreement with Ellis and Acton Bell for the publication of their novels see CB's correspondence with her own publishers, Smith, Elder & Co., after her sisters' deaths, 5th September, 13th September, 20th September, 16th October 1850, SLL II, 168–80.

226 EJB's judgement : CB to WSW, 22nd November 1848, SLL I, 463.

page

227 Failure of the *Poems* : CB to Wordsworth, Tennyson, De Quincey, 16th June 1847, SLL I, 329.

228 Prose work by Ellis and Acton : CB to WSW, 10th November 1847, SLL I, 366.

229 Books not well got up : CB to WSW, 14th December 1847, SLL I, 375.

229 AB's copy of AG : see Dr Charles A. Huguenin's article on Brontë MSS in Princeton University Library, BST 1955.

230 George Moore on AG : see *Conversations in Ebury Street*, 214–23.

231 Observation of character : AG, chap. I, 11 ; chap. IV, 36 ; chap. X, 79.

233 CB to WSW, 14th December 1847, SLL I, 375.

233 *Douglas Jerrolds' Weekly* : for the texts of the reviews of *Wuthering Heights* and *Agnes Grey*, see E. M. Weir's "Contemporary Reviews of the First Brontë Novels", BST 1947.

233 Lady Amberley : quoted from the text in Patricia Thomson's *The Victorian Heroine*, 53.

Chapter Seventeen

236 Lines, "God alters not . . ." : from "Self-Communion", 17th April 1848, WS/PEA, 287 ; Benson, 314.

237 PBB's condition : CB to EN, 31st December 1845, SLL I, 313 ; 14th April 1846, SLL I, 331.
   PBB to J. B. Leyland, 28th April 1846, BST 1925, 291.
   PBB to F. H. Grundy, 2nd May 1846, SLL I, 296.

238 Death of Mr Robinson : see *Scarborough Gazette* for 6th June 1846, "On the 26th ult, at Thorp Green the Rev. Edmund Robinson, aged 46."
   CB to EN, 17th June 1846, SLL I, 331.
   PBB to J. B. Leyland, June 1846, BST 1925, 293.

238 George Gooch : the Robinsons' coachman, see PBB to J. B. Leyland, June 1846, BST 1925, 293 ; PBB to F. H. Grundy, July 1846, SLL I, 297.

239 PBB's collapse at the *Bull* ; Duclaux, 145 ; Gaskell, 197.

239 PBB's intolerable conduct : CB to EN, 17th June 1848, SLL I, 332.

239 PBB's earlier use of opium : F. H. Grundy, *Pictures of the Past*, quoted in BST 1945, 280.

239 Mrs Robinson's intermediaries : PBB's letters, quoted above, to Grundy and Leyland.

240 PBB's hopes of marriage : PBB to J. B. Leyland, 24th (?) January 1847, BST 1945, 301.

240 PBB's creditors : PBB to J. B. Leyland, June or July 1846, BST 1925,

295 ; PBB to J. B. Leyland, 22nd July 1848, BST 1925, 309.
Gaskell speaking of Mrs Robinson writes, "She had sent him money—twenty pounds at a time . . .", 196.

240 Dr Crosby: for fuller evidence of the situation see Gérin, *Branwell Brontë*, 236, 272, 274–5, 285, 305.

241 The Misses Robinson : CB to EN, 1st March 1847, SLL I, 347.

241 The Robinsons' home life : examination of the *Scarborough Gazette* for the summer and autumn of 1847 shows the young people to have been constantly in residence there with their grandmother.

241 Mrs Robinson senior : see *Scarborough Gazettes* for 13th July and every subsequent week until 21st September 1848.

242 Mrs Robinson's plans : CB to EN, 28th January 1848, SLL I, 392 ; 18th August 1848, SLL I, 447 ; 28th July 1848, SLL I, 441.

243 Huntingdon on debt : TWH, chap. XXII, 181.

244 Mrs Hargrave : TWH, chap. XXVI, 223.

245 Esther Hargrave : TWH, chap. XLI, 358–9.

246 Helen Huntingdon's uncle : TWH, chap. XX, 171.

247 Lord Lowborough : TWH, chap. XXII, 182–3, 185–6.

248 Helen's self-knowledge : TWH, chap. XXX, 252.

249 Huntingdon's arrival : TWH, chap. XVIII, 148.

250 Change in Helen's once romantic temperament : TWH, chap. XXXI, 255 ; chap. XXXV, 301.

250 "He may drink himself dead" : TWH, chap. XXXVI, 309.

252 Huntingdon's character : TWH, chap. XXX, 245 ; chap. XXV, 219–20.

252 Education of boys : TWH, chap. III, 25–6.

253 CB on education of boys : letter to Miss Wooler, 30th January 1846, SLL I, 315.

253 Thackeray's lecture on Fielding : CB to Mrs Gaskell, SLL II, 325–6.

254 Husband's licence : TWH, chap. XXVII, 229.

254 Lord Lowborough : TWH, chap. XXXI, 263.

255 Scenes in home : TWH, chap. XXX, 252.

255 Huntingdon as embodiment of PBB : In support of my personal feelings that the comparison is unfounded I refer the reader to Chadwick, 356, whose opinion was based on that of the Haworth villagers who emphatically denied the resemblance.

257 Helen's aunt : TWH, chap. XX, 169–70.

258 Huntingdon's death-bed : TWH, chap. XLIX, 437.

Chapter Eighteen

259 Newby's letter to Ellis Bell : quoted from original in BPM, Haworth.

260 *Wuthering Heights* and AG attributed to CB : CB to WSW, 31st December 1847, SLL I, 378.

260 Further confusion of identity : CB to WSW, 22nd January 1848, SLL I, 389.

260 AB's contract with Newby : CB to George Smith, 18th September 1850 and 3rd December 1850, WS/BLFC III, 160, 185–6.

261 American confusion over authorship : see George Smith's recollections of CB in the *Cornhill Magazine*, December 1900, "We wrote to Currer Bell to say that we should be glad to be in a position to contradict the statement, adding at the same time that we were quite sure Mr Newby's assertion was untrue."

263 The London journey : for particulars relating to the journey see CB's letter to Mary Taylor, 4th September 1848, SLL I, 435–9.

263 Expenses of the journey : the details relating to the expenses on the London journey are contained in CB's small notebook bound in black leather and preserved at the BPM, Haworth.

265 Mr Smith's recollections : see above, *Cornhill Magazine* for December 1900.

Chapter Nineteen

270 Title : "Cup of Wrath" is taken from the last verse of AB's poem, "A Word to the Elect". For full text see chap. XV, 196–7 ; WS/PEA, 221.

270 Fatigue of the journey : CB to Mary Taylor, 4th September 1848, SLL I, 439.

270 AB's illnesses : CB to EN, 15th December 1846, SLL I, 341.

271 Idem : CB to EN, 15th December 1846, SLL I, 341 ; CB to Miss Wooler, 31st March 1848, SLL I, 406.

272 AB's health in 1847 : CB to EN, 7th October 1847, SLL I, 357.

273 AB's choice of subject in TWH : see CB's Biographical Notice of Ellis and Acton Bell, as above.

274 Lines, "Believe not those . . ." : from "The Narrow Way", written 27th April 1848, WS/PEA, 293–4 ; Benson, 308.

274 Lines, "Seek not thine honour here . . ." : loc. cit.

275 Notices of TWH : CB to WSW, 31st July 1848, SLL I, 442.

276 Preface to 2nd edition of TWH : quoted from Haworth edition of the works of the Brontës with Introduction by Mrs Humphrey Ward, Smith, Elder & Co., 1900.

page

277 PBB's Halifax creditors : PBB to J. B. Leyland, 22nd July 1848, BST 1925, 309.

278 Delirium tremens : idem.

278 Sheriff's Officer : CB to EN, 15th December 1846, SLL I, 341.

278 CB not speaking to PBB : " . . . after March 1846 Charlotte never addressed him again", Duclaux, 124 ; Chadwick states that she did not speak to him for weeks together, 361.

279 Lines, "Do I despise the timid deer . . ." : from EJB's poem "Well, some may hate, and some may scorn", dated 14th November 1839, Hatfield, 132 ; WS/PEA, 26.

279 "The Penitent" : dated 1845. In original MS the poem had no other title than "Fragment", WS/PEA, 255 ; Benson, 330.

280 The fire in PBB's room : John Greenwood's diary, BST 1951, 37–8.

281 Correspondence kept secret from PBB : CB to EN, 1st March 1847, SLL I, 347.

281 Anne of the *Black Bull* : Duclaux, 120, 145.

282 PBB's note to John Brown : BST 1925, 310.

282 Grundy's visit : for Grundy's last visit to PBB see his *Pictures of the Past,* as above.

283 PBB's change before death : CB to WSW, 6th October 1848, SLL I, 454–5.

284 The unkindness that had preceded death : Duclaux, 124 ; Chadwick, 361.

284 AB's letter to WSW : 29th September 1848, from original in British Museum (Ashley Library).

Chapter Twenty

286 Title : "Fortitude from Pain" is taken from AB's last lines, "To gather fortitude from pain and hope and holiness from wo [sic]", WS/PEA, 297 ; Benson, 367.

286 Cause of PBB's death : see BST 1934, 140 ; C. M. Edgerley's article on "Causes of death in the Brontë family", *British Medical Journal,* 2nd April 1932.

286 PBB's funeral : Haworth Parish Church registers for Thursday, 28th September 1848.

286 CB uneasy about her sisters' health : CB to EN, 29th October 1848, SLL I, 459–60 ; CB to WSW, 18th January 1849, SLL II, 21 ; SBC, 169.

287 CB's anticipation of AB's dying : CB to WSW, 4th June 1849, SBC, 185.

287 Details of EJB's illness : see CB's Biographical Notice of Ellis and Acton Bell prefixed to 1850 edition of her sisters' works, Smith, Elder & Co.

287 EJB's inner sanctuary : Professor Blondel in his masterly and perceptive

page

analysis of Emily Brontë expresses a similar thought : "... le secret d'Emily Brontë fut un désir constant et caché de lutter sur le plan de la vie imaginaire contre l'épreuve de la vie dans un monde étranger et hostile." (*Emily Brontë*, 27).

How fiercely Emily defended her "inner sanctuary" and resented any attempt at intrusion is also instanced by CB's confession to WSW in the letter of 31st July 1848 : "Ellis Bell will not endure to be alluded to under any other appellation than the 'nom de plume'. I committed a grand error in betraying his identity to you and Mr Smith." SLL I, 442.

288 EJB's last poem : "Why ask to know the date, the clime ?...", WS/PEA, 135 ; Benson, 210.

289 *Shirley* : CB to WSW, 18th October 1848, SLL I, 458.

290 The critiques : CB to WSW, 2nd November 1848, SLL I, 460.

290 Newby's announcement : CB to WSW, 7th December 1848, SLL II, 10.

291 *North American Review* : CB to WSW, 22nd November 1848, SLL I, 464.

292 Text of review : quoted from K. J. Fielding's article on "The Brontës and the *North American Review*", BST 1956, 17.

294 Marriage of Mary Robinson : see *The Yorkshireman*, 28th October 1848 : "On Thursday week (19th October) at Allestree near Derby, Samuel B. Clapham Esq. of Aireworth, Keighley, to Mary, youngest daughter of the late Rev. Edmund Robinson of Thorpe Green near Boroughbridge, and grand-daughter of the late Rev. T. Gisborne of Yoxall Lodge Staffordshire." The marriage certificate makes it clear that the bridegroom's name was Henry ; it was his father who was called Samuel Blakey Clapham. Henry Clapham died on 23rd June 1855 only seven years after his marriage.

294 The marriage of Mrs Robinson : thus reported in *The Yorkshireman*, 25th November 1848 : "On the 8th inst, by Special Licence, at the residence of Lady Bateman, at Bath, Sir Edward Dolman Scott, Bart, of Barr Hall, Staffordshire, to Lydia, widow of the late Rev. Edmund Robinson of Thorp Green near this city (York) and daughter of the late Rev. Thomas Gisborne of Yoxall Lodge."

295 Emerson's *Essays* : CB to WSW, 3rd March 1849, SLL II, 32.

295 The sprig of heather : Gaskell, 257.

296 Lines, "O Thou hast taken my delight ..." : from AB's last poem begun on 7th January 1849, BST 1932, 21-2, WS/PEA, 296.

297 EJB's funeral : Haworth Parish Church registers for 22nd December 1848.

297 Keeper at EJB's funeral : Gaskell, 259.

297 CB's concern for AB : CB to EN, 23rd December 1848, SLL II, 15 ; to WSW, 25th December 1848, SLL II, 16.

298 Dr Teale's visit : see EN's account, BST 1932, 21-2.

299 AB's last lines : quoted from original MS at BPM, Haworth, WS/PEA, 295.

page

301 *Chambers's Journal* : Gaskell, 203.

302 *Wuthering Heights* presented to EN: see letter of CB to EN, 22nd January 1849, SLL II, 22.

Chapter Twenty-One

303 AB's condition : CB to EN, 10th January 1849, SLL II, 19 ; CB to EN, 15th January 1849, SLL II, 20 ; CB to WSW, 18th January 1849, SLL II, 21 ; CB to WSW, 1st February 1849, SLL II, 22 ; CB to EN, 16th February 1849, SLL II, 28 ; CB to WSW, 11th March 1849, SLL II, 33.

304 Idem : CB to WSW, 18th January 1849, SLL II, 20 ; CB to WSW, 2nd March 1849, SLL II, 30.

304 EJB's illness : CB to EN, 20th April 1849, SLL II, 45.

304 Dr Teale's prescriptions : CB to WSW, 16th April 1849, SLL II, 43 ; CB to EN, 20th April 1849, SLL II, 45.

305 Hydropathy—CB to WSW, 16th April 1849, SLL II, 43.

305 Coming of spring : CB to WSW, 4th February 1849, SLL II, 25.

305 Books from London : CB to WSW, 4th February 1849, SLL II, 25 ; 5th April 1849, SLL II, 40.

305 Frederika Bremer (1802–65): Swedish novelist, much in vogue in England and English society.

306 *Shirley* : CB to WSW, 2nd April 1849, SLL II, 38.

306 No horror of death : AB to EN, 5th April 1849, BPM.

306 AB's weakness : CB to EN, 1st May 1849, SLL II, 46.

307 AB to EN : letter of 5th April 1849, BPM.

308 Miss Wooler's house at Scarborough : CB to Miss Wooler, 16th May 1849, SLL II, 48.

309 Miss Outhwaite's legacy : CB to EN, 20th May 1849, SLL II, 50.

309 Wood's Lodgings : regularly advertised in the *Scarborough Gazette* and in other local papers as well as in Theakston's *Guide*.

310 CB's anxiety over journey : CB to EN, 1st May 1849, SLL II, 46.

310 AB's emaciation : CB to Miss Wooler, 16th May 1849, SLL II, 49.

310 Shopping : CB to EN, 23rd May 1849, SLL II, 50, Gaskell 270.

310 CB's and AB's shopping-list : from notebook of expenses on Scarborough journey at BPM, Haworth.

311 CB's letter to EN : Gaskell, 270, where the date is given as 23rd May. Since this was the day on which the girls were due to set out for Scarborough the date is highly suspect. The last two sentences appear in CB's letter to EN, dated 20th May, SLL II, 50.

311 EN's account of journey from Leeds : Gaskell, 271.

page

311 AB's appearance : CB to EN, 16th May, 1849, SLL II, 49.

312 The journey : CB to WSW, 27th May 1849, SLL II, 51.

312 The *George Hotel* : EN specifically mentions their stay at the *George* in her account of AB's last journey (see T. Wemyss Reid's *Charlotte Brontë, A Monograph*), and entered the fact in her diary for 24th May 1849, to be seen at the BPM, Haworth.

This, of itself, would seem conclusive evidence that they did not stay at the *Old George Inn* in the Whip-ma-Whap-ma Gate as suggested in a footnote to D. W. L. Ake's drawing of the *Old George* in BST 1949, even without the supplementary evidence given me by Miss I. P. Pressley, M.A., Honorary Secretary of the York Georgian Society. The *George Hotel*, Coney Street, now disappeared, was, in Miss Pressley's opinion, far the likelier of the two hostelries for AB to choose, being the more select of the two. Moreover, it was from there that the coaches for Scarborough had started before the York–Scarborough Railway was opened on 7th July 1845. AB had accompanied her employers, the Robinsons, on their annual holidays to Scarborough since 1841 and would, therefore, have known the *George Hotel* from her previous journeys.

The "Banqueting Room", which was over the gateway, was wainscotted and had a panelled, plastered ceiling and bay windows containing painted glass shields of Charles II, James II, etc. It was preserved intact until the demolition of the *George* in 1861. See Benson's *History of York*, 1925.

312 AB at York Minster : Chadwick, 382. That she counted her first visit to the Minster a great event in her life is shown by her diary paper for July 1841. There is also an echo of its power over PBB in his letter of 24th (?) January 1847 to J. B. Leyland, BST 1925, 303.

313 Idem : see EN's recollections in her diary at BPM, Haworth, which contains the rough draft of her eventual report to T. Wemyss Reid for his *Charlotte Brontë*, a Monograph, 95-7.

313 CB's account-book : can be seen at the BPM, Haworth.

314 The Scarborough lodgings : CB to WSW, 27th May 1849, SLL II, 51.

315 The Baths : doubtless Harland's Baths, situated at the corner of Falconer's Road and Vernon Place, the nearest to the Cliff lodgings of any of the Baths in town, now pulled down and replaced by a filling station. There is an illustration of the Baths in Theakston's *Guide*, showing Christ Church, Vernon Place (p. 96).

315 AB's drive in donkey-carriage : Gaskell, 271 ; T. Wemyss Reid, 95. In EN's rough draft about the journey (see above), she mentions the drive and AB's recommendations to the donkey-boy, ". . . she was ever fond of dumb animals and would give up her own comfort for them." See EN's diary in the BPM, Haworth.

315 Scarborough sands : see AG, chap. XXIV, 181.

317 Glorious summer evening : AG, chap. XXV, 190-1.

317 Sunday evening : EN's recollections of the last evening, Gaskell, 272.

319 Lines, "There is a rest . . ." : quoted from AB's poem "Self-Communion" dated 17th April 1848, WS/PEA, 292 ; Benson, 321.

320 The doctor's wonder : CB to WSW, 13th June 1849, from original in British Museum (Ashley Library).

321 Cause of death : a copy of AB's death certificate can be seen at the BPM, Haworth.

321 AB's obituary notice : *Leeds Mercury*, 9th June 1849, "On Monday week [28th May] at Scarborough in her 29th year, Anne, daughter of the Rev. P. Bronte [sic], incumbent of Haworth."

321 AB's funeral : registers of Scarborough Parish Church for Wednesday, 30th May 1849.

322 CB's return to Haworth : letters to WSW, 25th June 1849, SLL II, 53 ; and to EN, 1st July 1849, SLL II, 55.

322 CB's memories of her sisters : CB to WSW, 13th June 1849, WS/BLFC II, 339–40.

Anne Brontë died intestate, leaving an estate assessed "under £600" : see Administration Paper "Of the Effects of Anne Brontë, Spinster, deceased" issued by the Probate Court of York, 5th September 1849, by which Mr Brontë was appointed Administrator.   Preserved at the BPM, Haworth.

A GENERAL BIBLIOGRAPHY OF WORKS
CONSULTED

BELL, CURRER : Biographical Notice of Ellis and Acton Bell, prefixed to the posthumous edition of their works. London : Smith, Elder & Co. 1850.

BELL, CURRER : A Memoir of Acton Bell, prefixed to the posthumous edition of her poems. London : Smith, Elder & Co. 1850.

BELL : *Poems by Currer, Ellis and Acton Bell*, 1st edition. London : Aylott & Jones, 1846.

BELL, ACTON : *Agnes Grey*, 1st edition, forming vol. III of *Wuthering Heights*. London : Thomas Cautley Newby, 1847.

BELL, ACTON : *The Tenant of Wildfell Hall*, 2nd edition, with Preface by the Author, in 3 vols. London : Thomas Cautley Newby, 1848.

THE BRONTË NOVELS : 6 vols. London : Smith, Elder & Co. 1893.

BRONTË POEMS : *The Poems of Emily Jane Brontë and Anne Brontë*, edited by T. J. Wise and J. A. Symington. Oxford, 1934.

BRONTË POEMS : Selections from the poetry of Charlotte, Emily, Anne and Branwell Brontë, edited by Arthur C. Benson. London, 1915.

BRONTË POEMS : *The Complete Poems of Anne Brontë*, edited by Clement K. Shorter with a Bibliographical Introduction by C. W. Hatfield. London, 1920.

BRONTË POEMS : *The Complete Poems of Emily Jane Brontë*, edited by C. W. Hatfield. Oxford, 1941.

BRONTË, CHARLOTTE : *The Twelve Adventurers and Other Stories*, edited by Clement K. Shorter. London, 1925.

BRONTË, CHARLOTTE: *Five Novelettes,* edited by Winifred Gérin. Folio Society, 1971.

BRONTË SOCIETY TRANSACTIONS : 13 vols, 68 parts. See separate list for articles particularly consulted.

BLONDEL, JACQUES : *Emily Brontë*, Expérience Spirituelle et Création Poétique. Presses Universitaires de France, 1955.

CHADWICK, ELLIS : *In the Footsteps of the Brontës*. London, 1914.

CHRISTIAN, MILDRED : "A Census of Brontë Manuscripts in the United States of America" reprinted from *The Trollopian*. London, 1947–9.

DIMNET, ERNEST : *Les Sœurs Brontë*. Paris, 1910.

COOPER, I. WILLIS: *The Brontës*. New York, 1933.

DUCLAUX, MARY : *Emily Brontë*, A Memoir. London, 1883.

ERSKINE STUART, J. A. : *The Brontë Country*. London, 1888.

GASKELL, ELIZABETH : *The Life of Charlotte Brontë*. Everyman edition. London, 1908.

GASKELL, ELIZABETH: *The Life of Charlotte Brontë*, edited by Winifred Gérin. Folio Press, 1971.

GÉRIN, WINIFRED: *Branwell Brontë: A Biography*. Edinburgh, 1961.

GÉRIN, WINIFRED: *Charlotte Brontë: The Evolution of Genius*. Clarendon Press, 1967.

GÉRIN, WINIFRED: *Emily Brontë: A Biography*. Clarendon Press, 1971.

GÉRIN, WINIFRED: *The Brontës (2 vols.)*. Longmans, 1974.

GRUNDY, F. H. ; *Pictures of the Past*. London : Griffith & Farrar, 1879.

HARRISON, G. ELSIE: *Methodist Good Companions*. London, 1935.

HARRISON, G. ELSIE: *Haworth Parsonage: A Study of Wesley and the Brontës*. London, 1937.

HARRISON, G. ELSIE : *The Clue to the Brontës*. London, 1948.

HARRISON, ADA, AND STANFORD, DEREK: *Anne Brontë: Her Life and Work*. London, 1959.

HOPE-DODDS, M.: "Gondalland". *Modern Language Review*, January 1923.

LEYLAND, F. A. : *The Brontë Family, with Special Reference to Patrick Branwell Brontë*. London, 1886.

LOCK, JOHN, AND DIXON, W. T.: *The Life, Letters and Times of the Rev. Patrick Brontë*. Edinburgh, 1965.

MOORE, GEORGE : *Conversations in Ebury Street*. London, 1930.

NUSSEY, ELLEN : "Reminiscences of Charlotte Brontë" reprinted from *Scribner's Magazine*, May 1871.

OLIPHANT, MRS: *Annals of a Publishing House*. London, 1837.

PADEN, W. D.: *An Investigation of Gondal*. New York, 1958.

RATCHFORD, FANNIE E. : *The Brontës' Web of Childhood*. Columbia University Press, 1941.

RATCHFORD, FANNIE E. : *Gondal's Queen*. Edinburgh, 1955.

RAYMOND, ERNEST : *In the Steps of the Brontës*. London, 1948.

REID, T. WEMYSS : *Charlotte Brontë, A Monograph*. London : Macmillan, 1877.

ROWNTREE, ARTHUR : *The History of Scarborough*. London, 1931.

ROYDE-SMITH, NAOMI : *The Mind of Mrs Sherwood*. London, 1946.

SCRUTON, WILLIAM : *Thornton and the Brontës*. Bradford, 1898.

SHORTER, CLEMENT K. : *The Brontës, Life and Letters*, edited by Clement K. Shorter. London, 1908.

SHORTER, CLEMENT K. : *The Brontës and their Circle*, edited by Clement K. Shorter. London : Hodder & Stoughton, 1896. London : Dent, 1914.

SIMPSON, CHARLES : *Emily Brontë.* London, 1929.

SINCLAIR, MAY : *The Three Brontës.* London, 1912.

SOUTHEY, ROBERT : *The Life of Wesley,* 3rd edition. London : Longmans, Green & Co. 1846.

SYMINGTON, J. A. : *A Catalogue of the Museum and Library, Haworth Parsonage Museum.* The Brontë Society, 1927.

TELFORD, JOHN : *The Life of John Wesley.* Kelly, revised edition, 1899.

THEAKSTON, S. W. : *Guide to Scarborough,* 8th edition, 1860.

THOMSON, PATRICIA : *The Victorian Heroine.* Oxford, 1956.

TURNER, J. HORSFALL : *Haworth, Past and Present.* Brighouse, 1879.

WISE, T. J. AND SYMINGTON, J. A. : *The Brontës, their Lives, Friendships and Correspondence,* edited by T. J. Wise and J. A. Symington. Oxford, 1932.

List of Periodicals, Journals, Newspapers consulted

The Arminian Magazine, 1798 ; *The Wesleyan Methodist Magazine,* 1799–1812 ; *The Yorkshireman,* 1845–9 ; *The Scarborough Gazette,* 1845–9 ; *The Scarborough Herald,* 1845–9 ; *The Cornhill Magazine,* December 1900 ; *The Bookman,* October 1904.

BRONTË SOCIETY TRANSACTIONS

1895 YATES, W.W., The Brontës at Dewsbury, p. 8.

1898 SCRUTON, W., Reminiscences of the late Miss Ellen Nussey, p. 23.

1899 NUSSEY, ELLEN, Reminiscences of Charlotte Brontë, reprinted by permission of *Scribner's Magazine*, May 1871, p. 58.

1923 HAMBLEY ROWE, J., The Maternal Relatives of the Brontës, p. 135.

1925 SYMINGTON, J. A., A Complete Transcript of the Leyland Manuscripts from the original documents in the collection of Col. Sir E. Brotherton, pp. 278–312.

1927 HATFIELD, C. W., Unpublished poems by Patrick Branwell Brontë, pp. 71–96.

1931 HATFIELD, C. W., Letter from the Rev. Patrick Brontë on the death of his wife, pp. 284–9.

1932 HATFIELD, C. W., The Last Verses written by Anne Brontë, pp. 20–6.

1933 HATFIELD, C. W., Letters of the Rev. Patrick Brontë to Mrs Gaskell, pp. 83–100.

1934 EDGERLEY, C. M., Causes of death in the Brontë family, p. 139.

1937 EDGERLEY, C. M., Life of Miss Branwell, p. 103.

1938 EDGERLEY, C. M., Life of Anne Brontë, p. 173.

1939 HATFIELD, C. W., The Relatives of Maria Branwell, p. 245.

1941 EDGERLEY, C. M., Tabitha Aykroyd, p. 62.

1945 OLSEN, T., The Weary are at Rest (Patrick Branwell Brontë), p. 269.

1946 M. C., Memories of Ellen Nussey, p. 41.

1946 WEIR, E. M., Cowan Bridge : new light on old documents, p. 16.

1947 WEIR, E. M., Contemporary Reviews of the first Brontë novels, p. 89.

1950 WHONE, CLIFFORD, Where the Brontës borrowed books : the Keighley Mechanics' Library, p. 344.

1952 BLAKELEY, The Rev. MAX, Memories of Margaret Wooler and her sisters, p. 113.

1952 WEIR, E. M., Brontë Manuscripts in the United States of America, p. 125.

1953 WEIR, E. M., Text of three letters by Anne Brontë, p. 193.

1953 CURTIS, DAME MYRA, Cowan Bridge School, p. 187.

1955 HUGUENIN, Dr. C., Brontëana at Princeton University, p. 391.

1956 FIELDING, K. J., The Brontës and the North American Review, p. 17.

1950   SUSAN BROOKE, M.A., F.S.A., Anne Brontë at Blake Hall, p.239.

1959   MARY VISICK, Anne Brontë's Last Poem, p.352.

1971   GUY SCHOFIELD, The Gentle Anne, p.1.

APPENDIX A

I ANNE BRONTË'S LITERARY REMAINS

Anne Brontë's literary remains consist of :

TWO NOVELS

1   *Agnes Grey*, published 1847
2   *The Tenant of Wildfell Hall*, published 1848

of which the original MSS have disappeared without leaving any trace. *Agnes Grey* was published as vol. III of Emily Brontë's *Wuthering Heights* in December 1847, and *The Tenant of Wildfell Hall* as a three-volume novel in June 1848, both by Thomas Cautley Newby of 72 Mortimer Street, Cavendish Square, London.

FIFTY-NINE POEMS

of which 24 were published in her lifetime :

21 in *Poems by Currer, Ellis and Acton Bell*, 1846
1 in *Fraser's Magazine*, August 1848
1 in *Agnes Grey*
1 in *The Tenant of Wildfell Hall*

The original MSS of some of these are preserved in the following places :

9 in the Brontë Parsonage Museum, Haworth
1 in the British Museum
9 in the Bonnell Collection, Philadelphia
9 in the J. Pierpont Morgan Library, New York
3 in the Berg Collection, New York Public Library
6 in the Henry Huntingdon Museum Library, San Marino, California

TWO DIARY PAPERS

written on Emily's birthday, 30th July 1841 and 1845. In the Law Collection now dispersed.

FOUR LETTERS

3 addressed to Ellen Nussey (preserved at the Brontë Parsonage Museum) dated   4th October 1847
26th January 1848
5th April 1849

1 addressed to Mr W. S. Williams (preserved in the British Museum, Ashley Library) dated 29th September 1848

II POEMS OF ANNE BRONTË PUBLISHED
IN HER LIFETIME

I   Twenty-one poems published in the volume *Poems by Currer, Ellis and Acton Bell*. London : Aylott & Jones, 1846.

1   A Reminiscence
2   The Arbour
3   Home
4   Vanitas Vanitatum
5   The Penitent
6   Music on Christmas Morn
7   Oh, weep not love ! . . .
8   If this be all. . . .
9   Memory
10 To Cowper
11 The Doubter's Prayer
12 A Word to the Elect
13 'Tis strange to think there was a time. . . .
14 The Consolation : Though bleak these woods. . . .
15 Lines Composed in a Wood on a Windy Day
16 Views of Life
17 Oh, I am very weary. . . .
18 The Student's Serenade
19 The Captive Dove
20 Self-Congratulation
21 Fluctuations

II Poems included in the text of *Agnes Grey* and *The Tenant of Wildfell Hall*

1   Oh, they have robbed me of the hope. . . .   (*Agnes Grey, chap. XVII*)
2   Farewell to Thee. . . .   (*The Tenant of Wildfell Hall, chap. XIX*)

III Poems published in periodicals

1   The Three Guides (*Fraser's Magazine*, August 1848)

III POEMS OF ANNE BRONTË PUBLISHED
IN POSTHUMOUS EDITIONS

I   Poems of Acton Bell, selected by Charlotte Brontë, in the posthumous edition of *Wuthering Heights* and *Agnes Grey*. London : Smith, Elder & Co., 1850.

1   Despondency
2   A Prayer
3   In Memory of a Happy Day in February
4   Confidence : Oppressed with sin and woe. . . .

5 The Narrow Way
6 Domestic Peace
7 Last Lines : I hoped that with the brave and strong. . . .

II   Edited by T. J. Wise and privately published, 1900

      1 Self-Communion

III   *Poems by Charlotte, Emily and Anne Brontë.* New York : Dodd, Mead
      & Co., 1902.

      1 The Captive's Dream
      2 The North Wind
      3 The Parting (I and II)
      4 Verses to a Child
      5 The Bluebell
      6 An Orphan's Lament
      7 Lines written at Thorp Green
      8 Song : We know where deepest lies the snow. . . .
      9 Song : Come to the Banquet
      10 Mirth and Mourning
      11 Weep not too much, my darling. . . .

IV   *Brontë Poems* : selections from the poetry of Charlotte, Emily, Anne and
      Branwell Brontë, edited with an introduction by A. C. Benson, including
      35 poems by Anne Brontë of which 5 were hitherto unpublished. London :
      John Murray, 1915.

      1 Night
      2 Dreams
      3 I dreamt last night, and in that dream. . . .
      4 Severed and gone, so many years. . . .
      5 Fragment : Yes, I will take a cheerful tone. . . .

V   *The Complete Poems of Anne Brontë*, for the first time collected, edited by
      C. K. Shorter, with an Introduction by C. W. Hatfield. London : Hodder
      & Stoughton, 1920.   54 titles.

VI   *The Poems of Emily Jane Brontë and Anne Brontë*, edited by T. J. Wise and
      J. A. Symington, Oxford : including "Retirement", hitherto ascribed to
      Emily Brontë but recognised by C. W. Hatfield as in Anne's handwriting
      in the original MS.   Shakespeare Head Press, 1934.   59 titles.

IV ANNE BRONTË'S GONDAL POEMS

I   SIGNED BY A GONDAL PSEUDONYM

     1838 24th Jan.   The Captive's Dream, *signed* Alexandrina Zenobia
     1838 26th Jan.   The North Wind, *signed* Alexandrina Zenobia
     1838 9th July   The Parting, I and II, *signed* Alexandrina Zenobia
     1838 21st Aug.   Verses to a Child, *signed* Alexandrina Zenobia
     1840 1st Jan.   Self-Congratulation, *signed* Olivia Vernon

1841　　1st Jan.　An Orphan's Lament, *signed* Alexandrina Zenobia
1844　　　Feb.　The Student's Serenade, *signed* Alexander Hybernia
1844　　16th Dec.　The Dungeon, *signed* Alexander Hybernia
1845　　1st Oct.　Stanzas : Oh, weep not love . . ., *signed* Zerona
1846　　15th July　Mirth and Mourning, *signed* Zerona
1846　　20th July　Weep not too much, my darling, *signed* A—E—
1846　　13th Aug.　The Power of Love, *signed* A—E—.
1846　　12th Sept.　I dreamt last night . . ., *signed* E—Z—

II　SIGNED IN HER OWN NAME ONLY

1836　　　Dec.　Verses by Lady Geralda, *signed* Anne Brontë
1837　　1st July　Alexander and Zenobia, *signed* Anne Brontë
1837　　　Oct.　A Voice from the Dungeon, *signed* Anne Brontë
1845　　24th Jan.　Call me away . . ., *signed* Anne Brontë

V EDITIONS OF ANNE BRONTË'S WORKS

1846　*Poems by Currer, Ellis and Acton Bell*. London : Aylott & Jones. (Including 21 poems by Acton Bell).

1847　*Agnes Grey*, a novel by Acton Bell, published jointly with *Wuthering Heights* by Ellis Bell. London : Thomas Cautley Newby.

1848　*The Tenant of Wildfell Hall* by Acton Bell, 3 vols., London : Thomas Cautley Newby.

1848　*The Tenant of Wildfell Hall* by Acton Bell, 2nd edition, with Preface by the Author. London : Thomas Cautley Newby, July 1848.

1848　*Poems by Currer, Ellis and Acton Bell*. London : Smith, Elder & Co.

1848　*Poems by Currer, Ellis and Acton Bell*, first American edition. Philadelphia : Lea & Blanchard.

1848　*Wuthering Heights* and *Agnes Grey*, first American edition. New York : Harper Bros.

1848　*The Tenant of Wildfell Hall*, first American edition, 1 vol., by "Acton Bell, author of Wuthering Heights [sic]", New York : Harper Bros.

1848　Poem by Acton Bell, "The Three Guides", *Fraser's Magazine*, August.

1850　Posthumous edition of *Agnes Grey*, together with a selection of the poems by Acton Bell, with a Memoir of the Author by Currer Bell, 1 vol. London : Smith, Elder & Co.

1915　*Brontë Poems*, including 9 by Anne Brontë hitherto unpublished (some poems incomplete), edited by A. C. Benson. London : John Murray.

1921　*The Complete Poems of Anne Brontë* (54 poems), edited by C. K. Shorter and C. W. Hatfield. London : Hodder & Stoughton.

1934　"The Shakespeare Head Brontë", edited T. J. Wise & J. A. Symington, *The Poems of Emily Jane Brontë and Anne Brontë* (59 poems of Anne). Oxford : The Shakespeare Head Press.

1926, 1932, 1938　*The Brontë Society Transactions*, texts of poems from original MSS.

1932　"The Shakespeare Head Brontë", *The Brontës, Their Lives, Friendships, and Correspondence*, in 4 vols., edited T. J. Wise & J. A. Symington, containing the text of 4 letters by Anne Brontë. Oxford : The Shakespeare Head Press.

APPENDIX B

Letter from Anne Brontë to the Rev. David Thom, D.D.

December 30, 1848

Dear Sir,—Ill-health must plead my excuse for this long delay in acknowledging your flattering communication; but, believe me, I am not the less gratified at the pleasure you have derived from my own and my relatives' work, and especially from the opinions they express. I have seen so little of controversial Theology that I was not aware the doctrine of Universal Salvation had so able and ardent an advocate as yourself; but I have cherished it from my very childhood—with a trembling hope at first, and afterwards with a firm and glad conviction of its truth. I drew it secretly from my own heart and from the Word of God before I knew that any other held it. And since then it has ever been a source of true delight to me to find the same views either timidly suggested or boldly advocated by benevolent and thoughtful minds; and I now believe there are many more believers than professors in that consoling creed. Why good men should be so adverse to admit it, I know not; into their own hearts at least, however they might object to its promulgation among the bulk of mankind. But perhaps the world is not ripe for it yet. I have frequently thought that since it has pleased God to leave it in darkness so long respecting this particular truth, and often to use such doubtful language as to admit of such a general misconception thereupon, he must have some good reason for it. We see how liable men are to yield to the temptation of the passing hour; how little the dread of future punishment—and still less the promise of future reward—can avail to make them forbear and wait; and if so many thousands rush into destruction with (as they suppose) the prospect of Eternal Death before their eyes—what might not the consequence be, if that prospect were changed for one of a limited season of punishment, far distant and unseen, however protracted and terrible it might be?

I thankfully cherish this belief; I honour those who hold it; and I would that all men had the same view of man's hopes and God's unbounded goodness as he has given to us, if it might be had with safety. But does not that "if" require some consideration? Should we not remember the weak brother and the infatuated slave of Satan and beware of revealing the truths too hastily to those as yet unable to receive them? But in these suggestions I am perhaps condemning myself, for in my last novel *The Tenant of Wildfell Hall*, I have given as many hints in support of the doctrine as I could venture to introduce into a work of that description. They are, however, *mere* suggestions, and as such I trust you will receive them, believing that I am well aware how much may be said in favour of boldly disseminating God's truth and leaving that to work its way. Only let our zeal be tempered with discretion, and while we labour let us humbly look to God who is able and certain to bring his great work to perfection in his own good time and manner.

Accept my best wishes in behalf of yourself and your important undertakings, and believe me to remain with sincere esteem,

Yours truly,
Acton Bell

INDEX

Abernathy, Mr, 50
Adam, Adolphe, 203
Aesop, 49, 51
Agnes Grey, 39, 43, 70, 72, 74, 75, 93, 97, 119, 122, 125–7, 134, 138, 145, 146, 148, 150, 151–2, 155–9, 161, 163, 166, 174–5, 176, 177, 182, 186, 191, 193, 194, 224, 225, 227, 228, 229, 230–3, 235, 259, 260, 261, 272, 276, 315
"Alexander and Zenobia", 106
Alexander Hybernia (Gondal), 59, 62, 64, 107, 218
Alexandia (Gondal), 64
Alexandrina Zenobia (Gondal), 59, 64, 107, 117–18, 218
Allbutt, the Rev. Thomas, 83
Allestree, Derbyshire, 294
Almedore (Gondal), 64
Alzerno (Gondal), 64, 117
Amberley, Lady, 233
American editions, 261–2, 290, 291–3
Anderson, Wilson, 116
Angora (Gondal), 64
Angria, 56, 88, 89, 105, 219, 279
Anne of the *Black Bull*, 256, 281
Annii (childhood plays), 49–51
"Appeal", 167, 222
Appleby, 136, 137
Arabian Nights, The, 49, 51, 71
"Arbour, The", 221
Arminian Magazine, The, 37
Arminian Methodism, 32
As You Like It, 70
Athenaeum, The, 223, 259
Atkinson, Mrs, 56, 83, 95, 111, 192
Atkinson, the Rev. Thomas, 3–4, 7, 11, 56, 76, 95, 99
Atkinsons, 14, 54, 82, 93
Atlas, The, 233–4
Auber, 203
Audubon, 70
Augustus Almeda (Gondal), 106
Augusta Geraldine (Gondal), 64, 218
Austen, Jane, 3, 139, 231, 233, 235
Aykroyd, Tabitha (Tabby), 7, 23, 40, 44, 45, 48, 50, 53, 60, 66, 69, 103–4, 106, 123, 133, 139, 165, 172, 210, 211, 219, 269, 272, 273, 297, 311, 322
Aylott & Jones, 219, 224, 225, 238, 290

Barber of Seville, 268
Bath, 243
Bay Horse Inn, Whixley, 153
Bayswater, 268
Beethoven, 74
Bell, Acton, 20, 219, 220, 223, 227, 228, 233, 234, 259–62, 266–7, 277, 290–3. (*See* Anne Brontë)
Bell, Currer, 219–20, 225, 227, 228, 234, 259, 260–2, 265, 267, 277, 289. (*See* Charlotte Brontë)
Bell, Ellis, 20, 219–20, 223, 227, 228, 234, 259, 260, 261, 262, 277, 290–1, 293. (*See* Emily Brontë)
Bennet (*Pride and Prejudice*), 139
Bentinck, Lord, 50
Bewick, 55, 70, 71
Birstall, 65, 83, 92–3, 108, 151, 321
Black Bull, Haworth, 238, 256, 281–3, 285
Blackwood's Magazine, 46, 71, 164
"Blackwood's Young Men's Magazine" (childhood plays), 52, 55–6
Blake Hall, 93, 120–2, 124, 128, 132, 133, 135, 137, 142, 150, 165, 176, 231
Blanche, Mlle, 214
Bland, John, 145
Bland, Mrs, 146
Bland, Susan, 145–6
Bloomfield, Fanny (*Agnes Grey*), 127–8
Bloomfield, Harriette (*Agnes Grey*), 127
Bloomfield, Mary Ann (*Agnes Grey*), 93, 127–9, 131
Bloomfield, Mr (*Agnes Grey*), 126, 134, 232
Bloomfield, Mrs (*Agnes Grey*), 125, 133–4
Bloomfield, Mrs (senior, *Agnes Grey*), 232
Bloomfield, Tom (*Agnes Grey*), 93, 127–8
Bloomfields (*Agnes Grey*), 73, 231
"Bluebell, The", 149
Böhler, Peter, 99
Boroughbridge, 152
Borrow, George, 305
Boswell, 70
Bowling Green Inn, Bradford, 152
Bradford, 1, 4, 8, 11, 81, 84, 111, 116, 124, 126, 151, 152, 190, 192, 211, 225, 286